GO!
with Microsoft®
Word 2007
Brief

Shelley Gaskin and Robert L. Ferrett

PEARSON

Prentice Hall

Upper Saddle River, New Jersey

This book is dedicated to my students, who inspire me every day, and to my husband, Fred Gaskin.
—Shelley Gaskin

I dedicate this book to my granddaughters, who bring me great joy and happiness: Clara and Siena.
—Robert L. Ferrett

Library of Congress Cataloging-in-Publication Data

Gaskin, Shelley.
  Go! with Microsoft Word 2007, brief / Shelley Gaskin and Robert L. Ferrett.
    p. cm.
  Includes index.
  ISBN-13: 978-0-13-512996-8
  ISBN-10: 0-13-512996-6
  1. Microsoft Word. 2. Word processing. I. Ferrett, Robert. II. Title.
Z52.5.M52G38 2008
005.52--dc22

2007011740

Vice President and Publisher: Natalie E. Anderson
Associate VP/Executive Acquisitions Editor,
  Print: Stephanie Wall
Executive Acquisitions Editor, Media: Richard Keaveny
Product Development Manager: Eileen Bien Calabro
Senior Editorial Project Manager: Laura Burgess
Development Editor: Ginny Munroe
Editorial Assistants: Becky Knauer, Lora Cimiluca
Executive Producer: Lisa Strite
Content Development Manager: Cathi Profitko
Senior Media Project Manager: Steve Gagliostro
Production Media Project Manager: Lorena Cerisano
Director of Marketing: Margaret Waples
Senior Marketing Manager: Jason Sakos
Marketing Assistants: Angela Frey, Kathryn Ferranti
Senior Sales Associate: Rebecca Scott

Managing Editor: Lynda J. Castillo
Manufacturing Production Project Manager:
  Wanda Rockwell
Production Editor: GGS Book Services
Photo Researcher: GGS Book Services
Manufacturing Buyer: Natacha Moore
Production/Editorial Assistant: Sandra K. Bernales
Design Director: Maria Lange
Art Director/Interior Design: Blair Brown
Cover Photo: Courtesy of Getty Images, Inc./Marvin
  Mattelson
Composition: GGS Book Services
Project Management: GGS Book Services
Cover Printer: Phoenix Color
Printer/Binder: RR Donnelley/Willard

Microsoft, Windows, Word, PowerPoint, Outlook, FrontPage, Visual Basic, MSN, The Microsoft Network, and/or other Microsoft products referenced herein are either trademarks or registered trademarks of Microsoft Corporation in the U.S.A. and other countries. Screen shots and icons reprinted with permission from the Microsoft Corporation. This book is not sponsored or endorsed by or affiliated with Microsoft Corporation.

Credits and acknowledgments borrowed from other sources and reproduced, with permission, in this textbook are as follows or on the appropriate page within the text.

Page 2: Getty Images, Inc. – Taxi; and page 86: iStockphoto.com; page 174: PhotoEdit, Inc.; page 260: Omni-Photo Communications, Inc.

10 9 8 7 6 5 4 3 2
ISBN 0-13-512996-6

Contents in Brief

Table of Contents

Letter from the Editor

Dear Instructors and Students,

The primary goal of the *GO!* Series is two-fold. The first goal is to help instructors teach the course they want in less time. The second goal is to provide students with the skills to solve business problems using the computer as a tool, for both themselves and the organization for which they might be employed.

The *GO!* Series was originally created by Series Editor Shelley Gaskin and published with the release of Microsoft Office 2003. Her ideas came from years of using textbooks that didn't meet all the needs of today's diverse classroom and that were too confusing for students. Shelley continues to enhance the series by ensuring we stay true to our vision of developing quality instruction and useful classroom tools.

But we also need your input and ideas.

Over time, the *GO!* Series has evolved based on direct feedback from instructors and students using the series. *We are the publisher that listens.* To publish a textbook that works for you, it's critical that we continue to listen to this feedback. It's important to me to talk with you and hear your stories about using *GO!* Your voice can make a difference.

My hope is that this letter will inspire you to write me an e-mail and share your thoughts on using the *GO!* Series.

Stephanie Wall
Executive Editor, *GO!* Series
stephanie_wall@prenhall.com

GO! System Contributors

We thank the following people for their hard work and support in making the *GO!* System all that it is!

Additional Author Support

Coyle, Diane	Montgomery County Community College
Fry, Susan	Boise State
Townsend, Kris	Spokane Falls Community College
Stroup, Tracey	Amgen Corporation

Instructor Resource Authors

Amer, Beverly	Northern Arizona University	Paterson, Jim	Paradise Valley Community College
Boito, Nancy	Harrisburg Area Community College	Prince, Lisa	Missouri State
Coyle, Diane	Montgomery County Community College	Rodgers, Gwen	Southern Nazarene University
Dawson, Tamara	Southern Nazarene University	Ruymann, Amy	Burlington Community College
Driskel, Loretta	Niagara County Community College	Ryan, Bob	Montgomery County Community College
Elliott, Melissa	Odessa College		
Fry, Susan	Boise State	Smith, Diane	Henry Ford Community College
Geoghan, Debra	Bucks County Community College	Spangler, Candice	Columbus State Community College
Hearn, Barbara	Community College of Philadelphia	Thompson, Joyce	Lehigh Carbon Community College
Jones, Stephanie	South Plains College	Tiffany, Janine	Reading Area Community College
Madsen, Donna	Kirkwood Community College	Watt, Adrienne	Douglas College
Meck, Kari	Harrisburg Area Community College	Weaver, Paul	Bossier Parish Community College
Miller, Cindy	Ivy Tech	Weber, Sandy	Gateway Technical College
Nowakowski, Tony	Buffalo State	Wood, Dawn	
Pace, Phyllis	Queensborough Community College	Weissman, Jonathan	Finger Lakes Community College

Super Reviewers

Brotherton, Cathy	Riverside Community College	Maurer, Trina	Odessa College
Cates, Wally	Central New Mexico Community College	Meck, Kari	Harrisburg Area Community College
		Miller, Cindy	Ivy Tech Community College
Cone, Bill	Northern Arizona University	Nielson, Phil	Salt Lake Community College
Coverdale, John	Riverside Community College	Rodgers, Gwen	Southern Nazarene University
Foster, Nancy	Baker College	Smolenski, Robert	Delaware Community College
Helfand, Terri	Chaffey College	Spangler, Candice	Columbus State Community College
Hibbert, Marilyn	Salt Lake Community College	Thompson, Joyce	Lehigh Carbon Community College
Holliday, Mardi	Community College of Philadelphia	Weber, Sandy	Gateway Technical College
Jerry, Gina	Santa Monica College	Wells, Lorna	Salt Lake Community College
Martin, Carol	Harrisburg Area Community College	Zaboski, Maureen	University of Scranton

Technical Editors

Janice Snyder
Joyce Nielsen
Colette Eisele
Janet Pickard
Mara Zebest
Lindsey Allen
William Daley

Student Reviewers

Allen, John	Asheville-Buncombe Tech Community College	Erickson, Mike	Ball State University
		Gadomski, Amanda	Northern Michigan University
Alexander, Steven	St. Johns River Community College	Gyselinck, Craig	Central Washington University
Alexander, Melissa	Tulsa Community College	Harrison, Margo	Central Washington University
Bolz, Stephanie	Northern Michigan University	Heacox, Kate	Central Washington University
Berner, Ashley	Central Washington University	Hill, Cheretta	Northwestern State University
Boomer, Michelle	Northern Michigan University	Innis, Tim	Tulsa Community College
Busse, Brennan	Northern Michigan University	Jarboe, Aaron	Central Washington University
Butkey, Maura	Central Washington University	Klein, Colleen	Northern Michigan University
Christensen, Kaylie	Northern Michigan University	Moeller, Jeffrey	Northern Michigan University
Connally, Brianna	Central Washington University	Nicholson, Regina	Athens Tech College
Davis, Brandon	Northern Michigan University	Niehaus, Kristina	Northern Michigan University
Davis, Christen	Central Washington University	Nisa, Zaibun	Santa Rosa Community College
Den Boer, Lance	Central Washington University	Nunez, Nohelia	Santa Rosa Community College
Dix, Jessica	Central Washington University	Oak, Samantha	Central Washington University
Moeller, Jeffrey	Northern Michigan University	Oertii, Monica	Central Washington University
Downs, Elizabeth	Central Washington University	Palenshus, Juliet	Central Washington University

Pohl, Amanda	Northern Michigan University	Shanahan, Megan	Northern Michigan University
Presnell, Randy	Central Washington University	Teska, Erika	Hawaii Pacific University
Ritner, April	Northern Michigan University	Traub, Amy	Northern Michigan University
Rodriguez, Flavia	Northwestern State University	Underwood, Katie	Central Washington University
Roberts, Corey	Tulsa Community College	Walters, Kim	Central Washington University
Rossi, Jessica Ann	Central Washington University	Wilson, Kelsie	Central Washington University
Shafapay, Natasha	Central Washington University	Wilson, Amanda	Green River Community College

Series Reviewers

Abraham, Reni	Houston Community College
Agatston, Ann	Agatston Consulting Technical College
Alexander, Melody	Ball Sate University
Alejandro, Manuel	Southwest Texas Junior College
Ali, Farha	Lander University
Amici, Penny	Harrisburg Area Community College
Anderson, Patty A.	Lake City Community College
Andrews, Wilma	Virginia Commonwealth College, Nebraska University
Anik, Mazhar	Tiffin University
Armstrong, Gary	Shippensburg University
Atkins, Bonnie	Delaware Technical Community College
Bachand, LaDonna	Santa Rosa Community College
Bagui, Sikha	University of West Florida
Beecroft, Anita	Kwantlen University College
Bell, Paula	Lock Haven College
Belton, Linda	Springfield Tech. Community College
Bennett, Judith	Sam Houston State University
Bhatia, Sai	Riverside Community College
Bishop, Frances	DeVry Institute—Alpharetta (ATL)
Blaszkiewicz, Holly	Ivy Tech Community College/Region 1
Branigan, Dave	DeVry University
Bray, Patricia	Allegany College of Maryland
Brotherton, Cathy	Riverside Community College
Buehler, Lesley	Ohlone College
Buell, C	Central Oregon Community College
Byars, Pat	Brookhaven College
Byrd, Lynn	Delta State University, Cleveland, Mississippi
Cacace, Richard N.	Pensacola Junior College
Cadenhead, Charles	Brookhaven College
Calhoun, Ric	Gordon College
Cameron, Eric	Passaic Community College
Carriker, Sandra	North Shore Community College
Cannamore, Madie	Kennedy King
Carreon, Cleda	Indiana University—Purdue University, Indianapolis
Chaffin, Catherine	Shawnee State University
Chauvin, Marg	Palm Beach Community College, Boca Raton
Challa, Chandrashekar	Virginia State University
Chamlou, Afsaneh	NOVA Alexandria
Chapman, Pam	Wabaunsee Community College
Christensen, Dan	Iowa Western Community College
Clay, Betty	Southeastern Oklahoma State University
Collins, Linda D.	Mesa Community College
Conroy-Link, Janet	Holy Family College
Cosgrove, Janet	Northwestern CT Community
Courtney, Kevin	Hillsborough Community College
Cox, Rollie	Madison Area Technical College
Crawford, Hiram	Olive Harvey College

Crawford, Thomasina	Miami-Dade College, Kendall Campus
Credico, Grace	Lethbridge Community College
Crenshaw, Richard	Miami Dade Community College, North
Crespo, Beverly	Mt. San Antonio College
Crossley, Connie	Cincinnati State Technical Community College
Curik, Mary	Central New Mexico Community College
De Arazoza, Ralph	Miami Dade Community College
Danno, John	DeVry University/Keller Graduate School
Davis, Phillip	Del Mar College
DeHerrera, Laurie	Pikes Peak Community College
Delk, Dr. K. Kay	Seminole Community College
Doroshow, Mike	Eastfield College
Douglas, Gretchen	SUNYCortland
Dove, Carol	Community College of Allegheny
Driskel, Loretta	Niagara Community College
Duckwiler, Carol	Wabaunsee Community College
Duncan, Mimi	University of Missouri-St. Louis
Duthie, Judy	Green River Community College
Duvall, Annette	Central New Mexico Community College
Ecklund, Paula	Duke University
Eng, Bernice	Brookdale Community College
Evans, Billie	Vance-Granville Community College
Feuerbach, Lisa	Ivy Tech East Chicago
Fisher, Fred	Florida State University
Foster, Penny L.	Anne Arundel Community College
Foszcz, Russ	McHenry County College
Fry, Susan	Boise State University
Fustos, Janos	Metro State
Gallup, Jeanette	Blinn College
Gelb, Janet	Grossmont College
Gentry, Barb	Parkland College
Gerace, Karin	St. Angela Merici School
Gerace, Tom	Tulane University
Ghajar, Homa	Oklahoma State University
Gifford, Steve	Northwest Iowa Community College
Glazer, Ellen	Broward Community College
Gordon, Robert	Hofstra University
Gramlich, Steven	Pasco-Hernando Community College
Graviett, Nancy M.	St. Charles Community College, St. Peters, Missouri
Greene, Rich	Community College of Allegheny County
Gregoryk, Kerry	Virginia Commonwealth State
Griggs, Debra	Bellevue Community College
Grimm, Carol	Palm Beach Community College
Hahn, Norm	Thomas Nelson Community College
Hammerschlag, Dr. Bill	Brookhaven College
Hansen, Michelle	Davenport University
Hayden, Nancy	Indiana University—Purdue University, Indianapolis

Hayes, Theresa — Broward Community College
Helfand, Terri — Chaffey College
Helms, Liz — Columbus State Community College
Hernandez, Leticia — TCI College of Technology
Hibbert, Marilyn — Salt Lake Community College
Hoffman, Joan — Milwaukee Area Technical College
Hogan, Pat — Cape Fear Community College
Holland, Susan — Southeast Community College
Hopson, Bonnie — Athens Technical College
Horvath, Carrie — Albertus Magnus College
Horwitz, Steve — Community College of Philadelphia
Hotta, Barbara — Leeward Community College
Howard, Bunny — St. Johns River Community
Howard, Chris — DeVry University
Huckabay, Jamie — Austin Community College
Hudgins, Susan — East Central University
Hulett, Michelle J. — Missouri State University
Hunt, Darla A. — Morehead State University, Morehead, Kentucky
Hunt, Laura — Tulsa Community College
Jacob, Sherry — Jefferson Community College
Jacobs, Duane — Salt Lake Community College
Jauken, Barb — Southeastern Community
Johnson, Kathy — Wright College
Johnson, Mary — Kingwood College
Johnson, Mary — Mt. San Antonio College
Jones, Stacey — Benedict College
Jones, Warren — University of Alabama, Birmingham
Jordan, Cheryl — San Juan College
Kapoor, Bhushan — California State University, Fullerton
Kasai, Susumu — Salt Lake Community College
Kates, Hazel — Miami Dade Community College, Kendall
Keen, Debby — University of Kentucky
Keeter, Sandy — Seminole Community College
Kern-Blystone, Dorothy Jean — Bowling Green State
Keskin, Ilknur — The University of South Dakota
Kirk, Colleen — Mercy College
Kleckner, Michelle — Elon University
Kliston, Linda — Broward Community College, North Campus
Kochis, Dennis — Suffolk County Community College
Kramer, Ed — Northern Virginia Community College
Laird, Jeff — Northeast State Community College
Lamoureaux, Jackie — Central New Mexico Community College
Lange, David — Grand Valley State
LaPointe, Deb — Central New Mexico Community College
Larson, Donna — Louisville Technical Institute
Laspina, Kathy — Vance-Granville Community College
Le Grand, Dr. Kate — Broward Community College
Lenhart, Sheryl — Terra Community College
Letavec, Chris — University of Cincinnati
Liefert, Jane — Everett Community College
Lindaman, Linda — Black Hawk Community College
Lindberg, Martha — Minnesota State University
Lightner, Renee — Broward Community College
Lindberg, Martha — Minnesota State University
Linge, Richard — Arizona Western College
Logan, Mary G. — Delgado Community College
Loizeaux, Barbara — Westchester Community College
Lopez, Don — Clovis-State Center Community College District

Lord, Alexandria — Asheville Buncombe Tech
Lowe, Rita — Harold Washington College
Low, Willy Hui — Joliet Junior College
Lucas, Vickie — Broward Community College
Lynam, Linda — Central Missouri State University
Lyon, Lynne — Durham College
Lyon, Pat Rajski — Tomball College
MacKinnon, Ruth — Georgia Southern University
Macon, Lisa — Valencia Community College, West Campus
Machuca, Wayne — College of the Sequoias
Madison, Dana — Clarion University
Maguire, Trish — Eastern New Mexico University
Malkan, Rajiv — Montgomery College
Manning, David — Northern Kentucky University
Marcus, Jacquie — Niagara Community College
Marghitu, Daniela — Auburn University
Marks, Suzanne — Bellevue Community College
Marquez, Juanita — El Centro College
Marquez, Juan — Mesa Community College
Martyn, Margie — Baldwin-Wallace College
Marucco, Toni — Lincoln Land Community College
Mason, Lynn — Lubbock Christian University
Matutis, Audrone — Houston Community College
Matkin, Marie — University of Lethbridge
McCain, Evelyn — Boise State University
McCannon, Melinda — Gordon College
McCarthy, Marguerite — Northwestern Business College
McCaskill, Matt L. — Brevard Community College
McClellan, Carolyn — Tidewater Community College
McClure, Darlean — College of Sequoias
McCrory, Sue A. — Missouri State University
McCue, Stacy — Harrisburg Area Community College
McEntire-Orbach, Teresa — Middlesex County College
McLeod, Todd — Fresno City College
McManus, Illyana — Grossmont College
McPherson, Dori — Schoolcraft College
Meiklejohn, Nancy — Pikes Peak Community College
Menking, Rick — Hardin-Simmons University
Meredith, Mary — University of Louisiana at Lafayette
Mermelstein, Lisa — Baruch College
Metos, Linda — Salt Lake Community College
Meurer, Daniel — University of Cincinnati
Meyer, Marian — Central New Mexico Community College
Miller, Cindy — Ivy Tech Community College, Lafayette, Indiana
Mitchell, Susan — Davenport University
Mohle, Dennis — Fresno Community College
Monk, Ellen — University of Delaware
Moore, Rodney — Holland College
Morris, Mike — Southeastern Oklahoma State University
Morris, Nancy — Hudson Valley Community College
Moseler, Dan — Harrisburg Area Community College
Nabors, Brent — Reedley College, Clovis Center
Nadas, Erika — Wright College
Nadelman, Cindi — New England College
Nademlynsky, Lisa — Johnson & Wales University
Ncube, Cathy — University of West Florida
Nagengast, Joseph — Florida Career College
Newsome, Eloise — Northern Virginia Community College Woodbridge
Nicholls, Doreen — Mohawk Valley Community College
Nunan, Karen — Northeast State Technical Community College

Odegard, Teri — Edmonds Community College
Ogle, Gregory — North Community College
Orr, Dr. Claudia — Northern Michigan University South
Otieno, Derek — DeVry University
Otton, Diana Hill — Chesapeake College
Oxendale, Lucia — West Virginia Institute of Technology

Paiano, Frank — Southwestern College
Patrick, Tanya — Clackamas Community College
Peairs, Deb — Clark State Community College
Prince, Lisa — Missouri State University-Springfield Campus
Proietti, Kathleen — Northern Essex Community College
Pusins, Delores — HCCC
Raghuraman, Ram — Joliet Junior College
Reasoner, Ted Allen — Indiana University—Purdue
Reeves, Karen — High Point University
Remillard, Debbie — New Hampshire Technical Institute
Rhue, Shelly — DeVry University
Richards, Karen — Maplewoods Community College
Richardson, Mary — Albany Technical College
Rodgers, Gwen — Southern Nazarene University
Roselli, Diane — Harrisburg Area Community College
Ross, Dianne — University of Louisiana in Lafayette
Rousseau, Mary — Broward Community College, South
Samson, Dolly — Hawaii Pacific University
Sams, Todd — University of Cincinnati
Sandoval, Everett — Reedley College
Sardone, Nancy — Seton Hall University
Scafide, Jean — Mississippi Gulf Coast Community College
Scheeren, Judy — Westmoreland County Community College
Schneider, Sol — Sam Houston State University
Scroggins, Michael — Southwest Missouri State University
Sever, Suzanne — Northwest Arkansas Community College
Sheridan, Rick — California State University-Chico
Silvers, Pamela — Asheville Buncombe Tech
Singer, Steven A. — University of Hawai'i, Kapi'olani Community College
Sinha, Atin — Albany State University
Skolnick, Martin — Florida Atlantic University
Smith, T. Michael — Austin Community College
Smith, Tammy — Tompkins Cortland Community Collge
Smolenski, Bob — Delaware County Community College
Spangler, Candice — Columbus State
Stedham, Vicki — St. Petersburg College, Clearwater
Stefanelli, Greg — Carroll Community College
Steiner, Ester — New Mexico State University
Stenlund, Neal — Northern Virginia Community College, Alexandria
St. John, Steve — Tulsa Community College

Sterling, Janet — Houston Community College
Stoughton, Catherine — Laramie County Community College
Sullivan, Angela — Joliet Junior College
Szurek, Joseph — University of Pittsburgh at Greensburg
Tarver, Mary Beth — Northwestern State University
Taylor, Michael — Seattle Central Community College
Thangiah, Sam — Slippery Rock University
Thompson-Sellers, Ingrid — Georgia Perimeter College
Tomasi, Erik — Baruch College
Toreson, Karen — Shoreline Community College
Trifiletti, John J. — Florida Community College at Jacksonville
Trivedi, Charulata — Quinsigamond Community College, Woodbridge
Tucker, William — Austin Community College
Turgeon, Cheryl — Asnuntuck Community College
Turpen, Linda — Central New Mexico Community College
Upshaw, Susan — Del Mar College
Unruh, Angela — Central Washington University
Vanderhoof, Dr. Glenna — Missouri State University-Springfield Campus
Vargas, Tony — El Paso Community College
Vicars, Mitzi — Hampton University
Villarreal, Kathleen — Fresno
Vitrano, Mary Ellen — Palm Beach Community College
Volker, Bonita — Tidewater Community College
Wahila, Lori (Mindy) — Tompkins Cortland Community College
Waswick, Kim — Southeast Community College, Nebraska
Wavle, Sharon — Tompkins Cortland Community College
Webb, Nancy — City College of San Francisco
Wells, Barbara E. — Central Carolina Technical College
Wells, Lorna — Salt Lake Community College
Welsh, Jean — Lansing Community College Nebraska
White, Bruce — Quinnipiac University
Willer, Ann — Solano Community College
Williams, Mark — Lane Community College
Wilson, Kit — Red River College
Wilson, Roger — Fairmont State University
Wimberly, Leanne — International Academy of Design and Technology
Worthington, Paula — Northern Virginia Community College
Yauney, Annette — Herkimer County Community College
Yip, Thomas — Passaic Community College
Zavala, Ben — Webster Tech
Zlotow, Mary Ann — College of DuPage
Zudeck, Steve — Broward Community College, North

About the Authors

Shelley Gaskin, Series Editor, is a professor of business and computer technology at Pasadena City College in Pasadena, California. She holds a master's degree in business education from Northern Illinois University and a doctorate in adult and community education from Ball State University. Dr. Gaskin has 15 years of experience in the computer industry with several Fortune 500 companies and has developed and written training materials for custom systems applications in both the public and private sector. She is also the author of books on Microsoft Outlook and word processing.

Robert L. Ferrett recently retired as the director of the Center for Instructional Computing at Eastern Michigan University, where he provided computer training and support to faculty. He has authored or co-authored more than 70 books on Access, PowerPoint, Excel, Publisher, WordPerfect, and Word. Before writing for the *GO! Series*, Bob was a series editor and author for the *Learn Series*. He has a bachelor's degree in psychology, a master's degree in geography, and a master's degree in interdisciplinary technology from Eastern Michigan University. Bob's doctoral studies were in instructional technology at Wayne State University. For fun, Bob teaches a four-week computers and genealogy class and has written genealogy and local history books.

Visual Walk-Through of the *GO!* System

The *GO!* System is designed for ease of implementation on the instructor side and ease of understanding on the student. It has been completely developed based on professor and student feedback.

The *GO!* System is divided into three categories that reflect how you might organize your course— **Prepare**, **Teach**, and **Assess**.

Prepare

GO!

Because the GO! System was designed and written by instructors like yourself, it includes the tools that allow you to Prepare, Teach, and Assess in your course. We have organized the GO! System into these three categories that match how you work through your course and thus, it's even easier for you to implement.

To help you get started, here is an outline of the first activities you may want to do in order to conduct your course.

There are several other tools not listed here that are available in the GO! System so please refer to your GO! Guide for a complete listing of all the tools.

Prepare
1. Prepare the course syllabus
2. Plan the course assignments
3. Organize the student resources

Teach
4. Conduct demonstrations and lectures

Assess
5. Assign and grade assignments, quizzes, tests, and assessments

PREPARE

1. Prepare the course syllabus
A syllabus template is provided on the IRCD in the **go07_syllabus_template** folder of the main directory. It includes a course calendar planner for 8-week, 12-week, and 16-week formats. Depending on your term (summer or regular semester) you can modify one of these according to your course plan, and then add information pertinent to your course and institution.

2. Plan course assignments
For each chapter, an Assignment Sheet listing every in-chapter and end-of-chapter project is located on the IRCD within the **go01_go!office2007intro_instructor_resources_by_chapter** folder. From there, navigate to the specific chapter folder. These sheets are Word tables, so you can delete rows for the projects that you choose not to assign or add rows for your own assignments—if any. There is a column to add the number of points you want to assign to each project depending on your grading scheme. At the top of the sheet, you can fill in the course information.

Transitioning to GO! Office 2007   Page 1 of 1

NEW

Transition Guide

New to *GO!*–We've made it quick and easy to plan the format and activities for your class.

GO! with Microsoft Office 2007 Introductory
SAMPLE SYLLABUS (16 weeks)

I. COURSE INFORMATION

Course No.:   Semester:
Course Title: Credits:
Course Hours:

Instructor: Office:
Office Hours:
Email: Phone:

II. TEXT AND MATERIALS
Before starting the course, you will need the following:

> GO! with Microsoft Office 2007 Introductory by Shelley Gaskin, Robert L. Ferrett, Alicia Vargas, Suzanne Marks ©2007, published by Pearson Prentice Hall. ISBN 0-13-167990-6

> Storage device for saving files (any of the following: multiple diskettes, CD-RW, flash drive, etc.)

III. WHAT YOU WILL LEARN IN THIS COURSE
This is a hands-on course where you will learn to use a computer to practice the most commonly used Microsoft programs including the Windows operating system, Internet Explorer for navigating the Internet, Outlook for managing your personal information and the four most popular programs within the Microsoft Office Suite (Word, Excel, PowerPoint and Access). You will also practice the basics of using a computer, mouse and keyboard. You will learn to be an intermediate level user of the Microsoft Office Suite.

Within the Microsoft Office Suite, you will use Word, Excel, PowerPoint, and Access. Microsoft Word is a word processing program with which you can create common business and personal documents. Microsoft Excel is a spreadsheet program that organizes and calculates accounting-type information. Microsoft PowerPoint is a presentation graphics program with which you can develop slides to accompany an oral presentation. Finally, Microsoft Access is a database program that organizes large amounts of information in a useful manner.

Syllabus Template

Includes course calendar planner for 8-,12-, and 16-week formats.

Assignment Sheet

One per chapter. Lists all possible assignments; add to and delete from this simple Word table according to your course plan.

File Guide to the *GO!* Supplements

Tabular listing of all supplements and their file names.

NEW

Assignment Planning Guide

Description of *GO!* assignments with recommendations based on class size, delivery mode, and student needs. Includes examples from fellow instructors.

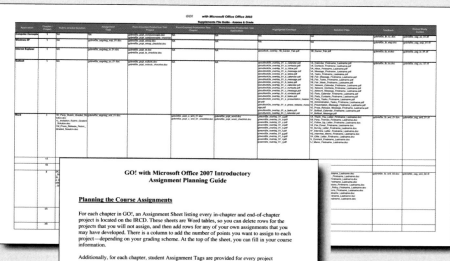

GO! with Microsoft Office 2007 Introductory
Assignment Planning Guide

Planning the Course Assignments

For each chapter in GO!, an Assignment Sheet listing every in-chapter and end-of-chapter project is located on the IRCD. These sheets are Word tables, so you can delete rows for the projects that you will not assign, and then add rows for any of your own assignments that you may have developed. There is a column to add the number of points you want to assign to each project—depending on your grading scheme. At the top of the sheet, you can fill in your course information.

Additionally, for each chapter, student Assignment Tags are provided for every project (including Problem Solving projects)—also located on the IRCD. These are small scoring checklists on which you can check off errors made by the student, and with which the student can verify that all project elements are complete. For campus classes, the student can attach the tags to his or her paper submissions. For online classes, many GO! instructors have the student include these with the electronic submission.

Deciding What to Assign

Front Portion of the Chapter—Instructional Projects: The projects in the front portion of the chapter, which are listed on the first page of each chapter, are the instructional projects. Most instructors assign all of these projects, because this is where the student receives the instruction and engages in the active learning.

End-of-Chapter—Practice and Critical Thinking Projects: In the back portion of the chapter (the gray pages), you can assign on a prescriptive basis; that is, for students who were challenged by the instructional projects, you might assign one or more projects from the two *Skills Reviews*, which provide maximum prompting and a thorough review of the entire chapter. For students who have previous software knowledge and who completed the instructional projects easily, you might assign only the *Mastery Projects*.

You can also assign prescriptively by Objective, because each end-of-chapter project indicates the Objectives covered. So you might assign, on a student-by-student basis, only the projects that cover the Objectives with which the student seemed to have difficulty in the instructional projects.

The five Problem Solving projects and the You and GO! project are the authentic assessments that pull together the student's learning. Here the student is presented with a "messy real-life situation" and then uses his or her knowledge and skill to solve a problem, produce a product, give a presentation, or demonstrate a procedure. You might assign one or more of the Problem

GO! Assignment Planning Guide   Page 1 of 1

Student Data Files

Music School Records discovers, launches, and and develops the careers of young artists in classical, jazz, and contemporary music. Our philosophy is to not only shape, distribute, and sell a music product, but to help artists create a career that can lats a lifetime. too often in the music industry, artists are forced to fit their music to a trend that is short-lived. Music School Records doesn't just follow trends, we take a long-term view of the music industry and help our artists develop a style and repertiore that is fluid and flexible and that will appeal to audiences for years and even decades.

The music industry is constantly changing, but over the last decade the changes have been enormous. New forms of entertainment such as DVDs, video games, and the Internet mean there are more competition for the leisure dollar in the market. New technologies give consomers more options for buying and listening to music, and they are demaning high quality recordings. Young consomers are comfortable with technology and want the music they love when and where they want it, no matter where they are or what they are doing.

Music School Records embraces new technologies and the sophisticated market of young music lovers. We believe that providing high quality recordings of truly talented artists make for more discerning listeners who will cherish the gift of music for the rest of their lives. The expertise of Music School Records includes:

- Insight into our target market and the ability to reach the desired audience
- The ability to access all current sources of music income
- A management team with years of experience in music commerce
- Innovative business strategies and artist development plans
- Investment in technology infrastructure for high quality recordings and business services
- Initiative and proactive management of artist careers

Online Study Guide for Students

Interactive objective-style questions based on chapter content.

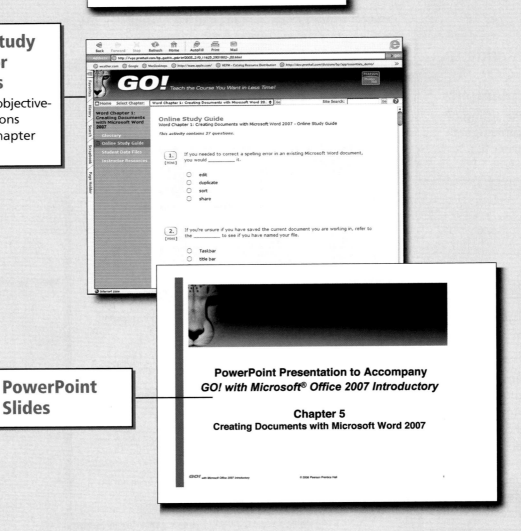

PowerPoint Slides

PowerPoint Presentation to Accompany
GO! with Microsoft® Office 2007 Introductory

Chapter 5
Creating Documents with Microsoft Word 2007

Student Textbook

Word 2007

5 chapter five

Creating Documents with Microsoft Word 2007

OBJECTIVES
At the end of this chapter you will be able to:

OUTCOMES
Mastering these objectives will enable you to:

1. Create and Save a New Document
2. Edit Text
3. Select, Delete, and Format Text
4. Print a Document

PROJECT 5A
Create, Edit, Save, and Print a Document

5. Navigate the Word Window
6. Add a Graphic to a Document
7. Use the Spelling and Grammar Checker
8. Preview and Print Documents, Close a Document, and Close Word
9. Use the Microsoft Help System

PROJECT 5B
Navigate the Word Window and Check Your Work

Word 237

Learning Objectives and Student Outcomes

Objectives are clustered around projects that result in student outcomes. They help students learn how to solve problems, not just learn software features.

Project-Based Instruction

Students do not practice features of the application; they create real projects that they will need in the real world. Projects are color coded for easy reference and are named to reflect skills the students will be practicing.

NEW

A and B Projects

Each chapter contains two instructional projects—A and B.

Music School Records

Music School Records was created to launch young musical artists with undiscovered talent in jazz, classical, and contemporary music. The creative management team searches internationally for talented young people, and has a reputation for mentoring and developing the skills of its artists. The company's music is tailored to an audience that is young, knowledgeable about music, and demands the highest quality recordings. Music School Records releases are available in CD format as well as digital downloads.

Getting Started with Microsoft Office Word 2007

A word processor is the most common program found on personal computers and one that almost everyone has a reason to use. When you learn word processing you are also learning skills and techniques that you need to work efficiently on a personal computer. You can use Microsoft Word to perform basic word processing tasks such as writing a memo, a report, or a letter. You can also use Word to complete complex word processing tasks, such as those that include sophisticated tables, embedded graphics, and links to other documents and the Internet. Word is a program that you can learn gradually, and then add more advanced skills one at a time.

Each chapter opens with a story that sets the stage for the projects the student will create; the instruction does not force the student to pretend to be someone or make up a scenario.

Each chapter has an introductory paragraph that briefs students on what is important.

Visual Summary

Shows students upfront what their projects will look like when they are done.

Project Summary

Stated clearly and quickly in one paragraph.

NEW

File Guide

Clearly shows students which files are needed for the project and the names they will use to save their documents.

Objective

The skills the student will learn are clearly stated at the beginning of each project and color coded to match projects listed on the chapter opener page.

Teachable Moment

Expository text is woven into the steps—at the moment students need to know it—not chunked together in a block of text that will go unread.

NEW

Screen Shots

Larger screen shots.

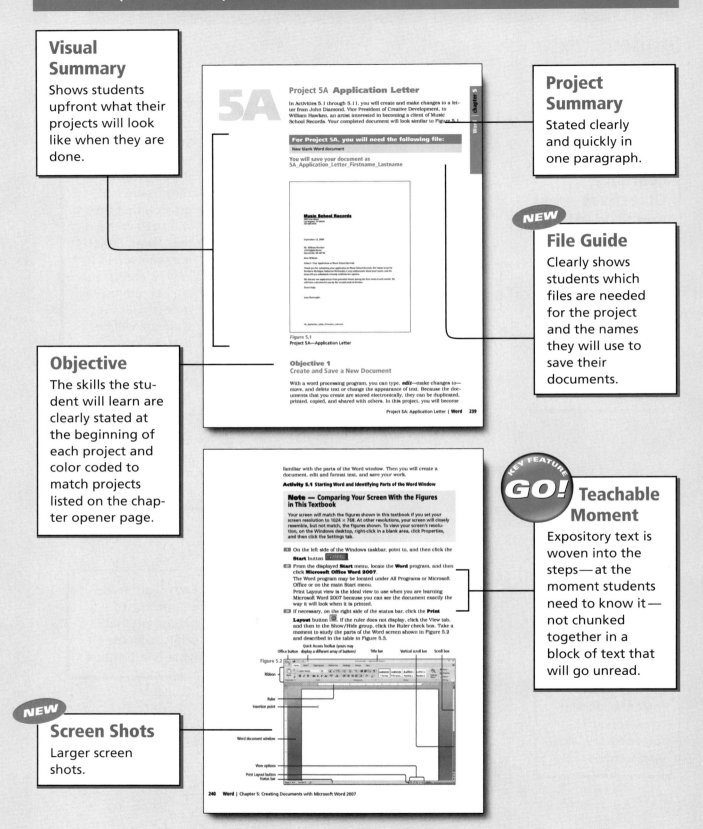

Steps

Color coded to the current project, easy to read, and not too many to confuse the student or too few to be meaningless.

GO! KEY FEATURE

Sequential Pagination

No more confusing letters and abbreviations.

---

8 Press **Enter** two more times.

In a business letter, insert two blank lines between the date and the inside address, which is the same as the address you would use on an envelope.

9 Type **Mr. William Hawken** and then press **Enter**.

The wavy red line under the proper name *Hawken* indicates that the word has been flagged as misspelled because it is a word not contained in the Word dictionary.

10 On two lines, type the following address, but do not press **Enter** at the end of the second line:

123 Eighth Street
Harrisville, MI 48740

Note — Typing the Address

Include a comma after the city name in an inside address. However, for mailing addresses on envelopes, eliminate the comma after the city name.

11 On the **Home tab**, in the **Styles group**, click the **Normal** button.

The Normal style is applied to the text in the rest of the document. Recall that the Normal style adds extra space between paragraphs; it also adds slightly more space between lines in a paragraph.

12 Press **Enter**. Type **Dear William:** and then press **Enter**.

This salutation is the line that greets the person receiving the letter.

13 Type **Subject: Your Application to Music School Records** and press **Enter**. Notice the light dots between words, which indicate spaces and display when formatting marks are displayed. Also, notice the extra space after each paragraph, and then compare your screen with Figure 5.6.

The subject line is optional, but you should include a subject line in most letters to identify the topic. Depending on your Word settings, a wavy green line may display in the subject line, indicating a potential grammar error.

GO! KEY FEATURE

Microsoft Procedural Syntax

All steps are written in Microsoft Procedural Syntax to put the student in the right place at the right time.

Note — Space Between Lines in Your Printed Document

The Cambria font, and many others, uses a slightly larger space between the lines than more traditional fonts like Times New Roman. As you progress in your study of Word, you will use many different fonts and also adjust the spacing between lines.

9 From the **Office** menu, click **Close**, saving any changes if prompted to do so. Leave Word open for the next project.

Another Way | **To Print a Document**

To Print a document:

• From the Office menu, click Print to display the Print dialog box (to be covered later), from which you can choose a variety of different options, such as printing multiple copies, printing on a different printer, and printing some but not all pages.

• Hold down **Ctrl** and then press **P**. This is an alternative to the Office menu command, and opens the Print dialog box.

• Hold down **Alt**, press **F**, and then press **P**. This opens the Print dialog box.

End You have completed Project 5A

End-of-Project Icon

All projects in the *GO! Series* have clearly identifiable end points, useful in self-paced or on-line environments.

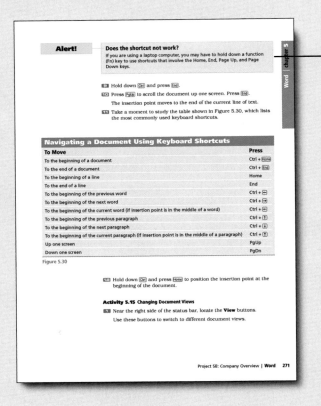

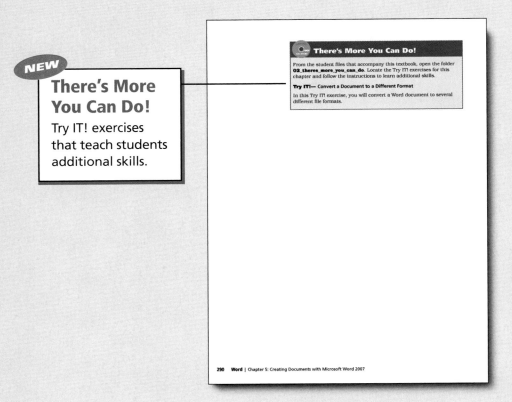

Alert box
Draws students' attention to make sure they aren't getting too far off course.

Another Way box
Shows students other ways of doing tasks.

More Knowledge box
Expands on a topic by going deeper into the material.

Note box
Points out important items to remember.

NEW

There's More You Can Do!
Try IT! exercises that teach students additional skills.

End-of-Chapter Material

Take your pick! Content-based or Outcomes-based projects to choose from. Below is a table outlining the various types of projects that fit into these two categories.

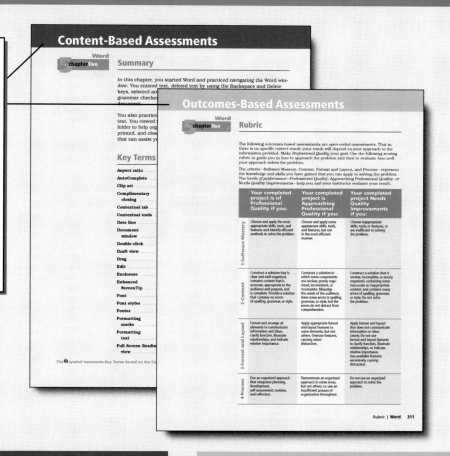

Content-Based Assessments
(Defined solutions with solution files provided for grading)

Project Letter	Name	Objectives Covered
N/A	Summary and Key Terms	
N/A	Multiple Choice	
N/A	Fill-in-the-blank	
C	Skills Review	Covers A Objectives
D	Skills Review	Covers B Objectives
E	Mastering Excel	Covers A Objectives
F	Mastering Excel	Covers B Objectives
G	Mastering Excel	Covers any combination of A and B Objectives
H	Mastering Excel	Covers any combination of A and B Objectives
I	Mastering Excel	Covers all A and B Objectives
J	Business Running Case	Covers all A and B Objectives

Outcomes-Based Assessments
(Open solutions that require a rubric for grading)

Project Letter	Name	Objectives Covered
N/A	Rubric	
K	Problem Solving	Covers as many Objectives from A and B as possible
L	Problem Solving	Covers as many Objectives from A and B as possible.
M	Problem Solving	Covers as many Objectives from A and B as possible.
N	Problem Solving	Covers as many Objectives from A and B as possible.
O	Problem Solving	Covers as many Objectives from A and B as possible.
P	You and GO!	Covers as many Objectives from A and B as possible
Q	GO! Help	Not tied to specific objectives
R	* Group Business Running Case	Covers A and B Objectives

* This project is provided only with the *GO! with Microsoft Office 2007 Introductory* book.

Teach (continued)

Objectives List

Most projects in the end-of-chapter section begin with a list of the objectives covered.

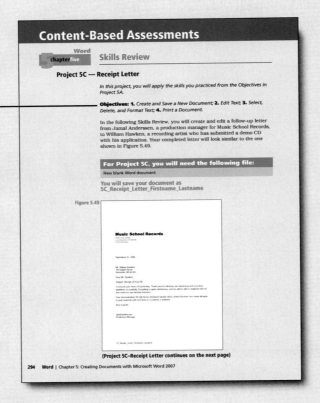

End of Each Project Clearly Marked

Clearly identified end points help separate the end-of-chapter projects.

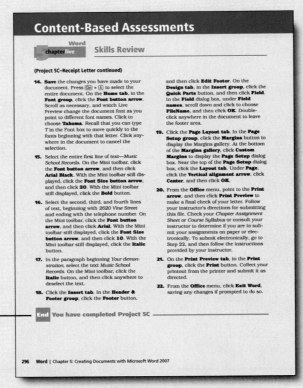

NEW

Rubric

A matrix that states the criteria and standards for grading student work. Used to grade open-ended assessments.

Outcomes-Based Assessments

Word chapter five **Rubric**

The following outcomes-based assessments are *open-ended assessments.* That is, there is no specific correct result; your result will depend on your approach to the information provided. Make *Professional Quality* your goal. Use the following scoring rubric to guide you in *how* to approach the problem and then to evaluate *how well* your approach solves the problem.

The *criteria*—Software Mastery, Content, Format and Layout, and Process—represent the knowledge and skills you have gained that you can apply to solving the problem. The *levels of performance*—Professional Quality, Approaching Professional Quality, or Needs Quality Improvements—help you and your instructor evaluate your result.

	Your completed project is of Professional Quality if you:	Your completed project is Approaching Professional Quality if you:	Your completed project Needs Quality Improvements if you:
1-Software Mastery	Choose and apply the most appropriate skills, tools, and features and identify efficient methods to solve the problem.	Choose and apply some appropriate skills, tools, and features, but not in the most efficient manner.	Choose inappropriate skills, tools, or features, or are inefficient in solving the problem.
2-Content	Construct a solution that is clear and well organized, contains content that is accurate, appropriate to the audience and purpose, and is complete. Provide a solution that contains no errors of spelling, grammar, or style.	Construct a solution in which some components are unclear, poorly organized, inconsistent, or incomplete. Misjudge the needs of the audience. Have some errors in spelling, grammar, or style, but the errors do not detract from comprehension.	Construct a solution that is unclear, incomplete, or poorly organized, containing some inaccurate or inappropriate content, and contains many errors of spelling, grammar, or style. Do not solve the problem.
3-Format and Layout	Format and arrange all elements to communicate information and ideas, clarify function, illustrate relationships, and indicate relative importance.	Apply appropriate format and layout features to some elements, but not others. Overuse features, causing minor distraction.	Apply format and layout that does not communicate information or ideas clearly. Do not use format and layout features to clarify function, illustrate relationships, or indicate relative importance. Use available features excessively, causing distraction.
4-Process	Use an organized approach that integrates planning, development, self-assessment, revision, and reflection.	Demonstrate an organized approach in some areas, but not others; or use an insufficient process of organization throughout.	Do not use an organized approach to solve the problem.

Rubric | **Word** 311

Outcomes-Based Assessments

Word chapter five   You and *GO!*

Project 5P — You and Go!

In this project, you will construct a solution by applying any combination of the skills you practiced from the Objectives in Projects 5A and 5B.

From the student files that accompany this textbook, open the folder **04_you_and_go**. Locate the You and *GO!* project for this chapter and follow the instructions to create a cover letter for your resume.

End You have completed Project 5P

GO! with Help

Project 5Q — *Go!* with Help

The Word Help system is extensive and can help you as you work. In this chapter, you used the Quick Access Toolbar on several occasions. You can customize the Quick Access Toolbar by adding buttons that you use regularly, making them quickly available to you from any tab on the Ribbon. In this project, you will use Help to find out how to add buttons.

1 **Start** Word. At the far right end of the Ribbon, click the **Microsoft Office Word Help** button. In the **Word Help** dialog box, click the **Search button arrow**, and then click **Offline Word Help**.

2 In the **Type words to search for** box, type Quick Access Toolbar and then press Enter.

3 From the list of search results, click **Customize the Quick Access Toolbar**.

4 Click each of the links to find out how to add buttons from the Ribbon and from the **Options** dialog box.

5 When you are through, **Close** the Help window, and then **Close** Word.

End You have completed Project 5Q

318 **Word** | Chapter 5: Creating Documents with Microsoft Word 2007

NEW

You and *GO!*

A project in which students use information from their own lives and apply the skills from the chapter to a personal task.

GO! with Help

Students practice using the Help feature of the Office application.

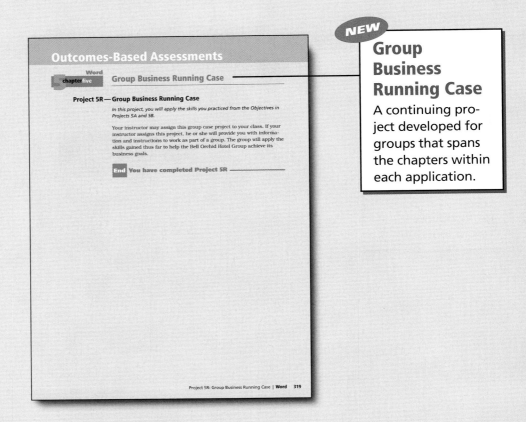

Group Business Running Case

A continuing project developed for groups that spans the chapters within each application.

Student CD includes:

- Student Data Files
- There's More You Can Do!
- Business Running Case
- You and *GO!*

Companion Web site

An interactive Web site to further student leaning.

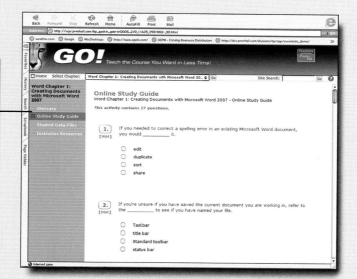

Online Study Guide

Interactive objective-style questions to help students study.

Teach (continued)

Annotated Instructor Edition

The Annotated Instructor Edition contains a full version of the student textbook that includes tips, supplement references, and pointers on teaching with the *GO!* instructional system.

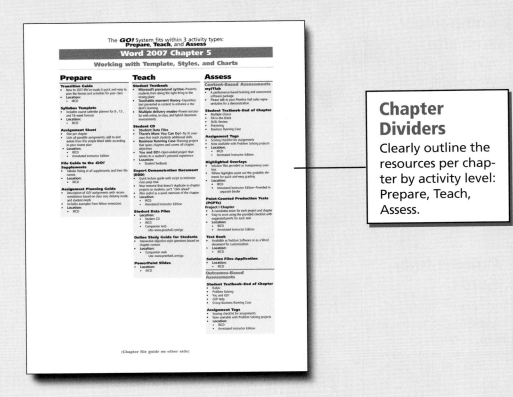

Chapter Dividers

Clearly outline the resources per chapter by activity level: Prepare, Teach, Assess.

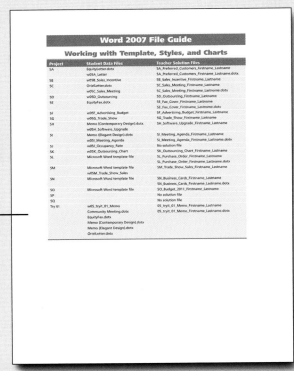

Instructor File Guide

Complete list of all Student Data Files and instructor Solution Files needed for the chapter.

Helpful Hints, Teaching Tips, Expand the Project

References correspond to what is being taught in the student textbook.

NEW

Full-Size Textbook Pages

An instructor copy of the textbook with traditional Instructor Manual content incorporated.

Figure 5.8

Teaching Tip

Saving files with spaces in the file name is an acceptable practice in Microsoft Word, but if students need to submit files electronically, they will need to use an underscore instead of a space in the file name.

Teaching Tip

It is important to give meaningful names to files and folders. One should be able to guess the purpose of a file or folder without looking inside it.

Expand the Project

Provide students with a few examples of files and ask them to suggest how to name them. What would you name the file and folder for the following examples?
- Homework from chemistry lab class today
- Résumé for an internship job at Jones, Inc.
- Letter to your congressional representative
- List of potential employers

More Knowledge

Renaming a Folder

You can also rename existing folders. To rename a folder, right-click the folder in the Save As dialog box, click Rename from the shortcut menu, and then type a new folder name. This procedure also works in My Computer or Windows Explorer. You can follow the same procedure to rename an individual file, as long as you do not modify the file extension.

B In the lower portion of the **Save As** dialog box, locate the **File name** box. If necessary, select or delete the existing text, and then in the **File name** box, using your own first and last names, type 5A_Application_Letter_Firstname_Lastname being sure to include the underscore—⧉ Shift + ⧉—instead of spaces between words, as shown in Figure 5.9.

Throughout this textbook, you will be instructed to save your files using the file name followed by your first and last names. Check with your instructor to see if there is some other file-naming arrangement for your course.

The Microsoft Windows operating system recognizes file names with spaces. However, some Internet file transfer programs do not. To facilitate sending your files over the Internet, using a course management system, in this textbook you will be instructed to save files using an underscore instead of a space. The underscore key is the shift of the ⧉ key—on most keyboards located two keys to the left of ← Bksp.

Project 5A: Application Letter | **Word** 247

Content-Based Assessments

Word

chapter five | Matching

Match each term in the second column with its correct definition in the first column. Write the letter of the term on the blank line in front of the correct definition.

___C___ **1.** The location in the Word window, indicated by a blinking vertical line, where text will be inserted when you start to type.

___F___ **2.** In the Word window, the location of the Minimize, Maximize/Restore Down, and Close buttons.

___O___ **3.** A button that represents the command to reveal nonprinting characters.

___K___ **4.** The action that takes place when the insertion point reaches the right margin and automatically moves down and to the left margin of the next line.

___B___ **5.** The process of setting the overall appearance of the text within the document.

___G___ **6.** To hold down the left mouse button and move the mouse pointer over text to select it.

___H___ **7.** A set of ... and sh...

A Draft
B Drag
C Font
D Footer
E Formatting
F Insertion point
G Keyboard shortcut
H Live preview
I Point
J Sans serif
K Serif
L Shortcut menu
M Show/Hide ¶

End-of-Chapter Concepts Assessments contain the answers for quick reference.

Content-Based Assessments

Word

chapter five | Fill in the Blank

Write the correct word in the space provided.

1. Microsoft Word 2007 is a word _Right_ program that you can use to perform tasks such as writing a memo, a report, or a letter.

2. Located at the bottom of the Word window, the bar that provides information such as page number and word count is referred to as the _Space_ bar.

3. Within the scroll bar, dragging the _Double Click_ downward causes the document on your screen to move up.

4. A toolbar above the Ribbon and to the right of the Office button, which can be customized by adding frequently used buttons, is called the _Blank Blank Blank_ (QAT).

5. Characters that display on the screen to show the location of paragraph marks, tabs, and spaces but that do not print are called _Space_ marks.

6. If you point to a button on the Ribbon, a _Help_ displays the name of the button.

7. A purple dotted line under an address or a date indicating that the information could be placed into another Office program such as Outlook is a _URL_.

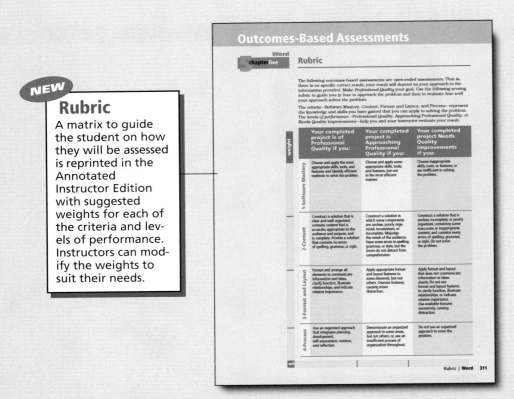

NEW

Rubric

A matrix to guide the student on how they will be assessed is reprinted in the Annotated Instructor Edition with suggested weights for each of the criteria and levels of performance. Instructors can modify the weights to suit their needs.

Assess

Assignment Tags

NEW

Scoring checklist for assignments. Now also available for Problem-Solving projects.

GO! with Microsoft® Office 2007

Assignment Tags for GO! with Office 2007
Word Chapter 5

| Name: | | Project: | **5A** |
| Professor: | | Course: | |

Task	Points	Your Score
Center text vertically on page	2	
Delete the word "really"	1	
Delete the words "try to"	1	
Replace "last" with "first"	1	
Insert the word "potential"	1	
Replace "John W. Diamond" with "Lucy Burrows"	1	
Change entire document to the Cambria font	2	
Change the first line of text to Arial Black 20 pt. font	2	
Bold the first line of text	2	
Change the 2nd through 4th lines to Arial 10 pt.	2	
Italicize the 2nd through 4th lines of text	2	
Correct/Add footer as instructed	2	
Circled information is incorrect or formatted incorrectly		
Total Points	**20**	**0**

| Name: | | Project: | **5B** |
| Professor: | | Course: | |

Task	Points	Your Score
Insert the file w05B_Music_School_Records	4	
Insert the Music Logo	4	
Remove duplicate "and"	2	
Change spelling and grammar errors (4)	8	
Correct/Add footer as instructed	2	
Circled information is incorrect or formatted incorrectly		
Total Points	**20**	**0**

| Name: | | Project: | **5C** |
| Professor: | | Course: | |

Task	Points	Your Score
Add four line letterhead	2	
Insert today's date	1	
Add address block, subject line, and greeting	2	
Add two-paragraph body of letter	2	
Add closing, name, and title	2	
In subject line, capitalize "receipt"	1	
Change "standards" to "guidelines"	1	
Insert "quite"	1	
Insert "all"	1	
Change the first line of text to Arial Black 20 pt. font	2	
Bold the first line of text	1	
Change the 2nd through 4th lines to Arial 10 pt.	1	
Italicize the 2nd through 4th lines of text	1	
Correct/add footer as instructed	2	
Circled information is incorrect or formatted incorrectly		
Total Points	**20**	**0**

| Name: | | Project: | **5D** |
| Professor: | | Course: | |

Task	Points	Your Score
Insert the file w05D_Marketing	4	
Bold the first two title lines	2	
Correct spelling of "Marketting"	2	
Correct spelling of "geners"	2	
Correct all misspellings of "allready"	2	
Correct grammar error "are" to "is"	2	
Insert the Piano image	4	
Correct/add footer as instructed	2	
Circled information is incorrect or formatted incorrectly		
Total Points	**20**	**0**

Highlighted Overlays

Solution files provided as transparency overlays. Yellow highlights point out the gradable elements for quick and easy grading.

Music School Records

2620 Vine Street
Los Angeles, CA 90028
323-555-0028

20 point Arial Black, bold and underline

10 point Arial, italic

September 12, 2009

Text vertically centered on page

Body of document changed to Cambria font, 11 point

Mr. William Hawken
123 Eighth Street
Harrisville, MI 48740

Dear William:

Subject: Your Application to Music School Records

Thank you for submitting your application to Music School Records. Our talent scout for Northern Michigan, Catherine McDonald, is very enthusiastic about your music, and the demo CD you submitted certainly confirms her opinion.

Word "really" deleted

We discuss our applications from potential clients during the first week of each month. We will have a decision for you by the second week of October.

Words "try to" deleted

Yours Truly,

Lucy Burroughs

Point-Counted Production Tests (PCPTs)

A cumulative exam for each **project**, **chapter**, and **application**. Easy to score using the provided checklist with suggested points for each task.

GO! with Microsoft® Office 2007 Introductory

Point-Counted Production Test—Project for GO! with Microsoft® Office 2007 Introductory Project 5A

Instructor Name: _____

Course Information: _____

1. Start Word 2007 to begin a new blank document. Save your document as 5A_Cover_Letter_Firstname_Lastname Remember to save your file frequently as you work.

2. If necessary, display the formatting marks. With the insertion point blinking in the upper left corner of the document to the left of the default first paragraph mark, type the current date (you can use AutoComplete).

3. Press Enter three times and type the inside address:

   Music School Records
   2620 Vine Street
   Los Angeles, CA 90028

4. Press Enter three times, and type Dear Ms. Burroughs:

   Press Enter twice, and type Subject: Application to Music School Records

   Press Enter twice, and type the following text (skipping one line between paragraphs):

   I read about Music School Records in Con Brio magazine and I would like to inquire about the possibility of being represented by your company.

   I am very interested in a career in jazz and am planning to relocate to the Los Angeles area in the very near future. I would be interested in learning more about the company and about available opportunities.

   I was a member of my high school jazz band for three years. In addition, I have been playing in the local coffee shop for the last two years. My demo CD, which is enclosed, contains three of my most requested songs.

   I would appreciate the opportunity to speak with you. Thank you for your time and consideration. I look forward to speaking with you about this exciting opportunity.

5. Press Enter three times, and type the closing Sincerely, Press enter four times, and type your name.

6. Insert a footer that contains the file name.

7. Delete the first instance of the word *very* in the second body paragraph, and insert the word modern in front of *jazz*.

Copyright © 2008 Pearson Prentice Hall   Page 1 of 1

Test Bank

Available as TestGen Software or as a Word document for customization.

Chapter 5: Creating Documents with Microsoft Word 2007

Multiple Choice:

1. With word processing programs, how are documents stored?

   A. On a network

   B. On the computer

   C. Electronically

   D. On the floppy disk

   Answer: C   **Reference:** Objective 1: Create and Save a New Document   **Difficulty:** Moderate

2. Because you will see the document as it will print, _____ view is the ideal view to use when learning Microsoft Word 2007.

   A. Reading

   B. Normal

   C. Print Layout

   D. Outline

   Answer: C   **Reference:** Objective 1: Create and Save a New Document   **Difficulty:** Moderate

3. The blinking vertical line where text or graphics will be inserted is called the:

   A. cursor.

   B. insertion point.

   C. blinking line.

   D. I-beam.

   Answer: B   **Reference:** Objective 1: Create and Save a New Document   **Difficulty:** Easy

Music School Records

Music School Records discovers, launches, and develops the careers of young artists in classical, jazz, and contemporary music. Our philosophy is to not only shape, distribute, and sell a music product, but to help artists create a career that can last a lifetime. Too often in the music industry, artists are forced to fit their music to a trend that is short-lived. Music School Records does not just follow trends, we take a long-term view of the music industry and help our artists develop a style and repertoire that is fluid and flexible and that will appeal to audiences for years and even decades.

The music industry is constantly changing, but over the last decade, the changes have been enormous. New forms of entertainment such as DVDs, video games, and the Internet mean there is more competition for the leisure dollar in the market. New technologies give consumers more options for buying and listening to music, and they are demanding high quality recordings. Young consumers are comfortable with technology and want the music they love when and where they want it, no matter where they are or what they are doing.

Music School Records embraces new technologies and the sophisticated market of young music lovers. We believe that providing high quality recordings of truly talented artists make for more discerning listeners who will cherish the gift of music for the rest of their lives. The expertise of Music School Records includes:

- Insight into our target market and the ability to reach the desired audience
- The ability to access all current sources of music income
- A management team with years of experience in music commerce
- Innovative business strategies and artist development plans
- Investment in technology infrastructure for high quality recordings and business services

pagexxxix_top.docx

Solution Files–Application and PDF format

Online Assessment and Training

myitlab is Prentice Hall's new performance-based solution that allows you to easily deliver outcomes-based courses on Microsoft Office 2007, with customized training and defensible assessment. Key features of myitlab include:

A *true* "system" approach: myitlab content is the same as in your textbook.

Project-based *and* skills-based: Students complete real-life assignments.

Advanced reporting *and* gradebook: These include student click stream data.

***No* installation required:** myitlab is completely Web-based. You just need an Internet connection, small plug-in, and Adobe Flash Player.

Ask your Prentice Hall sales representative for a demonstration or visit:

www.prenhall.com/myitlab

chapter**one**

Creating Documents with Microsoft Word 2007

OBJECTIVES

At the end of this chapter you will be able to:

1. Create and Save a New Document
2. Edit Text
3. Select, Delete, and Format Text
4. Print a Document

OUTCOMES

Mastering these objectives will enable you to:

PROJECT 1A
Create, Edit, Save, and Print a Document

5. Navigate the Word Window
6. Add a Graphic to a Document
7. Use the Spelling and Grammar Checker
8. Preview and Print Documents, Close a Document, and Close Word
9. Use the Microsoft Help System

PROJECT 1B
Navigate the Word Window and Check Your Work

Music School Records

Music School Records was created to launch young musical artists with undiscovered talent in jazz, classical, and contemporary music. The creative management team searches internationally for talented young people, and has a reputation for mentoring and developing the skills of its artists. The company's music is tailored to an audience that is young, knowledgeable about music, and demands the highest quality recordings. Music School Records releases are available in CD format as well as digital downloads.

Getting Started with Microsoft Office Word 2007

A word processor is the most common program found on personal computers and one that almost everyone has a reason to use. When you learn word processing you are also learning skills and techniques that you need to work efficiently on a personal computer. You can use Microsoft Word to perform basic word processing tasks such as writing a memo, a report, or a letter. You can also use Word to complete complex word processing tasks, such as those that include sophisticated tables, embedded graphics, and links to other documents and the Internet. Word is a program that you can learn gradually, and then add more advanced skills one at a time.

Project 1A **Application Letter**

In Activities 1.1 through 1.11, you will create and make changes to a letter from John Diamond, Vice President of Creative Development, to William Hawken, an artist interested in becoming a client of Music School Records. Your completed document will look similar to Figure 1.1.

For Project 1A, you will need the following file:

New blank Word document

You will save your document as
1A_Application_Letter_Firstname_Lastname

Music School Records
2620 Vine Street
Los Angeles, CA 90028
323-555-0028

September 12, 2009

Mr. William Hawken
123 Eighth Street
Harrisville, MI 48740

Dear William:

Subject: Your Application to Music School Records

Thank you for submitting your application to Music School Records. Our talent scout for Northern Michigan, Catherine McDonald, is very enthusiastic about your music, and the demo CD you submitted certainly confirms her opinion.

We discuss our applications from potential clients during the first week of each month. We will have a decision for you by the second week of October.

Yours truly,

Lucy Burroughs

1A_Application_Letter_Firstname_Lastname

Figure 1.1
Project 1A—Application Letter

Objective 1
Create and Save a New Document

With a word processing program, you can type, *edit*—make changes to— move, and delete text or change the appearance of text. Because the documents that you create are stored electronically, they can be duplicated, printed, copied, and shared with others. In this project, you will become familiar with the parts of the Word window. Then you will create a document, edit and format text, and save your work.

Activity 1.1 Starting Word and Identifying Parts of the Word Window

> **Note — Comparing Your Screen with the Figures in This Textbook**
>
> Your screen will match the figures shown in this textbook if you set your screen resolution to 1024 × 768. At other resolutions, your screen will closely resemble, but not match, the figures shown. To view your screen's resolution, on the Windows desktop, right-click in a blank area, click Properties, and then click the Settings tab.

1 On the left side of the Windows taskbar, point to, and then click the **Start** button [*start*].

2 From the displayed **Start** menu, locate the **Word** program, and then click **Microsoft Office Word 2007**.

The Word program may be located under All Programs or Microsoft Office or on the main Start menu.

Print Layout view is the ideal view to use when you are learning Microsoft Word 2007 because you can see the document exactly the way it will look when it is printed.

3 If necessary, on the right side of the status bar, click the **Print Layout** button [🔲]. If the ruler does not display, click the View tab, and then in the Show/Hide group, click the Ruler check box. Take a moment to study the parts of the Word screen shown in Figure 1.2 and described in the table in Figure 1.3.

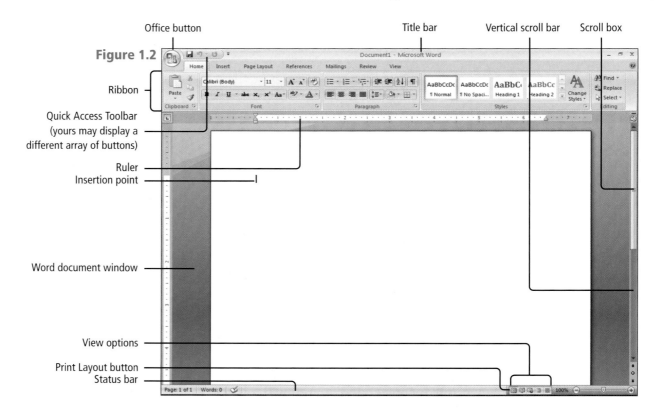

Figure 1.2

Office button · Title bar · Vertical scroll bar · Scroll box · Ribbon · Quick Access Toolbar (yours may display a different array of buttons) · Ruler · Insertion point · Word document window · View options · Print Layout button · Status bar

Microsoft Word Screen Elements

Screen Element	Description
Insertion point	Indicates, with a blinking vertical line, where text or graphics will be inserted.
Office button	Displays a list of commands related to things you can do *with* a document, such as opening, saving, printing, or sharing.
Quick Access Toolbar (QAT)	Displays buttons to perform frequently used commands with a single click. Frequently used commands in Word include Save, Undo, Redo, and Print. For commands that *you* use frequently, you can add additional buttons to the Quick Access Toolbar.
Ribbon	Organizes commands on tabs, and then groups the commands by topic for performing related document tasks.
Ruler	Displays the location of margins, indents, columns, and tab stops for the selected paragraph(s).
Scroll box	Provides a visual indication of your location in a document. It can also be used with the mouse to drag a document up and down to reposition the document.
Status bar	Displays, on the left side, the page and line number, word count, and the Proof button. On the right side, displays buttons to control the look of the window. The status bar can be customized to include other information.
Title bar	Displays the name of the document and the name of the program. The Minimize, Maximize/Restore Down, and Close buttons are grouped on the right side of the title bar.
Vertical scroll bar	Enables you to move up and down in a document to display text that is not visible.
View options	Contains buttons for viewing the document in Print Layout, Full Screen Reading, Web Layout, Outline, or Draft views, and also displays controls to Zoom Out and Zoom In.
Word document window	Displays the active document.

Figure 1.3

Alert! — **Does your screen differ?**

The appearance of the screen can vary, depending on various settings that were established when Office 2007 was installed. Additionally, the Quick Access Toolbar can display any combination of buttons.

Activity 1.2 Beginning a New Document and Displaying Formatting Marks

When you start the Word program, you need only start typing to create a new document. As you work on a document, save your changes frequently—the Save button is always available on the Quick Access Toolbar.

1 On the title bar, notice that *Document1* displays.

Word displays the file name of a document in both the title bar at the top of the screen and on a button in the Windows taskbar at the lower edge of the screen—including new unsaved documents. The new unsaved document displays *Document* followed by a number; the number depends on how many times you have started a new document during your current Word session.

2 In the displayed blank document, determine if a paragraph symbol (¶) displays in the upper left corner of the document, as shown in Figure 1.4. If you do *not* see the paragraph symbol, on the Ribbon, on the **Home tab**, in the **Paragraph group**, click the **Show/Hide ¶** button ¶ to display the formatting marks.

When you press Enter, Spacebar, or Tab on your keyboard, characters display in your document to represent these keystrokes. These characters do not print and are referred to as ***formatting marks*** or ***nonprinting characters***. Because formatting marks guide your eye in a document—like a map and road signs guide you along a highway—these marks will display throughout this instruction.

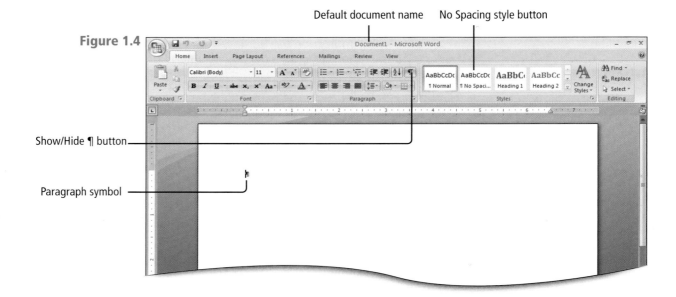

Default document name   No Spacing style button

Figure 1.4

Show/Hide ¶ button

Paragraph symbol

3 Click the **Show/Hide ¶** button ¶ to turn off the display of nonprinting characters. Then, click the **Show/Hide ¶** button ¶ one more time to turn it on again.

The Show/Hide ¶ button is referred to as a ***toggle button***—you can click the button one time to turn it on and click it again to turn it off.

4 On the **Home tab**, in the **Styles group**, click the **No Spacing** style button.

By default, Word adds spacing after each paragraph. In a business letter, the address block should be single-spaced, with no spacing after each paragraph. The No Spacing button applies a style to the text that removes extra spacing. A ***style*** is a set of formatting characteristics—such as line spacing, space after paragraphs, font, and font style—that can be applied to text, paragraphs, tables, or lists.

Activity 1.3 Entering Text and Inserting Blank Lines

Business letters follow a standard format and contain the following parts: the current date—the ***date line***; the name and address of the person receiving the letter—the ***inside address***; a greeting—the ***salutation***; an optional subject—the ***subject line***; the body of the letter; a closing line—the ***complimentary closing***; and the ***writer's identification***, which includes the name or job title (or both) of the writer. Some letters also include the initials of the person who typed the letter, and a list of ***enclosures***—documents included with the letter. In this activity, you will begin to enter the text of a business letter.

1 With the insertion point blinking in the upper left corner of the document to the left of the default first paragraph mark, type **Music School Records** and then press Enter.

2 Type the following text, and then press Enter after each line:

2620 Vine Street
Los Angeles, CA 90028
323-555-0028

3 Press Enter five more times, type **Sept** and then compare your screen with Figure 1.5.

A ***ScreenTip*** displays *September (Press ENTER to Insert)*. This feature, called ***AutoComplete***, assists you in typing. After you type the first few characters, AutoComplete suggests commonly used words and phrases to enter. A ScreenTip is a small note, activated by holding the pointer over a button or other screen object, which displays information about a screen element.

Figure 1.5

ScreenTip

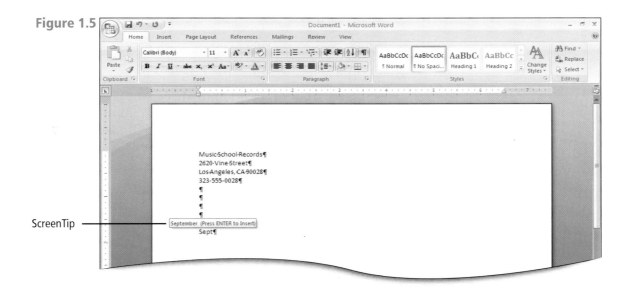

4 To finish the word *September*, press Enter. Press Spacebar, type **12, 2009** and then press Enter. If you are completing this activity during the month of September, AutoComplete may offer to fill in the current date. To ignore the suggestion, type as indicated.

The first paragraph is complete and the insertion point is positioned at the beginning of the next line. A paragraph is created when you press Enter. Thus, a paragraph can be a single line like this date line, or a blank line.

5 Press ⌨Enter two more times.

In a business letter, insert two blank lines between the date and the inside address, which is the same as the address you would use on an envelope.

6 Type **Mr. William Hawken** and then press ⌨Enter.

The wavy red line under the proper name *Hawken* indicates that the word has been flagged as misspelled because it is a word not contained in the Word dictionary.

7 On two lines, type the following address, but do not press ⌨Enter at the end of the second line:

**123 Eighth Street
Harrisville, MI 48740**

Note — Typing the Address

Include a comma after the city name in an inside address. However, for mailing addresses on envelopes, eliminate the comma after the city name.

8 On the **Home tab**, in the **Styles group**, click the **Normal** button.

The Normal style is applied to the text in the rest of the document. Recall that the Normal style adds extra space between paragraphs; it also adds slightly more space between lines in a paragraph.

9 Press ⌨Enter. Type **Dear William:** and then press ⌨Enter.

This salutation is the line that greets the person receiving the letter.

10 Type **Subject: Your Application to Music School Records** and press ⌨Enter. Notice the light dots between words, which indicate spaces and display when formatting marks are displayed. Also, notice the extra space after each paragraph, and then compare your screen with Figure 1.6.

The subject line is optional, but you should include a subject line in most letters to identify the topic. Depending on your Word settings, a wavy green line may display in the subject line, indicating a potential grammar error.

Light dots indicate spaces resulting
from pressing the space bar on your keyboard

Figure 1.6

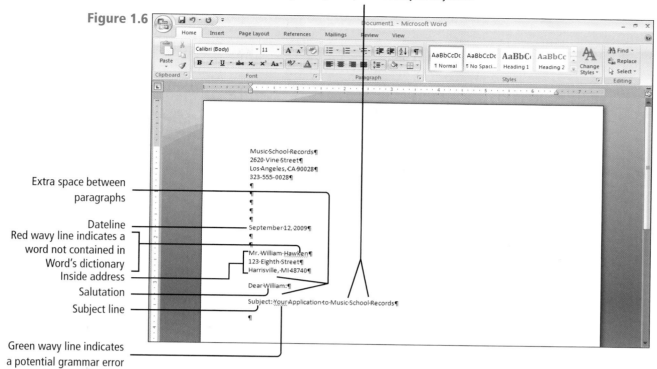

Extra space between
paragraphs

Dateline
Red wavy line indicates a
word not contained in
Word's dictionary
Inside address
Salutation
Subject line

Green wavy line indicates
a potential grammar error

Activity 1.4 Creating Folders for Document Storage and Saving a Document

In the same way that you use file folders to organize your paper documents, Windows uses a hierarchy of electronic folders to keep your electronic files organized. When you save a document file, the Windows operating system stores your document permanently on a storage medium. Changes that you make to existing documents, such as changing text or typing in new text, are not permanently saved until you perform a Save operation.

1 In the upper left corner of your screen, click the **Office** button, and from the displayed menu, point to the words **Save As**—not the Save As arrow—and click.

2 In the displayed **Save As** dialog box, at the right edge of the **Save in** box, click the **Save in arrow** to view a list of the drives available to you, as shown in Figure 1.7.

Figure 1.7

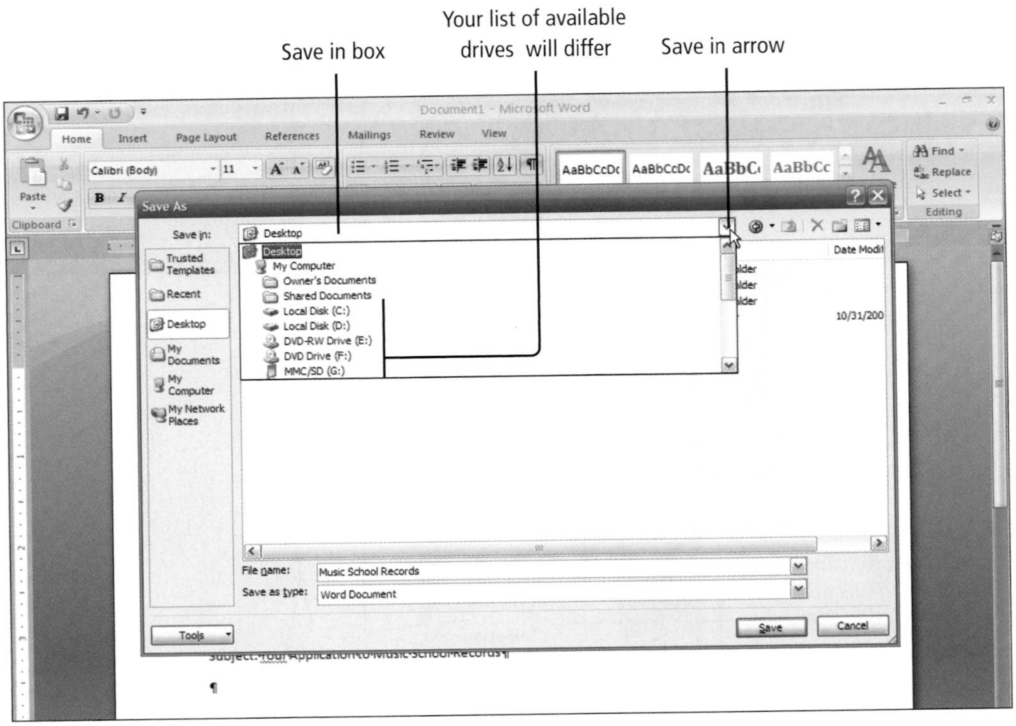

Save in box

Your list of available drives will differ

Save in arrow

---

3 Navigate to the drive on which you will be storing your folders and projects for this chapter—for example, a USB flash drive that you have connected, a shared drive on a network, or the drive designated by your instructor or lab coordinator.

4 In the **Save As** dialog box, on the toolbar, click the **Create New Folder** button ⬚. In the displayed **New Folder** dialog box, in the **Name** box, type **Word Chapter 1** as shown in Figure 1.8, and then click **OK**.

The new folder name displays in the Save in box, indicating that the folder is open and ready to store your document.

Figure 1.8

New folder name   Create New Folder button

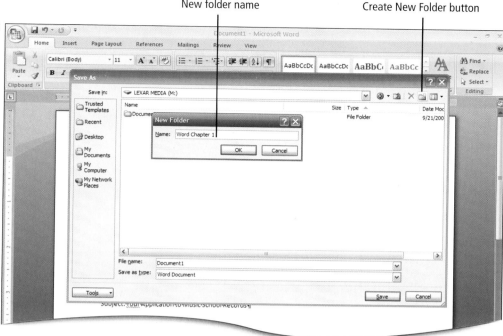

More Knowledge
Renaming a Folder

You can also rename existing folders. To rename a folder, right-click the folder in the Save As dialog box, click Rename from the shortcut menu, and then type a new folder name. This procedure also works in My Computer or Windows Explorer. You can follow the same procedure to rename an individual file, as long as you do not modify the file extension.

5 In the lower portion of the **Save As** dialog box, locate the **File name** box. If necessary, select or delete the existing text, and then in the **File name** box, using your own first and last names, type **1A_Application_Letter_Firstname_Lastname** being sure to include the underscore—⟨⇧ Shift⟩ + ⟨-⟩—instead of spaces between words, as shown in Figure 1.9.

Throughout this textbook, you will be instructed to save your files using the file name followed by your first and last names. Check with your instructor to see if there is some other file-naming arrangement for your course.

The Microsoft Windows operating system recognizes file names with spaces. However, some Internet file transfer programs do not. To facilitate sending your files over the Internet, using a course management system, in this textbook you will be instructed to save files using an underscore instead of a space. The underscore key is the shift of the ⟨-⟩ key—on most keyboards located two keys to the left of ⟨←Bksp⟩.

Figure 1.9

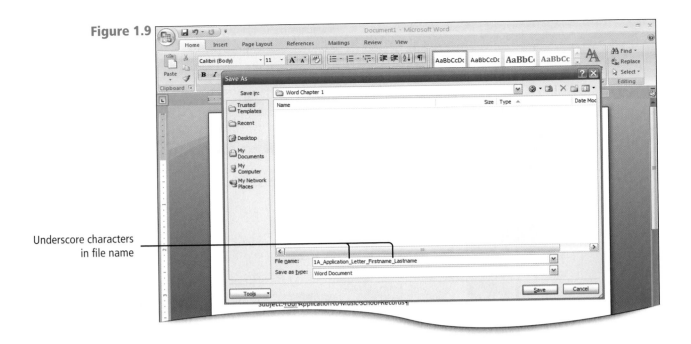

Underscore characters
in file name

6 In the lower portion of the **Save As** dialog box, click the **Save** button, or press [Enter]. The file extension .*docx* may or may not display, depending on your Word settings.

Your file is saved on the storage device that you selected, and it is contained in the *Word Chapter 1* folder with the new file name. The new file name also displays in the title bar.

7 As you type the following text, press the [Spacebar] only one time at the end of a sentence: **Thank you for submitting your application to Music School Records. Our talent scout for Northern Michigan, Catherine McDonald, is really very enthusiastic about your music, and the demo CD you submitted certainly confirms her opinion.** Press [Enter].

As you type, the insertion point moves to the right, and when it approaches the right margin, Word determines whether or not the next word in the line will fit within the established right margin. If the word does not fit, Word will move the whole word down to the next line. This feature is called ***wordwrap***, and means that you do not press [Enter] until you reach the end of a paragraph.

Note — Spacing Between Sentences

Although you may have learned to press [Spacebar] two times at the end of a sentence, it is common practice now to space only one time between sentences.

8 Type **We discuss our applications from clients during the last week of each month. We will try to have a decision for you by the second week of October.**

9 Press Enter. Type **Yours truly,** and then press Enter.

10 Press Enter again, and then type **John W. Diamond** and then compare your screen with Figure 1.10.

As you reach the bottom of the screen, the page scrolls up to enable you to read what you are typing.

Figure 1.10

One space between sentences

Body of the letter

Complimentary closing

Extra line

Writer's identification

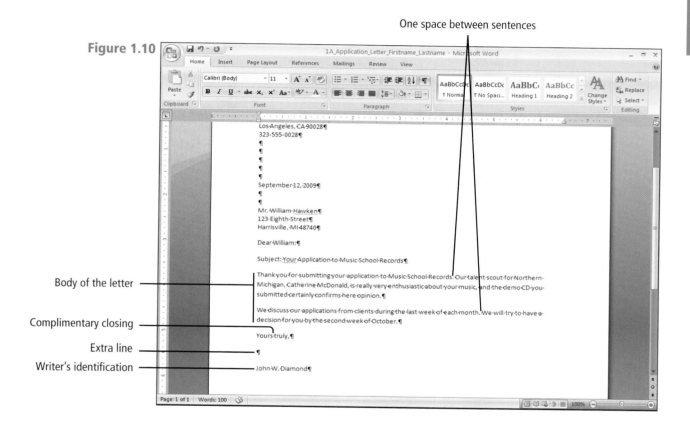

11 On the Ribbon, click the **Page Layout tab**. In the **Page Setup group**, click the **Margins** button to display the **Margins gallery**, as shown in Figure 1.11.

A *gallery* displays a list of potential results.

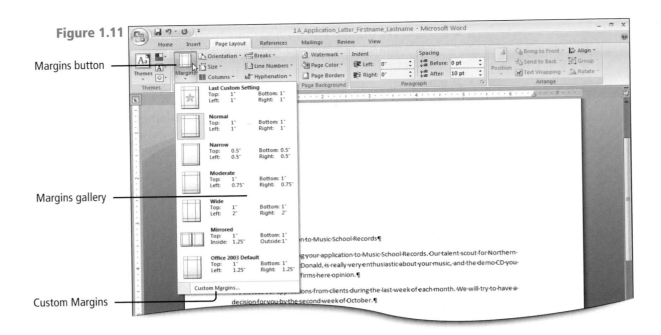

Figure 1.11

Margins button

Margins gallery

Custom Margins

12 At the bottom of the **Margins gallery**, click **Custom Margins** to display the **Page Setup** dialog box.

13 Near the top of the **Page Setup** dialog box, click the **Layout tab**. Under **Page**, click the **Vertical alignment arrow**, and then click **Center**. Compare your dialog box to Figure 1.12.

Layout tab

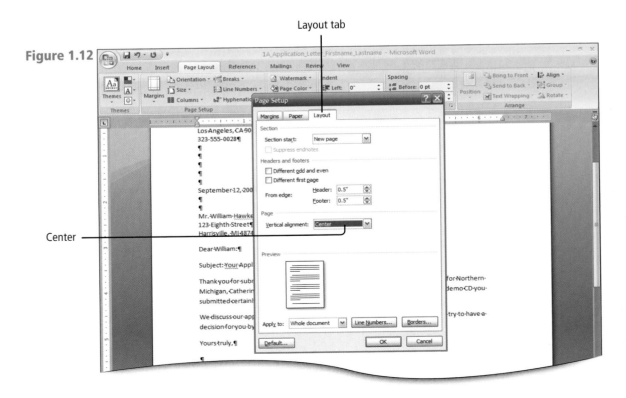

Figure 1.12

Center

14 In the lower right corner of the **Page Setup** dialog box, click **OK**.

The text is centered vertically on the page. This makes the letter more visually appealing.

15 On the **Quick Access Toolbar,** click the **Save** button 🖫 to save the changes you have made to the letter since your last save operation.

More Knowledge

Letter Placement

According to the *Gregg Reference Manual*, Tenth Edition (Sabin, 2005), a one-page letter typed on blank stationery may be centered vertically in this manner. If you are using letterhead stationery, leave at least a 0.5-inch space between the letterhead and the first element typed. Always consult trusted references when deciding on the proper formats for your personal and professional documents.

Objective 2
Edit Text

When you change text or formatting in a document, you are editing the text. Two commonly used editing tools are the Delete key and the Backspace key. The Backspace and Delete keys on your keyboard are used to remove text from the screen one character at a time. Backspace removes a character to the left of the insertion point; Delete removes a character to the right of the insertion point. You can also insert characters in the middle of existing text.

Activity 1.5 Editing Text with the Delete and Backspace Keys

1 Using the vertical scroll bar, scroll as necessary to view the paragraph beginning *Thank you.* In the middle of the second line of the paragraph, click to position your insertion point to the left of the *v* in the word *very* and then press ←Bksp. Compare your screen with Figure 1.13.

The space between the words *really* and *very* is removed.

Insertion point

Figure 1.13

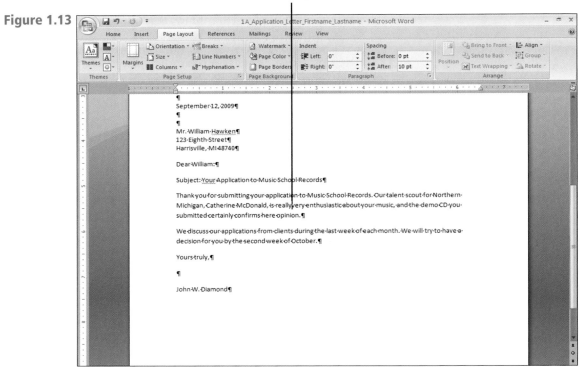

The document shows a Microsoft Word window with the following letter text:

September 12, 2009¶

Mr. William Hawken¶
123 Eighth Street¶
Harrisville, MI 48740¶

Dear William:¶

Subject: Your Application to Music School Records¶

Thank you for submitting your application to Music School Records. Our talent scout for Northern Michigan, Catherine McDonald, is really very enthusiastic about your music, and the demo CD you submitted certainly confirms here opinion.¶

We discuss our applications from clients during the last week of each month. We will try to have a decision for you by the second week of October.¶

Yours truly,¶

¶

John W. Diamond¶

2 With the insertion point between the two words, press ←Bksp six times.

The word *really* is removed. Be sure there is only one dot—recall that dots are the formatting marks that indicate spaces—between *is* and *very*. You can see that when editing text, it is useful to display formatting marks.

3 In the paragraph beginning *We discuss*, in the first line, locate the phrase *try to* and then click to position the insertion point to the left of the word *to*.

4 Press ←Bksp four times to remove the word *try* and the extra space. Press Delete three times, and then compare your screen with Figure 1.14.

The word *to* at the right of the insertion point is removed, along with the space following the word. Be sure there is only one dot (space) between *will* and *have*.

Figure 1.14

One space

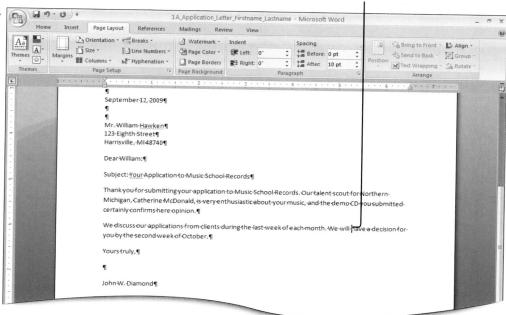

5 On the **Quick Access Toolbar,** click the **Save** button [icon] to save the changes you have made to the letter since your last save operation.

Activity 1.6 Inserting New Text

When you place the insertion point in the middle of a word or sentence and start typing, the existing text moves to the right to make space for your new keystrokes. This is called **_insert mode_** and is the default setting in Word.

1 In the paragraph beginning _We discuss_, in the first line, click to place the insertion point to the left of the letter _c_ in the word _clients_.

2 Type **potential** and then press Spacebar.

As you type, the existing text moves to the right to make space for your new keystrokes.

3 In the last line of the document, click to place the insertion point to the left of _John W. Diamond_.

4 Type **Lucy Burroughs** and then press Delete until the name _John W. Diamond_ is removed.

5 Compare your screen with Figure 1.15.

Figure 1.15

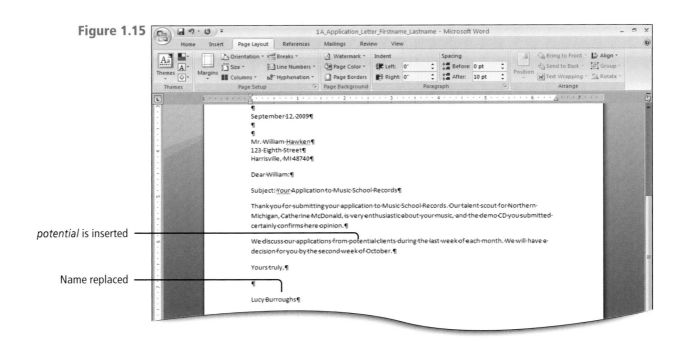

potential is inserted —

Name replaced —

6 **Save** 📁 the changes you have made to your document.

Objective 3
Select, Delete, and Format Text

Selecting text refers to highlighting, by dragging with your mouse, areas of text so that the text can be edited, formatted, copied, or moved. Word recognizes a selected area of text as one unit, to which you can make changes. **Formatting text** is the process of setting the overall appearance of the text within the document by changing the layout, color, shading, emphasis, or font characteristics of text.

Activity 1.7 Selecting and Deleting Text

1 In the paragraph beginning *Thank you*, position the 🔲 pointer to the left of *Thank*, hold down the left mouse button, and then drag to the right to select the first sentence including the ending period and its following space as shown in Figure 1.16. Release the mouse button.

The first sentence of the paragraph is selected, and a **Mini toolbar** displays above and to the right of the selected text. **Dragging** is the technique of holding down the left mouse button and moving over an area of text. Selected text is indicated when the background changes to a light blue or gray. The Mini toolbar displays buttons that are commonly used with the selected object. When you move the pointer away from the Mini toolbar, it fades from view. Selecting text may require some practice. If you are not satisfied with your result, click anywhere in the document and begin again.

Figure 1.16

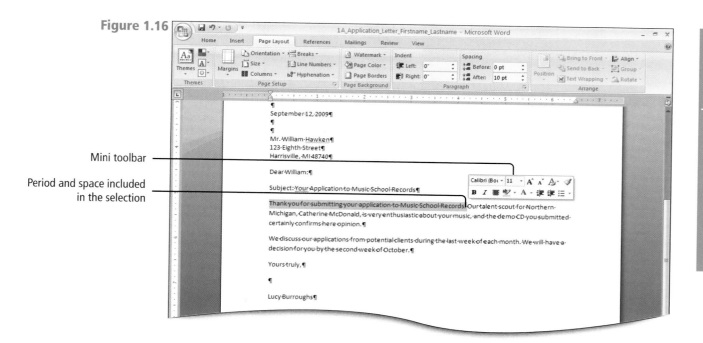

Mini toolbar

Period and space included in the selection

Word | chapter 1

2 Click anywhere in the document to deselect the sentence. Then, in the same sentence, move the pointer over the word *Music* and ***double-click***—click the left mouse button two times in rapid succession.

The entire word is selected and the Mini toolbar displays. Double-clicking takes a steady hand. The speed of the two clicks is not difficult (although you only have about a second between clicks), but you must hold the mouse perfectly still between the two clicks. If you are not satisfied with your result, try again.

3 Click anywhere in the document to deselect the word *Music*. Then, in the paragraph that begins *We discuss*, move the pointer over the word *last* and double-click. Type **first** and notice that when you type the first letter, the selected word is deleted.

4 In the paragraph beginning *Thank you*, move the pointer over the word *Music* and triple-click the left mouse button.

The entire paragraph is selected. You can triple-click anywhere in a paragraph to select the entire paragraph; keeping the mouse perfectly still between the clicks will guarantee the desired result.

5 Hold down Ctrl and press A to select the entire document, as shown in Figure 1.17.

Holding down Ctrl and typing a letter to perform a command is called a ***keyboard shortcut***. There are many keyboard shortcuts for selecting text. Take a moment to study the shortcuts shown in the table in Figure 1.18.

Figure 1.17

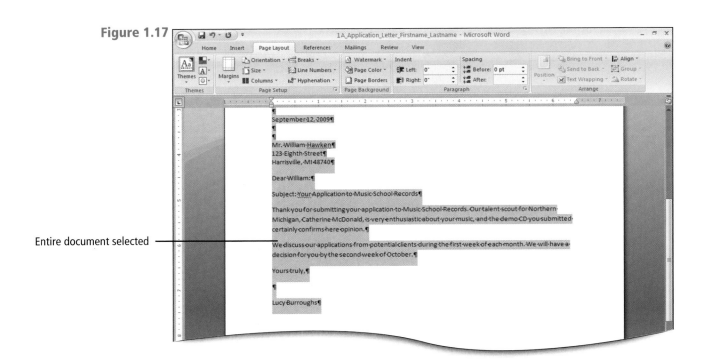

Entire document selected

Selecting Text in a Document

To Select	Do This
A portion of text	Click to position the insertion point at the beginning of the text you want to select, hold down ⇧ Shift, and then click at the end of the text you want to select. Alternatively, hold down the left mouse button and drag from the beginning to the end of the text you want to select.
A word	Double-click the word.
A sentence	Hold down Ctrl and click anywhere in the sentence.
A paragraph	Triple-click anywhere in the paragraph; or, move the pointer to the left of the line, into the margin area. When the ⟰ pointer displays, double-click.
A line	Move the pointer to the left of the line. When the ⟰ pointer displays, click one time.
One character at a time	Position the insertion point to the left of the first character, hold down ⇧ Shift, and press → or ← as many times as desired.
A string of words	Position the insertion point to the left of the first word, hold down ⇧ Shift and Ctrl, and then press → or ← as many times as desired.
Consecutive lines	Position the insertion point to the left of the first word, hold down ⇧ Shift and press ↑ or ↓.
Consecutive paragraphs	Position the insertion point to the left of the first word, hold down ⇧ Shift and Ctrl and press ↑ or ↓.
The entire document	Hold down Ctrl and press A or move the pointer to the left of the line. When the ⟰ pointer displays, triple-click.

Figure 1.18

6 Click anywhere in the document to cancel the text selection. **Save** 🖫 your work.

Activity 1.8 Changing Font and Font Size

A *font* is a set of characters with the same design and shape. There are two basic types of fonts—serif and sans serif. *Serif fonts* contain extensions or lines on the ends of the characters. Examples of serif fonts include Cambria, Times New Roman, and Garamond. *Sans serif fonts* do not have lines on the ends of characters. Examples of sans serif fonts include Calibri, Arial, and Comic Sans MS. The table in Figure 1.19 shows examples of serif and sans serif fonts.

Examples of Serif and Sans Serif Fonts

Serif Fonts	Sans Serif Fonts
Cambria	Calibri
Times New Roman	Arial
Garamond	Comic Sans MS

Figure 1.19

1 Hold down Ctrl and press A to select the entire document.

2 With the document selected, click the **Home tab**, and then in the **Font group**, click the **Font button arrow** [Cambria ▾]. At the top of the **Font** gallery, under **Theme Fonts**, point to—but do not click—**Cambria**. Notice that the font in the document changes to a preview of the Cambria font, as shown in Figure 1.20.

This is an example of *Live Preview*—a technology that shows the results of applying an editing or formatting change as you move the pointer over the results presented in a gallery or list. Here, Live Preview changes the selected text to the Cambria font, even though you did not click the font name.

A *theme* is a predefined set of colors, fonts, lines, and fill effects that look good together and that can be applied to your entire document or to specific items—for example, to a paragraph or table. As you progress in your study of Word, you will use more theme features.

Figure 1.20

Font button arrow   List of fonts   Live Preview displays the
document in the chosen font

Theme Fonts

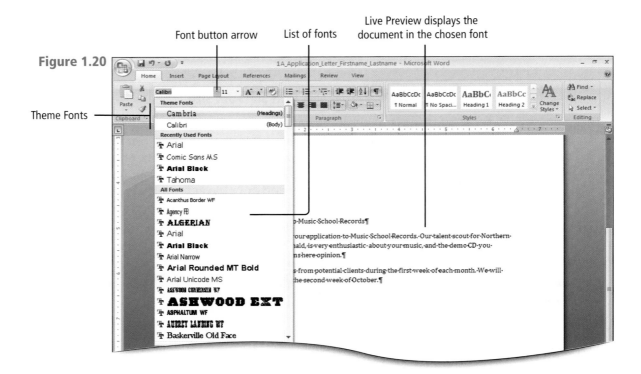

3 Click **Cambria** to apply the font to the entire document. On the Ribbon, in the **Font group**, click the **Font Size button arrow** `12 ▾`, click **12**, and then click anywhere to cancel the selection. Move the pointer into the left margin area, slightly to the left of the first line of the document—*Music School Records*. When the ⤢ pointer displays, click one time to select the entire first line of text.

Fonts are measured in **points**, with one point equal to 1/72 of an inch. A higher point size indicates a larger font size. For large amounts of text, font sizes between 10 point and 12 point are good choices. Headings and titles are often formatted by using a larger font size. The word *point* is abbreviated as **pt**.

4 On the Mini toolbar, click the **Font button arrow** `Cambria ▾`, scroll down if necessary, and then click **Arial Black**.

5 With the Mini toolbar still displayed, click the **Font Size button arrow** `12 ▾`, and then click **20**.

6 Position the ⤢ pointer to the left of the second line of the document—*2620 Vine Street*. Drag down to select the second, third, and fourth lines of the document, ending with the telephone number.

7 On the Mini toolbar, click the **Font button arrow** `Cambria ▾`, and then click **Arial**. With the Mini toolbar still displayed, click the **Font Size button arrow** `12 ▾`, and then click **10**. Click anywhere to cancel the selection and close the Mini toolbar, and then compare your screen with Figure 1.21.

Figure 1.21

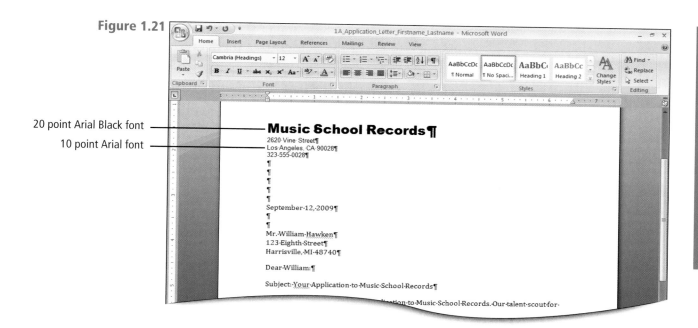

20 point Arial Black font

10 point Arial font

Note — To Move Quickly in a Long List

The list of available fonts is frequently very long. You can move quickly to any font by typing the first (or even first and second) letter of the font after you click the Font button arrow.

8 **Save** 💾 the changes you have made to your document.

More Knowledge

Viewing Keyboard Shortcuts

The key combinations for Control keyboard shortcuts are identified in the ScreenTip for each button. The Alt keyboard shortcuts are displayed by pressing and then releasing the Alt key.

Activity 1.9 Adding Emphasis to Text

Font styles emphasize text and are a visual cue to draw the reader's eye to important text. Font styles include bold, italic, and underline, although underline is not commonly used for emphasis. You can add emphasis to existing text, or you can turn the emphasis on before you start typing the word or phrase, and then turn it off.

1 Point anywhere in the first line of text—*Music School Records*—and triple-click to select the paragraph. Then, on the displayed Mini toolbar, click the **Bold** button **B** to apply bold emphasis to the paragraph that forms the first line of the letterhead.

2 On the **Home tab**, in the **Font group**, click the **Underline** button **U** .

Another Way — **To Apply Font Styles**

There are two other methods used to apply font styles:

- From the keyboard, use the keyboard shortcuts of Ctrl + B for bold, Ctrl + I for italic, or Ctrl + U for underline.
- From the Font tab of the Font dialog box, click the desired font styles.

3 Position the pointer to the left of the second line of the document—*2620 Vine Street*. Drag down to select the second, third, and fourth lines of the document, ending with the telephone number.

4 On the displayed Mini toolbar, click the **Italic** button *I* to apply italic emphasis to the paragraph that forms the remainder of the letterhead. Click anywhere to cancel the selection.

5 From the **Office** menu , point to the **Print arrow**, and then click **Print Preview**. Alternatively, press Ctrl + F2 to display the Print Preview. Compare your screen with Figure 1.22.

The Ribbon displays the Print Preview *program tab*, which replaces the standard set of tabs when you switch to certain authoring modes or views, including Print Preview. Print Preview displays the entire page and enables you to see what the document will look like when printed.

Figure 1.22

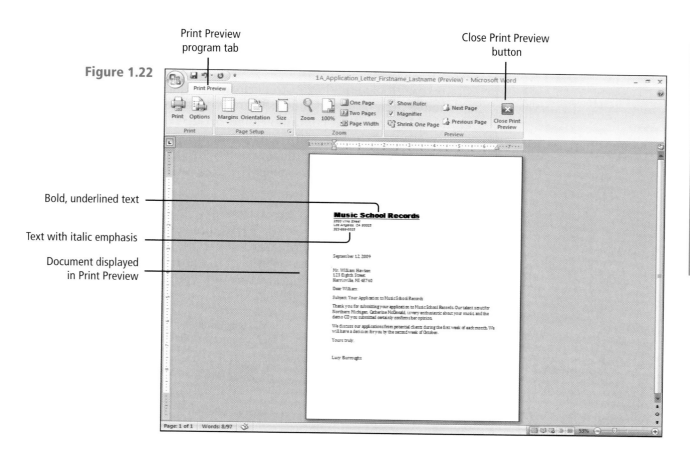

Print Preview program tab

Close Print Preview button

Bold, underlined text

Text with italic emphasis

Document displayed in Print Preview

6 On the **Print Preview tab**, in the **Preview group**, click the **Close Print Preview** button, and then **Save** 💾 your changes.

Objective 4
Print a Document

Information in headers and footers helps identify a document when it is printed. A *header* is information that prints at the top of every page, and a *footer* is information that prints at the bottom of every page.

Activity 1.10 Accessing Headers and Footers

1 Click the **Insert tab**, and then, in the **Header & Footer group**, click the **Footer** button.

Another Way ── **To Open a Footer**

Scroll to the bottom of the page, right-click near the bottom edge of the page, and then click Edit Footer to open the footer area.

2 At the bottom of the **Footer gallery,** click **Edit Footer**.

The footer area displays with the insertion point blinking at the left edge of the footer area. Because the footer area is active, *contextual tools* named *Header & Footer Tools* display and add contextual tabs—in this case the Design tab—next to the standard tabs on the Ribbon.

Contextual tools enable you to perform specific commands related to the active area or selected object, and display one or more *contextual tabs* that contain related *groups* of commands that you will need when working with the type of area or object that is selected. Contextual tools display only when needed for a selected area or object; when you deselect the area or object, the contextual tools no longer display.

3 On the **Design tab**, in the **Insert group**, click the **Quick Parts** button, and then click **Field**. In the **Field** dialog box, under **Field names**, use the vertical scroll bar to examine the items that you can insert in a header or footer, as shown in Figure 1.23. You will work with fields more as you progress through your study of Word.

Quick Parts button   Inserts filename   Header and Footer Tools Design tab   Field dialog box

Figure 1.23

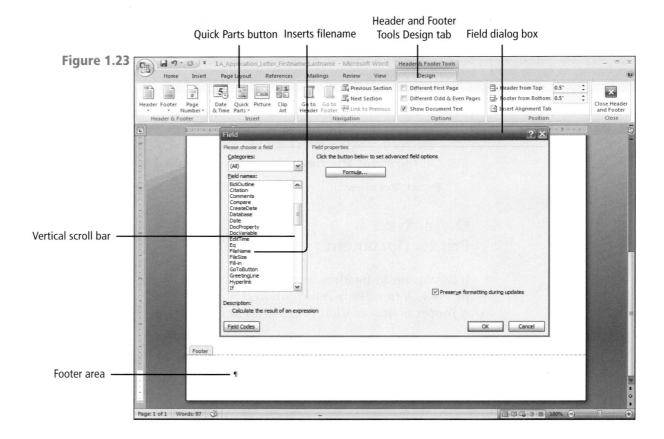

Vertical scroll bar

Footer area

4 In the **Field names** list, scroll as necessary to locate and click **FileName**, and then click **OK**.

The file name displays in the Footer box. The file extension *.docx* may or may not display, depending on your Windows settings.

5 Double-click anywhere in the document to leave the footer area. Scroll down until you can see the footer, and then compare your screen with Figure 1.24. Alternatively, in the Close group, click the Close Header & Footer button.

The footer displays in gray. Because it is a proper name and is likely not in Word's dictionary, your name in the footer may display with wavy red lines.

Figure 1.24

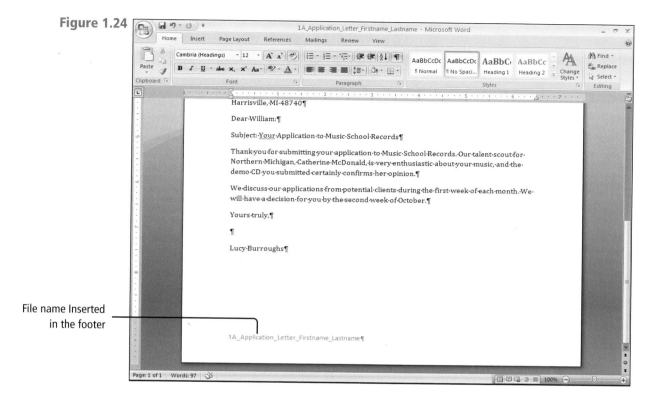

File name Inserted in the footer

6 **Save** 💾 your changes.

More Knowledge

Moving to the Header or Footer

To quickly edit an existing header or footer, double-click in the header or footer area. This will display the Header & Footer contextual tools and place the insertion point at the beginning of the header or footer. The file name field that you inserted will display with a gray background.

Activity 1.11 Printing a Document

1 Check your *Chapter Assignment Sheet* or *Course Syllabus*, or consult your instructor, to determine if you are to submit your assignments on paper or electronically, using your college's course information management system. To submit electronically, go to Step 3, and then follow the instructions provided by your instructor.

2 Click the **Office** button 🔘, point to the **Print arrow**, and then click **Quick Print**.

One copy of your document prints on the default printer connected to your system. The formatting marks that indicate spaces and paragraphs do not print.

Note — Space Between Lines in Your Printed Document

The Cambria font, and many others, uses a slightly larger space between the lines than more traditional fonts like Times New Roman. As you progress in your study of Word, you will use many different fonts and also adjust the spacing between lines.

3 From the **Office** menu 🔘, click **Close**, saving any changes if prompted to do so. Leave Word open for the next project.

Another Way

To Print a Document

To Print a document:

- From the Office menu, click Print to display the Print dialog box (to be covered later), from which you can choose a variety of different options, such as printing multiple copies, printing on a different printer, and printing some but not all pages.

- Hold down Ctrl and then press P. This is an alternative to the Office menu command, and opens the Print dialog box.

- Hold down Alt, press F, and then press P. This opens the Print dialog box.

End You have completed Project 1A

Project 1B Company Overview

In Activities 1.12 through 1.23 you will create a document that describes the mission of Music School Records. You will add a graphic image to the document, and insert text from another document. Your completed document will look similar to Figure 1.25.

For Project 1B, you will need the following files:

w01B_Music_School_Records
w01B_Music_Logo

You will save your document as
1B_Company_Overview_Firstname_Lastname

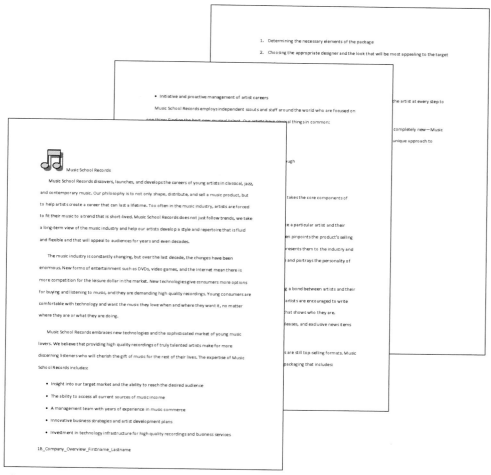

Figure 1.25
Project 5B—Company Overview

Objective 5
Navigate the Word Window

Most Word documents are longer than the Word window—some are wider than the window. Use the scroll bars to *navigate*—move around in—a document. Keyboard shortcuts provide additional navigation techniques that you cannot accomplish with scroll bars. For example, using keyboard shortcuts, you can move the insertion point to the beginning or end of a word, line, paragraph, or document.

Activity 1.12 Opening and Closing an Existing Document

1 If necessary, **Start** [*start*] Word. From the **Office** menu [icon], click **Open**.

2 In the **Open** dialog box, click the **Look in arrow** at the right edge of the **Look in** box to view a list of the drives available on your system.

3 Navigate to the location where the student files for this textbook are stored, which may be on a CD that came with your textbook or in some other location designated by your instructor. Locate **w01B_Music_School_Records** and click to select it. Then, in the lower right corner of the **Open** dialog box, click the **Open** button. Alternatively, double-click the file name. If necessary, on the Home tab, in the Paragraph group, click the Show/Hide ¶ button [¶] to display the nonprinting characters.

The document displays in the Word window. This text will be inserted into a new document in Activity 1.13.

4 From the **Office** menu [icon], click **Close** to close the document and leave Word open.

Activity 1.13 Inserting Existing Text into a New Document

1 From the **Office** menu [icon], click **New** to display the **New Document** dialog box. The *Blank document* button is selected by default. Compare your screen with Figure 1.26.

Blank document button

Figure 1.26

New Document dialog box

Create button

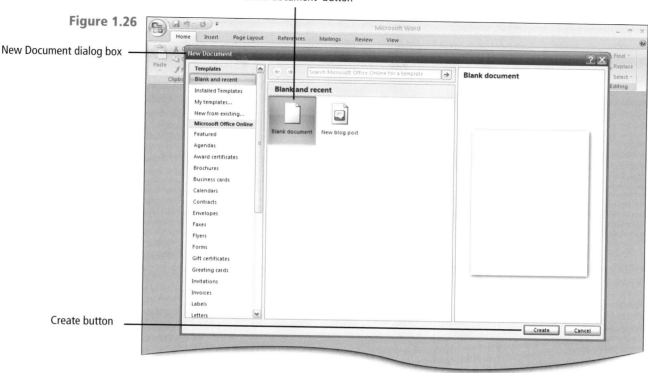

2 In the lower right corner of the **New Document** dialog box, click **Create** to create a new document. Type **Music School Records** and then press Enter.

3 On the Ribbon, click the **Insert tab**. In the **Text group**, click the **Object button arrow**, and then click **Text From File**.

4 In the displayed **Insert File** dialog box, navigate to the location where the student files for this textbook are stored. Locate **w01B_Music_School_Records**, click to select it, and then in the lower right corner, click the **Insert** button. Compare your screen with Figure 1.27.

A copy of the text from the w01B_Music_School_Records document is inserted into the blank document, the last page of the three-page document displays, and the insertion point displays at the end of the inserted text. The original w01B_Music_School_Records document remains intact and undisturbed. The page number, total number of pages in the document, and number of words in the document display in the status bar.

Object button

Figure 1.27

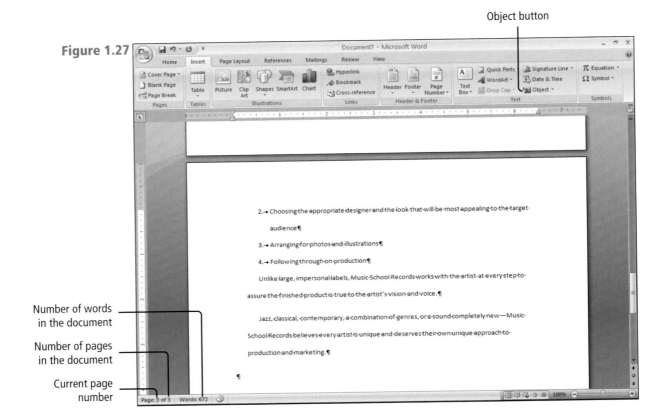

Number of words in the document

Number of pages in the document

Current page number

5 Press ←Bksp to delete the blank line at the end of the document. On the **Quick Access Toolbar**, click the **Save** button 🖫 . In the displayed **Save As** dialog box, click the **Save in arrow** and navigate to your **Word Chapter 1** folder.

Recall that because this is a new unnamed document—*Document2* or some other number displays in the title bar—the *Save As* dialog box displays so that you can name and designate a storage location for the document. The first line of text in the document displays in the *File name* box.

6 In the **File name** box, delete any existing text, and then using your own first and last names, type **1B_Company_Overview_Firstname_Lastname** and then click **Save**.

7 On the **Insert tab**, in the **Header & Footer group**, click the **Footer** button. At the bottom of the displayed **Footer gallery**, click **Edit Footer**. Alternatively, right-click near the bottom edge of the page, and then from the shortcut menu, click Edit Footer.

A *shortcut menu* is a context-sensitive menu that displays commands relevant to the selected object.

8 On the **Design tab**, in the **Insert group**, click the **Quick Parts** button, and then click **Field**. In the **Field** dialog box, under **Field names**, locate and click **FileName**, and then click **OK**.

9 Double-click anywhere in the document to leave the footer area. Alternatively, in the Close group, click the Close Header & Footer button. **Save** 🖫 your document.

Activity 1.14 Navigating a Document

1 At the right of your screen, in the vertical scroll bar, locate the **up scroll arrow** at the top of the scroll bar as shown in Figure 1.28. Then, click the **up scroll arrow** five times. Notice that the document scrolls up one line at a time. Also, notice that the scroll box is near the bottom of the vertical scroll bar.

Up scroll arrow

Figure 1.28

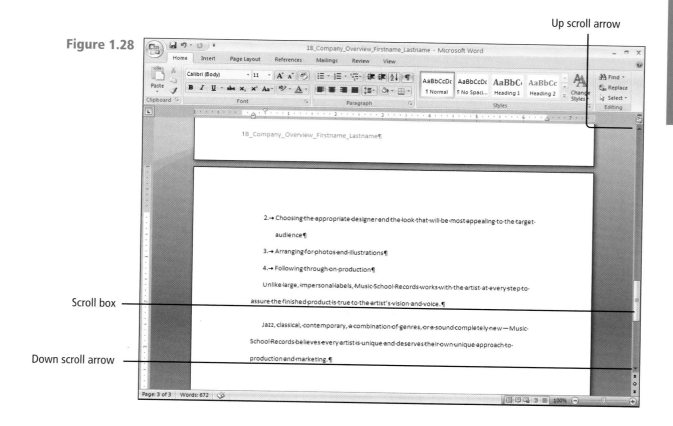

Scroll box

Down scroll arrow

2 Point to the **up scroll arrow** again. Click and hold down the mouse button for several seconds.

The document text scrolls up continuously, one line at a time.

3 At the top of the vertical scroll bar, point to the **up scroll arrow**, and then click and hold down the mouse button until you have scrolled to the beginning of the document. As you do so, notice that the scroll box moves up in the scroll bar—like an elevator going to the top floor.

4 Near the top of the vertical scroll bar, point to the **scroll box**, and then press and hold down the left mouse button. Compare your screen with Figure 1.29.

A ScreenTip displays, indicating the page number. The page number and total number of pages in the document are displayed in the status bar—in this case page 1 of 3 pages.

ScreenTip

Figure 1.29

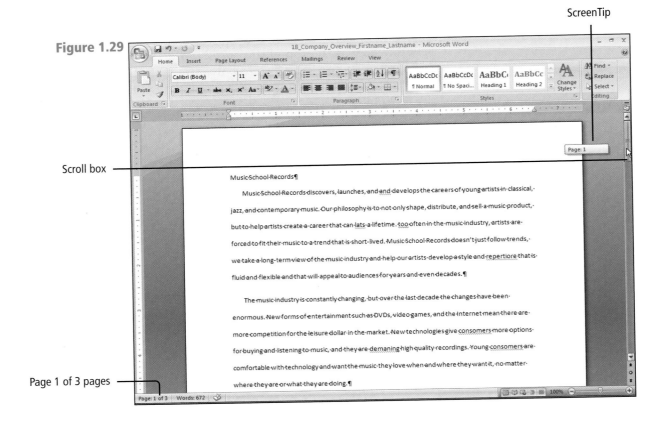

Scroll box

Page 1 of 3 pages

5 Drag the **scroll box** slowly down to the bottom of the scroll bar. As you do so, notice that the ScreenTip changes as each new page reaches the top of the screen.

6 Release the mouse button, and then click in the dark area just above the scroll box.

The document scrolls up one screen. This is a quick way to scan a document.

7 Practice clicking in the area above and below the scroll box.

Another Way — **To Scroll Through a Document**

If your mouse has a small wheel button between the left and right mouse buttons, you can scroll up and down in the document by rotating the wheel.

8 On your keyboard, hold down [Ctrl] and press [Home].

The beginning of the document displays, and the insertion point moves to the left of the first word in the document. In this document, Word has flagged some spelling, grammar, and contextual errors (red, green, and blue wavy lines), which you will correct in Activity 1.19.

Does the shortcut not work?

If you are using a laptop computer, you may have to hold down a function (Fn) key to use shortcuts that involve the Home, End, Page Up, and Page Down keys.

9 Hold down Ctrl and press End.

10 Press PgUp to scroll the document up one screen. Press End.

The insertion point moves to the end of the current line of text.

11 Take a moment to study the table shown in Figure 1.30, which lists the most commonly used keyboard shortcuts.

Navigating a Document Using Keyboard Shortcuts

To Move	Press
To the beginning of a document	Ctrl + Home
To the end of a document	Ctrl + End
To the beginning of a line	Home
To the end of a line	End
To the beginning of the previous word	Ctrl + ←
To the beginning of the next word	Ctrl + →
To the beginning of the current word (if insertion point is in the middle of a word)	Ctrl + ←
To the beginning of the previous paragraph	Ctrl + ↑
To the beginning of the next paragraph	Ctrl + ↓
To the beginning of the current paragraph (if insertion point is in the middle of a paragraph)	Ctrl + ↑
Up one screen	PgUp
Down one screen	PgDn

Figure 1.30

12 Hold down Ctrl and press Home to position the insertion point at the beginning of the document.

Activity 1.15 Changing Document Views

1 Near the right side of the status bar, locate the **View** buttons.

Use these buttons to switch to different document views.

To View Documents

There are five ways to view your document on the screen. Each view is useful in different situations.

- *Print Layout view* displays the page borders, margins, text, and graphics as they will look when you print the document. Most Word users prefer this view for most tasks, and it is the default view.

- *Full Screen Reading view* creates easy-to-read pages that fit on the screen to increase legibility. This view does not represent the pages as they would print. Each screen page is labeled with a screen number, rather than a page number.

- *Web Layout view* shows how the document will look when saved as a Web page and viewed in a Web browser.

- *Outline view* shows the organizational structure of your document by headings and subheadings and can be collapsed and expanded to look at individual sections of a document.

- *Draft view* simplifies the page layout for quick typing, and shows a little more text on the screen than the Print Layout view. Graphics, headers, and footers do not display.

2 Click the **Draft** button.

3 Click the **Full Screen Reading** button.

Text displays in a side-by-side format, and can be read like a book.

4 Near the upper right corner of the screen, click the **Close** button.

In this view you can see all of the elements that will display on paper when you print the document. The instructions in this textbook will use Print Layout view for most documents.

Activity 1.16 Using the Zoom Slider

To *zoom* means to increase or decrease the viewing area of the screen. You can zoom in to look closely at a particular section of a document, and then zoom out to see a whole page on the screen. You can also zoom to view multiple pages on the screen.

1 On the right side of the status bar, just to the right of the View buttons, drag the **Zoom slider** to the right until you have zoomed to approximately 150%, as shown in Figure 1.31.

Figure 1.31

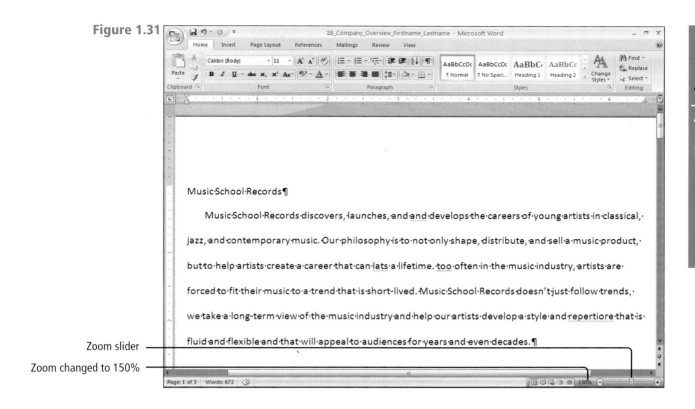

Zoom slider

Zoom changed to 150%

2 Drag the **Zoom slider** to the left until you have zoomed to approximately 40%, as shown in Figure 1.32. Notice that as the pages get smaller, multiple pages display.

Figure 1.32

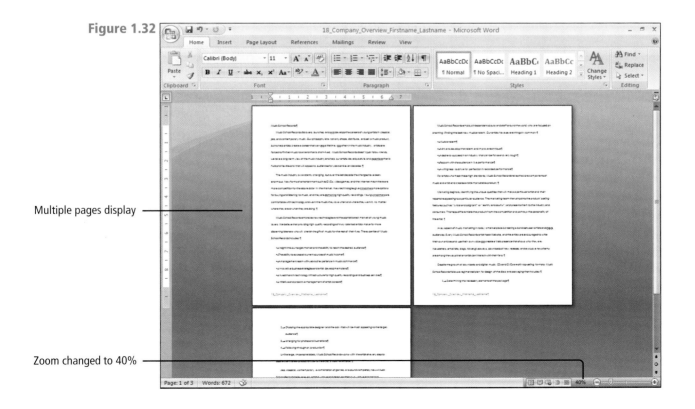

Multiple pages display

Zoom changed to 40%

3 Drag the **Zoom slider** to the right until you have zoomed to a page size with which you are comfortable—typically 100%.

As you work on various documents, you can adjust the zoom to best display the document.

Another Way ── **To Change the Zoom**

You can click the page percentage label to the right of the View buttons to open the Zoom dialog box. The Zoom dialog box enables you to specify the exact page percentage you want to use. It also enables you to stretch the page to the width of the screen, or display several pages at one time.

Activity 1.17 Splitting Windows and Arranging Panes

Word enables you to split the screen, which enables you to look at two different parts of the same document at the same time. In a long document, this is convenient for viewing both the first page and the last page at the same time. You can also view two different documents side by side and make comparisons between the two.

1 Hold down Ctrl and press Home to move the insertion point to the beginning of the document. On the Ribbon, click the **View tab**, and then, in the **Window group**, click the **Split** button. Notice that a **split bar** displays near the middle of the document area, with a move pointer ⬍ on the bar. The split bar indicates the location of the border between the windows. Compare your screen to Figure 1.33.

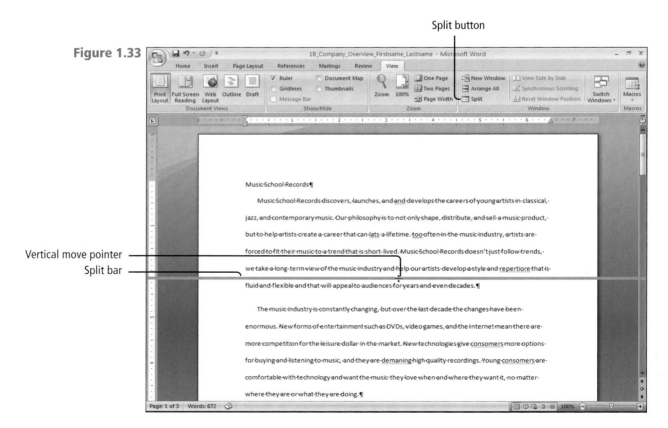

Figure 1.33

2 Drag the split bar to just below the fifth line of text—including the title—that contains the phrase *that is short lived*, and then click to position the split bar. Notice that both the top and bottom halves of the screen display rulers, and two different parts of the same document display in the two document windows, as shown in Figure 1.34. If you don't see the rulers, on the **View** tab, in the **Show/Hide** group, click the **Ruler** check box.

Different areas of the
same document

Figure 1.34

Split bar extends
across the screen

Two document windows

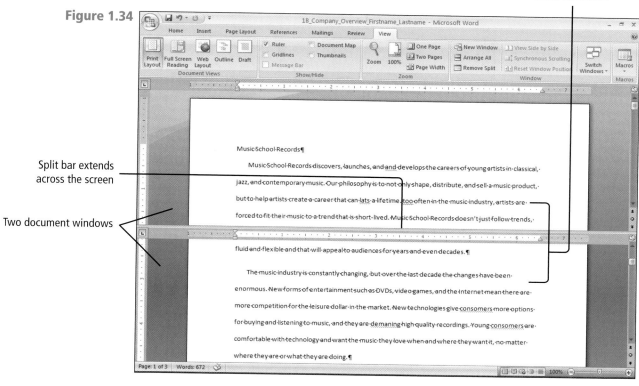

3 Using the top vertical scroll bar, scroll down and up in the top window. Notice that the portion of the document displayed in the top window moves independently from the portion of the document displayed in the bottom window.

4 Using the bottom vertical scroll bar, scroll up and down in the bottom window.

5 On the **View tab**, in the **Window group**, click the **Remove Split** button to return to a single document window.

6 From the **Office** menu , click **Open**. Locate and open the **1A_Application_Letter** document that you created in Project 1A.

7 Click the **View tab**, and then in the **Window group**, click the **View Side by Side** button to display both documents at the same time, as shown in Figure 1.35. Alternatively, in the Window group, you can click the Arrange All button to arrange the two documents in horizontal windows that look similar to the two document windows you created by using the split box.

With two documents open, you can edit both at the same time, or move text or objects between the documents.

Figure 1.35

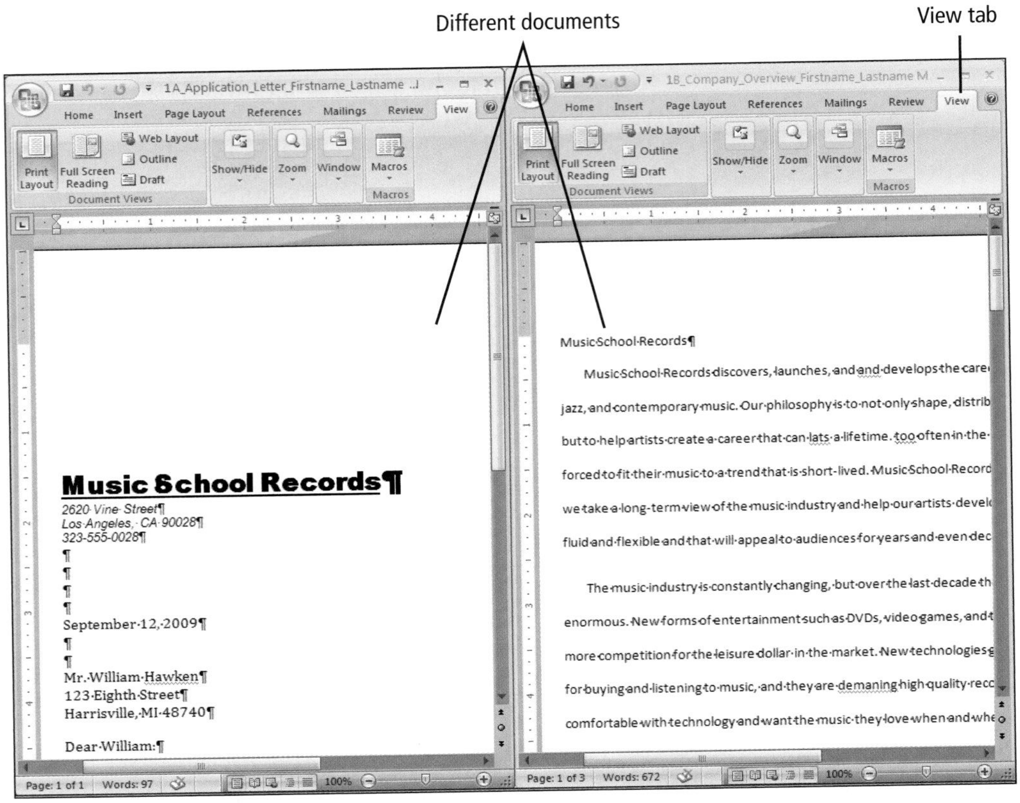

Different documents   View tab

8 On the title bar of the document on the left, click the **Close** button ☒ to close the letter. Notice that the **1B_Company_Overview** window is maximized when the other window is closed.

Objective 6
Add a Graphic to a Document

Graphics can be inserted into a document from many sources. *Clip art* images—predefined graphics included with Microsoft Office or down-loaded from the Web—can make your document more interesting and visually appealing.

Activity 1.18 Inserting Clip Art

1 Press Ctrl + Home to move the insertion point to the beginning of the document. Press Spacebar three times, and then press ← three times to move the insertion point back to the beginning of the line.

2 Click the **Insert tab**, and then in the **Illustrations group**, click the **Clip Art** button.

3 In the displayed **Clip Art** task pane, in the **Search for** box, type **Music** and then in the **Search in** box, be sure **All collections** is selected. Click the **Results should be arrow**, and clear all the check boxes except **Clip Art**. Click **Go**, and then compare your screen with Figure 1.36. If necessary, scroll up to view the first displayed music images.

Figure 1.36

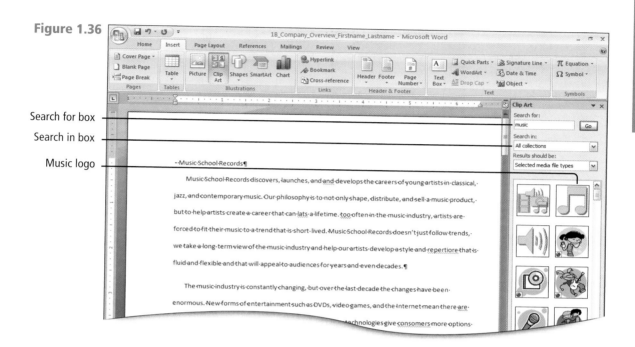

Search for box

Search in box

Music logo

4 Click the **music logo** clip art image. Notice that the image displays over the text.

5 Right-click the image, and then from the displayed shortcut menu, click **Format AutoShape**. In the displayed **Format AutoShape** dialog box, on the **Layout tab**, under **Wrapping style**, click **In line with text**, which will treat the clip art image as a text character.

6 In the **Format AutoShape** dialog box, click the **Size tab**. Under **Scale**, click the **Lock aspect ratio** check box. In the **Height** box, select the current value and then type **30** to reduce the image to 30% of its original size. Compare your dialog box to Figure 1.37.

The **aspect ratio** of an object is the relationship of its height to its width. If you lock the aspect ratio, changing either the height or width of an object will resize the object proportionally.

Figure 1.37

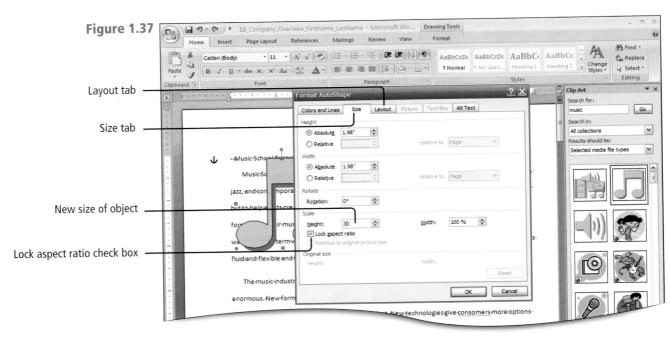

Layout tab
Size tab
New size of object
Lock aspect ratio check box

7 At the bottom of the **Format AutoShape** dialog box, click **OK**, and then click anywhere in the document to deselect the image. Compare your screen with Figure 1.38.

Figure 1.38

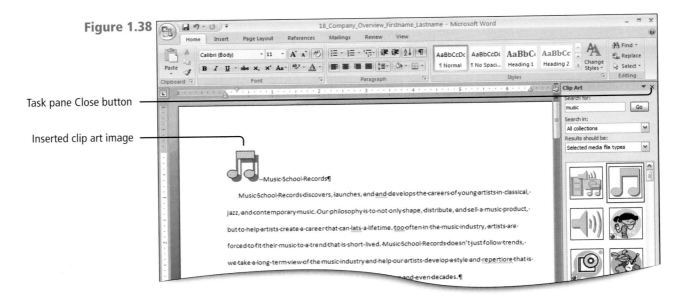

Task pane Close button
Inserted clip art image

8 **Close** ☒ the **Clip Art** task pane, and then **Save** 🖫 your document.

Objective 7
Use the Spelling and Grammar Checker

As you type, Word compares your words to those in the Word dictionary and compares your phrases and punctuation to a list of grammar rules. Words that are not in the Word dictionary are marked with a wavy red underline. Phrases and punctuation that differ from the grammar rules are marked with a wavy green underline. Because a list of grammar rules applied by a computer program can never be exact, and because a computer dictionary cannot contain all known words and proper names, you will need to check any words flagged by Word as misspellings or grammar errors.

Word will also place a blue wavy underline under a word that is spelled correctly but used incorrectly, such as the misuse of *their*, *there*, and *they're*. However, Word will not flag the word *sign* as misspelled, even though you intended to type *sing a song* rather than *sign a song*, because both are legitimate words contained within Word's dictionary, but not variations of the same word.

Activity 1.19 Checking Individual Spelling and Grammar Errors

One way to check spelling and grammar errors flagged by Word is to right-click the flagged word or phrase and, from the displayed shortcut menu, choose a suitable correction or instruction.

1 Scan the text on the screen to locate green, red, and blue wavy underlines.

Note — Activating Spelling and Grammar Checking

If you do not see any wavy red, green, or blue lines under words, the automatic spelling and/or grammar checking has been turned off on your system. To activate the spelling and grammar checking, display the Office menu, click Word Options, and then in the list, click Proofing. Under *When correcting spelling in Office programs*, click the first four check boxes. Under *When correcting spelling and grammar in Word*, click the first four check boxes, and then click the Writing Style arrow and click Grammar & Style. Under *Exceptions for*, clear both check boxes. To display the flagged spelling and grammar errors, click the Recheck Document button, and then close the dialog box.

2 In the first line of the paragraph that begins *Music School Records discovers*, locate the word *and* with the wavy red underline. Point to the word and **right-click**—click the right mouse button to display a shortcut menu, as shown in Figure 1.39.

A shortcut menu displays under the Mini toolbar. Word identified a duplicate word, and provides two suggestions—*Delete Repeated Word* or *Ignore*. The second option is included because sometimes the same word will be correctly used two times in succession.

Word flagged with red wavy underline

Figure 1.39

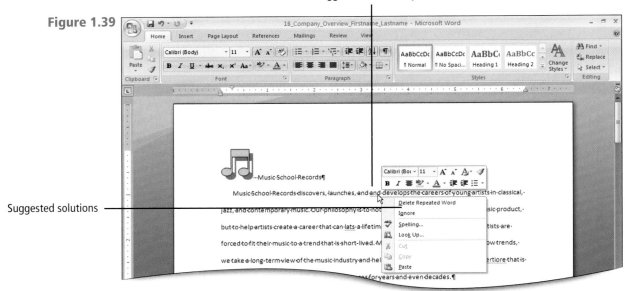

Suggested solutions

3 From the shortcut menu, click **Delete Repeated Word** to delete the duplicate word.

4 In the third line of the same paragraph, locate and right-click the misspelled word *lats*, and then compare your screen to Figure 1.40.

In this instance, Word has identified a misspelled word. Suggested replacements are shown at the top of the shortcut menu.

Figure 1.40

Suggested replacements

Word flagged with wavy red underline

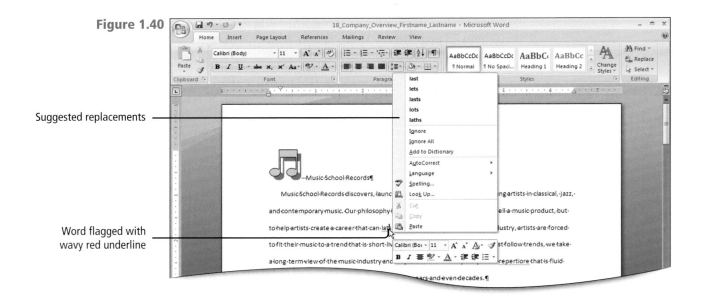

5 At the top of the shortcut menu, click **last** to replace the misspelled word.

6 In the third line of the same paragraph, locate and right-click the word *too* that has a wavy green underline.

The wavy green underline indicates a grammar error; in this case, a word at the beginning of a sentence that should be capitalized.

7 In the same paragraph, from the shortcut menu, click **Too** to capitalize the word.

8 Scroll down to display the bottom of **Page 2**. In the paragraph beginning *A key aspect*, notice that two words have wavy blue underlines.

The wavy blue underline indicates a word that is recognized by the dictionary, but may be the wrong form of the word—in this case *there* is incorrectly used instead of *their*, and *too* is used instead of *to*.

9 In the paragraph beginning *A key aspect*, right-click *there*, and then from the shortcut menu, click **their**. In the same paragraph, right-click *too*, and then from the shortcut menu, click **to**.

10 **Save** 🖫 the changes you have made to your document.

Activity 1.20 Checking Spelling and Grammar in an Entire Document

Initiating the spelling and grammar checking feature from the Ribbon displays the Spelling and Grammar dialog box, which provides more options than the shortcut menus.

1 Scan the document to locate red, green, and blue wavy underlines. Notice the icon of a red X over a book in the status bar, which indicates that the document contains flagged entries that need to be addressed.

2 Press [Ctrl] + [Home] to move the insertion point to the beginning of the document. Click the **Review tab**, and then in the **Proofing group**, click the **Spelling & Grammar** button to begin to check the document.

The first suggested error is a potential grammar error—using a passive voice.

Alert!

Do your spelling and grammar selections differ?

The errors that are flagged by Word depend on the Proofing settings. Not all of the potential errors listed in this activity may appear in your spelling and grammar check. Your document may also display errors not noted here. If you run across flagged words or phrases that aren't included here, click the Ignore Once button to move to the next potential error.

3 In the **Spelling and Grammar** dialog box, click the **Ignore Once** button. If necessary, point to the title bar of the dialog box, and then drag the dialog box out of the way so you can see the misspelled word *repertoire*, which is selected. Compare your screen with Figure 1.41.

Under Not in Dictionary, the misspelled word displays in red, and under Suggestions, a suggested change is presented.

Figure 1.41

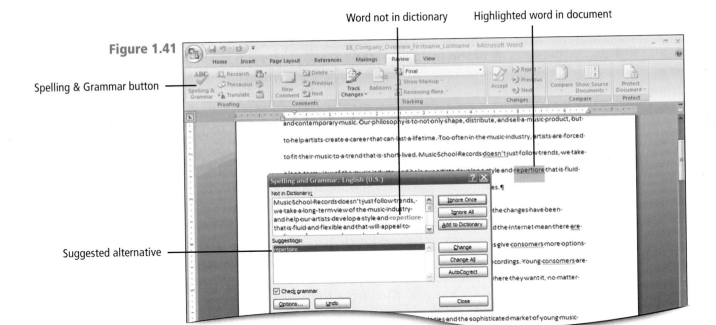

Spelling & Grammar button

Word not in dictionary

Highlighted word in document

Suggested alternative

4 Take a moment to study the spelling and grammar options available in the **Spelling and Grammar** dialog box as shown in the table in Figure 1.42.

Spelling and Grammar Dialog Box Buttons

Button	Action
Ignore Once	Ignores the identified word one time, but flags it in other locations in the document.
Ignore All	Discontinues flagging any instance of the word anywhere in the document.
Add to Dictionary	Adds the word to a custom dictionary, which can be edited. This option does not change the built-in Office dictionary.
Change	Changes the identified word to the word highlighted under Suggestions.
Change All	Changes every instance of the word in the document to the word highlighted under Suggestions.
AutoCorrect	Adds the flagged word to the AutoCorrect list, which will subsequently correct the word automatically if misspelled in any documents typed in the future.
Ignore Rule (Grammar)	Ignores the specific rule used to determine a grammar error and removes the green wavy line.
Next Sentence (Grammar)	Moves to the next identified error.
Explain (Grammar)	Displays the rule used to identify a grammar error.
Options	Displays the Proofing section of the Word Options dialog box.

Figure 1.42

5 If necessary, under **Suggestions**, click to select **repertoire**, and then click the **Change** button. Compare your screen with Figure 1.43.

The correction is made and the next identified error is highlighted, which is a contraction use error. Under Contraction Use, the entire sentence displays, with the contraction *doesn't* displayed in green. The suggested replacement—*does not*—displays in the Suggestions box. Recall that because of the settings on your computer, your spelling and grammar selections may differ.

Grammar error

Figure 1.43

Suggested replacement

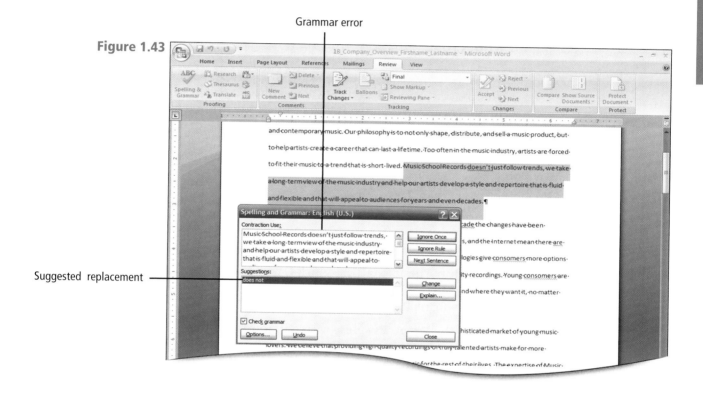

6 Under **Suggestions**, be sure **does not** is selected, and then click the **Change** button.

The correction is made and the next identified error is highlighted, which is a grammar error. Under Comma Use, the entire sentence displays. The suggested change is to add a comma.

7 Under **Suggestions**, be sure **decade,** is selected, and then click the **Change** button.

The error is corrected, and the next potential error displays, a Subject-Verb Agreement grammar error.

8 Under **Suggestions**, be sure **is** is selected, and then click the **Change** button.

The error is corrected, and the next potential error displays. The word *comsomers* is misspelled twice in two successive sentences.

9 Under **Suggestions**, be sure **consumers** is selected, and then click the **Change All** button to change all instances of the misspelled word.

10 Continue to the end of the document. Change *demaning* to **demanding**, and then click **Ignore Once** for any other marked words or phrases.

A message indicates that the spelling and grammar check is complete. If your program is configured to display readability statistics, a Readability Statistics dialog box displays instead.

11 Click **OK** to close the dialog box, and then **Save** 🖫 your changes.

Objective 8
Preview and Print Documents, Close a Document, and Close Word

While you create your document, displaying the Print Preview helps to ensure that you are getting the result you want. Before printing, make a final preview to be sure the document layout is what you intended.

Activity 1.21 Previewing and Printing a Document

1 Press ⌨Ctrl + ⌨Home to move the insertion point to the beginning of the document. From the **Office** menu 🔘, point to the **Print arrow**, and then click **Print Preview**. Alternatively, press ⌨Ctrl + ⌨F2.

One or more pages of your document display exactly as they will print. The formatting marks, which do not print, are not displayed. The size of the preview depends on the zoom level used the last time the Print Preview window was opened.

2 In the **Print Preview** window, move the mouse pointer anywhere over the document. Notice that the pointer becomes a magnifying glass with a plus in it, indicating that you can magnify the view, as shown in Figure 1.44.

If you are viewing multiple pages, you may have to click on a page before the magnifying glass displays.

Magnifying glass pointer

Figure 1.44

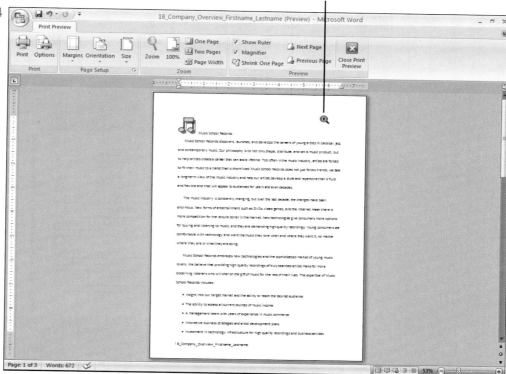

3 Move the pointer over the upper portion of the first page of the document and click one time.

The top portion of the document is magnified making it easier to read. The pointer changes to a magnifying glass with a minus sign.

4 Click anywhere on the document to zoom out. On the right side of the status bar, drag the **Zoom slider** to the left until you can see all three pages, as shown in Figure 1.45.

All three pages of the document display on the screen. The footers display on the bottom of each page.

Figure 1.45

One Page button

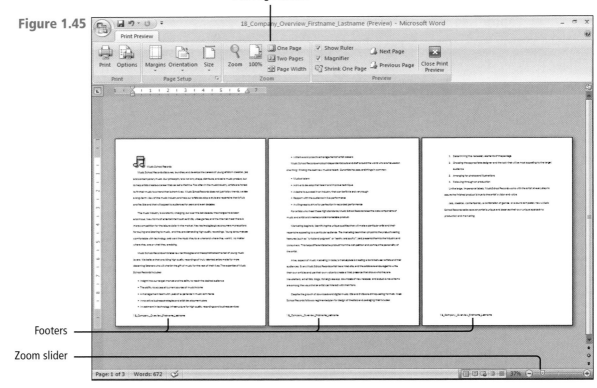

Footers

Zoom slider

5 On the **Print Preview tab**, in the **Zoom group**, click the **One Page** button to display a single page of the document.

6 In the **Preview group**, click the **Close Print Preview** button.

7 From the **Office** menu, click **Print**, and then compare your screen with Figure 1.46.

The Print dialog box displays. Here you can specify which pages to print and how many copies you want. Additional command buttons for Options and Properties provide more printing choices. The printer that displays will be the printer that is selected for your computer.

Figure 1.46

Selected printer

Number of copies

Current page option

Pages to print

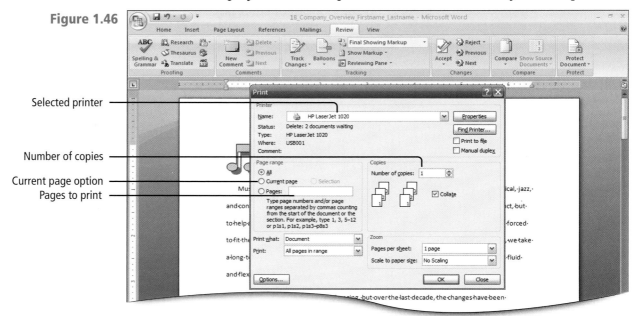

8 In the displayed **Print** dialog box, under **Copies**, change the number of copies to 2 by typing **2** in the text box, or by clicking the **spin box up arrow**.

A **spin box** is a small box with upward- and downward-pointing arrows that enables you to move—spin—through a set of values by clicking.

9 Under **Page range**, click the **Current page** option button, and then, at the bottom of the **Print** dialog box, click **OK** if you want to print two copies of the first page. If you do not want to print, click **Cancel**.

Activity 1.22 Closing a Document and Closing Word

1 Check your *Chapter Assignment Sheet* or *Course Syllabus* or consult your instructor to determine if you are to submit your assignments on paper or electronically. To submit electronically, go to Step 3, and then follow the instructions provided by your instructor.

2 From the **Office** menu, click **Print**. At the bottom of the displayed **Print** dialog box, click **OK**. Collect your printout from the printer and submit it as directed.

3 From the **Office** menu, click **Close**, saving any changes if prompted to do so.

The document closes, but the Word program remains open.

4 At the far right edge of the title bar, click the **Close** button ☒ to exit the Word program.

Objective 9
Use the Microsoft Help System

As you work with Word, you can get assistance by using the Help feature. You can type key words and phrases and Help will provide you with information and step-by-step instructions for performing tasks.

Activity 1.23 Getting Help

Word Help is available on your computer, online at the Microsoft Web site, and on your screen with enhanced ScreenTips.

1 **Start** Word. On the Ribbon, click the **Page Layout tab**, and then in the **Page Setup group**, point to—but do not click—the **Hyphenation** button.

The ScreenTip for this button has more information than just the name, including a link to the topic in the Help system. This is called an **Enhanced ScreenTip**, and is part of the Microsoft Office 2007 Help system.

2 Move your pointer to the right side of the Ribbon and click the **Microsoft Office Word Help** button. In the **Word Help** dialog box, click the **Search button arrow**, and then under **Content from this computer**, click **Word Help**.

This search for Help will be restricted to the Help installed on your computer. Depending on your Word settings, the glossary on the left of the Word Help dialog box may not display.

3 To the left of the **Search** button, click in the **Type words to search for** box, type **save a file** and then press [Enter].

A list of related topic displays, as shown in Figure 1.47. Your list may differ.

Search button arrow   Search results   Help button

Figure 1.47

Words to search for

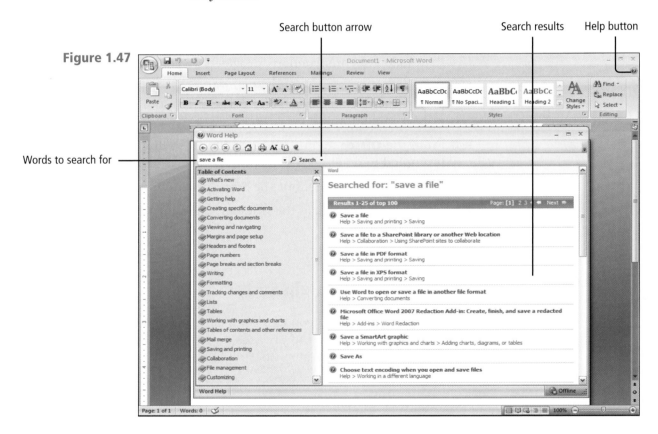

4 From the displayed list, point to, and then click **Save a file**.

5 Under **What do you want to do?** click **Use Word to open or save a file in another file format**—the wording for this topic may vary. Scroll to the bottom of the displayed Help. Notice that step-by-step instructions are given, as shown in Figure 1.48.

Figure 1.48

Instructions for saving a document under another format

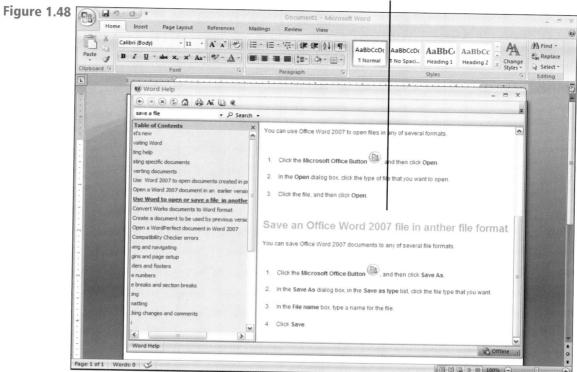

6 In the upper right corner of the Word Help window, click the **Close**

button ☒. From the **Office** menu 🔘, click **Exit Word** to close the
Word program.

End **You have completed Project 1B**

There's More You Can Do!

From My Computer, navigate to the student files that accompany this textbook. In the folder **02_theres_more_you_can_do_pg1_36**, locate and open the folder for this chapter. Open and print the instructions for this project, which are provided to you in Adobe PDF format.

Try IT!— Convert a Document to a Different Format

In this Try IT! exercise, you will convert a Word document to several different file formats.

Content-Based Assessments

Summary

In this chapter, you started Word and practiced navigating the Word window. You entered text, deleted text by using the Backspace and Delete keys, selected and replaced text, and inserted text. The spelling and grammar checker tools were demonstrated, and an image was added to a document.

You also practiced changing font style and size and adding emphasis to text. You viewed the header and footer areas, and created a chapter folder to help organize your files. Each document was saved, previewed, printed, and closed. Finally, the Help program was introduced as a tool that can assist you in using Word.

Key Terms

The ● symbol represents Key Terms found on the Student CD in the 02_theres_more_you_can_do folder for this chapter.

Content-Based Assessments

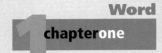
Matching

Match each term in the second column with its correct definition in the first column. Write the letter of the term on the blank line in front of the correct definition.

_____ **1.** The location in the Word window, indicated by a blinking vertical line, where text will be inserted when you start to type.

_____ **2.** In the Word window, the location of the Minimize, Maximize/Restore Down, and Close buttons.

_____ **3.** A button that represents the command to reveal nonprinting characters.

_____ **4.** The action that takes place when the insertion point reaches the right margin and automatically moves down and to the left margin of the next line.

_____ **5.** The process of setting the overall appearance of the text within the document.

_____ **6.** To hold down the left mouse button and move the mouse pointer over text to select it.

_____ **7.** A set of characters (letters and numbers) with the same design and shape.

_____ **8.** A unit of measure to describe the size of a font.

_____ **9.** A font type, such as Calibri or Arial that does not have lines on the ends of characters.

_____ **10.** A font type, such as Cambria or Times New Roman, that has extensions or lines on the ends of the characters.

_____ **11.** The term that refers to pressing one or more keys to navigate a window or execute commands.

_____ **12.** This feature changes the selected text when the pointer points to a button or list item to preview what the text will look like if the button or list item is clicked.

_____ **13.** A reserved area for text and graphics that displays at the bottom of each page in a document or section of a document.

_____ **14.** A view that simplifies the page layout for quick typing and can show more text on a smaller screen.

_____ **15.** A context-sensitive list that displays when you click the right mouse button.

A Draft

B Drag

C Font

D Footer

E Formatting

F Insertion point

G Keyboard shortcut

H Live Preview

I Point

J Sans serif

K Serif

L Shortcut menu

M Show/Hide ¶

N Title bar

O Wordwrap

Content-Based Assessments

Fill in the Blank

Write the correct word in the space provided.

1. Microsoft Word 2007 is a word _____ program that you can use to perform tasks such as writing a memo, a report, or a letter.

2. Located at the bottom of the Word window, the bar that provides information such as page number and word count is referred to as the _____ bar.

3. Within the scroll bar, dragging the _____ _____ downward causes the document on your screen to move up.

4. A toolbar above the Ribbon and to the right of the Office button, which can be customized by adding frequently used buttons, is called the _____ _____ _____ (QAT).

5. Characters that display on the screen to show the location of paragraph marks, tabs, and spaces but that do not print are called _____ marks.

6. If you point to a button on the Ribbon, a(n) _____ displays the name of the button.

7. In a business letter, the address of the recipient is called a(n) _____ address.

8. When you select text, the _____ toolbar displays buttons that are commonly used with the selected object.

9. Before text can be edited, changed, formatted, copied, or moved, it must first be _____

10. To add emphasis to text, use the _____ or _____ or _____ command, each of which has a button on the Ribbon.

11. The view that displays the page borders, margins, text, and graphics is the _____ _____ view.

12. The View buttons are located on the right side of the _____ bar.

13. To enlarge or decrease the viewing area of the document, use the _____ _____ on the status bar.

14. Graphic images, of which some are included with Word, that can be inserted in the document are called _____ art.

15. To display a shortcut menu, click the _____ mouse button.

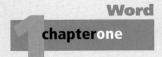

Skills Review

Project 1C — Receipt Letter

In this project, you will apply the skills you practiced from the Objectives in Project 1A.

Objectives: 1. *Create and Save a New Document;* **2.** *Edit Text;* **3.** *Select, Delete, and Format Text;* **4.** *Print a Document.*

In the following Skills Review, you will create and edit a follow-up letter from Jamal Anderssen, a production manager for Music School Records, to William Hawken, a recording artist who has submitted a demo CD with his application. Your completed letter will look similar to the one shown in Figure 1.49.

For Project 1C, you will need the following file:

New blank Word document

You will save your document as
1C_Receipt_Letter_Firstname_Lastname

Figure 1.49

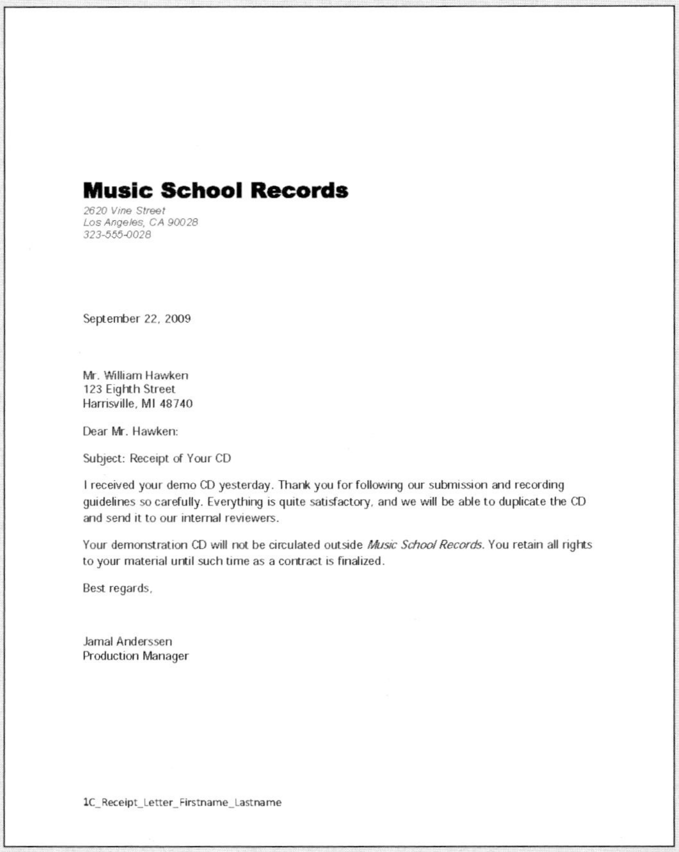

Music School Records
2620 Vine Street
Los Angeles, CA 90028
323-555-0028

September 22, 2009

Mr. William Hawken
123 Eighth Street
Harrisville, MI 48740

Dear Mr. Hawken:

Subject: Receipt of Your CD

I received your demo CD yesterday. Thank you for following our submission and recording guidelines so carefully. Everything is quite satisfactory, and we will be able to duplicate the CD and send it to our internal reviewers.

Your demonstration CD will not be circulated outside *Music School Records*. You retain all rights to your material until such time as a contract is finalized.

Best regards,

Jamal Anderssen
Production Manager

1C_Receipt_Letter_Firstname_Lastname

(Project 1C–Receipt Letter continues on the next page)

(Project 1C–Receipt Letter continued)

1. **Start** Word. If necessary, on the Ribbon, in the **Paragraph group**, click the **Show/Hide ¶** button to display the formatting marks. In the status bar, use the **Zoom slider** to adjust the page width to display both the left and right page margins.

2. On the **Home tab**, in the **Styles group**, click the **No Spacing** style. With the insertion point blinking in the upper left corner of the document to the left of the default first paragraph mark, type **Music School Records** and then press [Enter]. Type the following text and press [Enter] after each line:

   **2620 Vine Street
   Los Angeles, CA 90028
   323-555-0028**

3. Press [Enter] five more times. Begin typing today's date and let AutoComplete assist in your typing by pressing [Enter] when the ScreenTip displays. Press [Enter] four times. Type the inside address on three lines:

   **Mr. William Hawken
   123 Eighth Street
   Harrisville, MI 48740**

4. On the **Quick Access Toolbar**, click the **Save** button. In the **Save As** dialog box, click the **Save in arrow**, and then navigate to your **Word Chapter 1** folder. In the displayed **File name** box, using your own first and last names, type **1C_Receipt_Letter_Firstname_Lastname** and then click **Save**.

5. On the **Home tab**, in the **Styles group**, click the **Normal** style. Press [Enter], type the salutation **Dear Mr. Hawken:** and then press [Enter].

6. Type **Subject: receipt of Your CD** and then press [Enter]. Then using just one space following the periods at the end of sentences, type the following text:

I received your demo CD yesterday. Thank you for following our submission and recording standards so carefully. Everything is satisfactory, and we will be able to duplicate the CD and send it to our internal reviewers.

7. Press [Enter] to begin a new paragraph, and then type the following:

   Your demonstration CD will not be circulated outside Music School Records. You retain the rights to your material until such time as a contract is finalized.

8. Press [Enter], type the closing **Best regards,** and then press [Enter] two times.

9. On the **Quick Access Toolbar**, click the **Save** button to save your changes. On the **Home tab**, in the **Styles group**, click the **No Spacing** button. Finish the letter by typing the writer's identification on two lines:

   **Jamal Anderssen
   Production Manager**

10. If necessary, drag the vertical scroll box to the top of the scroll bar to view the upper portion of the document. In the *Subject* line, position the insertion point to the left of *receipt*, and then press the **Delete** button. Type **R** to capitalize *Receipt*.

11. In the paragraph beginning *I received*, double-click the word **standards** to select it, and then type **guidelines**

12. In the same paragraph, position the insertion point to the left of the word *satisfactory*. Type **quite** and then press [Spacebar] one time.

13. In the paragraph beginning *Your demonstration*, click to position the insertion point to the left of *rights*, press the **Backspace** button four times. Type **all** and then press [Spacebar] to change the phrase to *retain all rights*.

(Project 1C–Receipt Letter continues on the next page)

(Project 1C–Receipt Letter continued)

14. **Save** the changes you have made to your document. Press Ctrl + A to select the entire document. On the **Home tab**, in the **Font group**, click the **Font button arrow**. Scroll as necessary, and watch Live Preview change the document font as you point to different font names. Click to choose **Tahoma**. Recall that you can type *T* in the Font box to move quickly to the fonts beginning with that letter. Click anywhere in the document to cancel the selection.

15. Select the entire first line of text—*Music School Records*. On the Mini toolbar, click the **Font button arrow**, and then click **Arial Black**. With the Mini toolbar still displayed, click the **Font Size button arrow**, and then click **20**. With the Mini toolbar still displayed, click the **Bold** button.

16. Select the second, third, and fourth lines of text, beginning with *2620 Vine Street* and ending with the telephone number. On the Mini toolbar, click the **Font button arrow**, and then click **Arial**. With the Mini toolbar still displayed, click the **Font Size button arrow**, and then click **10**. With the Mini toolbar still displayed, click the **Italic** button.

17. In the paragraph beginning *Your demonstration*, select the text *Music School Records*. On the Mini toolbar, click the **Italic** button, and then click anywhere to deselect the text.

18. Click the **Insert tab**. In the **Header & Footer group**, click the **Footer** button,

and then click **Edit Footer**. On the **Design tab**, in the **Insert group**, click the **Quick Parts** button, and then click **Field**. In the **Field** dialog box, under **Field names**, scroll down and click to choose **FileName**, and then click **OK**. Double-click anywhere in the document to leave the footer area.

19. Click the **Page Layout tab**. In the **Page Setup group**, click the **Margins** button to display the Margins gallery. At the bottom of the **Margins gallery**, click **Custom Margins** to display the **Page Setup** dialog box. Near the top of the **Page Setup** dialog box, click the **Layout tab**. Under **Page**, click the **Vertical alignment arrow**, click **Center**, and then click **OK**.

20. From the **Office** menu, point to the **Print arrow**, and then click **Print Preview** to make a final check of your letter. Follow your instructor's directions for submitting this file. Check your *Chapter Assignment Sheet* or *Course Syllabus* or consult your instructor to determine if you are to submit your assignments on paper or electronically. To submit electronically, go to Step 22, and then follow the instructions provided by your instructor.

21. On the **Print Preview tab,** in the **Print** group, click the Print button. Click **OK**, and then **Close** Print Preview. Collect your printout from the printer and submit it as directed.

22. From the **Office** menu, click **Exit Word**, saving any changes if prompted to do so.

 You have completed Project 1C —————————————

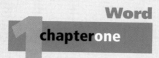

Content-Based Assessments

Word
chapter one | Skills Review

Project 1D — Marketing

In this project, you will apply the skills you practiced from the Objectives in Project 1B.

Objectives: 5. *Navigate the Word Window;* **6.** *Add a Graphic to a Document;* **7.** *Use the Spelling and Grammar Checker;* **8.** *Preview and Print Documents, Close a Document, and Close Word;* **9.** *Use the Microsoft Help System.*

In the following Skills Review, you will edit a document that details the marketing and promotion plan for Music School Records. Your completed document will look similar to Figure 1.50.

For Project 1D, you will need the following files:

New blank Word document
w01D_Marketing
w01D_Piano

You will save your document as
1D_Marketing_Firstname_Lastname

Figure 1.50

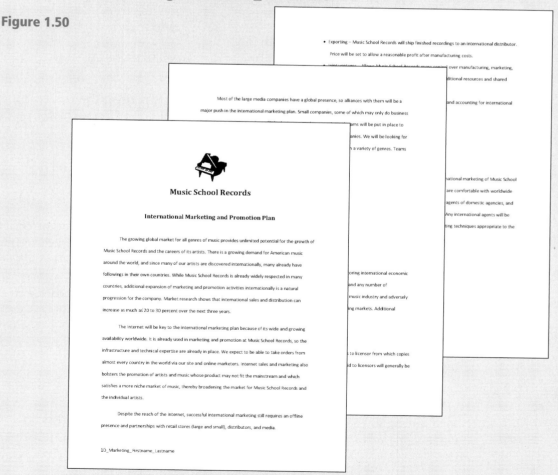

(Project 1D–Marketing continues on the next page)

Content-Based Assessments

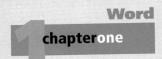

(Project 1D–Marketing continued)

1. **Start** Word and be sure a new blank document is displayed. If necessary, on the Ribbon, in the **Paragraph group**, click the **Show/Hide ¶** button to display the formatting marks. In the status bar, use the **Zoom slider** to adjust the page width to display both the left and right page edges.

2. On the **Quick Access Toolbar**, click the **Save** button. In the **Save As** dialog box, click the **Save in arrow**, and then navigate to your **Word Chapter 1** folder. In the **File name** box, using your own first and last names, type **1D_Marketing_Firstname_Lastname** and then click **Save**.

3. Click the **Insert tab**. In the **Header & Footer group**, click the **Footer** button to display the Footer gallery. At the bottom of the **Footer gallery**, click **Edit Footer**. Click the **Design tab**. In the **Insert group**, click the **Quick Parts** button, and then click **Field**. In the **Field** dialog box, under **Field names**, scroll down and click **FileName**, and then click **OK**. Double-click anywhere in the document to leave the footer area.

4. Click the **Insert tab**. In the **Text group**, click the **Object button arrow**, and then click **Text From File**. In the displayed **Insert File** dialog box, navigate to the location where the student files for this textbook are stored. Locate and click to select **w01D_Marketing**, and then click the **Insert** button to insert the text.

5. Press ⌫Bksp to remove the blank line at the end of the document. Use the vertical scroll bar to examine the document. When you are finished, hold down Ctrl + Home to move to the beginning of the document.

6. **Save** your document. Move the ⌐ pointer into the margin area to the left of the title *Music School Records* and drag down to

select the title, the blank line, and the second title that begins *International Marketting*. Be sure to include the blank line between the two titles. On the Mini toolbar, click the **Bold** button. Click anywhere in the document to deselect the text.

7. In the second title line, notice that the word *Marketting* is marked as misspelled. Right-click *Marketting*, and from the shortcut menu, click **Marketing**. In the first line of the paragraph that begins *The growing global*, right-click *geners*, and from the shortcut menu, locate and click **genres**.

8. Click the **Review tab**, and then, in the **Proofing group**, click the **Spelling & Grammar** button to open the **Spelling and Grammar** dialog box. The first word flagged is *allready*. Notice that this word is misspelled several times in the document.

9. In the **Spelling and Grammar** dialog box, click the **Change All** button to correct all occurrences of this misspelled word. The next potential error—a subject-verb agreement problem—is highlighted. Notice that two suggested corrections are listed. If necessary, click **is a growing demand,** and then click the **Change** button.

10. If a Passive Voice error is identified next, click Ignore Once. In the paragraph that begins *The Internet will be key*, another potential grammar problem is highlighted. Click the **Ignore Once** button to leave the sentence the way it was written. Correct the spelling error for the word *Millenium*, and then click the **Ignore Once** button until you reach the end of the document. When a message box tells you the check is complete, click **OK**.

11. Hold down Ctrl and press Home to move to the beginning of the document, and then

(Project 1D–Marketing continues on the next page)

Content-Based Assessments

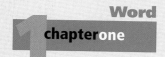

(Project 1D–Marketing continued)

press ⏎ to add a blank line. Click to position the insertion point in the new blank line.

12. Click the **Microsoft Office Word Help** button. In the **Word Help** dialog box, click the **Search button arrow**, and then under **Content from this computer**, click **Word Help**. In the **Type words to search for** box, type **graphic file types** and then press ⏎. In the search results, click **Types of media files you can add** and examine the list of graphic file types that can be added to a Word document.

13. Close the **Word Help** window, and then click the **Insert tab**. In the **Illustrations group**, click the **Picture** button. In the displayed **Insert Picture** dialog box, navigate to the student files that accompany this textbook, click the **w01D_Piano** file, and then click **Insert**.

14. **Save** your changes. Check your *Chapter Assignment Sheet* or *Course Syllabus* or consult your instructor to determine if you are to submit your assignments on paper or electronically. To submit electronically, go to Step 16, and then follow the instructions provided by your instructor.

15. From the **Office** menu, point to the **Print arrow**, and then click **Print Preview** to make a final check of your document. On the **Print Preview tab**, in the **Print group**, click the **Print** button, and from the displayed **Print** dialog box, click **OK**. Then, in the **Preview group**, click the **Close Print Preview** button. Collect your printout from the printer and submit as directed.

16. From the **Office** menu, click **Close**. At the right end of the title bar, click the **Close** button to close Word.

End **You have completed Project 1D** ————————

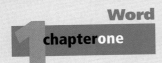

Mastering Word

Project 1E — School Tour

In this project, you will apply the skills you practiced from the Objectives in Project 1A.

Objectives: 1. *Create and Save a New Document;* **2.** *Edit Text;* **3.** *Select, Delete, and Format Text;* **4.** *Print a Document;* **7.** *Use the Spelling and Grammar Checker.*

In the following Mastering Word project, you will write a thank-you letter to the Dean of the Music Center School of Atlanta to thank him for a tour of his school's facilities. You will leave enough room at the top of the page to print it on preprinted company letterhead stationery. Your completed document will look similar to Figure 1.51.

For Project 1E, you will need the following file:

New blank Word document

You will save your document as
1E_School_Tour_Firstname_Lastname

Figure 1.51

September 29, 2009

Dr. Adair Leake, Dean
Music Center School of Atlanta
1395 Peachtree Street, Suite 1850
Atlanta, GA 30309

Dear Dr. Leake:

Thank you for the tour of your school's facilities and for the opportunity to watch the jazz piano recital. I was very impressed with the methods you are using to draw new and interesting sounds from the students in the piano program. **Music School Records** intends to send a team from *Artists & Repertoire* to the school over the next few months to meet with some of these students individually to determine their next steps in their music careers.

I enjoyed meeting you and the students, and I look forward to talking with you again soon. Please send my regards to the students.

Sincerely,

Lisa Ivanko
Talent Developer

1E_School_Tour_Firstname_Lastname

(Project 1E–School Tour continues on the next page)

Content-Based Assessments

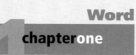

Mastering Word

(Project 1E–School Tour continued)

1. **Start** Word and be sure a new blank document displays. Display formatting marks, and be sure your screen displays both the left and right document edges. Save the document in your **Word Chapter 1** folder as **1E_School_Tour_Firstname_Lastname** Open the document footer area and add the file name to the footer.

2. Use the letter formatting skills you practiced in Project 1A to create a letter. Begin with the current date. Then, on the **Home tab**, apply the **No Spacing** style. Add the appropriate number of blank lines, and then add the following inside address (at the end of the last line of the address, apply the **Normal** style).

   Dr. Adair Leake, Dean
   Music Center School of Atlanta
   1395 Peachtree Street, Suite 1850
   Atlanta, GA 30309

3. Add the salutation **Dear Dr. Leake:** and then type the following paragraphs, saving your work frequently. Be sure to space only one time following end-of-sentence punctuation:

   Thank you for the tour of your school's facilities and for the opportunity to watch the jazz piano recital. I was very impressed with the methods you are using to draw new and interesting sounds from the students in the piano program. Music School Records intends to send a team from Artists & Repertoire to the school over the next few

   months to meet with some of these students individually to determine their next steps in their music careers.

   I liked meeting you and the students, and I very much look forward to talking with you again soon. Please send my regards to the students.

4. **Save** your document. Use the appropriate spacing, add the complimentary closing **Sincerely,** and then add the following writer's identification:

   Lisa Ivanko
   Talent Developer

5. In the paragraph beginning *I liked meeting you*, use either Delete or ←Bksp to change *liked* to **enjoyed** In the same paragraph, select the text *very much* and then press Delete to remove this phrase.

6. In the paragraph beginning *Thank you for the tour*, in the third line, locate the text *Music School Records* and add **Bold** emphasis. In the same sentence, locate *Artists & Repertoire* and add **Italic** emphasis.

7. Select the entire document. Change the **Font** to **Arial**, and the **Font Size** to **12**. Center the letter vertically on the page.

8. Check the spelling and grammar. Preview the document and then print it, or submit it electronically as directed. **Close** the document, and then **Close** Word.

 You have completed Project 1E ————————————

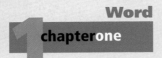

Word

chapterone

Mastering Word

Project 1F — Scouting Trip

In this project, you will apply the skills you practiced from the Objectives in Project 1B.

Objectives: 5. *Navigate the Word Window;* **6.** *Add a Graphic to a Document;* **7.** *Use the Spelling and Grammar Checker;* **8.** *Preview and Print Documents, Close a Document, and Close Word.*

In the following Mastering Word project, you will edit a memo from one of Music School Records' talent developers highlighting her third quarter accomplishments. Your completed document will look similar to Figure 1.52.

For Project 1F, you will need the following files:

w01F_Scouting_Trip
w01F_Piano

You will save your document as 1F_Scouting_Trip_Firstname_Lastname

Figure 1.52

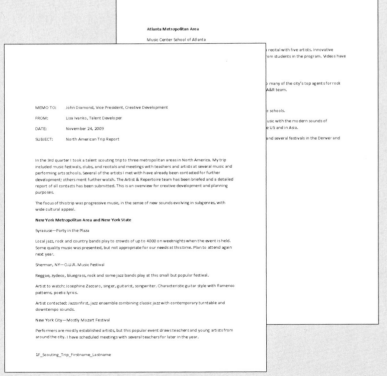

(Project 1F–Scouting Trip on the next page)

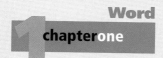

chapter one

Word

Mastering Word

(Project 1F–Scouting Trip continued)

1. Locate and open the document **w01F_Scouting Trip**. Display formatting marks, display the ruler, and be sure your screen displays both the left and right document edges. **Save** the file in your **Word Chapter 1** folder as **1F_Scouting_Trip_Firstname_Lastname** and add the file name to the footer.

There are numerous acceptable memo formats. This format is an example from the *Gregg Reference Manual* (Sabin, 2005). Always consult a trusted reference manual or Business Communication textbook when formatting business documents.

2. Use the vertical scroll bar to examine the document. Notice the potential spelling and grammar errors that have been flagged. Also notice that there is a heading—*Atlanta Metropolitan Area*—at the bottom of the first page that should be placed at the top of the second page.

3. On the **View tab**, in the **Window group**, click the **Split** button to split the screen and use the vertical scroll bars in the top and bottom windows to display the Subject line in the top window, and the last line of the first page—*Atlanta Metropolitan Area*—in the bottom window.

4. Position the insertion point at the end of the *Subject* line and press [Enter]. Notice that the *Atlanta Metropolitan Area* heading moves to the top of the second page. Scroll within the bottom window if necessary to view the top of page 2. Then, close the split screen. As you progress in your study of Microsoft Word, you will discover other ways to manually end a page and move text to the next page.

5. View the document in **Full Screen Reading** view. Return to **Print Layout** view and use the **Zoom slider** to display two pages on the screen. Zoom back to a comfortable document size.

6. In the first line of the memo, the word *Creative* may be flagged as a potential grammar error. If so, use the shortcut menu to Ignore Once. In the *FROM:* line, use the shortcut menu to ignore the flagged word *Ivanko*.

7. Open the **Spelling and Grammar** dialog box to check the remainder of the potential spelling and grammar errors. Although there are a number of uncommon words and proper names that are flagged because they are not in Word's dictionary, there are only two additional errors—the misspelled word *focuss* and the grammar error *Videos has been*. Correct these errors, and ignore any other names, words, or phrases that are flagged. **Save** your work.

8. Move to the end of the document. Place the insertion point at the end of the last paragraph—the one beginning *My next trip*—and then press [Enter]. Locate and insert the **w01F_Piano** image.

9. Preview the memo to see how it will print on paper. If you are to submit the document on paper, print and submit it as directed. If you are to submit the document electronically, follow your instructor's directions. **Close** the document and **Close** Word.

End **You have completed Project 1F** —————

Mastering Word

Project 1G — Contract

In this project, you will apply the skills you practiced from the Objectives in Projects 1A and 1B.

Objectives: 2. *Edit Text;* **3.** *Select, Delete, and Format Text;* **4.** *Print a Document;* **5.** *Navigate the Word Window;* **7.** *Use the Spelling and Grammar Checker;* **8.** *Preview and Print Documents, Close a Document, and Close Word.*

In the following Mastering Word project, you will edit a contract between a client and Music School Records. Your completed document will look similar to Figure 1.53.

For Project 1G, you will need the following file:

w01G_Contract

You will save your document as
1G_Contract_Firstname_Lastname

Figure 1.53

The Second Party is required to present an individualized promotional plan for the Artist in the Chicago Metropolitan Area. Upon approval of the plan, Music School Records will release the above-mentioned products and allow access to the Artist. The Second Party ... an implementation and sales figures to

... e Second Party will be paid an amount ... ago Metropolitan Area during the ... e year after the contract has been

... ubject to renewal and/or revision at

...'s fees.
... Los Angeles, County of Los Angeles,

... l: _____
... l: _____

Contract for Services

PARTIES TO THE CONTRACT
The First Party's name is Music School Records, a Corporation.

The Second Party's name is **Evie Chardan**, an individual proprietor.

WHO HAS TO DO WHAT
Music School Records and **Evie Chardan** agree to the following:
Music School Records will provide the Second Party various marketing materials and recordings of **Evie Chardan** (the Artist) for the purposes of publicizing and promoting the Artist to music stores in the Chicago metropolitan area.

The materials provided by Music School Records may include printed brochures, promotional CDs, pre-loaded digital music players, advertising copy, Artist fact sheets, photographs, and press clips. Also available as requested will be low-value promotional items such as buttons, stickers, and other trinkets.

Music School Records will also provide, with proper notice and approval of venue, access to the Artist for press conferences, interviews, media appearances, and performances. All such personal appearances will be subject to Music School Records' contract with the Artist.

Music School Records is responsible for the accuracy of all printed materials. Music School Records is also

The Second Party will take all legally required actions and professionally appropriate care in protecting the copyrights of Music School Records and the Artist. The Second Party is responsible for the health and safety of the Artist while at appearances arranged by the Second Party. If the Artist is a minor, the Second Party will follow all applicable laws relating to care and work of a minor.

The Second Party will be responsible for writing/producing and releasing press clips (print, audio and video) following any promotional events. The Second Party is responsible for the accuracy of such releases and clips. Other promotional actions are expected to include, but are not limited to:

• Announcements and listings in local press entertainment calendars
• Arrangement of and public service announcements for charity events
• Mailings, faxes, and phone calls to local press, club owners, music store managers, etc.
• Any necessary local Web presence

1G_Contract_Firstname_Lastname

(Project 1G–Contract continues on the next page)

(Project 1G–Contract continued)

1. Locate and open the document **w01G_Contract**. **Save** the document in your **Word Chapter 1** folder as **1G_Contract_Firstname_Lastname** and then add the file name to the footer. Display formatting marks, display the ruler, and set the page width to a comfortable size for you.

2. If necessary, move to the beginning of the document, type **Contract for Services** and press Enter. Select *Contract for Services*, change the **Font Size** to **18** points, and apply **Bold** emphasis.

3. Use the **Spelling and Grammar** checker to correct the errors in the document. There are several misspellings of the word *responsibel* and a subject-verb agreement error—*are* instead of *is*. Ignore all other flagged items.

4. Locate the three headings in uppercase letters. Select each one and add **Bold** emphasis. Recall that when you select the text, the Mini toolbar displays with the Bold button on it.

5. Locate the black lines in the document that represent blanks to be filled in. In the line beginning *The Second Party's name*, select the long line, but not the comma following it. Type **Evie Chardan** and notice that as you type, your typing will be displayed in bold. On the next two long lines, use the same technique to type **Evie Chardan** again.

6. On page 2, in the paragraph beginning *For services provided*, select the line and type **12** Select the line following *This agreement will be in force for*, type **2** and then remove *months/* so that the sentence reads *in force for 2 years.*

7. **Save** your changes. At the end of the contract, under *Signed*, select the text *Music School Records*, and then on the Mini toolbar, change the font size to **10** and add **Bold** emphasis. **Save** your changes. Preview the document and then print it, or submit it electronically as directed. **Close** the document, and then **Close** Word.

End **You have completed Project 1G**

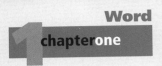

Mastering Word

Project 1H—Invitation

In this project, you will apply the skills you practiced from the Objectives in Projects 1A and 1B.

Objectives: 1. *Create and Save a New Document;* **2.** *Edit Text;* **3.** *Select, Delete, and Format Text;* **4.** *Print a Document;* **5.** *Navigate the Word Window;* **6.** *Add a Graphic to a Document;* **7.** *Use the Spelling and Grammar Checker;* **8.** *Preview and Print Documents, Close a Document, and Close Word.*

In the following Mastering Word project, you will create a new letter to a talent agent, and then insert and edit text from a file. Your completed document will look similar to Figure 1.54.

For Project 1H, you will need the following files:

New blank Word document

w01H_Invitation

w01H_Letterhead

You will save your document as
1H_Invitation_Firstname_Lastname

Figure 1.54

Music School Records

2620 Vine Street

Los Angeles, CA 90028

323-555-0028

Musicschoolrecords.com

September 30, 2009

Ms. Caroline Westbrook
Artists' Workshop Agency
249 Fifth Avenue #2700
New York, NY 10001

Dear Ms. Westbrook:

Thank you for the introduction to your client, Ms. Evie Chardan. Our representatives were very impressed with the quality of Ms. Chardan's music, stage presence, and obvious rapport with the young audience for which she performed. It is certainly our pleasure to invite Ms. Chardan to consider a recording contract with **Music School Records**.

Upon your approval, we will draft a standard contract for your and Ms. Chardan's attorneys' review. The contract will be subject to the laws of California and will include language outlining the term of the contract, guaranteed minimum payments per year, and obligations of the artist and **Music School Records**. As part of the standard contract we do require a period of exclusivity regarding the artist's recording, and this period is subject to negotiation.

Please call me as soon as possible to confirm your client's agreement to draft the contract. We are looking forward to working with you again and playing a key role in the development of Ms. Chardan's career.

Sincerely,

John Diamond
Vice President, Creative Development

1H_Invitation_Firstname_Lastname

(Project 1H–Invitation continues on the next page)

Word

chapterone

Mastering Word

(Project 1H–Invitation continued)

1. **Start** Word and be sure a new blank document is displayed. Display formatting marks, display the ruler, and be sure your screen displays both the left and right document edges. **Save** the document in your **Word Chapter 1** folder as 1H_Invitation_Firstname_Lastname Open the document footer and add the file name.

2. Locate and insert the file **w01H_Letterhead**. Be sure the insertion point is positioned at the second blank line below the letterhead, and then type the current date. Using the skills you practiced in Project 1A, be sure the address style is set to **No Spacing**, and then add the following inside address and salutation:

   Ms. Caroline Westbrook
   Artists' Workshop Agency
   249 Fifth Avenue #2700
   New York, NY 10001

3. Change the style back to **Normal**, press Enter, and then type **Dear Ms. Westbrook:** Press Enter, and then locate and insert the file **w01H_Invitation**. Add the following paragraph at the end of the document:

   Please call me as soon as possible to confirm your client's agreement to draft the contract. We are looking forward to working with you again and playing a key role in the development of Ms. Chardan's career.

4. Using appropriate spacing, add the complimentary closing **Sincerely,** and then add the following writer's identification:

   John Diamond
   Vice President, Creative Development

5. **Save** your changes. Be sure grammar errors are flagged in the document. In the paragraph beginning *Thank you*, in the second sentence, correct the grammar error *was*, and then type **very** between *were* and *impressed*. In the third line of the same paragraph, add **certainly** between *It is* and *our pleasure*. In the last sentence of the same paragraph, change *sign* to **consider**

6. Use the **Spelling and Grammar** checker to correct the errors in the document. There is one error—the misspelled word *qualty*. Ignore all other flagged items.

7. At the end of the paragraph beginning *Thank you for the introduction*, locate the text *Music School Records* and add **Bold** emphasis. In the paragraph beginning *Upon your approval*, add **Bold** emphasis to *Music School Records*.

8. Select the entire document. Change the **Font** to **Cambria**. **Save** your changes.

9. Preview the document and then print it, or submit it electronically as directed. **Close** the file, and then **Close** Word.

End **You have completed Project 1H**

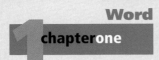
Word
chapter one

Mastering Word

Project 1I—Fax Cover

In this project, you will apply the skills you practiced from the Objectives in Projects 1A and 1B.

Objectives: 1. *Create and Save a New Document;* **2.** *Edit Text;* **3.** *Select, Delete, and Format Text;* **4.** *Print a Document;* **5.** *Navigate the Word Window;* **6.** *Add a Graphic to a Document;* **7.** *Use the Spelling and Grammar Checker;* **8.** *Preview and Print Documents, Close a Document, and Close Word.*

In the following Mastering Word project, you will create a cover sheet for a facsimile (fax) transmission. When sending a fax, it is common practice to include a cover sheet with a note describing the pages that will follow. Your completed document will look similar to Figure 1.55.

For Project 1I, you will need the following files:

New blank Word document
w01I_Fax_Cover
w01I_Fax_Machine

You will save your document as
1I_Fax_Cover_Firstname_Lastname

Figure 1.55

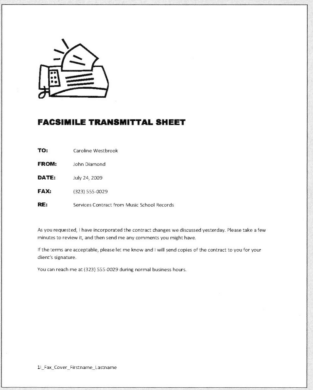

(Project 1I–Fax Cover on the next page)

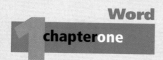

Mastering Word

(Project 1I–Fax Cover continued)

1. Start Word and be sure a new blank document is displayed. Display formatting marks and rulers, and be sure your screen displays both the left and right document edges. **Save** the document in your **Word Chapter 1** folder as **1I_Fax_Cover_Firstname_Lastname** Open the document footer and add the file name to the footer.

2. Press [Enter] two times and then move to the top of the document. Locate and insert the **w01I_Fax_Machine** clip art image. Press [Ctrl] + [End]. Press [CapsLock], type **FACSIMILE TRANSMITTAL SHEET** and then press [Enter] two times. Press [CapsLock] again.

3. Locate and insert the file **w01I_Fax_Cover**. Move to the blank line at the end of the document, and then type **You can reach me at (323) 555-0029 during normal business hours. Save** your work.

4. Select the text *FACSIMILE TRANSMITTAL SHEET*. Change the **Font Size** to **16**, and the **Font** to **Arial Black**. Change the font of the line headings *TO:, FROM:, DATE:, FAX:,* and *RE:* to **Arial Black**.

5. In the paragraph that begins *As you requested*, select and delete the text *on the telephone*. In the same paragraph, replace the phrase *look it over* with **review it** and, in the same sentence, add an **s** to *comment*.

6. There are several grammar and spelling errors that need to be corrected. Right-click on the duplicate or misspelled words and correct as necessary. In the paragraph beginning *If the term are*, select the **terms are** option. **Save** your changes.

7. Use [Ctrl] + [Home] to navigate to the beginning of the document. Proofread the fax cover to be sure you have made all necessary corrections.

8. Preview the document. Print and submit as directed, or submit the document electronically according to your instructor's directions. **Close** the document and **Close** Word.

End **You have completed Project 1I**

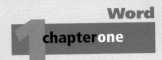

Project 1J—Business Running Case

In this project, you will apply the skills you practiced in Projects 1A and 1B.

From My Computer, navigate to the student files that accompany this textbook. In the folder **03_business_running_case_pg37_86**, locate and open the folder for this chapter. Open and print the instructions for this project, which are provided to you in Adobe PDF format. Follow the instructions and use the skills you have gained thus far to assist Jennifer Nelson in meeting the challenges of owning and running her business.

Outcomes-Based Assessments

Rubric

The following outcomes-based assessments are *open-ended assessments*. That is, there is no specific correct result; your result will depend on your approach to the information provided. Make *Professional Quality* your goal. Use the following scoring rubric to guide you in *how* to approach the problem and then to evaluate *how well* your approach solves the problem.

The *criteria*—Software Mastery, Content, Format and Layout, and Process—represent the knowledge and skills you have gained that you can apply to solving the problem. The *levels of performance*—Professional Quality, Approaching Professional Quality, or Needs Quality Improvements—help you and your instructor evaluate your result.

	Your completed project is of Professional Quality if you:	Your completed project is Approaching Professional Quality if you:	Your completed project Needs Quality Improvements if you:
1-Software Mastery	Choose and apply the most appropriate skills, tools, and features and identify efficient methods to solve the problem.	Choose and apply some appropriate skills, tools, and features, but not in the most efficient manner.	Choose inappropriate skills, tools, or features, or are inefficient in solving the problem.
2-Content	Construct a solution that is clear and well organized, contains content that is accurate, appropriate to the audience and purpose, and is complete. Provide a solution that contains no errors of spelling, grammar, or style.	Construct a solution in which some components are unclear, poorly organized, inconsistent, or incomplete. Misjudge the needs of the audience. Have some errors in spelling, grammar, or style, but the errors do not detract from comprehension.	Construct a solution that is unclear, incomplete, or poorly organized, containing some inaccurate or inappropriate content; and contains many errors of spelling, grammar, or style. Do not solve the problem.
3-Format and Layout	Format and arrange all elements to communicate information and ideas, clarify function, illustrate relationships, and indicate relative importance.	Apply appropriate format and layout features to some elements, but not others. Overuse features, causing minor distraction.	Apply format and layout that does not communicate information or ideas clearly. Do not use format and layout features to clarify function, illustrate relationships, or indicate relative importance. Use available features excessively, causing distraction.
4-Process	Use an organized approach that integrates planning, development, self-assessment, revision, and reflection.	Demonstrate an organized approach in some areas, but not others; or, use an insufficient process of organization throughout.	Do not use an organized approach to solve the problem.

Outcomes-Based Assessments

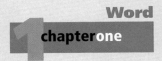
Problem Solving

Project 1K — Services

In this project, you will construct a solution by applying any combination of the skills you practiced from the Objectives in Projects 1A and 1B.

For Project 1K, you will need the following file:

New blank Word document

**You will save your document as
1K_Services_Firstname_Lastname**

Using the information provided, compose a form letter from Lucy Burroughs—founder and CEO of Music School Records—that explains the services offered by the company. Music School Records is located at 2620 Vine Street, Los Angeles, CA 90028, (323) 555-0028. The tone of the letter should be positive and sales-oriented. The letter should answer the question "Why do I need this service?" As you write the letter, use the information in Project 1B that describes the company. The letter should contain three paragraphs—an introductory paragraph, a second paragraph describing the services offered, and a closing paragraph.

The letter should include the appropriate business letter components, and should be in the proper business format. Add the file name to the footer. Check the letter for spelling or grammar errors. Save the letter as **1K_Services_Firstname_Lastname** and submit it as directed.

End **You have completed Project 1K** ——————————

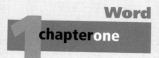

Problem Solving

Project 1L—Survey Form

In this project, you will construct a solution by applying any combination of the skills you practiced from the Objectives in Projects 1A and 1B.

For Project 1L, you will need the following file:

New blank Word document

You will save your document as
1L_Survey_Form_Firstname_Lastname

In Project 1L, you will create a brief survey form to be filled out by potential clients of Music School Records. The purpose of the survey form is to do a quick screening of applicants to be sure they are a match for the company before they talk to a field representative or send in a demo recording.

The target audience will be high school and college students, and young performers already working in their field. The form should include information that may be important to a screening committee, including the student's:

- Place of residence
- Current school (if any)
- Type of talent (instrument, voice)
- Genre of music
- Professional experience (if any)
- Awards and other types of public recognition

Include any other topics you feel would be helpful in a brief survey form. The form should list the topics down the left side of the page, and should leave three or four blank lines between each so the person filling out the form will have enough space to write.

Add the file name to the footer. Check the survey form for spelling or grammar errors. Save the document as **1L_Survey_Form_Firstname_Lastname** and submit it as directed.

End You have completed Project 1L

Problem Solving

Project 1M—Press Release

In this project, you will construct a solution by applying any combination of the skills you practiced from the Objectives in Projects 1A and 1B.

For Project 1M, you will need the following files:

New blank Word document
w01M_Music_Logo

You will save your document as
1M_Press_Release_Firstname_Lastname

In Project 1M, you will write a press release to announce the opening of an East Coast location for Music School Records. The information for the press release should be taken from the following information about the company:

Music School Records is located at 2620 Vine Street, Los Angeles, CA 90028, (323) 555-0028. The new office will be located in Manhattan at 250 5th Avenue #1460, New York, NY 10001, (212) 555-9124.

Music School Records is owned by Lucy Burroughs, who founded the company in 1994. The company was created to launch young musical artists with undiscovered talent in jazz, classical, and contemporary music. The creative management team searches internationally for talented young people, and has a reputation for mentoring and developing the skills of its artists. The company's music is tailored to an audience that is young, knowledgeable about music, and demands the highest quality recordings. Music School Records releases are available in CD format as well as digital downloads.

For artists who meet the company's high standards, Music School Records takes the core components of music and artist and creates a total marketable product. Marketing begins by identifying the unique qualities that will make a particular artist and their repertoire appealing to a particular audience. The marketing team then pinpoints the product's selling features and presents them to the industry and consumers. This helps differentiate the product from the competition and portrays the personality of the artist.

A key aspect of music marketing in today's marketplace is creating a bond between artists and audiences. Every Music School Records artist has a Web site, and the artists are encouraged to write their own articles and use their own voice to create a Web presence that shows who they are. Newsletters, email lists, blogs, ticket giveaways, downloads of new releases, and exclusive news items are among the ways that an artist can interact with their fans.

(Project 1M—Press Release continues on the next page)

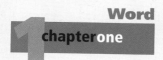

Problem Solving

(Project 1M–Press Release continued)

To complete this assignment:

- Insert a clip art image as the company logo at the top of the page. Find one of your own, or use **01M_Music_Logo**, which is included in your student files.

- Add the contact information of the person writing the press release, which should be in either the upper-right or upper-left corner of the release. It should look similar to the address block you typed in Project 1A, but with the addition of a telephone number. Use the name of the owner and the address and telephone number from the previous information.

- Add a **For Immediate Release** line before the body of the press release, but lower on the page than the address block. Format the line so it stands out from the rest of the text.

- Create an interesting title for the press release, and place it below the *For Immediate Release* line.

- Use the preceding information to create a two- or three-paragraph press release, with a space between each paragraph.

- Save the document as **1M_Press_Release_Firstname_Lastname** and add the file name to the footer.

The press release should include the most important information first, and should be simple and straightforward. For example, the information about the new location should come in the first paragraph, and the general information about the company should be presented in the second paragraph. A quote from the owners may make an interesting highlight in the third paragraph—you will need to create an appropriate quote.

 End **You have completed Project 1M** ————————

Outcomes-Based Assessments

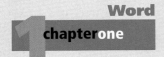
Problem Solving

Project 1N—Holidays

In this project, you will construct a solution by applying any combination of the skills you practiced from the Objectives in Projects 1A and 1B.

> **For Project 1N, you will need the following files:**
>
> New blank Word document
> w01N_Musical_Score

You will save your document as
1N_Holidays_Firstname_Lastname

In Project 1N, you will write a memo to announce the days that Music School Records will be closed for holidays in the upcoming year. Use a memo format that you like. If you are unsure of what should be contained in the memo heading, search **memo format** on the Internet. Most memos have at least four lines at the top—Date, To, From, and Subject.

The memo should be from Mahadevan Ropa, Vice President for Business Development, to all employees at the Los Angeles office. Include an opening paragraph that mentions the reason for the memo, and then identify seven or eight holidays for which the office will be closed. Choose any typical holidays that you want to include. If you are not sure of the dates of holidays, or which ones to include, search the Web, using as search terms the year and the word *holidays*.

Add the file name to the footer. Check the memo for spelling or grammar errors. Add the **w01N_Musical_Score** image where appropriate. Save the document as **1N_Holidays_Firstname_Lastname** and submit it as directed.

 You have completed Project 1N ————————————

Outcomes-Based Assessments

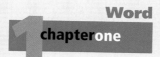

Word

chapterone

Problem Solving

Project 1O — Concert

In this project, you will construct a solution by applying any combination of the skills you practiced from the Objectives in Projects 1A and 1B.

For Project 1O, you will need the following files:

New blank Word document
w01O_Singer

You will save your document as
1O_Concert_Firstname_Lastname

In Project 1O, you will write a letter inquiring about a venue for an upcoming concert featuring three new clients of Music School Records. The following information is necessary to complete the letter:

- Contact person: Jamie Buchanan, Manager, Prince Island Auditorium
- Address: 112 Forkbend Rd., Los Angeles, California, 90030
- Performer 1: Jimmie O'Farrell, trumpet
- Performer 2: Alicia Jones, singer
- Performer 3: The Sturgeon Pointers, instrumental trio
- Musical style: Jazz/Pop fusion
- Desired date: second or third week in June
- Letter from: John Diamond, VP, Creative Development, Music School Records (323-555-0028)

Use the letter format you practiced in Project 1A to create a letter to Jamie Buchanan. The letter should be an inquiry about the availability of the auditorium during the specified time. All three of the performers are from the West Coast, and have recently become clients of Music School Records. Each performer or group will be releasing debut CDs just before the anticipated concert date.

Add the **w01O_Singer** image included with your student files. Add the file-name to the footer. Check the memo for spelling or grammar errors. Save the document as **1O_Concert_Firstname_Lastname** and submit it as directed.

End **You have completed Project 1O** _____

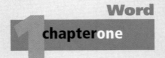

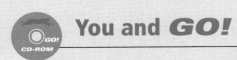 You and *GO!*

Project 1P — You and *GO!*

In this project, you will construct a solution by applying any combination of the skills you practiced from the Objectives in Projects 1A and 1B.

From My Computer, navigate to the student files that accompany this textbook. In the folder **04_you_and_go_pg87_102**, locate and open the folder for this chapter. Open and print the instructions for this project, which are provided to you in Adobe PDF format. Follow the instructions to create a cover letter for your resume.

 You have completed Project 1P ⎯⎯⎯⎯⎯⎯⎯⎯⎯

GO! with Help

Project 1Q — *GO!* with Help

The Word Help system is extensive and can help you as you work. In this chapter, you used the Quick Access Toolbar on several occasions. You can customize the Quick Access Toolbar by adding buttons that you use regularly, making them quickly available to you from any tab on the Ribbon. In this project, you will use Help to find out how to add buttons.

1 **Start** Word. At the far right end of the Ribbon, click the **Microsoft Office Word Help** button. In the **Word Help** window, click the **Search button arrow**, and then click **Word Help**.

2 In the **Type words to search for** box, type **Quick Access Toolbar** and then press Enter.

3 From the list of search results, click **Customize the Quick Access Toolbar**.

4 Click each of the links to find out how to add buttons from the Ribbon and from the **Options** dialog box.

5 When you are through, **Close** the Help window, and then **Close** Word.

 You have completed Project 1Q ⎯⎯⎯⎯⎯⎯⎯⎯⎯

Outcomes-Based Assessments

Group Business Running Case

Project 1R—Group Business Running Case

In this project, you will apply the skills you practiced from the Objectives in Projects 1A and 1B.

Your instructor may assign this group case project to your class. If your instructor assigns this project, he or she will provide you with information and instructions to work as part of a group. The group will apply the skills gained thus far to help the Bell Orchid Hotel Group achieve its business goals.

 End **You have completed Project 1R** _____

chaptertwo

2

Formatting and Organizing Text

OBJECTIVES

At the end of this chapter you will be able to:

OUTCOMES

Mastering these objectives will enable you to:

1. Change Document and Paragraph Layout
2. Change and Reorganize Text
3. Create and Modify Lists

PROJECT 2A
Format Text and Use Lists

4. Insert and Format Headers and Footers
5. Insert Frequently Used Text
6. Insert and Format References

PROJECT 2B
Create a Research Paper

GHS Law Partners

GHS Law Partners specializes in patent and intellectual property law and government contracts, serving clients in the e-commerce, computer technology, pharmaceutical, and health care fields. The firm researches and prepares patents, litigates intellectual property infringement, handles licensing disputes, and prepares appeals. In the growing area of government contracts, the firm counsels its clients regarding United States government policymaking and prepares contracts according to government procurement policies. The firm's experienced staff of attorneys includes many who have formerly worked as prosecutors, federal court law clerks, and United States patent inspectors and procurement contract attorneys.

Formatting and Organizing Text

Typing text is just the beginning of the process of creating an effective, professional-looking document. Microsoft Word provides many tools for formatting paragraphs and documents. For example, there are tools to create shortcuts for entering commonly used text, and quick ways to copy, cut, and move text. Word also provides tools to create specialized formats, such as footnotes, bulleted and numbered lists, and indented paragraphs.

In this chapter, you will edit a seminar announcement, and then you will create and format a research paper.

Project 2A **Seminar**

In Activities 2.1 through 2.15, you will edit an announcement from GHS Law Partners about an upcoming Intellectual Property Seminar. Your completed document will look similar to Figure 2.1.

For Project 2A, you will need the following file:

w02A_Seminar

You will save your document as
2A_Seminar_Firstname_Lastname

GHS Law Partners
Intellectual Property Seminar for Business Attorneys

July 12, 2009
Atlanta, GA
Draft Announcement

GHS Law Partners will present its fifth annual Intellectual Property Seminar for Business Attorneys in Atlanta, GA, on July 12, 2009. This event is intended for attorneys who want to expand their knowledge of intellectual property in order to better serve their clients. Intellectual property law affects every kind of business and clients' rights, obligations, and strategies. GHS Law Partners believes that sharing knowledge and expertise in this area of law enhances the business climate and improves the ability of business-focused firms to serve their diverse client base.

Some states confer Continuing Legal Education credits for this seminar. Each attendee will receive a complete set of all seminar materials along with an Intellectual Property textbook written by one of our partners. Audio tapes and DVDs of selected sessions will also be available.

The three morning sessions will focus on copyrights:

1. Introduction to Copyrights
2. Copyright FAQs
3. Current Issues in Copyrights

Lunch will feature a panel discussion of GHS attorneys and other trademark experts. Among the topics discussed will be:

™ Use of trademarks
™ Trademark enforcement
™ Avoiding dilution of trademark

The four afternoon sessions will cover patents:

1. Patent Basics
2. Understanding Trade Secrets and Patent Protection
3. Current Issues in Patents
4. Business Considerations in Patents and Trademarks

Questions and discussion are encouraged at all sessions, and attendees are reminded that such discussions should be kept confidential to protect the wide array of clients represented by the group.

Registration will open on April 1, 2009, and is limited to 400 attendees. Discounted rates are available at several nearby hotels. A "dine-around" dinner will be arranged at several local restaurants for those who want to participate.

If you would like a brochure containing much more detailed information about the topics to be covered in the upcoming Intellectual Property Seminar, contact Melissa Rosella at (404) 555-0022. You can also register online at www.ghslaw.com/ipseminar.

2A_Seminar_Firstname_Lastname

Figure 2.1
Project 2A—Seminar

Objective 1
Change Document and Paragraph Layout

Document layout includes *margins*—the space between the text and the top, bottom, left, and right edges of the paper. Paragraph layout includes line spacing, indents, and tabs. In Word, the information about paragraph formats is stored in the paragraph mark at the end of a paragraph. When you press the Enter key, the new paragraph mark contains the formatting of the previous paragraph, unless you take steps to change it.

Activity 2.1 Setting Margins

You can change each of the four page margins—top, bottom, left, and right—independently. You can also change the margins for the entire document at one time or change the margins for only a portion of the document.

> ### Note — Comparing Your Screen with the Figures in This Textbook
>
> Your screen will match the figures shown in this textbook if you set your screen resolution to 1024 × 768. At other resolutions, your screen will closely resemble, but not match, the figures shown. To view your screen's resolution, on the Windows desktop, right-click in a blank area, click Properties, and then click the Settings tab.

1 **Start** Word. From your student files, locate and open the document **w02A_Seminar**.

2 From the **Office** menu 🔲, display the **Save As** dialog box, click the **Save in arrow**, and then navigate to the location where you are saving your files. In the upper right corner of the dialog box, click the **Create New Folder** button 🔲. In the **Name** box, name the new folder **Word Chapter 2** and then click **OK**.

3 In the **File name** box, delete the existing text. Using your own name, type **2A_Seminar_Firstname_Lastname** and then click **Save**. If necessary, in the Paragraph group, click the Show/Hide ¶ button to display formatting marks. Set the page width to display the left and right page edges.

4 On the Ribbon, click the **Page Layout tab**. In the **Page Setup group**, click the **Margins** button, and then at the bottom of the **Margins gallery**, click **Custom Margins**.

5 In the displayed **Page Setup** dialog box, press Tab as necessary to select the value in the **Left** box, and then, with *1.25″* selected, type **1**

This action will change the left margin to 1 inch on all pages of the document. You do not need to type the inch (″) mark.

6 Press Tab to select the measurement in the **Right** box, type **1** and then compare your screen with Figure 2.2. Notice that the new margins will be applied to the entire document.

Figure 2.2

New left margin   New right margin

Margins applied to entire document

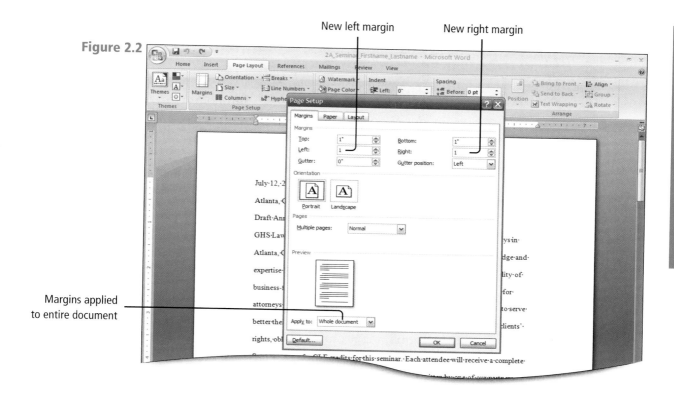

7 In the lower right corner of the dialog box, click **OK** to apply the new margins and close the dialog box. If the ruler below the Ribbon is not displayed, at the top of the vertical scroll bar, click the **View Ruler** button. Compare your screen with Figure 2.3.

View Ruler button

Figure 2.3

Document width of 6.5" displays in white on ruler

New right margin
New left margin

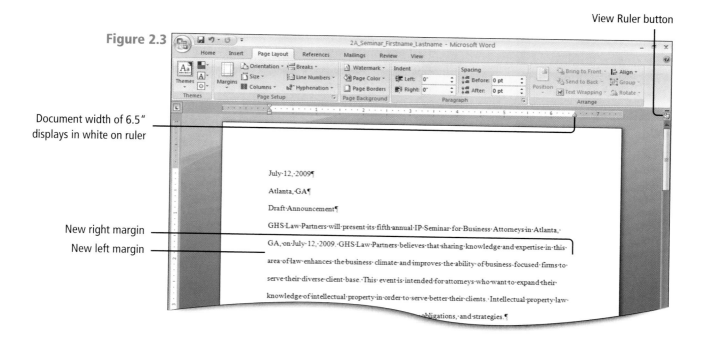

8 Scroll to view the bottom of **Page 1**. Near the bottom edge of the page, right-click, and then click **Edit Footer** to display the footer area.

This shortcut provides a quick way to display either the footer or header area. Because the insertion point is in the footer area, *Header & Footer Tools* displays, and the Design tab is added to the standard tabs on the Ribbon.

9 On the **Design tab**, in the **Insert group**, click the **Quick Parts** button, and then click **Field**. In the **Field** dialog box, under **Field names**, locate and click **FileName**, and then click **OK**.

10 Double-click anywhere in the document to close the footer area.

Save 🖫 your document.

Activity 2.2 Aligning Text

Alignment is the placement of paragraph text relative to the left and right margins. Most paragraph text uses *left alignment*—aligned at the left margin, leaving the right margin uneven. Three other types of paragraph alignment are available: *center alignment*—centered between the left and right margins; *right alignment*—aligned on the right margin; and *justified alignment*—text aligned on both the left and right margins. Examples are shown in the table in Figure 2.4.

Paragraph Alignment Options

Alignment	Button	Description and Example
Align Text Left	▤	Align Text Left is the default paragraph alignment in Word. Text in the paragraph aligns at the left margin, and the right margin is uneven.
Center	▤	Center alignment aligns text in the paragraph so that it is centered between the left and right margins.
Align Text Right	▤	Align Text Right is used to align text at the right margin. Using Align Text Right, the left margin, which is normally even, is uneven.
Justify	▤	The Justify alignment option adds additional space between words so that both the left and right margins are even. Justify is often used when formatting newspaper-style columns.

Figure 2.4

1 Press [Ctrl] + [Home] to place the insertion point at the beginning of the document. Type **GHS Law Partners Intellectual Property Seminar for Business Attorneys** and then press [Enter].

2 Click to place the insertion point anywhere in the first line of the document—the title that you just typed that begins *GHS Law Partners*. On the **Home tab**, in the **Paragraph group**, click the **Center** button ▤.

The first paragraph, which is a title, is centered. To format a paragraph, you just need to have the insertion point somewhere in the paragraph—you do not need to select all of the text in the paragraph.

3 Move the pointer into the left margin area to the left of the second line of text that begins *July 12* until the ⬚ pointer displays. Drag down to select that line and the two lines following it, ending with *Draft Announcement*, and then on the Mini toolbar, click the **Center** button ▤. Compare your screen with Figure 2.5.

A paragraph consists of a paragraph mark and all the text in front of it. To format multiple paragraphs, they must all be selected.

First four lines centered

Figure 2.5

Center button

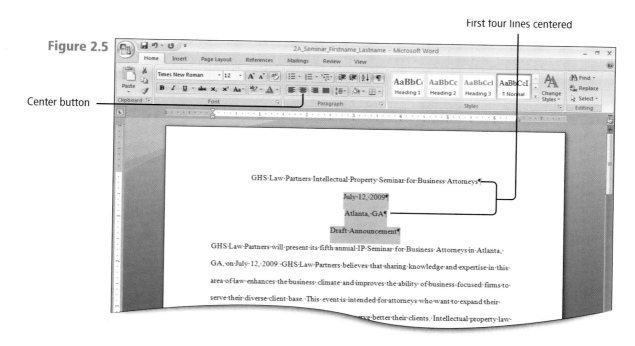

4 Move the pointer into the left margin area to the left of the fifth line of text that begins *GHS Law Partners will present* until the ⬚ pointer displays. Then, drag down to select this line of text and the next eight lines of text—including the line that ends *will also be available.*

5 In the **Paragraph group**, click the **Justify** button ▤, and then compare your screen with Figure 2.6.

Both the left and right edges of the paragraphs are even. The other paragraphs are not affected.

Figure 2.6

Right edge aligned

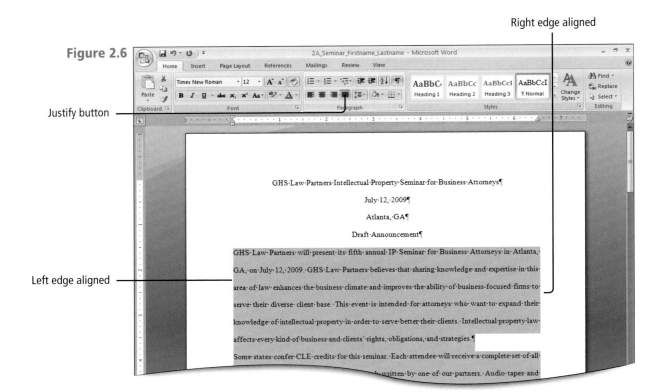

Justify button

Left edge aligned

6 Because justified text is better used in narrow columns, with the text still selected, in the **Paragraph group**, click the **Align Text Left** button . Click anywhere in the document to deselect the text. **Save** the document.

Activity 2.3 Changing Line Spacing

Line spacing is the distance between lines of text in a paragraph. A single-spaced paragraph of 12-point text accommodates six lines in a vertical inch. If you double-space the same text, each line will be 24 points high—12 points of text, 12 points of space—and will accommodate only three lines in a vertical inch as shown in the table in Figure 2.7. The default Word setting—Multiple—uses 14 points between lines of 12-point text resulting in single line spacing that is 1.15 (about 1 $\frac{1}{6}$) line spacing.

Paragraph Alignment Options

Spacing	Example
Single (1.0)	Most business documents are single-spaced. This means that the spacing between lines is just enough to separate the text.
Multiple with 1.15 line spacing	The default line spacing in Microsoft Word 2007 is 1.15, which is equivalent to single spacing with an extra 1/6 line added between lines.
Double (2.0)	Many college research papers and reports, and many draft documents that need space for notes, are double-spaced; there is space for a full line of text between each document line.

Figure 2.7

1 Press Ctrl + Home to place the insertion point at the beginning of the document. In the left margin area, display the ⬚ pointer and drag down to select the first four lines of text—the four centered title lines.

2 In the **Paragraph group**, click the **Line Spacing** button ⬚, and then compare your screen with Figure 2.8.

A check mark next to 2.0 indicates that the selected paragraphs are double-spaced.

Double-spacing

Figure 2.8

Line Spacing button

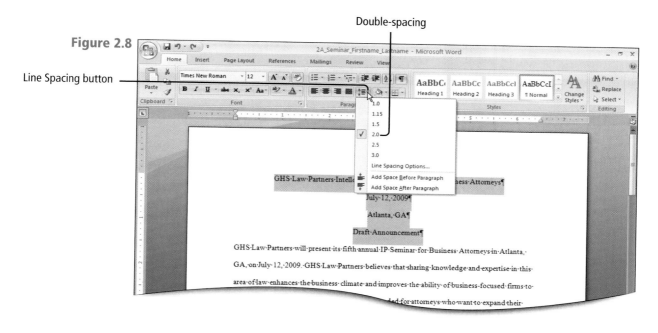

3 In the **Line spacing** list, click **1.0** to change the line spacing of the first four paragraphs.

4 Click to place the insertion point in the paragraph that begins *GHS Law Partners will present*. In the **Paragraph group**, click the **Line Spacing** button ⬚, and then click **1.0**. Compare your screen with Figure 2.9.

Recall that you do not have to select the whole paragraph to change the paragraph formatting. The first five paragraphs of the document are single-spaced.

Figure 2.9

First five paragraphs of the document are single-spaced

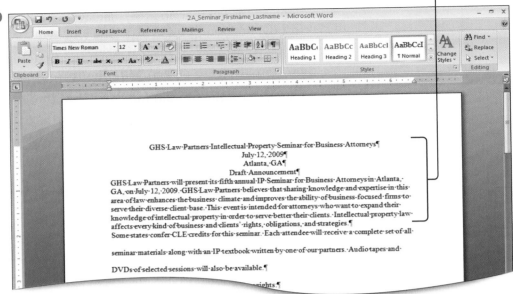

5 Save 💾 the changes you have made to your document.

Activity 2.4 Adding Space After Paragraphs

Adjusting paragraph spacing from the Paragraph dialog box enables you to control the space before or after paragraphs using points as the unit of measure. Recall that there are 72 points per inch. The Word default adds 10-pt. spacing after each paragraph. The document you are working on has no extra spacing after each paragraph.

1 Press Ctrl + Home to place the insertion point at the beginning of the first line of text in the document. In the **Paragraph group**, click the **Dialog Box Launcher** 🔲. Alternatively, click the Line spacing button, and then click Line Spacing Options from the displayed list.

2 In the displayed **Paragraph** dialog box, click the **Indents and Spacing tab**. Under **Spacing**, in the **After** spin box, click the **up spin arrow** two times, and then compare your screen with Figure 2.10.

The value in the box changes from 0 pt to 12 pt. A **spin box** is a small box with an upward- and downward-pointing arrow that lets you move (spin) through a set of values by clicking. The up and down arrows, called **spin box arrows**, increment the point size by six points at a time. Alternatively, type a number of your choice directly into the spin box.

Figure 2.10

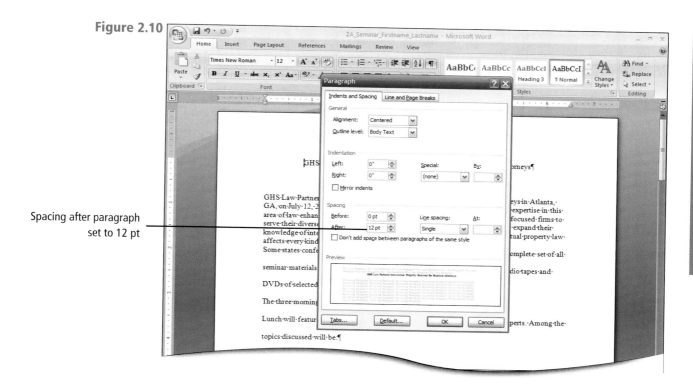

Spacing after paragraph set to 12 pt

▣ Click **OK** to add a 12-pt space after the paragraph.

▣ In the *Draft Announcement* paragraph, click to position the insertion point anywhere in the paragraph. In the **Paragraph group**, click the **Dialog Box Launcher** 🔲. Under **Spacing**, in the **After** box, click the **up spin arrow** one time to change the value in the box from *0 pt* to **6 pt**. Click **OK**.

▣ In the paragraph beginning *GHS Law Partners will present*, click to position the insertion point anywhere in the paragraph. In the **Paragraph group**, display the **Paragraph** dialog box. Under **Spacing**, set **After** to **6 pt**, and then click **OK**. Compare your screen with Figure 2.11.

Figure 2.11

6-pt. spacing after each paragraph

12-pt. spacing after the first paragraph

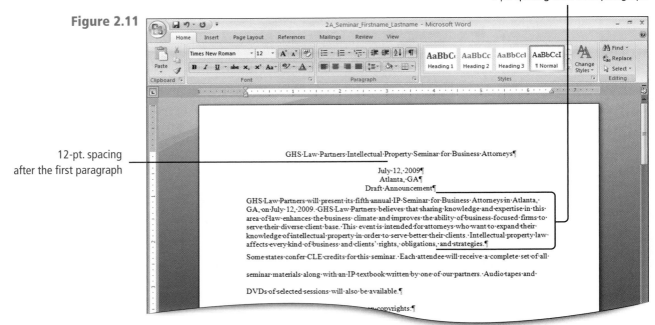

6 **Save** the changes you have made to your document.

Activity 2.5 Using the Format Painter

Use the ***Format Painter*** to copy the formatting of specific text or of a paragraph and then apply it in other locations in your document.

1 Click anywhere in the paragraph that begins *GHS Law Partners will present*. On the **Home tab**, in the **Clipboard group**, click the **Format Painter** button. Point to the paragraph that begins *Some states confer*, and then compare your screen with Figure 2.12.

The pointer takes the shape of a paintbrush, and contains the formatting information from the paragraph where the insertion point is positioned. Instructions on how to turn the Format Painter off display in the status bar.

Figure 2.12

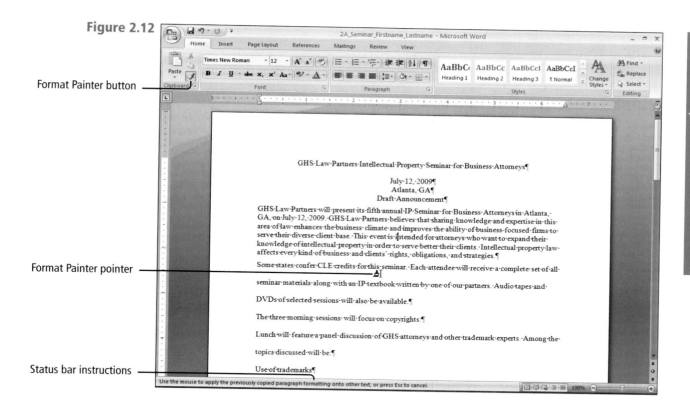

Format Painter button

Format Painter pointer

Status bar instructions

2 Click the ▲I pointer one time.

The paragraph formatting from the original paragraph—single-spacing, 6-pt space after the paragraph—is copied to this paragraph. The Format Painter is no longer active.

3 With the insertion point in the recently formatted paragraph, double-click the **Format Painter** button ✐ to use the Format Painter multiple times.

4 Move the ▲I pointer to the paragraph that begins *The three morning sessions*, and then click one time.

The paragraph formatting from the original paragraph is copied to this paragraph, and the Format Painter remains active.

5 Move the ▲I pointer over the paragraph that begins *Lunch will feature*, and then click one time.

6 Using the down scroll arrow, locate and click in the paragraph that begins *The four afternoon sessions*. Use the Format Painter to change the formatting of the last three paragraphs, starting with the paragraph that begins *Registration will open*. Compare your screen with Figure 2.13.

Figure 2.13

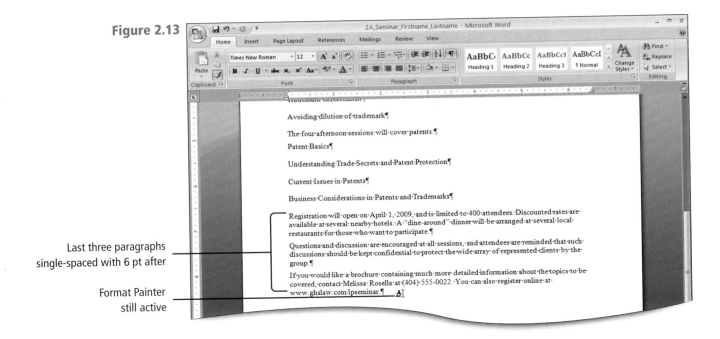

Last three paragraphs single-spaced with 6 pt after

Format Painter still active

7 In the **Clipboard group**, click the **Format Painter** button to turn the command off. Alternatively, press [Esc] to turn off the Format Painter feature. **Save** your document.

Objective 2
Change and Reorganize Text

Changing and reorganizing text is accomplished using Word features such as the Find and Replace dialog box and the ***Office Clipboard***, a temporary storage area that holds text. You can ***copy*** text to move it to the Office Clipboard, which leaves the original text in place, or ***cut*** text, which removes it from its original location. Then, you can **_paste_**—insert—the contents of the Office Clipboard in a new location. The keyboard shortcuts for these commands are shown in the table in Figure 2.14.

Keyboard Shortcuts for Editing Text

Keyboard Shortcut	Action
Ctrl + X	Cut text or graphic and move it to the Office Clipboard.
Ctrl + C	Copy text or graphic and move it to the Office Clipboard.
Ctrl + V	Paste the contents of the Office Clipboard.
Ctrl + Z	Undo an action.
Ctrl + Y	Redo an action.
Ctrl + F	Find text.
Ctrl + H	Find and replace text.

Figure 2.14

Activity 2.6 Finding and Replacing Text

Finding and then replacing text is a quick way to make the same change more than one time in a document. For example, if you consistently misspell someone's last name, Word can search for all instances of the name and replace it with the correct spelling.

1 Press Ctrl + Home to position the insertion point at the beginning of the document.

When you initiate a find operation or a find and replace operation, the search begins from the location of the insertion point and proceeds to the end of the document. If you begin a search in the middle of a document, Word will prompt you to return to the beginning of the document and continue the operation.

2 On the **Home tab**, in the **Editing group**, click the **Find** button. In the **Find and Replace** dialog box, in the **Find what** box, type **CLE** which is an acronym for _Continuing Legal Education_.

You can use the Find command to move quickly to a specific location in a document if you know that a word or phrase is located in the document.

3 In the **Find and Replace** dialog box, click the **Find Next** button to select the first occurrence of _CLE._

4 In the **Find and Replace** dialog box, click **Cancel**. Press Ctrl + Home to position the insertion point at the beginning of the document.

In the **Editing group**, click the **Replace** button. Alternatively, in the Find and Replace dialog box, click the Replace tab.

5 If necessary, in the displayed **Find and Replace** dialog box, in the **Find what** box, type **CLE** and then in the **Replace with** box, type **Continuing Legal Education**

6 Click the **More** button to expand the dialog box, and then under **Search Options**, click to select the **Match case** and **Find whole words only** check boxes. Click **Find Next**, and then compare your screen with Figure 2.15.

By searching for whole words only, you will avoid changing the search text if it occurs in the middle of a word—for example, *CLEVELAND*. By matching case, you not only instruct the program to look for text in the same case, but you also instruct the program to replace text using the same case as the text in the Replace with box.

Find what box   Replace with box

Figure 2.15

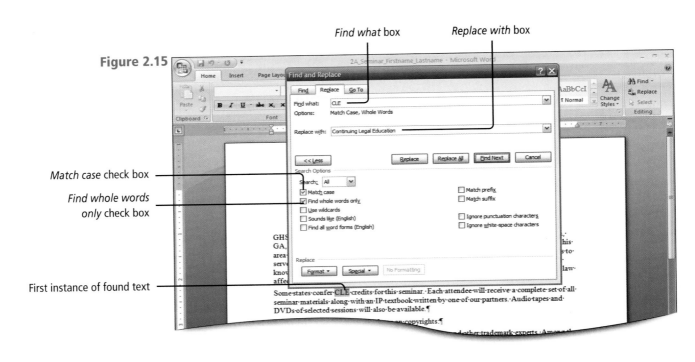

Match case check box

Find whole words only check box

First instance of found text

7 In the **Find and Replace** dialog box, click the **Replace** button.

The text is replaced, and a message indicates that Word has finished searching the document; no other instances of the search text were found.

8 Click **OK** to close the message box. In the **Find what** box, type **IP** and in the **Replace with** box, type **Intellectual Property**

9 Click **Replace All**.

A message displays, indicating that two replacements have been made.

10 Click **OK** to close the message box. Clear the two **Search Options** check boxes, click the **Less** button, and then click **Close** to close the **Find and Replace** dialog box. **Save** your document.

Activity 2.7 Cutting, Copying, and Pasting Text

You can move text from one location in a document to a different location in the same document with the Cut and Paste commands. Use the Cut command to move text out of the document to the Office Clipboard—the temporary storage location for text or graphics. Then, use the Paste command to paste the contents of the Office Clipboard to the new location. The Copy command moves a copy of selected text to the Office Clipboard, which you can then paste to another location. Unlike the Cut command, the Copy command does not remove the selected text from its original location.

1 Near the end of the document, locate the paragraph that begins *Questions and discussion*, and then double-click to select the word *represented*.

2 On the **Home tab**, in the **Clipboard group**, click the **Cut** button. Alternatively, right-click on the selected text and click Cut from the shortcut menu; or, press Ctrl + X.

The selected text is removed from the document and moved to the Office Clipboard.

Note — The Difference Between Using Delete, Backspace, and Cut

When you use the Cut command to remove text, it is moved to the Office Clipboard and can be pasted into the same—or a different—document. When you use Delete or Backspace to remove text, the text is not moved to the Office Clipboard. The only way you can retrieve text removed with Delete or Backspace is by using the Undo command.

3 In the same line of text, click to position the insertion point between *clients* and *by*. In the **Clipboard group**, click the **Paste** button. Alternatively, right-click on the selected text and click Paste from the shortcut menu; or, press Ctrl + V. Adjust the spacing before and after the word if necessary.

The text is placed at the insertion point, but also remains on the Office Clipboard. The Paste Options button displays below the pasted word. When you click the button, a list displays that lets you determine how the information is pasted into your document. The available options depend on the type of content you are pasting, the program you are pasting from, and the format of the text where you are pasting.

4 Point to the **Paste Options** button until its ScreenTip *Paste Options* displays, click the button, and then compare your screen with Figure 2.16.

A short menu provides commands related specifically to the Paste command. You can determine whether you want to format the pasted text the same as the surrounding text or retain its original formatting. Performing another screen action will cancel the display of the button; alternatively, press Esc to cancel its display.

Pasted text

Figure 2.16

Figure 2.16

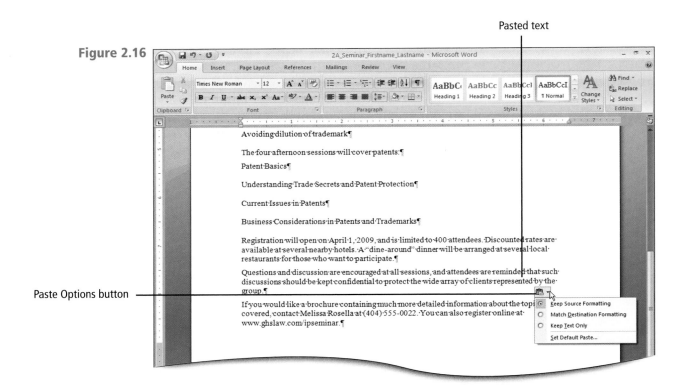

Paste Options button

5 Click anywhere in the document to close the **Paste Options** menu and retain the same formatting.

6 Locate the paragraph that begins *Registration will open*, and then triple-click to select the entire paragraph. Alternatively, select the paragraph by dragging with your mouse, but be sure to include the paragraph mark.

7 In the **Clipboard group**, click the **Cut** button. Locate the paragraph that begins *If you would like* and position the insertion point at the beginning of that paragraph. In the **Clipboard group**, click the **Paste** button to paste the text in the new location.

Alert! **If the Clipboard Task Pane Opens**

The Clipboard task pane may display on your screen depending on the options that have been set for the Office Clipboard on your computer. If the task pane opens, click the Close button on the task pane title bar.

8 Press Ctrl + Home. In the first title line, select *Intellectual Property Seminar*. In the **Clipboard group**, click the **Copy** button. Press Ctrl + End to move to the end of the document.

9 In the last paragraph, locate the word *covered* and position the insertion point between the word and the following comma. Press Spacebar, type **in the upcoming** and then press Spacebar. In the **Clipboard group**, click the **Paste** button, and then compare your screen with Figure 2.17.

The copied text is inserted in the new location, but is not removed from the original location. The Paste Options button displays below the pasted text.

Figure 2.17

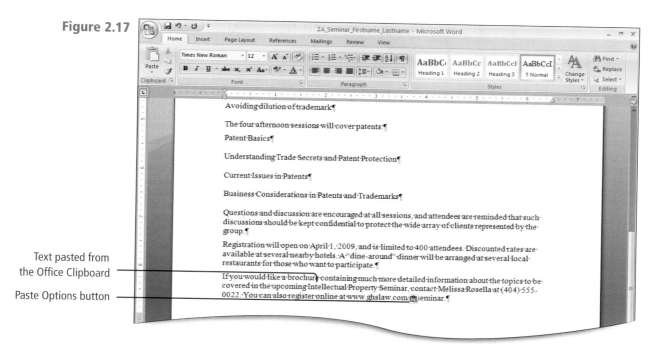

Text pasted from the Office Clipboard

Paste Options button

10 **Save** ◲ the changes you have made to your document.

Activity 2.8 Moving Text to a New Location

Another method of moving text is the ***drag-and-drop*** technique, which uses the mouse to drag selected text from one location to another. This method is useful if the text to be moved is on the same screen as the destination location.

1 Press Ctrl + Home to position the insertion point at the beginning of the document. In the fifth line of the paragraph that begins *GHS Law Partners will present*, locate and select *better*.

2 Point to the selected word to display the ◳ pointer as shown in Figure 2.18.

better selected

Figure 2.18

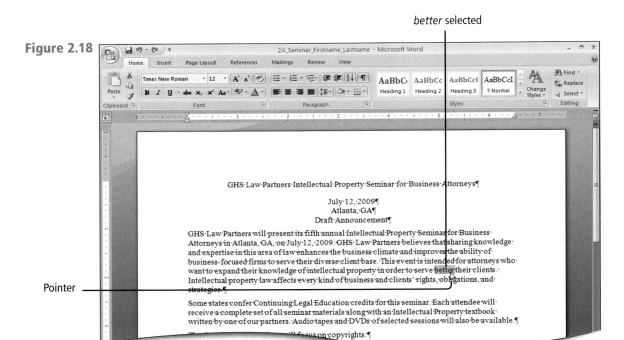

Pointer

3 Hold down the left mouse button and drag to the left until the dotted vertical line that floats next to the pointer is positioned to the left of the word *serve* in the same line, and then release the left mouse button.

4 Click anywhere to deselect the text, and then compare your screen with Figure 2.19.

The word is moved to the insertion point location. The vertical line of the pointer assists you in dropping the moved text in the place where you want it. The small box attached to the pointer indicates that there is text attached to the pointer.

Figure 2.19

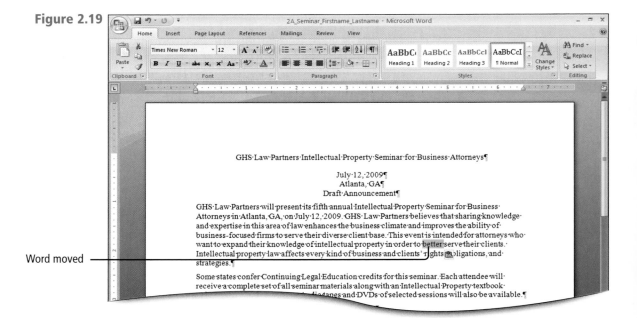

Word moved

5 In the same paragraph, point to the second sentence—the one that begins *GHS Law Partners believes*. Hold down Ctrl and click one time to select the entire sentence.

6 Point to the selected sentence to display the ⬚ pointer, and then drag down to the end of the paragraph and position the vertical line to the right of the period at the end of *obligations, and strategies*, as shown in Figure 2.20.

Figure 2.20

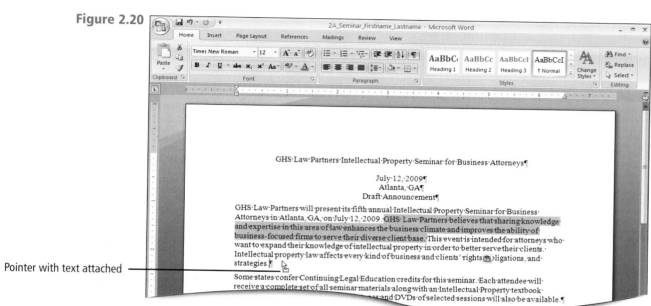

Pointer with text attached

7 Release the mouse button, and click anywhere in the document to deselect the text. The sentence you moved becomes the last sentence in the paragraph. Notice that a space was automatically added before the sentence.

8 **Save** 🖫 the changes you have made to your document.

More Knowledge
Drag and Drop Using the Right Mouse Button

You can also drag and drop using the right mouse button. Select the text, point to the selected text and hold the right mouse button down, and then drag to a new location. A shortcut menu displays, giving you the option of moving the text to the new location, copying the text to the new location, or creating a link.

Activity 2.9 Undoing and Redoing Changes

You can undo one or more actions that you made to an active document. An Undo action can be reversed with the Redo command.

1 In the fourth paragraph, *Draft Announcement*, double-click *Draft* to select it, and then press Delete.

2 On the **Quick Access Toolbar**, click the **Undo** button 🔄.

The word you deleted returns to its original location.

3 On the **Quick Access Toolbar**, click the **Undo** button two times.

The sentence you dragged and dropped returns to its original location, and the words *serve* and *better* are switched back to their original locations, as shown in Figure 2.21.

Undo button

Figure 2.21

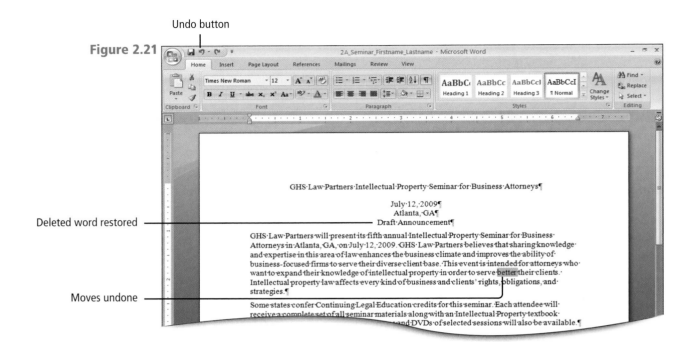

Deleted word restored

Moves undone

4 On the **Quick Access Toolbar**, click the **Redo** button two times.

The words are switched back, and the sentence moves back to the end of the paragraph. Clicking the Undo and Redo buttons changes one action at a time.

5 On the **Quick Access Toolbar**, click the **Undo button arrow**.

A list of changes displays showing all of the changes made since you last opened your document. From the displayed list, you can click any of the actions and undo it, but all of the changes above the one you select will also be undone.

6 Click anywhere in the document to close the Undo button list without undoing any other actions.

Activity 2.10 Inserting Nonbreaking Spaces and Hyphens

When you want to keep two words together regardless of where they fall in a paragraph, use a ***nonbreaking space***, which will wrap both words even if only the second word would normally wrap to the next line. For example, if the words *Mt. McKinley* fall at the end of a line so that *Mt.* is on one line and *McKinley* moves to the next, inserting a nonbreaking space will treat the two words as one so that they are not split between two lines. Similarly, you may have a hyphenated term, such as a postal code with the four-digit extension. If you want that term to be treated as one entity, use a nonbreaking hyphen.

1 Press [Ctrl] + [End] to move to the end of the document. Locate the paragraph that begins *If you would like*, and then click to position the insertion point at the end of the second line.

2 In the telephone number, delete the hyphen. While holding down both [Ctrl] and [⇧ Shift], press [_] one time. Alternatively, on the Insert tab, in the Symbols group, click Symbol, and then click More Symbols. In the displayed Symbol dialog box, click the Special Characters tab, click Nonbreaking hyphen, and then click Close.

The hyphen is replaced with a ***nonbreaking hyphen***; the telephone number will not break at the hyphen if you edit the paragraph. The nonbreaking hyphen is indicated by a slightly longer, slightly higher line than a standard hyphen, but prints as a normal hyphen.

3 At the end of the second line, after the telephone number area code, delete the space. While holding down both [Ctrl] and [⇧ Shift], press [Spacebar] one time. Compare your screen with Figure 2.22.

This combination of keys inserts a nonbreaking space. The result of inserting the nonbreaking space and nonbreaking hyphen is that the telephone number is treated as one word, so when Word applies its word-wrapping rules, the number is kept together on the same line. The nonbreaking space is indicated by an open circle rather than the dot normally used to indicate a space, but prints as a normal space.

The telephone number stays together

Figure 2.22

Nonbreaking space indicator

Nonbreaking hyphen indicator

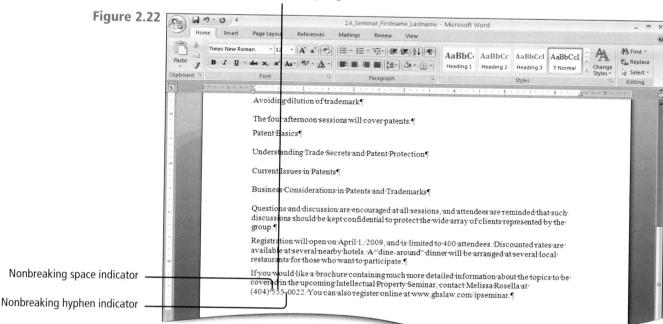

4 In the same sentence, locate and select the word *Seminar*, and then press Delete. Notice that the telephone number moves to the previous line as one word.

5 On the **Quick Access Toolbar**, click the **Undo** button to reinsert the deleted word. **Save** your changes.

Activity 2.11 Entering a Line Break

You can end a line of text with a ***manual line break***, which moves the insertion point to the next line without creating a new paragraph. For example, if your paragraph style includes space before or after paragraphs, you may want to begin a new line without adding the additional space.

1 Press Ctrl + Home to move to the beginning of the document. Position the pointer in the left margin area, and then select the first four lines of text—the four centered title lines.

2 On the Mini toolbar, click the **Bold** button **B**. Then, on the Mini toolbar, click the **Font Size button arrow** 12, and then click **14**.

3 In the first title line, notice the 12-point spacing after the first paragraph. Then, select the space between *Partners* and *Intellectual* and press Delete.

4 Hold down Shift, and then press Enter. Compare your screen with Figure 2.23.

By using a manual line break, the 12-pt spacing after the paragraph is not inserted, because a new paragraph is not created; rather, a new line within the same paragraph is created. The bent arrow at the end of the first line indicates an inserted line break.

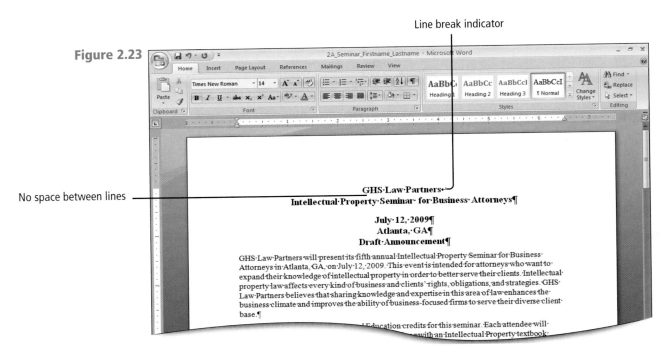

Figure 2.23

Line break indicator

No space between lines

5 **Save** your changes.

Objective 3
Create and Modify Lists

Word displays lists of information in two ways. A **bulleted list** uses **bullets**, which are text symbols such as small circles or check marks, to introduce each piece of information. **Numbered lists** use consecutive numbers or letters to introduce each item in a list. Use bulleted lists when the items in the list can be displayed in any order; use numbered lists for items that have definite steps, a sequence of actions, or are in chronological order.

Activity 2.12 Creating a Bulleted List

1 Locate the *Use of trademarks* paragraph, and then move the pointer into the left margin area to display the [🖉] pointer. Drag down to select this paragraph and the next two paragraphs.

2 On the Mini toolbar, click the **Bullets** button [≔ ▾]. Alternatively, on the Home tab, in the Paragraph group, click the Bullets button.

The default bullet is a large, round, black dot. Your bullet symbols may differ, depending on which bullets were most recently used on your computer.

3 With the bulleted list still selected, in the **Paragraph group**, click the **Increase Indent** button [🖅] one time. Click anywhere in the document to deselect the text.

The bulleted list is indented another 0.25 inch to the right.

4 Move the pointer into the left margin area to the left of the *Use of trademarks* paragraph until the [🖉] pointer displays. Then, drag down to select this paragraph and the next paragraph.

5 In the **Paragraph group**, click the **Line spacing button arrow** [⭥≡▾] and notice that the items are double-spaced. Click **1.0** to single-space the selected text, click anywhere in the document to deselect the text, and then compare your screen with Figure 2.24.

6 **Save** [💾] your changes.

Figure 2.24

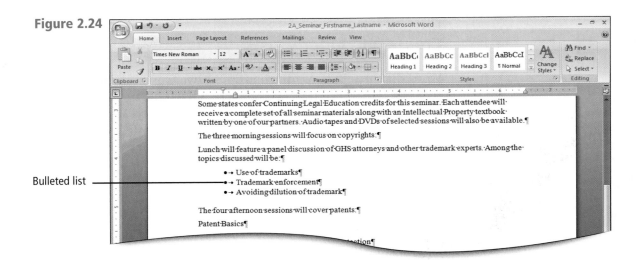

Bulleted list

Activity 2.13 Using AutoFormat To Create a Numbered List

In the previous activity, you created a list using existing text. In this activity, you will create a new list. Because the list items are the names of sessions in sequential order, you will number the items using Word's Numbering command.

1 Locate the paragraph that begins *The three morning sessions*, and then position the insertion point at the end of that paragraph. Press [Enter] to create a blank line.

This paragraph retains the formatting of the previous paragraph, which is stored in the paragraph mark you just created when you pressed [Enter]. Recall that formatting carries forward to a new paragraph mark unless you take specific steps to change the formatting for the newly created paragraph.

2 From the **Office** menu [icon], in the lower right corner click **Word Options**. In the list on the left side of the **Word Options** dialog box, click **Proofing**. Under **AutoCorrect options**, click the **AutoCorrect Options** button.

3 In the displayed **AutoCorrect** dialog box, click the **AutoFormat As You Type tab**, and then compare your screen with Figure 2.25.

AutoFormat As You Type is a Word feature that anticipates formatting based on what you type. There are several formatting options; each can be turned on or off independently of the others.

Figure 2.25

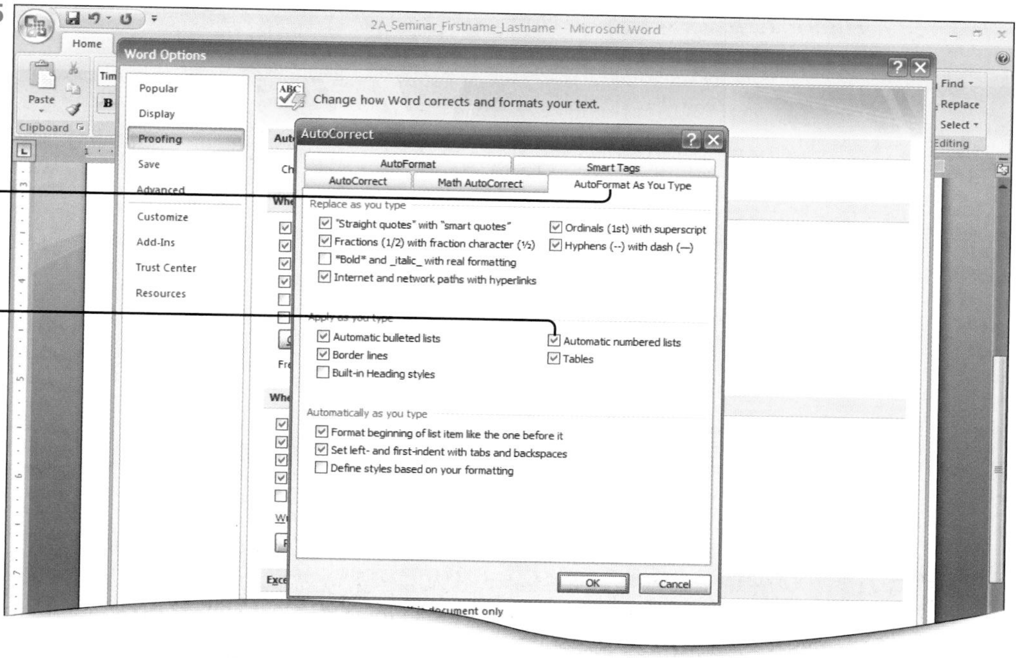

AutoFormat As You Type tab

Automatic numbered lists check box

4 Under **Apply as you type**, if it is not selected, select the **Automatic numbered lists** check box, and then click **OK**. At the bottom of the **Word Options** dialog box, click **OK**.

5 Type **1.** and press Spacebar. Be sure to type the period after the number.

Word determines that this paragraph is the first item in a numbered list and formats the new paragraph following it accordingly. The space after the number changes to a tab, and the AutoCorrect Options button displays to the left of the list item.

6 Click the **AutoCorrect Options** button, and then compare your screen with Figure 2.26.

From the displayed list, you can remove the automatic formatting in this instance, or stop using the Automatic numbered lists option in this document. You also have the option to open the AutoCorrect dialog box to *Control AutoFormat Options*.

Figure 2.26

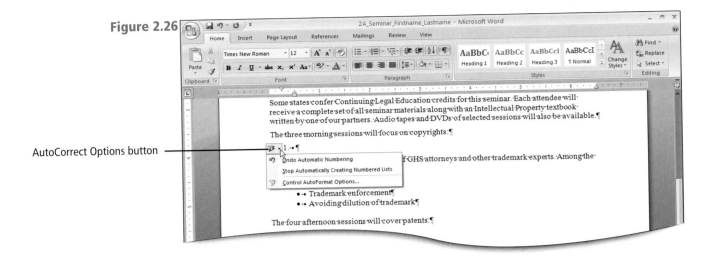

AutoCorrect Options button

7 Click the **AutoCorrect Options** button to close the menu without selecting any of the commands. Type **Introduction to Copyrights** and press Enter. Notice that the second number and a tab are added to the next line.

8 Type **Copyright FAQs** and press Enter. Type **Current Issues in Copyrights** and press Enter. Compare your screen with Figure 2.27.

Figure 2.27

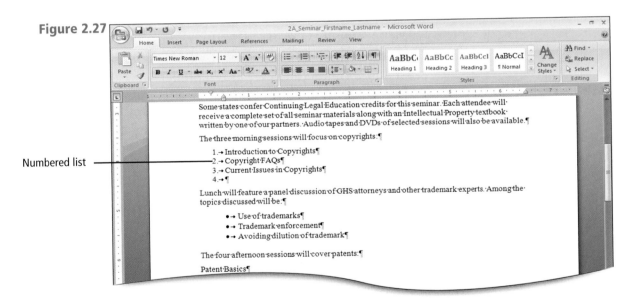

Numbered list

9 Press ←Bksp to turn off the list. Then, press ←Bksp three more times to remove the blank line.

More Knowledge

To End a List

When you end a list and press Enter, the next line will be formatted as a list item. To turn the list off, you can press ←Bksp, click the Numbering or Bullets button, or press Enter a second time. Both list buttons—Numbering and Bullets—act as *toggle buttons*; that is, clicking the button one time turns the feature on, and clicking the button again turns the feature off.

10 Select all three items in the numbered list. In the **Paragraph group**, click the **Increase Indent** button ![icon] one time to move the list 0.25 inch to the right.

11 **Save** ![icon] your document.

Activity 2.14 Formatting Lists

Each item in a list is a separate paragraph and can be formatted in the same way other paragraphs are formatted. The Format Painter can also be used to create lists.

1 In the bulleted list, click anywhere in the last bulleted item, which begins *Avoiding dilution*. Display the **Paragraph** dialog box. Under **Spacing**, click the **Line spacing arrow**, and then click **Single**. Under **Spacing**, in the **After** spin box, click the **up spin arrow** one time to add **6-pt** spacing, and then click **OK**. Compare your screen with Figure 2.28.

The last item in the bulleted list now has the same formatting as the last item in the numbered list.

Figure 2.28

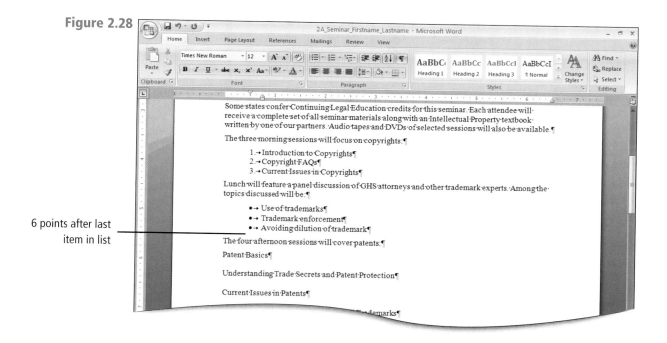

6 points after last item in list

2 In the first item of the numbered list, click anywhere to place the insertion point. In the **Clipboard group**, click the **Format Painter** button .

3 Move the pointer to the *Patent Basics* one-line paragraph, and then click one time. Notice that the *Patent Basics* paragraph takes on the formatting characteristics of the first item in the numbered list, and the numbering continues with the number *4*. Also notice that the Format Painter pointer no longer displays.

4 In the **Clipboard group**, double-click the **Format Painter** button .

Use the pointer to change the paragraph beginning *Understanding Trade*.

The Format Painter pointer still displays. When you double-click the Format Painter button, it remains active until you turn it off.

5 Use the pointer to change the paragraphs that begin *Current Issues* and *Business Considerations*. Then, in the **Clipboard group**, click the **Format Painter** button to turn it off. Alternatively, press Esc to turn off the Format Painter.

6 Move to **item number 4** in the list—*Patent Basics*—and then right-click. Notice that the displayed shortcut menu contains list-formatting commands, as shown in Figure 2.29.

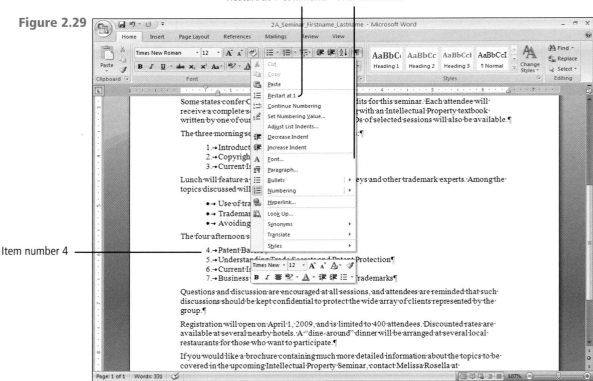

Figure 2.29

Restart at 1 command   Shortcut menu

Item number 4

7 From the shortcut menu, click **Restart at 1**.

The numbering is restarted for the second numbered list.

8 **Save** 🖫 your document.

More Knowledge

Using Multiple Levels in a Numbered List

If your numbered list contains two levels of information, type all of the list entries using automatic numbering. When you have completed the list, select the items that are at the lower level and click the Increase Indent button. The top level will retain the *1, 2, 3* format, while the lower level will use an *a, b, c* format.

Activity 2.15 Customizing Bullets

You are not restricted to the bullet symbol that displays when you click the Bullets button. You can use any symbol from any font on your computer for your bullet character.

1 Select the three bulleted points, and then right-click anywhere in the selected text. From the shortcut menu, point to **Bullets**. Notice that a gallery displays showing recently used bullets and a library of popular bullet shapes, as shown in Figure 2.30.

Figure 2.30

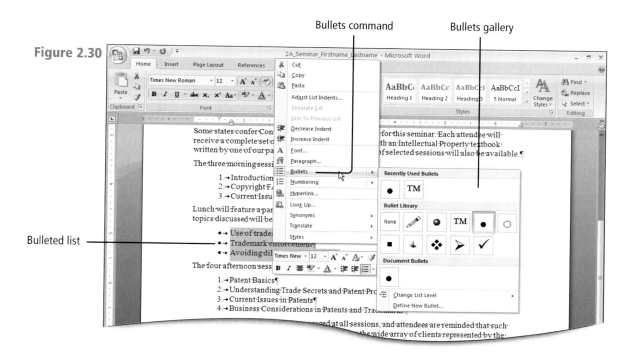

2 At the bottom of the **Bullets gallery**, click **Define New Bullet**. In the **Define New Bullet** dialog box, click the **Symbol** button.

3 In the displayed **Symbol** dialog box, be sure *Symbol* displays in the **Font** box. Scroll to the bottom of the list of symbols, and then in the third row from the bottom, click the trademark^(TM) symbol, as shown in Figure 2.31.

Symbol font

Figure 2.31

Trademark symbol

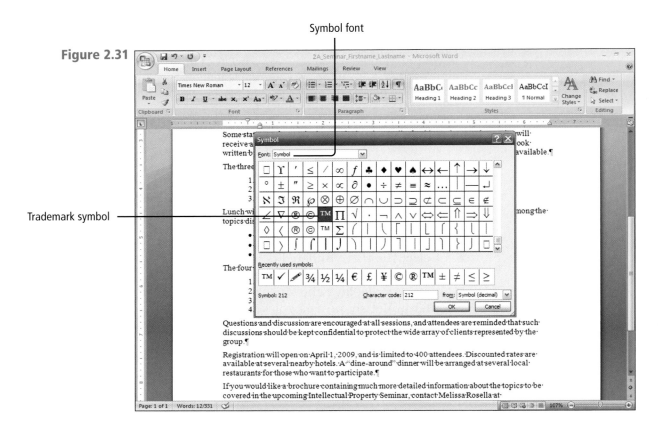

4 At the bottom of the **Symbol** dialog box, click **OK**. At the bottom of the **Define New Bullet** dialog box, click **OK**. Click anywhere to deselect the list. Notice that the bullets change to a trademark symbol, as shown in Figure 2.32. **Save** your document.

Figure 2.32

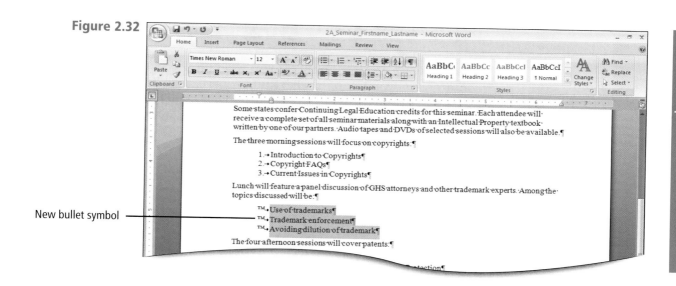

New bullet symbol

5 From the **Office** menu [icon], point to the **Print arrow**, and then click **Print Preview** to make a final check of your document. Check your Chapter Assignment Sheet or Course Syllabus or consult your instructor to determine if you are to submit your assignments on paper or electronically. To submit electronically, go to Step 7, and then follow the instructions provided by your instructor.

6 On the **Print Preview tab**, in the **Print group**, click the **Print** button. Click **OK**, **Close** the **Print Preview** and submit your printout as directed.

7 **Close** your document, and then **Close** Word.

End You have completed Project 2A ─────────

Project 2B **Law Overview**

In Activities 2.16 through 2.24, you will edit a research paper, which contains an overview of intellectual property law. This paper was created by a student intern of GHS Law Partners, and will later be modified for inclusion in an information packet for potential clients. Your completed document will look similar to Figure 2.33.

For Project 2B, you will need the following file:

w02B_Law_Overview

You will save your document as 2B_Law_Overview_Firstname_Lastname

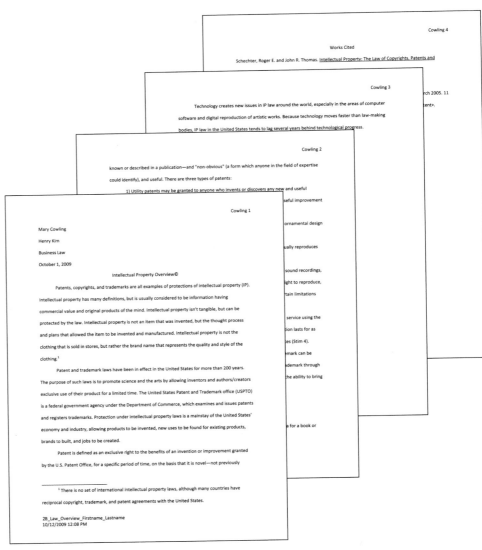

Figure 2.33
Project 2B—Law Overview

Objective 4
Insert and Format Headers and Footers

Text that you insert into a header or footer displays on every page of a document. Within a header or footer, you can add automatic page numbers, dates, times, the file name, and pictures.

Activity 2.16 Inserting and Formatting Page Numbers

1 **Start** Word. From your student files, locate and open the document **w02B_Law_Overview**. Display formatting marks, display the ruler, and set the page width to display the left and right page edges. Be sure all document margins are set to **1"**. **Save** the file in your **Word Chapter 2** folder as **2B_Law_Overview_Firstname_Lastname**

Note — Standard Styles for Research Papers

When you write a research paper or a report for college or business, you will probably be asked to follow a format prescribed by one of the standard style guides. The two most commonly used styles are those created by the *Modern Language Association (MLA)* and the *American Psychological Association (APA)*; there are several others. This project uses the MLA style.

2 Press Ctrl + A to select all of the text in the document. Right-click the selected text, and then from the shortcut menu, click **Paragraph**. In the displayed **Paragraph** dialog box, under **Spacing**, click the **After down spin arrow** two times to set the space after to **0**. Click the **Line spacing arrow**, and then click **Double**. Click **OK**.

The MLA style uses 1-inch margins and double spacing throughout the document, with no extra space between paragraphs.

3 Press Ctrl + Home to move to the beginning of the document. Type **Mary Cowling** and press Enter, and then type **Henry Kim** and press Enter. Type **Business Law** and press Enter, and then type **October 1, 2009** and press Enter.

The first line in an MLA research paper is the name of the author; the second is the name of the person for whom the report is prepared—often the professor of a class. The third line contains the name of the class, and the fourth line contains the date.

4 Type **Intellectual Property Overview** and then press Enter. Press ↑ to place the insertion point in the line you just typed. In the **Paragraph group**, click the **Center** button, and then compare your screen with Figure 2.34.

Title centered

Figure 2.34

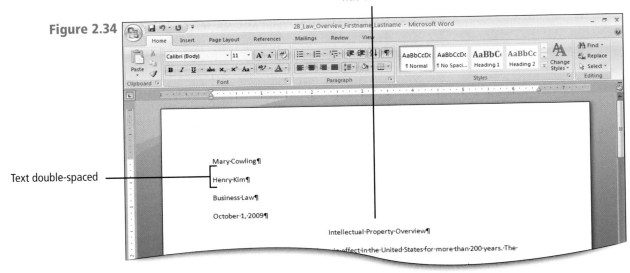

Text double-spaced

Mary·Cowling¶

Henry·Kim¶

Business·Law¶

October·1,·2009¶

Intellectual·Property·Overview¶

in·effect·in·the·United·States·for·more·than·200·years.·The·

5 Move the pointer to the top edge of **Page 1** and right-click. Click **Edit Header**, and then in the header area, type **Cowling** and then press [Spacebar].

6 On the **Design tab**, in the **Insert group**, click the **Quick Parts** button, and then click **Field**. In the **Field** dialog box, under **Field names**, locate and click **Page**. Under **Field properties**, click the first page number style—**1, 2, 3**. Compare your screen with Figure 2.35.

Page number format   Design tab

Figure 2.35

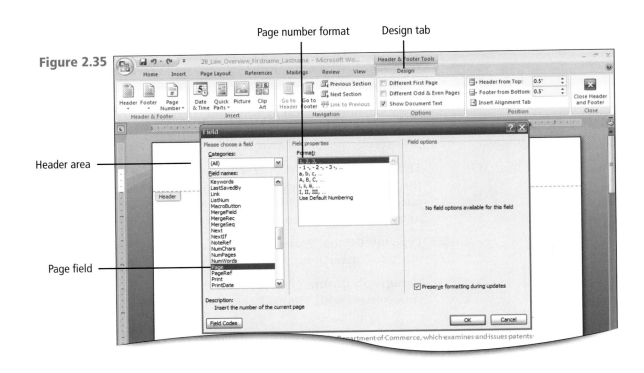

Header area

Page field

7 Click **OK** to place the page number at the insertion point location. Click the **Home tab**, and then in the **Paragraph group**, click the **Align Text Right** button. Compare your screen with Figure 2.36.

Figure 2.36

Name and page number inserted

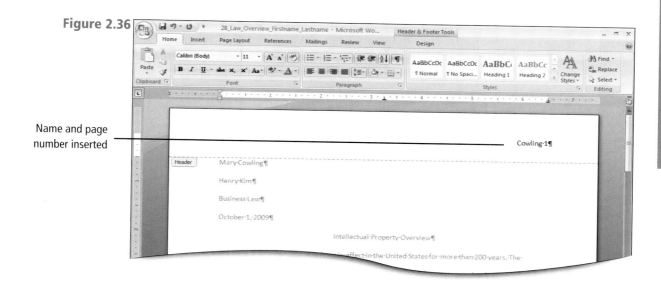

8 Click the **Design tab**, and then in the **Navigation group**, click the **Go to Footer** button. In the **Insert group**, click the **Quick Parts** button, and then click **Field**. In the **Field** dialog box, under **Field names**, locate and click **FileName**, and then click **OK**.

9 Double-click anywhere outside the footer area, and then press Ctrl + Home to move to the top of the document. **Save** your changes.

More Knowledge

Suppressing the Page Number on the First Page of a Document

Some style guidelines may require that the page number on the first page be hidden from view—suppressed. To hide the information contained in the header and footer areas on Page 1 of a document, double-click in the header or footer area. On the Design tab, in the Options group, click the Different First Page check box.

Activity 2.17 Inserting the Current Date and Time

The current date, time, or both can be inserted anywhere in a document. When you are working on a research paper, which will likely be revised several times, put the date and time in the footer to help identify the various revisions you will make. Then, remove the date and time before submitting the paper.

1 Use the vertical scroll bar to scroll to the bottom of the first page of the document to view the footer area. Double-click in the footer area, and notice that the **FileName** field is shaded in gray.

2 Click to position the insertion point to the right of the file name, and then press Enter to move the insertion point to the next line.

3 On the **Design tab**, in the **Insert group**, click the **Date & Time** button.

4 In the displayed **Date and Time** dialog box, locate and click the date and time format that displays the date in a *10/01/2009 4:43 PM* (or *AM*) format, as shown in Figure 2.37. The numbers in your dialog box will vary.

Selected format (your date and time will vary)

Figure 2.37
Date & Time button

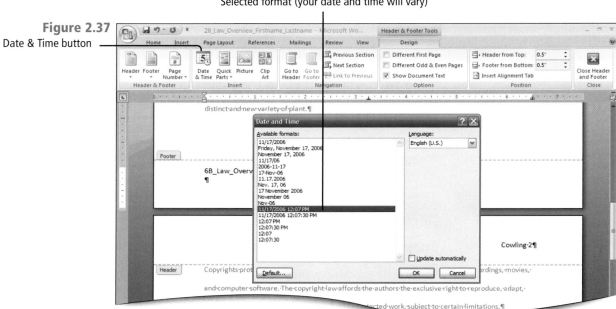

Note — Automatically Update the Date

At the bottom of the Date and Time dialog box, you can select the *Update automatically* check box to have Word update the date every time you open the document.

5 In the **Date and Time** dialog box, click **OK**. Double-click anywhere outside the footer area, and then press (Ctrl) + (Home) to move to the top of the document.

6 **Save** your changes.

Objective 5
Insert Frequently Used Text

AutoCorrect corrects common spelling errors as you type. When you type a word incorrectly, for example *teh*, Word automatically changes it to *the*. You can add words that you frequently misspell to the AutoCorrect list. You can also add shortcuts to phrases you type often. Another type of frequently used text includes various symbols, such as the trademark symbol™ or copyright symbol ©. These are accessed from the Symbols group on the Insert tab.

Activity 2.18 Recording AutoCorrect Entries

You probably have words that you frequently misspell. You can add these to the AutoCorrect list for automatic correction.

1 From the **Office** menu , click **Word Options**. In the **Word Options** list, click **Proofing**, and then under **AutoCorrect options**, click the **AutoCorrect Options** button.

2 In the **AutoCorrect** dialog box, click the **AutoCorrect tab**. Under **Replace**, type **intellectaul** and under **With**, type **intellectual** Compare your screen with Figure 2.38.

If another student has already added this AutoCorrect entry, the Add button will change to a Replace button.

Figure 2.38

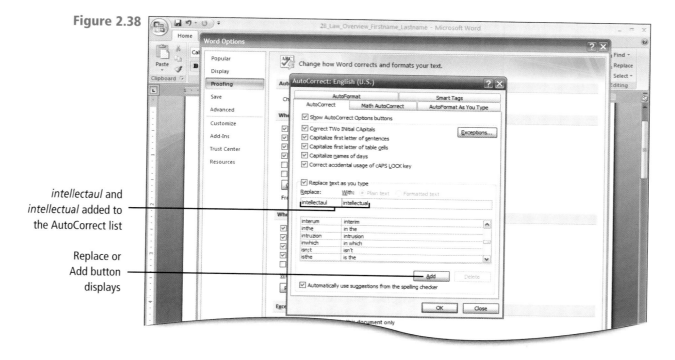

intellectaul and *intellectual* added to the AutoCorrect list

Replace or Add button displays

3 Click **Add**. If the entry already exists, click Replace instead, and then click Yes. Click **OK** two times to close the dialog boxes.

4 Near the top of the document, locate the paragraph beginning *Patent and trademark laws*, and then click to position the insertion point at the beginning of the paragraph. Scroll to the end of the document, hold down ⇧Shift, and then click to the right of the last paragraph mark. Scroll up to see the top of the document. Right-click the selected text, and then from the shortcut menu, click **Paragraph**. On the **Indents and Spacing tab**, under **Indentation**, click the **Special arrow**, and then click **First line**. Under **Indentation**, in the **By** box, be sure *0.5″* displays. Compare your screen with Figure 2.39.

Indenting—moving the beginning of the first line of a paragraph to the right or left of the rest of the paragraph—provides visual cues to the reader to help break the document up and make it easier to read. The MLA style uses 0.5-inch indents at the beginning of the first line of every paragraph.

Indentation will be applied to the *First line* of the paragraph

Figure 2.39

First line will be indented 0.5 (one-half) inch

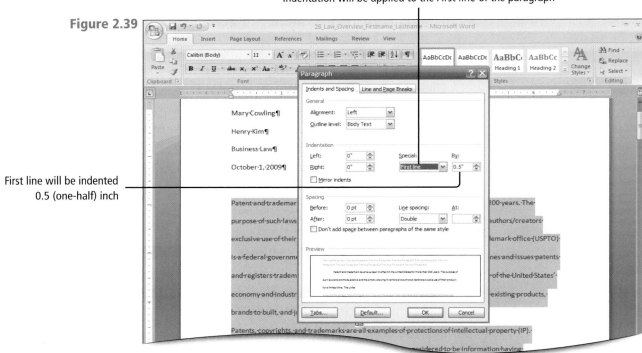

5 Click **OK** to close the dialog box. Near the top of the document, locate the paragraph beginning *Patent and trademark laws*, and then click to position the insertion point at the beginning of the paragraph. Press Enter, and then press ↑ to place the insertion point in the blank line. Type **Patents, copyrights, and trademarks are all examples of protections of** and then press Spacebar.

6 Type **intellectaul** and watch the screen as you press Spacebar. Notice that the misspelled word is automatically corrected.

7 Click in the corrected word, and then notice the blue line that displays under the word. Move the pointer over the blue line until the **AutoCorrect Options** button displays, and then click the button. Compare your screen with Figure 2.40.

Corrected word

Figure 2.40

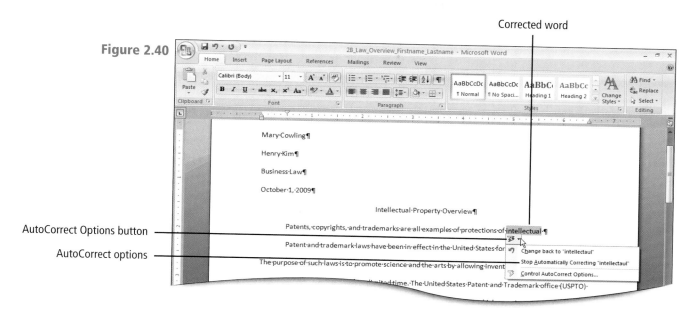

AutoCorrect Options button ———

AutoCorrect options ———

8 Click anywhere in the document to close the **AutoCorrect Options** menu without selecting a command. Locate the word *intellectual* that you just corrected and position the insertion point at the end of that line. Type **property (IP).** and then press [Spacebar].

9 Type the remainder of the paragraph, and then compare your screen with Figure 2.41:

Intellectual property has many definitions, but is usually considered to be information having commercial value and original products of the mind. Intellectual property isn't tangible, but can be protected by the law. Intellectual property is not an item that was invented, but the thought process and plans that allowed the item to be invented and manufactured. Intellectual property is not the clothing that is sold in stores, but rather the brand name that represents the quality and style of the clothing.

Figure 2.41

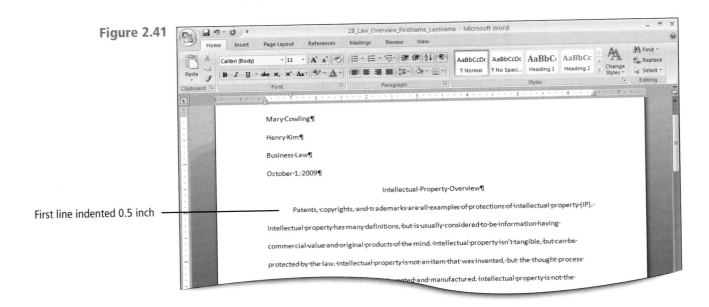

First line indented 0.5 inch

10 **Save** 💾 your changes.

More Knowledge
AutoCorrect Shortcuts

The AutoCorrect replacement is most commonly used to correct spelling errors, but it can also be used to expand shortcut text into longer words or phrases. In the Replace box, type a shortcut phrase, and type the full phrase in the With box. When setting up an AutoCorrect shortcut, it is best not to use shortcut text that is an actual word or a commonly used abbreviation. Even though you can reverse an AutoCorrect replacement by using the AutoCorrect Options shortcut menu, it is best to avoid the problem by adding a letter to the shortcut text. For example, if you type both *GHS* and *GHS Law Partners* frequently, you may want to add ghsx (or just ghx) as an AutoCorrect shortcut for the text *GHS Law Partners*.

Activity 2.19 Inserting Symbols

There are many symbols that are used occasionally, but not often enough to put on a standard keyboard. These symbols can be found on, and inserted from, the Symbols group on the Insert tab.

1 Use the vertical scroll bar to move down in the document to display the bottom half of **Page 1**. In the paragraph that begins *Patent is defined*, in the second line, locate the word *novel*, and then place the insertion point just to the right of the word. Press `Delete` two times to remove the space and the left parenthesis.

The phrase that follows *novel* should be separated by a dash rather than parentheses.

2 Click the **Insert tab**, and then in the **Symbols group**, click the **Symbol** button. At the bottom of the **Symbol gallery**, click **More**

Symbols. In the **Symbol** dialog box, click the **Special Characters tab**. Be sure the **Em Dash** is selected. In the lower right corner of the dialog box, click **Insert**, and then compare your screen with Figure 2.42.

An *em dash* is the default symbol in the list of commonly used symbols. An em dash is the word processing name for a long dash in a sentence. An em dash in a sentence marks a break in thought, similar to a comma but stronger. The keyboard shortcuts for inserting the commonly used symbols display to the right of the character name.

Keyboard shortcuts   Inserted em dash

Figure 2.42

Em dash

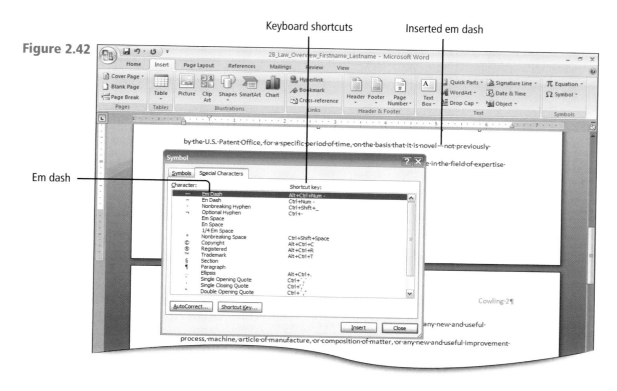

3 If necessary, click the title bar of the dialog box, and then drag the dialog box out of the way so you can see the third line of the same paragraph. With the **Symbol** dialog box still open, to the right of *in a publication*, remove the right parenthesis, the comma, and the space; and then click the **Insert** button again. At the bottom of the **Symbol** dialog box, click **Close**.

4 Press Ctrl + Home to move to the beginning of the document. Place the insertion point to the right of the title text *Intellectual Property Overview*, and then type **(c)** Alternatively, on the Insert tab, in the Symbol group, click the Symbol button, and then click the last item in the first row—the copyright symbol. Compare your document with Figure 2.43.

Your typed text *(c)* changes to the copyright symbol ©. Although this symbol is available from the Symbol gallery, it is also included in Word's AutoCorrect list. The parentheses are necessary for AutoComplete to insert a Copyright symbol. Notice that if you point to the copyright symbol, the AutoCorrect Options button displays, which enables you to remove the copyright symbol and display *(c)* instead.

Figure 2.43

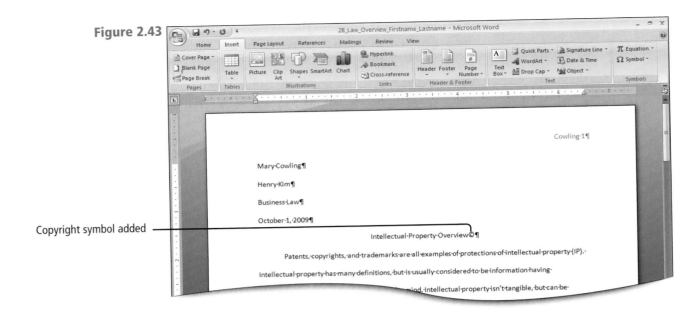

Copyright symbol added

5 **Save** 💾 your changes.

Objective 6
Insert and Format References

Reports frequently include information taken from other sources, and these must be credited. Within report text, numbers mark the location of *references*—information that has been taken from another source. The numbers refer to *footnotes*—references placed at the bottom of the page containing the reference, or *endnotes*—references placed at the end of a document or chapter.

When footnotes or endnotes are included in a report, a page listing the references is included. Such a list is commonly titled **Works Cited**, **Bibliography**, **Sources**, or References.

Activity 2.20 Inserting Footnotes

Footnotes can be added as you type the document or after the document is complete. Footnotes do not need to be entered in order, and if one footnote is removed, Word renumbers the remaining footnotes automatically.

1 Scroll to view **Page 2** and locate the paragraph that begins *Copyrights protect*. At the end of the paragraph, position the insertion point following the period.

2 Click the **References tab**, and then in the **Footnotes group**, click **Insert Footnote**.

A footnote area is created at the bottom of the page, and a footnote number is added to the text at the insertion point location. Footnote 1 is placed at the top of the footnote area, and the insertion point is moved to the right of the number. A short blank line is added just above the footnote area. You do not need to type the footnote number.

3 Type **According to the United States Copyright Office, abstractions, such as an idea for a book or movie, are not subject to copyright law.** and then compare your screen with Figure 2.44.

This is an explanatory footnote, giving additional information that does not fit well in the body of the report. The new footnote is single-spaced, even though the document text is double-spaced.

Figure 2.44

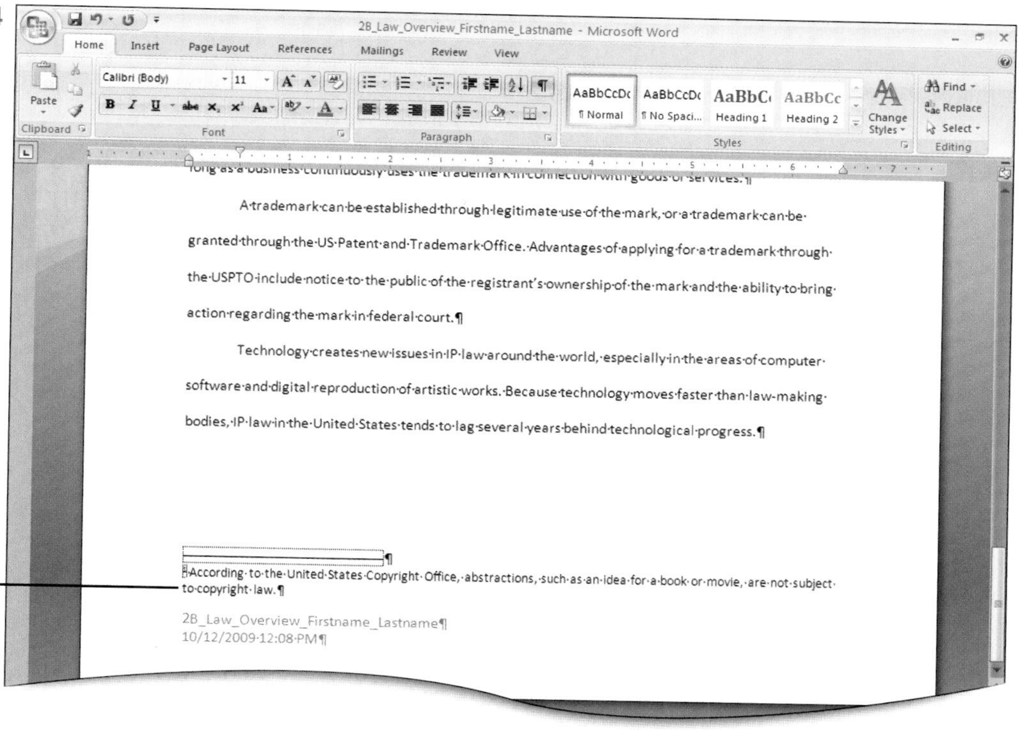

Footnote text, single- spaced

4 Press Ctrl + Home to move to the beginning of the document. Locate the paragraph that begins *Patents, copyrights*. At the end of the paragraph, position the insertion point following the period.

This sentence refers to the *protections* of intellectual property, and the report's author wants to clarify the scope of protections by adding a reference.

5 In the **Footnotes group**, click the **Insert Footnote** button. Type **There is no set of international intellectual property laws, although many countries have reciprocal copyright, trademark, and patent agreements with the United States.** Notice that the footnote you just added is the new footnote *1*, while the other footnote is renumbered as footnote *2*.

6 **Save** your changes.

More Knowledge

Using Symbols Rather Than Numbers for Notes

Instead of using numbers to designate footnotes, you can use standard footnote symbols. The seven traditional symbols, available from the Footnote and Endnote dialog box, in order, are * (asterisk), † (dagger), ‡ (double dagger), § (section mark), ‖ (parallels), ¶ (paragraph mark), and # (number or pound sign). This sequence can be continuous (this is the default setting), or can begin anew with each page.

Activity 2.21 | Modifying a Footnote Style

Microsoft Word contains built-in paragraph formats called *styles*, which can be applied to a paragraph with one command. The default style for footnote text is a single-spaced paragraph that uses a 10-point Calibri font and no indents. MLA style specifies double-spaced text in all areas of a research paper—including footnotes. According to the MLA style, footnotes must also be indented 0.5 inch.

In this activity, you will modify the footnote style so that all of your inserted footnotes are formatted according to MLA guidelines.

1 Scroll to view the bottom of **Page 1** and right-click anywhere in the footnote text. From the shortcut menu, click **Style**. Compare your screen with Figure 2.45.

The Style dialog box displays, listing the styles currently in use in the document, in addition to some of the word processing elements that come with special built-in styles. Because you right-clicked on the footnote text, the selected style is the Footnote Text paragraph style.

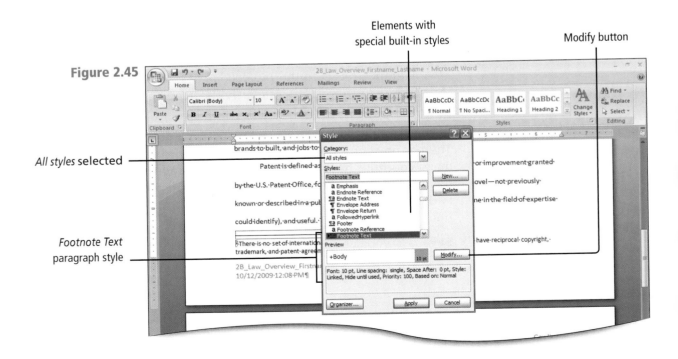

Figure 2.45

Elements with special built-in styles

Modify button

All styles selected

Footnote Text paragraph style

2 In the displayed **Style** dialog box, click the **Modify** button. In the **Modify Style** dialog box, locate the small Formatting toolbar in the center of the dialog box, click the **Font Size button arrow**, click **11**, and then compare your screen with Figure 2.46.

Font Size button arrow

Formatting toolbar in the Modify Style dialog box

Figure 2.46

Format button

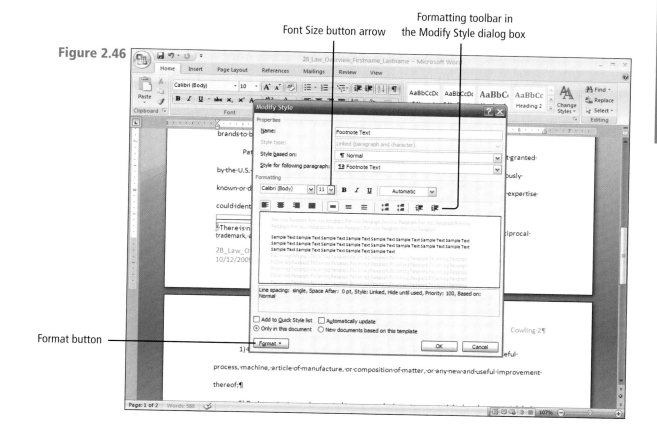

3 In the lower left corner of the dialog box, click the **Format** button, and then click **Paragraph**. In the displayed **Paragraph** dialog box, under **Indentation**, click the **Special arrow**, and then click **First line**. If necessary, change the By box to 0.5".

4 Under **Spacing**, click the **Line spacing button arrow**, and then click **Double**. Alternatively, line spacing can be adjusted using the Modify Style toolbar. Compare your dialog box with Figure 2.47.

First line indent

Figure 2.47

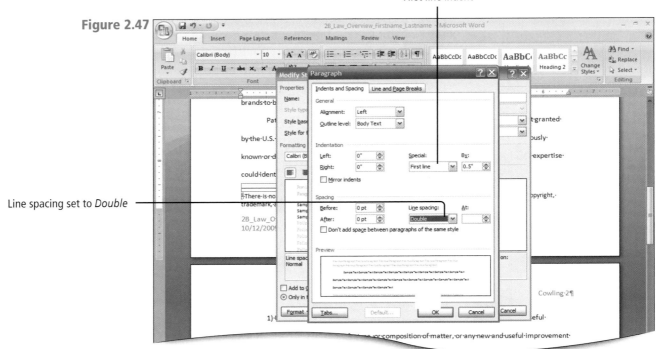

Line spacing set to *Double*

5 Click **OK** to close the **Paragraph** dialog box, click **OK** to close the **Modify Style** dialog box, and then click **Apply** to apply the new style and close the **Style** dialog box. Compare your screen with Figure 2.48.

Your inserted footnotes are formatted with the new Footnote Text paragraph style; any new footnotes that you insert will also use this format.

Footnote text double-spaced

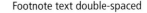

Figure 2.48

First line indented

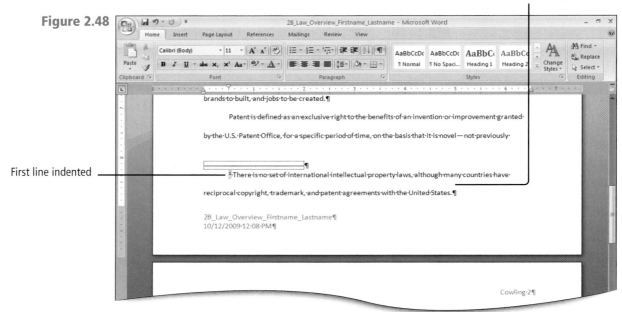

6 Scroll to view the bottom of **Page 2** to confirm that the new format was also applied to the second footnote, and then **Save** 🖫 the changes you have made to your research paper.

By modifying the formats of the existing Footnote style, the new formats were applied to any text in the document that had the Footnote style applied.

Activity 2.22 Adding Citations

When writing a long research paper, you will likely reference numerous books, articles, and Web sites. Some of your research sources may be referenced many times, others only one time.

References to sources within the text of your research paper are indicated in an *abbreviated* manner. However, as you enter a reference for the first time, you can also enter the *complete* information about the source. Then, when you have finished your paper, you will be able to automatically generate the list of sources that must be included at the end of your research paper.

1 On **Page 2** of the document, locate the paragraph that begins *Copyrights protect*, and then position the insertion point at the end of the paragraph, but before the period. Click the **References tab** to begin the process of inserting a citation.

A **citation** is a list of information about a source, usually including the name of the author, the full title of the work, the year of publication, and other publication information.

2 In the **Citations & Bibliography group**, click the **Style button arrow**, and then click **MLA** to insert a reference using MLA style. Click the **Insert Citation** button, and then click **Add New Source**. Be sure **Book** is selected as the **Type of Source**. Add the following information, and then compare your screen with Figure 2.49:

Author:	**Schechter, Roger E.; Thomas, John R.**
Title:	**Intellectual Property: The Law of Copyrights, Patents and Trademarks**
Year:	**2003**
City:	**St. Paul, MN**
Publisher:	**West Publishing Company**

Insert Citation button on the Ribbon

Figure 2.49

Source type

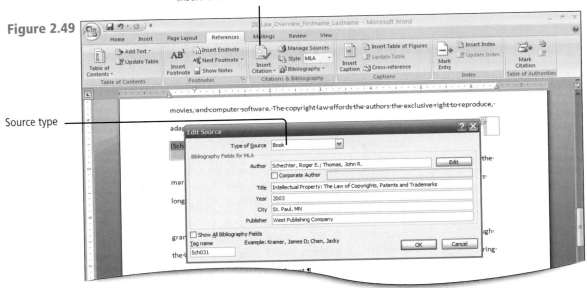

In the MLA style, references to items on the Works Cited page are placed in ***parenthetical references***—references that include the last name of the author or authors and the page number in the referenced source, which you add to the reference. No year is indicated, and there is no comma between the name and the page number.

3 Click **OK** to insert the reference. Click to select the reference, and notice that a small box surrounds the reference and an arrow displays in the lower right corner of the box. Click this **Citation Options arrow**, and then from the displayed list of options, click **Edit Citation**. In the displayed **Edit Citation** dialog box, under **Add**, in the **Pages** box, type **2** to indicate that you are citing from page 2 of this source. Compare your screen with Figure 2.50. Notice that the citation wraps from one line to the next, so the citation box also wraps between lines.

Page number of the citation

Figure 2.50

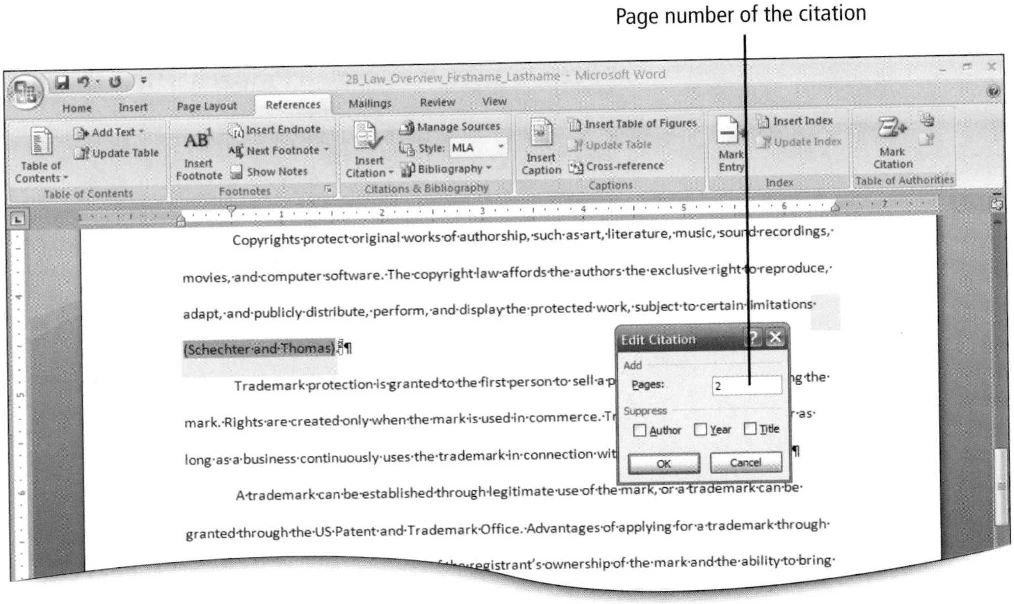

4 Click **OK** to display the page number of the citation. In the next paragraph, which begins *Trademark protection*, position the insertion point at the end of the paragraph, but before the period. In the **Citations & Bibliography group**, click the **Insert Citation** button, and then click **Add New Source**. Be sure **Book** is selected as the **Type of Source**, and then add the following information:

Author:	**Stim, Richard W.**
Title:	**Trademark Law**
Year:	**2000**
City:	**Stamford, CT**
Publisher:	**Thomson Delmar Learning**

5 Click **OK**. Click to select the reference, click the **Citation Options arrow**, and then click **Edit Citation**. In the displayed **Edit Citation** dialog box, under **Add**, in the **Pages** box, type **4** to indicate that you are citing from page 4 of this source. Click **OK**.

6 On the same page, locate the paragraph that begins *3) Plant patents*. At the end of that sentence, click to position the insertion point before the period. In the **Citations & Bibliography group**, click the **Insert Citation** button, and then click **Add New Source**. Click the **Type of Source arrow**, scroll down, and select **Web site** from the list. Under **Bibliography Fields for MLA**, click to select the **Corporate Author** check box.

When the author of a cited work is a corporation, the parenthetical reference is handled differently.

7 Type the following information:

Corporate Author:	**United States Patent and Trademark Office**
Name of Web Page:	**General Information Concerning Patents**
Year:	**2005**
Month:	**March**
Day:	**22**
Year Accessed:	**2009**
Month Accessed:	**October**
Day Accessed:	**11**
URL:	**http://www.uspto.gov/web/offices/pac/doc/general/index.html#patent**

8 Click **OK** to insert the reference, and then compare your screen with Figure 2.51.

A parenthetical reference is added. Because of the changing nature of Web sites, the citation includes the date the site was accessed. Also, because the cited Web page has no page numbers, only the author name is used in the parenthetical reference.

Figure 2.51

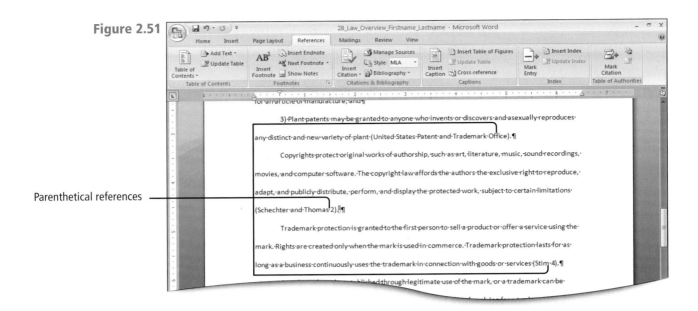

Parenthetical references

9 On the **References tab**, in the **Citations & Bibliography group**, click the **Manage Sources** button, and then compare your screen with Figure 2.52.

The Source Manager dialog box displays. You may have fewer sources, more sources, or different sources. Other citations on your computer display in the Master List box. The citations for the current document display in the Current List box. If you use the same sources regularly, you can copy sources from your Master List to the current document. You can also edit sources and preview the citations using the selected style.

Citations in the current document

Figure 2.52

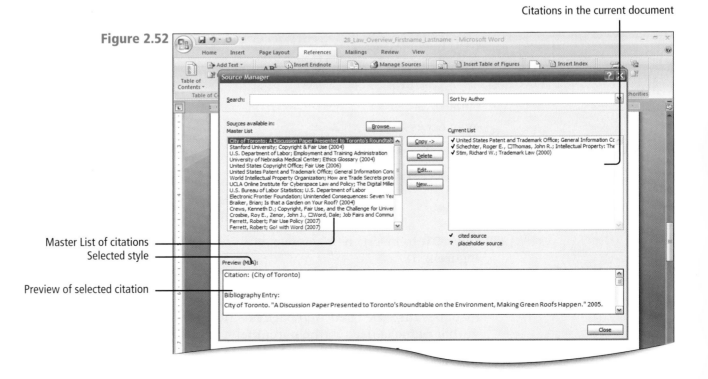

Master List of citations
Selected style

Preview of selected citation

10 At the bottom of the **Source Manager** dialog box, click **Close**. **Save** your changes.

Activity 2.23 Creating a Reference Page

It is common to include, at the end of a report, a list of each source referenced. *Works Cited* is the reference page heading used in the MLA style guidelines. Other styles may refer to this page as a *Bibliography* (Business Style) or *References* (APA Style).

1 Press Ctrl + End to move the insertion point to the end of the document. Hold down Ctrl and then press Enter to insert a manual page break.

2 Type **Works Cited** and then press Enter. On the **References tab**, in the **Citations & Bibliography group**, be sure **MLA** displays in the **Style** box.

3 In the **Citations & Bibliography group**, click the **Bibliography** button, and then click **Insert Bibliography** to insert the citations you typed earlier.

The bibliography is inserted as a field, and the field is linked to the citations Source Manager. The references are sorted alphabetically by author name.

4 In the bibliography, move the pointer to the left of the first entry—beginning *Schechter, Roger*—to display the pointer. Drag down to select all three references. Right-click the selected text, and then click **Paragraph**.

5 Under **Indentation**, click the **Special arrow**, and then click **Hanging**. Under **Spacing**, click the **Line spacing button arrow**, and then click **Double**. Under **Spacing**, in the **After** box, type **0** and then click **OK**.

The text is double-spaced, and the first line of each entry extends 0.5 inch to the left of the remaining lines of the entry. This is called a ***hanging indent***, and the lines are double-spaced according to MLA guidelines.

6 At the top of the last page, right-click the *Works Cited* title, and then click **Paragraph**. In the displayed **Paragraph** dialog box, under **General**, click the **Alignment arrow**, and then click **Centered**. Under **Indentation**, click the **Special arrow**, and then click **(none)**. Click **OK**, and then compare your screen with Figure 2.53.

In MLA style, the *Works Cited* title is aligned and centered. The first line indent of 0.5 inch was removed to center the title between the left and right margins.

Figure 2.53

Works Cited title centered

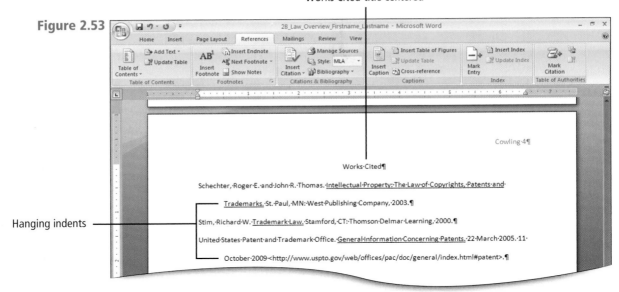

Hanging indents

7 **Save** 💾 your document.

Activity 2.24 Managing Document Properties

Document properties refer to the detailed information about your Word document file that can help you identify or organize your electronic files. Document property information is stored in the ***Document Information Panel***, and can include the document title, the name of the author, the subject of the document, and keywords that will help you search for the document in your computer system.

1 From the **Office** menu 🔲, point to **Prepare**, and then click **Properties** to display the **Document Information Panel**.

2 In the **Author** box, type your name, if necessary.

3 In the **Title** box, type **Intellectual Property Law**

4 In the **Keywords** box, type **copyright, patent, trademark** and then compare your screen with Figure 2.54. Notice that not all boxes need to be filled in.

Figure 2.54

Keywords

Close button

Author

Title

Document Information Panel

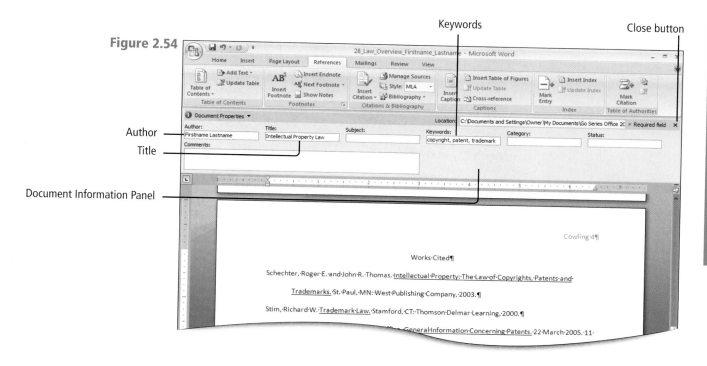

5 On the right side of the **Document Information Panel**, click the **Close** button ⊠. **Save** 🖫 your document.

6 From the **Office** menu 🗐, point to the **Print arrow**, and then click **Print Preview** to make a final check of your research paper. Check your *Chapter Assignment Sheet* or your *Course Syllabus* or consult your instructor to determine if you are to submit your assignments on paper or electronically. To submit electronically, go to Step 8, and then follow the instructions provided by your instructor.

7 On the **Print Preview tab**, in the **Print group**, click the **Print** button, click **OK**, and then click **Close Print Preview**.

8 From the **Office** menu, click **Exit Word**, saving any changes if prompted to do so.

End **You have completed Project 2B** ————————

There's More You Can Do!

From My Computer, navigate to the student files that accompany this textbook. In the folder **02_theres_more_you_can_do_pg1_36**, locate and open the folder for this chapter. Open and print the instructions for this project, which are provided to you in Adobe PDF format.

Try IT!—Add a Custom Entry to the Quick Part Gallery

In this Try IT! exercise, you will add a custom entry to the Quick Part gallery.

Content-Based Assessments

Summary

You can change the format of pages by setting different margins, and change the format of paragraphs by changing indents, line spacing, and the spacing after paragraphs. To apply formats from one paragraph to others, use the Format Painter. You can also format paragraphs by creating numbered and bulleted lists and modifying the bullets.

Use commands such as Cut and Paste, or techniques such as the drag-and-drop operation, to move and copy text. Use the Find and Replace dialog box to locate text that you want to modify. Some formatting in Word can be performed automatically using AutoCorrect and AutoComplete.

When creating reports, use the header and footer areas to add page numbers or to insert the date, time, or file name. Reports also require adding footnotes or endnotes and a reference page to list other sources of information cited within the report.

Key Terms

The ● symbol represents Key Terms found on the Student CD in the 02_theres_more_you_can_do folder for this chapter.

Content-Based Assessments

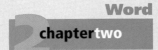

Matching

Match each term in the second column with its correct definition in the first column by writing the letter of the term on the blank line in front of the correct definition.

_____ **1.** The most commonly used text alignment, where text is aligned at the left margin, leaving the right margin uneven.

_____ **2.** The alignment of text centered between the left and right margins.

_____ **3.** Text that is aligned on both the left and right margins.

_____ **4.** The distance between lines of text in a paragraph.

_____ **5.** A small box with upward- and downward-pointing arrows that let you move rapidly through a set of values.

_____ **6.** A Word tool with which you can copy the formatting of specific text, or of a paragraph, to text in another location in the document.

_____ **7.** A temporary storage area that holds text or graphics that have been cut or copied, and that can subsequently be placed in another location in the document or in another Office program.

_____ **8.** The action of removing selected text from a document and moving it to the Office Clipboard.

_____ **9.** A small button that displays beneath pasted text, and lets you determine how the information is pasted into your document.

_____ **10.** Text symbols such as small circles or check marks used to introduce items in a list.

_____ **11.** A Word feature that automatically corrects common typing and spelling errors as you type, such as changing _teh_ to _the._

_____ **12.** The word processing name for a long dash in a sentence that marks a break in thought, similar to a comma but stronger.

_____ **13.** In a report or research paper, references placed at the bottom of a report page containing the source of the reference.

_____ **14.** A term used to describe a list of referenced works placed at the end of a research paper or report when using the MLA style.

_____ **15.** An indent style in which the first line of a paragraph extends to the left of the remaining lines; this indent style is commonly used for bibliographic entries.

A AutoCorrect

B Bullets

C Center alignment

D Cutting

E Em dash

F Footnotes

G Format Painter

H Hanging indent

I Justified alignment

J Left alignment

K Line spacing

L Office Clipboard

M Paste Options

N Spin box

O Works Cited

Content-Based Assessments

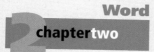

Fill in the Blank

Write the correct answer in the space provided.

1. The space between the text and the top, bottom, left, and right edges of the paper is known as the _____.

2. The placement of paragraph text relative to the left and right margins is known as the _____.

3. When you paste text, the text is moved from the _____ and placed where the insertion point is positioned.

4. The keyboard shortcut used to copy text is Ctrl + _____.

5. When you drag text and then drop it in another location, the text is _____ from one place to another.

6. When you click the Redo button, it reverses the action of the _____ button.

7. To keep two words together as one unit, so that Word does not split them at the end of a line, insert a(n) _____ space.

8. To move the insertion point to the next line without pressing Enter and without creating a new paragraph, insert a manual _____.

9. A list of items with each item introduced by a consecutive number to indicate definite steps, a sequence of actions, or chronological order is a(n) _____ list.

10. In a report or research paper, a reference placed at the end of a report is called a(n) _____.

11. If you need to add ™ or ® or © to a document, display the _____ dialog box.

12. A set of formatting characteristics that can be applied to a paragraph with one shortcut command is known as a(n) _____.

13. In the MLA report style, references placed in parentheses within the report text that includes the last name of the author or authors and the page number in the referenced source, are called

    _____.

14. A list of information about a reference source, usually including the name of the author, the full title of the work, the year of publication, a Web address, and other publication information, is called a(n)

    _____.

15. The detailed information about a document that can help you identify or organize your files, including author name, title, and keywords, is called the Document _____.

Content-Based Assessments

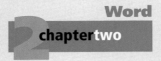

Skills Review

Project 2C — Patent Search

In this project, you will apply the skills you practiced from the Objectives in Project 2A.

Objectives: 1. *Change Document and Paragraph Layout;* **2.** *Change and Reorganize Text;* **3.** *Create and Modify Lists.*

In the following Skills Review, you will edit a document describing the patent search process performed by GHS Law Partners. Your completed document will look similar to the one shown in Figure 2.55.

For Project 2C, you will need the following file:

w02C_Patent_Search

You will save your document as
2C_Patent_Search_Firstname_Lastname

Figure 2.55

permit storage of information about large numbers of chips having complex designs.

e, CA); Hubbell; Earl (Los
alo Alto, CA); Cheung;
an Jose, CA)

ra, CA)

2000

to drawings and figures

of patent searches, such as infringement
can reveal whether a product already in
rches, conducted as part of large research
recent developments in a particular area.

GHS Law Partners
Patent Search Process and Procedures

GHS Law Partners conducts patent searches on behalf of its clients. Patent searches are conducted before preparing the patent application in order to discern if a similar product or process has been patented already. If a similar patent is discovered, the client's pending patent application can be abandoned before too much time or money is invested in it; or, the information in the existing patent can be used to modify the patent application or change its focus.

Patents are grouped into numerous classifications covering all areas of technology. The search process can be time consuming and expensive, but it is valuable for clients to have a search conducted by experts before investing millions of dollars in a new product or process. The number of patents granted by the United States Patent and Trademark Office is large, and has been growing every year. According to the USPTO, in 1963, 48,971 patents were granted. In 2004, 181,302 patents were granted.

GHS Law Partners conducts three main portions of the patent search:

1. Organize the search and determine whether manual searches will be needed in addition to electronic searches. Manual searches may be needed for older technologies not available in the USPTO databases.
2. Run electronic searches and/or manually search at USPTO depository libraries or the USPTO main office in Virginia.
3. Examine the patent documents.

GHS Law Partners employs experts in many fields who will examine the patent documents for their similarity to the new product or process. Patent documents consist of:

- Reference section
- Abstract – for example:

United States Patent 6,826,296

Balaban, et al. November 30, 2004

Method and system for providing a probe array chip design database

Abstract

Systems and method for organizing information relating to the design of polymer probe array chips including oligonucleotide array chips. A database model is provided which organizes information interrelating probes on a chip, genomic items investigated by the chip, and sequence information relating to the design of the chip. The model is readily translatable into database languages such as SQL. The database model scales to

2C_Patent_Search_Firstname_Lastname

(Project 2C–Patent Search continues on the next page)

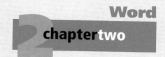

(Project 2C–Patent Search continued)

1. **Start** Word. Locate and open the file **w02C_Patent_Search**, and then save the file in your **Word Chapter 2** folder as **2C_Patent_Search_Firstname_Lastname** Display formatting marks and rulers, and adjust the page width to display both the left and right page edges.

2. Click the **Page Layout tab**, click the **Margins** button, and then at the bottom of the **Margins gallery**, click **Custom Margins**. In the displayed **Page Setup** dialog box, press Tab as necessary to select the value in the **Left** box. With *1.25"* selected, type **1** and then press Tab. In the **Right** box, change the value from *1.25"* to **1** and click **OK**.

3. Click the **Insert tab**. In the **Header & Footer group**, click the **Footer** button, and then click **Edit Footer**. On the **Design tab**, in the **Insert group**, click the **Quick Parts** button, and then click **Field**. In the **Field** dialog box, under **Field names**, locate and click **FileName**, and then click **OK**. Double-click anywhere in the document to close the footer area. **Save** your document.

4. Select the first line of the document. On the Mini toolbar, click the **Center** button, and then click the **Bold** button.

5. Right-click anywhere in the paragraph beginning *GHS Law Partners conducts patent*, and then from the shortcut menu, click **Paragraph**. In the displayed **Paragraph** dialog box, under **Indentation**, click the **Special arrow**, and then click **First line**. Under **Spacing**, in the **After** spin box, click the **up spin arrow** to change the spacing from *10 pt* to **12 pt**. Under **Spacing**, click the **Line spacing button arrow**, and then click **Single**. Click **OK** to close the Paragraph dialog box.

6. With the insertion point in the paragraph beginning *GHS Law Partners conducts patent*, in the **Clipboard group**, double-click the **Format Painter** button. Move the ![pointer] pointer to the paragraph beginning *The search process* and click one time. Use the **Format Painter** to format the paragraph that begins *GHS Law Partners conducts three*, the paragraph beginning *GHS Law Partners employs*, and the last paragraph in the document, beginning *GHS Law Partners can also*. In the **Clipboard group**, click the **Format Painter** button again to turn it off.

7. **Save** your changes. Press Ctrl + Home to position the insertion point at the beginning of the document. On the right side of the **Home tab**, in the **Editing group**, click the **Replace** button. In the **Find and Replace** dialog box, in the **Find what** box, type **USPTO** and in the **Replace with** box, type **United States Patent and Trademark Office**

8. In the **Find and Replace** dialog box, click the **More** button, and then under **Search Options**, if necessary, click to select the **Match case** check box. Click **Find Next** to find the first instance of *USPTO*, and then click the **Replace** button. **Close** the dialog box.

9. In the fourth line of the document, double-click to select the word *already*, and then in the **Clipboard group**, click the **Cut** button. Move the pointer to the right of the next word in the sentence—*patented*—and then click the **Paste** button. In the next paragraph, beginning *The search process*, hold down Ctrl and click to select the last sentence, beginning *Patents are grouped*. In the **Clipboard group**, click the **Cut** button. Move the insertion point to the beginning of the same paragraph, and then click

(Project 2C–Patent Search continues on the next page)

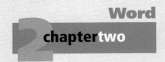
(Project 2C–Patent Search continued)

the **Paste** button. Adjust spacing at the end of the pasted sentence as necessary.

10. In the fifth paragraph beginning *Examine the patent*, select the entire paragraph, including the paragraph mark. Drag the paragraph down to the beginning of the paragraph beginning *GHS Law Partners employs*. In the same paragraph, select *Examine* and replace it with **Study**

11. On the **Quick Access Toolbar**, click the **Undo** button to remove *Study* and replace it with *Examine*. Click the **Undo** button one more time to move the paragraph back to its original location, and then click the **Redo** button to move it back to its new location.

12. Near the top of **Page 2**, in the paragraph beginning *Appl. No.: 737838*, select the space before *2000*. Hold down Ctrl and ⇧ Shift, and then press Spacebar to add a nonbreaking space. Use the same procedure to add a nonbreaking space between *December* and *14* to keep the date together if the line is edited.

13. Press Ctrl + Home to move to the top of the document. Right-click the title, and then click **Paragraph**. Under **Spacing**, in the **After** box, click the **up spin arrow** two times to change the value in the box from *10 pt* to **18 pt**. Click the **Line spacing button arrow**, and then click **Single**. Click **OK** to close the dialog box. In the title, click to the left of **Patent**, and then remove the space between *Partners* and *Patent*. Hold down ⇧ Shift and press Enter to enter a manual line break. **Save** your document.

14. In the middle of **Page 1**, point to the left of the paragraph beginning *Organize the*

search, and then drag down to select the next four lines, including the line beginning *Examine the patent*. On the **Home tab**, in the **Paragraph group**, click the **Numbering** button.

15. Below the numbered list, select the two paragraphs that begin *Reference section* and *Abstract*. In the **Paragraph group**, click the **Bullets** button. Use the same procedure to add bullets to the four paragraphs near the end of the document beginning *Field and background* and ending with *Inventor's description*.

16. On **Page 1**, below the second bulleted point, point to the left of the paragraph beginning *United States Patent*, and then drag down to select the text through the paragraph beginning *Appl. No.*—the line above the second part of the bulleted list. In the **Paragraph group**, click the **Increase Indent** button two times. **Save** your document.

17. From the **Office** menu, click the **Print arrow**, and then click **Print Preview** to make a final check of your document. Check your *Chapter Assignment Sheet* or *Course Syllabus* or consult your instructor to determine if you are to submit your assignments on paper or electronically. To submit electronically, go to Step 19, and then follow the instructions provided by your instructor.

18. On the **Print Preview tab**, click the **Print** button, click **OK**, and then click **Close Print Preview**.

19. From the **Office** menu, click **Exit Word**, saving any changes if prompted to do so.

 End **You have completed Project 2C**

Word

chaptertwo

Skills Review

Project 2D — Copyright Law

In this project, you will apply the skills you practiced from the Objectives in Project 2B.

Objectives: 4. *Insert and Format Headers and Footers;* **5.** *Insert Frequently Used Text;* **6.** *Insert and Format References.*

In the following Skills Review, you will edit a short research paper about the Digital Millennium Copyright Act. This paper was written by an intern at GHS Law Partners. Your completed document will look similar to Figure 2.56.

For Project 2D, you will need the following files:

New blank Word document
w02D_Copyright_Law

You will save your document as
2D_Copyright_Law_Firstname_Lastname

Figure 2.56

LaFleur 3

Works Cited

Electronic Frontier Foundation. *Unintended Consequences: Seven Years under the DMCA.* 13 April 2006.

_consequences.html>.

LaFleur 2

• Requires that the Register of Copyrights recommend to Congress policies to promote
distance education through digital technologies.

This federal statute addresses a number of copyright issues created by the increasing use of the

Because the DMCA is relatively

by copyright experts. There is

Partners' clients. For example, one

tended consequences (Electronic

LaFleur 1

Yvan LaFleur

Henry Kim

Business Law

October 21, 2009

Digital Millennium Copyright Act

In 1998, the United States Congress passed the Digital Millennium Copyright Act. The Act was
intended to address emerging technologies that allowed the circumvention of copyright protections and
growing copyright violations on the internet. According to the UCLA Online Institute for Cyberspace Law
and Policy (UCLA Online Institute for Cyberspace Law and Policy), the act generally:

• Makes it a crime to circumvent anti-piracy measures built into most commercial software.
• Outlaws the manufacture, sale, or distribution of code-cracking devices used to illegally copy
software.
• Does permit the cracking of copyright protection devices, however, to conduct encryption
research, assess product interoperability, and test computer security systems.
• Provides exemptions from anti-circumvention provisions for nonprofit libraries, archives, and
educational institutions under certain circumstances.
• In general, limits Internet service providers from copyright infringement liability for simply
transmitting information over the Internet. Service providers, however, are expected to
remove material from users' Web sites that appears to constitute copyright infringement.
• Limits liability of nonprofit institutions of higher education—when they serve as online
service providers and under certain circumstances—for copyright infringement by faculty
members or graduate students.
• Requires that "webcasters" pay licensing fees to record companies.

2D_Copyright_Law_Firstname_Lastname
November 14, 2009

the DMCA since its introduction in

ur clients. Our attorneys have

e implications of new legislation

pproach to copyright law, doing

blems and litigation.

Desk Reference, 8th Edition.

n Copyright Act. 8 February

.htm>.

Fair Use.

(Project 2D–Copyright Law continues on the next page)

(Project 2D–Copyright Law continued)

1. **Start** Word and be sure a new blank document is displayed. Display formatting marks, and display both the left and right page edges. Be sure the **Top**, **Bottom**, **Left**, and **Right** margins are set to **1** inch.

2. On the **Quick Access Toolbar**, click the **Save** button. In the **Save As** dialog box, navigate to your **Word Chapter 2** folder. Name your file **2D_Copyright_Law_ Firstname_Lastname** and then click **Save**.

3. Type **Yvan LaFleur** and press Enter, and then type **Henry Kim** and press Enter. Type **Business Law** and press Enter, and then type **October 21, 2009** and press Enter. Click the **Home tab**, and then in the **Paragraph group**, click the **Center** button, type **Digital Millennium Copyright Act** and press Enter. Then, in the **Paragraph group**, click the **Align Text Left** button.

4. Click the **Insert tab**. In the **Header & Footer group**, click **Header**, and then click **Edit Header**. In the header area, type **LaFleur** and then press Spacebar. On the **Design tab**, in the **Insert group**, click the **Quick Parts** button, and then click **Field**. In the **Field** dialog box, under **Field names**, locate and click **Page**. Under **Field properties**, click the first page number style—**1, 2, 3**, and then click **OK**. Click the **Home tab**, and then in the **Paragraph group**, click the **Align Text Right** button.

5. Click the **Design tab**, and then in the **Navigation group**, click the **Go To Footer** button. In the **Insert group**, click the **Quick Parts** button, and then click **Field**. In the **Field** dialog box, under **Field names**, locate and click **FileName**, and then click **OK**. Press Enter to create a new line in the footer.

6. In the **Insert group**, click the **Date & Time** button. In the **Date and Time** dialog box, locate and click the date and time format that displays the date in a *November 14, 2009* format. Click **OK**. Recall that the date in your dialog box will vary. Double-click anywhere in the document to close the footer area. **Save** your changes.

7. Press Ctrl + End to move to the end of the document. Click the **Insert tab**. In the **Text group**, click the **Object button arrow**, and then click **Text From File**. Navigate to your student files, select **w02D_Copyright_Law**, and then click **Insert**. Press ←Bksp to remove the empty paragraph at the end of the document. Press Ctrl + A to select the entire document. On the **Home tab**, in the **Paragraph group**, click the **Line spacing** button, and then click **2.0**. Click the **Page Layout tab**, and then in the **Paragraph group**, click the **After down spin arrow** to set the space after to **0**. Click anywhere in the document to deselect the text.

8. From the **Office** menu, click **Word Options**. Click **Proofing**, and then under **AutoCorrect options**, click the **AutoCorrect Options** button. In the **AutoCorrect** dialog box, under **Replace**, type **intruzion** and under **With**, type **intrusion** and then click **OK** two times to close both dialog boxes.

9. Locate the last bulleted item near the end of the document, and then click to place the insertion point to the right of the space after *computer*. Watch the screen as you type **intruzion** and then press Spacebar to see the AutoCorrect feature work.

10. On **Page 1**, locate the bulleted item that begins *Limits liability*. In the first line,

(Project 2D–Copyright Law continues on the next page)

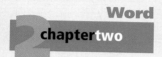
(Project 2D–Copyright Law continued)

select the two hyphens. On the **Insert tab**, in the **Symbols group**, click the **Symbol** button, and then click **More Symbols**. In the **Symbol** dialog box, click the **Special Characters tab**. Be sure the **Em dash** is selected, and then click **Insert**. Repeat this procedure to replace the two hyphens in the second line of the same bulleted item with an em dash. Click **Close** to close the **Symbol** dialog box.

11. Scroll to view the middle of **Page 2**, locate the first bulleted item that begins *Jeopardizing*, and then position the insertion point following the last quotation mark. Click the **References tab**, and then in the **Footnotes group**, click the **Dialog Box Launcher**. In the **Footnote and Endnote** dialog box, under **Location**, be sure **Footnotes** is selected. Under **Format**, in the **Custom mark** box, type an asterisk (*) and then click **Insert**. Type **See GHS Law Partners internal memorandum** *The Changing Face of Fair Use.*

12. At the bottom of **Page 2**, right-click the footnote text, and then from the shortcut menu, click **Style**. In the **Style** dialog box, click **Modify**, change the **Font Size** to **11** and then click **OK**. **Close** the **Style** dialog box.

13. In the middle of **Page 2**, in the paragraph that begins *This federal statute*, at the end of the first sentence, click to place the insertion point before the period. Click the **References tab**. In the **Citations & Bibliography group**, be sure **MLA** style is selected, click the **Insert Citation** button, and then click **Add New Source**. Click the **Type of Source arrow**, and then click **Book**. Add the following book citation:

Author: **Stim, Richard W.**

Title: **Patent, Copyright & Trademark: An Intellectual Property Desk Reference, 8th Edition**

Year: **2006**

City: **Berkeley, CA**

Publisher: **NOLO**

14. Click **OK** to insert the reference. If prompted to Update an existing reference, click Yes. Click to select the reference, click the **Citation Options arrow**, and then click **Edit Citation**. In the displayed **Edit Citation** dialog box, under **Add**, in the **Pages** box, type **227** and then click **OK** to insert the page number. **Save** your document.

15. Move to the top of the document. In the paragraph beginning *In 1998*, in the last line of the paragraph, place the insertion point after the word *Policy*, but before the comma. In the **Citations & Bibliography group**, click the **Insert Citation** button, and then click **Add New Source**. Click the **Type of Source arrow**, and then scroll down and select **Web site** from the list. Under **Bibliography Fields for MLA**, select the **Corporate Author** check box. Type the following information:

Corporate Author: **UCLA Online Institute for Cyberspace Law and Policy**

Name of Web Page: **The Digital Millennium Copyright Act**

Year: **2001**

Month: **February**

Day: **8**

Year Accessed: **2009**

Month Accessed: **November**

Day Accessed: **14**

URL: **http://www.gseis. ucla.edu/iclp/dmca1. htm**

(Project 2D–Copyright Law continues on the next page)

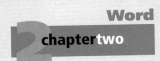
Word
Skills Review

(Project 2D–Copyright Law continued)

16. Click **OK** to insert the reference. If you are prompted to update an existing reference, click Yes.

17. Move to **Page 2** and locate the paragraph beginning *This federal statute*. At the end of the last sentence, after *unintended consequences*, place the insertion point before the comma. In the **Citations & Bibliography group**, click the **Insert Citation** button, and then click **Add New Source**. Under **Type of Source**, be sure **Web site** is selected. Under **Bibliography Fields for MLA**, select the **Corporate Author** check box. Type the following information:

Corporate Author:	**Electronic Frontier Foundation**
Name of Web Page:	**Unintended Consequences: Seven Years under the DMCA**
Year:	**2006**
Month:	**April**
Day:	**13**
Year Accessed:	**2009**
Month Accessed:	**November**
Day Accessed:	**14**
URL:	**http://www.eff.org/IP/ DMCA/?f=unintended_ consequences.html**

18. Click **OK** to insert the reference. If you are prompted to update an existing reference, click Yes.

19. **Save** your document. Hold down Ctrl and press End to move to the end of the document. Hold down Ctrl and press Enter to insert a manual page break. Type **Works Cited** and press Enter. On the **References tab**, in the **Citations & Bibliography group**, be sure **MLA** displays in the **Style** box.

20. In the **Citations & Bibliography group**, click the **Bibliography** button, and then click **Insert Bibliography** to insert the citations you typed earlier. Select the three references, right-click the selected text, and then click **Paragraph**.

21. Under **Indentation**, click the **Special arrow**, and then click **Hanging**. Under **Spacing**, click the **Line spacing button arrow**, and then click **Double**. Under **Spacing**, in the **After** box, type **0** and then click **OK**.

22. Right-click the *Works Cited* title, and then click **Paragraph**. In the displayed **Paragraph** dialog box, under **General**, click the **Alignment arrow**, and then click **Centered**. Under **Indentation**, click the **Special arrow**, and then click **(none)**. Click **OK**.

23. From the **Office** menu, point to **Prepare**, and then click **Properties**. In the displayed **Document Information Panel**, in the **Author** box, type your name, and in the **Title** box, type **Digital Millennium Copyright Act** On the right side of the **Document Information Panel**, click the **Close** button.

24. From the **Office** menu, point to the **Print arrow**, and then click **Print Preview** to make a final check of your document. Check your *Chapter Assignment Sheet* or *Course Syllabus* or consult your instructor to determine if you are to submit your assignments on paper or electronically. To submit electronically, go to Step 26, and then follow the instructions provided by your instructor.

(Project 2D–Copyright Law continues on the next page)

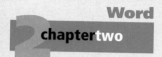

Skills Review

(Project 2D–Copyright Law continued)

25. On the **Print Preview tab**, click the **Print** button, click **OK**, and then click **Close Print Preview**.

26. From the **Office** menu, click **Exit Word**, saving any changes if prompted to do so.

 You have completed Project 2D _____

Word
chapter two

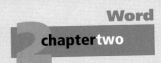

Mastering Word

Project 2E — New Services

In this project, you will apply the skills you practiced from the Objectives in Project 2A.

Objectives: 1. *Change Document and Paragraph Layout;* **2.** *Change and Reorganize Text;* **3.** *Create and Modify Lists.*

In the following Mastering Word project, you will edit a memo about law firm expansion from Rachel Glazer to the staff of GHS Law Partners. Your completed document will look similar to Figure 2.57.

For Project 2E, you will need the following files:

New blank Word document
w02E_New_Services

You will save your document as
2E_New_Services_Firstname_Lastname

Figure 2.57

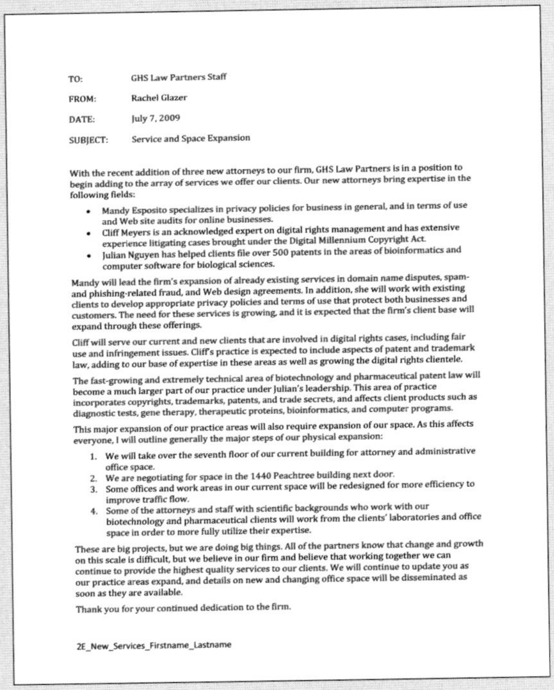

TO: GHS Law Partners Staff

FROM: Rachel Glazer

DATE: July 7, 2009

SUBJECT: Service and Space Expansion

With the recent addition of three new attorneys to our firm, GHS Law Partners is in a position to begin adding to the array of services we offer our clients. Our new attorneys bring expertise in the following fields:

- Mandy Esposito specializes in privacy policies for business in general, and in terms of use and Web site audits for online businesses.
- Cliff Meyers is an acknowledged expert on digital rights management and has extensive experience litigating cases brought under the Digital Millennium Copyright Act.
- Julian Nguyen has helped clients file over 500 patents in the areas of bioinformatics and computer software for biological sciences.

Mandy will lead the firm's expansion of already existing services in domain name disputes, spam- and phishing-related fraud, and Web design agreements. In addition, she will work with existing clients to develop appropriate privacy policies and terms of use that protect both businesses and customers. The need for these services is growing, and it is expected that the firm's client base will expand through these offerings.

Cliff will serve our current and new clients that are involved in digital rights cases, including fair use and infringement issues. Cliff's practice is expected to include aspects of patent and trademark law, adding to our base of expertise in these areas as well as growing the digital rights clientele.

The fast-growing and extremely technical area of biotechnology and pharmaceutical patent law will become a much larger part of our practice under Julian's leadership. This area of practice incorporates copyrights, trademarks, patents, and trade secrets, and affects client products such as diagnostic tests, gene therapy, therapeutic proteins, bioinformatics, and computer programs.

This major expansion of our practice areas will also require expansion of our space. As this affects everyone, I will outline generally the major steps of our physical expansion:

1. We will take over the seventh floor of our current building for attorney and administrative office space.
2. We are negotiating for space in the 1440 Peachtree building next door.
3. Some offices and work areas in our current space will be redesigned for more efficiency to improve traffic flow.
4. Some of the attorneys and staff with scientific backgrounds who work with our biotechnology and pharmaceutical clients will work from the clients' laboratories and office space in order to more fully utilize their expertise.

These are big projects, but we are doing big things. All of the partners know that change and growth on this scale is difficult, but we believe in our firm and believe that working together we can continue to provide the highest quality services to our clients. We will continue to update you as our practice areas expand, and details on new and changing office space will be disseminated as soon as they are available.

Thank you for your continued dedication to the firm.

2E_New_Services_Firstname_Lastname

(Project 2E–New Services continues on the next page)

Content-Based Assessments

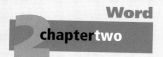
(Project 2E–New Services continued)

1. **Start** Word and be sure a new blank document is displayed. Display formatting marks and the rulers, and be sure your screen displays both the left and right document edges. **Save** the document in your **Word Chapter 2** folder as **2E_New_Services_Firstname_Lastname** Open the document footer and add the file name to the footer.

2. As you type the following text, press `Tab` two times after *TO*, and *FROM*, and *DATE* and one time after *SUBJECT*. Press `Enter` one time after each line.

TO:	**GHS Law Partners Staff**
FROM:	**Rachel Glazer**
DATE:	**July 7, 2009**
SUBJECT:	**Service and Space Expansion**

3. In the blank line below the SUBJECT line, from your student files, insert the file **w02E_New_Services**. Delete the blank line at the end of the document. Select and single-space the inserted text. On the **Page Layout tab**, in the **Paragraph group**, change the spacing **After** to **0 pt**.

4. Near the top of the document, select the three paragraphs beginning *Mandy Esposito, Cliff Meyers*, and *Julian Nguyen*. Create a bulleted list from the selected paragraphs.

5. Near the bottom of **Page 1**, select the four paragraphs beginning *We will take over, We are negotiating, Some offices*, and *Some of the attorneys*. Create a numbered list from the selected paragraphs.

6. Display the **Find and Replace** dialog box. Click the **More** button and select the **Match case** and the **Find whole words only** check boxes. Replace **DMCA** with **Digital Millennium Copyright Act** and then clear the two check boxes you selected. **Close** the dialog box.

7. Near the middle of **Page 1**, in the paragraph beginning *The fast-growing*, use drag and drop to switch the words *pharmaceutical* and *biotechnology*.

8. Add **24-pt** spacing after the SUBJECT line.

9. Near the top of the document, locate and click in the paragraph beginning *With the recent addition*, and then add **6-pt** spacing after the paragraph. Use the **Format Painter** to apply the same formatting to all the other paragraphs in the document, *excluding* the four heading lines and the lists.

10. Add **6-pt** spacing after the last item in each list. Then, select all of the text in the document and change the **Font** to **Cambria**.

11. Near the bottom of the document, in the paragraph beginning *All of the partners*, cut the last sentence in the paragraph—beginning *These are big projects*, but not including the paragraph mark—and then move it to the beginning of the same paragraph. Adjust spacing if necessary.

12. **Save** your document. Preview the document and then print it, or submit it electronically as directed. **Close** the file, and then **Close** Word.

End **You have completed Project 2E**

Word

chaptertwo

Mastering Word

Project 2F — Employee Agreement

In this project, you will apply the skills you practiced from the Objectives in Project 2B.

Objectives: 4. *Insert and Format Headers and Footers;* **5.** *Insert Frequently Used Text;* **6.** *Insert and Format References.*

In the following Mastering Word project, you will edit a report on employer/employee intellectual property ownership. Your completed document will look similar to Figure 2.58.

For Project 2F, you will need the following file:

w02F_Employee_Agreement

You will save your document as
2F_Employee_Agreement_Firstname_Lastname

Figure 2.58

(Project 2F–Employee Agreement continues on the next page)

Content-Based Assessments

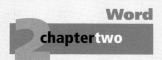
(Project 2F–Employee Agreement continued)

1. **Start** Word. Locate and open the file **w02F_Employee_Agreement**. Display formatting marks and rulers, and adjust the page width to display both the left and right page edges. Change all document margins to **1** inch.

2. Select the entire document and change the **Line spacing** to **2.0**, and the **Font Size** to **11** pt. **Save** your file in your **Word Chapter 2** folder as **2F_Employee_Agreement_Firstname_Lastname**

3. Move to the beginning of the document. Type the following, pressing Enter after each line:

   Siena Rusk
   Henry Kim
   Business Law
   December 17, 2009

4. Center the fifth line document title that begins *Employer/Employee.* Open the header area, type **Rusk** and then add a space and insert the **Page** field, using the **1, 2, 3** format. Right align the header text.

5. Open the footer area, and then add the **FileName** field. Press Enter, and then insert the current date field, using the *December 17, 2009* date format.

6. Select all of the document text except the first five lines. Indent the first line of each paragraph **0.5 inches**.

7. Open the **Word Options** dialog box, click **Proofing**, and then under **AutoCorrect options**, click the **AutoCorrect Options** button. **Replace tradmark With trademark** and then close both dialog boxes. Near the top of the document, in the sixth line of the paragraph that begins *The majority of,* position the insertion point after the space following *writings,* type **tradmark** and then

add a comma and a space to test the AutoCorrect entry.

8. In the first line of the same paragraph, select the two hyphens and use the **Symbol** dialog box to replace them with an **em dash**. Repeat this procedure in the second line of the same paragraph.

9. In the second line of the same paragraph, position the insertion point before the period. following *individuals.* Insert a footnote with the text **This is not true of the U.S. Federal Government.** Right-click the footnote and display the **Style** dialog box. Modify the **Footnote Text** style **Font** to **Cambria**, and the **Font Size** to **11**.

10. Near the bottom of **Page 1**, at the end of the fourth line in the paragraph that begins *Employees also often have,* position the insertion point to the right of the quotation mark that follows *trade secret.* Insert the following **Web site** citation, using **MLA** style. Be sure to select the **Corporate Author** check box:

Corporate Author:	**University of Nebraska Medical Center**
Name of Web Page:	**Ethics Glossary**
Year:	**2004**
Month:	**February**
Day:	**3**
Year Accessed:	**2009**
Month Accessed:	**November**
Day Accessed:	**22**
URL:	**http://www.unmc.edu/ethics/words.html#T**

(Project 2F–Employee Agreement continues on the next page)

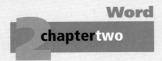

(Project 2F—Employee Agreement continued)

11. **Save** your document. At the end of the same paragraph, use the same procedure to add the following **Web site** citation:

Corporate Author:	**World Intellectual Property Organization**
Name of Web Page:	**How are Trade Secrets Protected?**
Year:	**2006**
Month:	**June**
Day:	**25**
Year Accessed:	**2009**
Month Accessed:	**November**
Day Accessed:	**17**
URL:	**http://www.wipo. int/sme/en/ip_ business/trade_secrets/ protection.htm**

12. **Save** your document. At the end of the second-to-last paragraph of the document, beginning *Disputes regarding ownership*, position the insertion point at the end of the paragraph. Use the same procedure to add the following **Book** citation:

Author:	**Leonard, Gregory K.; Stiroh, Lauren J.**
Title:	**Economic Approaches to Intellectual Property Policy, Litigation, and Management**
Year:	**2006**
City:	**New York, NY**
Publisher:	**NERA Economic Consulting**

13. Select the citation and add the page numbers **106–7**

14. **Save** your document. Move to the end of the document and insert a manual page break. Type **Works Cited** and press Enter. Center the *Works Cited* title and remove the first line indent. Position the insertion point in the blank line below *Works Cited*.

15. On the **References tab**, click the **MLA** style, and then insert a **Bibliography**. Select the bibliography field. Display the **Paragraph** dialog box, double-space the selected text, and then apply a hanging indent.

16. **Save** your changes. Preview the document, and then print it, or submit it electronically as directed. **Close** the file, and then **Close** Word.

End You have completed Project 2F

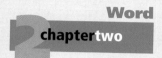

Content-Based Assessments

Word

chaptertwo

Mastering Word

Project 2G — Disputes

In this project, you will apply the skills you practiced from the Objectives in Projects 2A and 2B.

Objectives: 1. *Change Document and Paragraph Layout;* **2.** *Change and Reorganize Text;* **3.** *Create and Modify Lists;* **4.** *Insert and Format Headers and Footers;* **5.** *Insert Frequently Used Text;* **6.** *Insert and Format References.*

In the following Mastering Word project, you will edit an internal document on domain name disputes for GHS Law Partners. Your completed document will look similar to Figure 2.59.

> ### For Project 2G, you will need the following file:
>
> w02G_Disputes

You will save your document as 2G_Disputes_Firstname_Lastname

Figure 2.59

INTERNAL DISTRIBUTION ONLY

GHS Law Partners and Internet Domain Name Disputes

Domain names are Web site addresses used to direct Internet users to a particular site. Companies and organizations prefer to use a domain name that is easily identifiable with their company, service, or brand. Such domain names are easy to remember and often become identified with the company itself. Because Web sites are now an accepted and important part of almost every company's operations and a huge profit-driver, the right to use a particular domain name has become an issue in intellectual property.

Domain names are registered to various owners on a first-come, first-served basis. Under current law, a company like GHS Law Partners does not have automatic right to the terms *GHS*, *law*, or *partners* in a domain name simply because that is the name of the business. Because anyone can register a domain name, registration of a domain name before someone else registers it is an important part of business strategy.

Registering a Web site name is inexpensive, but the names are highly valuable to businesses. This has resulted in what is called *cybersquatting*—registering a domain name with little intention of creating a Web site and assuming the name will be valuable enough to another entity to force them to buy it at a much greater price than was paid to register it. As WIPO, the World Intellectual Property Organization describes it, "As the holders of these registrations, cybersquatters often then put the domain names up for auction, or offer them for sale directly to the company or person involved, at prices far beyond the cost of registration. Alternatively, they often keep the registration and use the good name of the person or business associated with that domain name to attract business for their own sites."

When domain name disputes arise for GHS Law Partners' clients, we work under the Uniform Domain Name Dispute Resolution Policy (UDRP), which was developed by WIPO for domain name disputes worldwide. In cases under this policy, the following factors are considered:

1. Whether the domain name is identical or confusingly similar to a trademark or service mark in which the complainant has rights.
2. Whether the respondent has any rights or legitimate interests in the domain name (for example, the legitimate offering of goods and services under the same name).
3. Whether the domain name was registered and is being used in bad faith.[1]

The policy defines "bad faith" in part as "circumstances indicating that you have registered or you have acquired the domain name primarily for the purpose of selling, renting, or otherwise transferring the domain name registration to the complainant who is the owner of the trademark or service mark or to a competitor of that complainant, for valuable

[1] http://www.wipo.int/about-ip/en/studies/publications/domain_names.htm

2G_Disputes_Firstname_Lastname

INTERNAL DISTRIBUTION ONLY

...ket costs directly related to the

...on both sides of domain name
...nd have relationships with other
...ts in these disputes regardless of the

(Project 2G–Disputes continues on the next page)

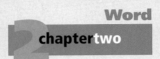

Mastering Word

(Project 2G—Disputes continued)

1. Locate and open the file **w02G_Disputes**. **Save** the file in your **Word Chapter 2** folder as **2G_Disputes_Firstname_Lastname** and then add the file name to the footer. Display formatting marks, and set the page width to a comfortable size for you.

2. Select the document title, increase the **Font Size** to **14** points, and add **Bold** emphasis. Select all of the text in the document, change the font to **Cambria**, change the line spacing to **1.0**, and then add **6 pt.** spacing after each paragraph.

3. Change the top margin to **1.5** inches and the other margins to **1** inch. Open the document header, type **INTERNAL DISTRIBUTION ONLY** and then **Center** the header. Change the header font to **Cambria**.

4. Near the top of the document, in the paragraph beginning *Because Web sites*, select the first sentence of the paragraph and move it to the end of the same paragraph.

5. In the paragraph that begins *Registering a Web site*, locate the two hyphens (--) after the word *cybersquatting*, and then replace the hyphens with an **em dash**.

6. **Save** your changes. Use the **Find and Replace** dialog box to locate the second occurrence of *World Intellectual Property Organization*, replace it with **WIPO** and then remove the word *the* preceding WIPO.

7. Near the bottom of **Page 1**, select the three paragraphs that begin with *Whether*. Change the selected paragraphs to a numbered list, and **Increase Indent** one time.

8. At the end of the third item in the list, after the period following *bad faith*, insert the following footnote:

    http://www.wipo.int/about-ip/en/ studies/publications/domain_names.htm

9. At the bottom of **Page 1**, at the end of the paragraph beginning *The policy defines*, insert the following footnote:

    http://www.icann.org/udrp/udrp-policy-24oct99.htm

10. Modify the **Footnote** style to use the **Cambria** font, and **11** point font size.

11. **Save** your changes. Preview the document, and then print it, or submit it electronically as directed. **Close** the file, and then **Close** Word.

End **You have completed Project 2G**

Project 2H — Trademarks

In this project, you will apply the skills you practiced from the Objectives in Projects 2A and 2B.

Objectives: 1. *Change Document and Paragraph Layout;* **2.** *Change and Reorganize Text;* **3.** *Create and Modify Lists;* **4.** *Insert and Format Headers and Footers;* **5.** *Insert Frequently Used Text;* **6.** *Insert and Format References.*

In the following Mastering Word project, you will edit a handout on trademarks and commercial identifiers prepared by GHS Law Partners. Your completed document will look similar to Figure 2.60.

For Project 2H, you will need the following files:

New blank Word document
w02H_Trademarks

You will save your document as
2H_Trademarks_Firstname_Lastname

Figure 2.60

GHS LAW PARTNERS

s kept in commercial use and is not being

usiness and intellectual property law,
ial identifiers and their value to your
ous types of marks and enable you to
ness for years to come.

GHS LAW PARTNERS

Trademarks and Commercial Identifiers

Trademarks—also known as commercial identifiers or marks—can be words, phrases, logos, symbols, or images. Sometimes a trademark is made up of two or more of these. You can look at just about any product and see one or more trademarks. A trademark is used to identify a product as being unique to the company that owns it, so therefore trademarks are extremely valuable to their owners. A trademark can be identified with a company to indicate quality, flavor, scent, innovation, or any number of "ideas" that a company wishes to express.

Exclusive rights to a mark are partially established through commercial use, such as:

- Entering the mark on state or county records
- Applying the mark to signs and promotional materials
- Using the mark on letterhead, business cards, and Web sites

Marks can also be registered with the United States Patent and Trademark Office (USPTO), which gives companies more leverage should a dispute arise over a mark. The mark will return a result during trademark searches, discouraging others from trying to claim the mark as their own, and registration puts the burden of proof of originality on any infringer.

A company may hold hundreds of trademarks. Microsoft provides a Web page listing its many trademarked names for games, software, fonts, brands, etc., along with information on how to cite each name. Microsoft also provides a page titled "General Microsoft Trademark Guidelines," that provides very specific instructions on referencing Microsoft trademarks and logos in any kind of publication.

Some trademarked names become so common in the language that they can become generic. This can be financially harmful to a company because the word or phrase is no longer necessarily associated with its creator. Some common name brands that have become generic include:

- ™ Jacuzzi for hot tub
- ™ Xerox for copiers
- ™ Band-Aid for adhesive
- ™ AstroTurf for artificial grass

and desist letters (which often end the case)

Skilled intellectual property attorneys like those at GHS Law Partners are helpful to companies at every stage in the trademark process. In the design phase, our attorneys perform thorough searches for similar phrases or logos, preventing resources from being spent on an idea unlikely to achieve registration. Once design is complete, GHS Law Partners assists in the preparation and filing of the registration application and work with the USPTO to resolve objection and answer questions. After

2H_Trademarks_Firstname_Lastname
11/24/2009 6:00 PM

(Project 2H–Trademarks continues on the next page)

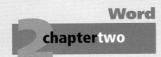

(Project 2H–Trademarks continued)

1. **Start** Word and be sure a new blank document is displayed. Display formatting marks and display both the left and right page edges. Change the top margin to **2** inches and the other margins to **1** inch.

2. Type **Trademarks and Commercial Identifiers** and press Enter. Select the title and increase the **Font Size** to **14 pt**, add **Bold** emphasis, and **Center** the title. **Save** the file in your **Word Chapter 2** folder as **2H_Trademarks_Firstname_Lastname** and then add the file name to the footer. With the footer open, insert a blank line under the **FileName** field, and then insert the **Date** field in the format *6/26/2009 5:15 PM*. Close the footer.

3. Place the insertion point in the blank line below the title. Locate and insert the file **w02H_Trademarks**. Remove the blank line at the end of the document. Select all of the text in the document—including the title—change the line spacing to **1.0**, and add **12-pt.** spacing after each paragraph.

4. Open the document header, type **GHS LAW PARTNERS** and then **Center** the header. Select the header text and change the font to **Arial Black, 28 pt**.

5. Near the top of **Page 2**, position the insertion point at the end of the paragraph that begins *Skilled intellectual property*. Display the **Footnote and Endnote** dialog box, and then change the footnote mark from a number to an asterisk (*). Insert a footnote and type **If infringements or disputes arise, we handle all details from cease and desist**

letters (which often end the case) through litigation.

6. **Save** your changes and move to the beginning of the document. Use the **Find and Replace** dialog box to find the word **allow** and then replace it with **enable**

7. Near the top of the document, in the paragraph beginning *Trademarks, also known as*, delete the comma and space after *Trademarks* and insert an **em dash**. In the same line, after *marks*, delete the comma and space and insert an **em dash**.

8. Near the bottom of **Page 1**, select the four lines of trademarked names, beginning with *Xerox*. Change the selected paragraphs to a bulleted list, and increase the indent one time. With the bullets still selected, right-click any of the list items, display the **Define New Bullet** dialog box, and then change the bullet type to a trademark symbol (TM).

9. Near the top of **Page 1**, select the three lines beginning with *Entering the mark* and ending with *Using the mark*. Change the selected paragraphs to a bulleted list using black dots for bullets, and increase the indent one time.

10. In the bottom bulleted list, select the fourth bullet point—*Jacuzzi*—and move it up so it becomes the first bullet point.

11. **Save** your changes. Preview the document, and then print it, or submit it electronically as directed. **Close** the file, and then **Close** Word.

End You have completed Project 2H

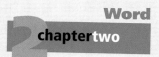

Word

chaptertwo

Mastering Word

Project 2I — Fair Use

In this project, you will apply the skills you practiced from all the Objectives in Projects 2A and 2B.

Objectives: 1. *Change Document and Paragraph Layout;* **2.** *Change and Reorganize Text;* **3.** *Create and Modify Lists;* **4.** *Insert and Format Headers and Footers;* **5.** *Insert Frequently Used Text;* **6.** *Insert and Format References.*

In the following Mastering Word project, you will edit a report on fair use of copyrighted material, created by summer intern Clara Madison for GHS Law Partners. Your completed document will look similar to Figure 2.61.

For Project 2I, you will need the following files:

New blank Word document
w02I_Fair_Use

You will save your document as
2I_Fair_Use_Firstname_Lastname

Figure 2.61

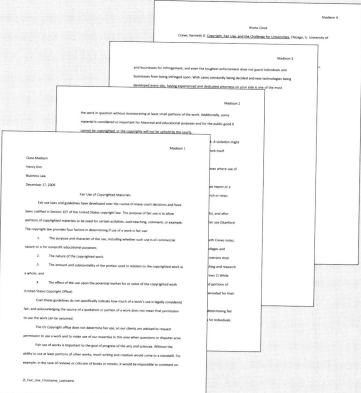

(Project 2I–Fair Use continues on the next page)

(Project 2I–Fair Use continued)

1. **Start** Word and be sure a new blank document is displayed. Display formatting marks and the rulers, and display the left and right document edges. If necessary, change all document margins to **1** inch. **Save** the document as **2I_Fair_Use_ Firstname_Lastname** Open the document footer and add the file name to the footer.

2. Move to the document header. In the header area, type **Madison** and then add a space and the page number, using the **1, 2, 3** format. Right align the header text.

3. Move to the beginning of the document. Type the following, pressing Enter after each line:

   Clara Madison
   Henry Kim
   Business Law
   December 17, 2009
   Fair Use of Copyrighted Materials

4. Center the last paragraph you typed—*Fair Use of Copyrighted Materials*. In the blank line below the centered title, insert the **w02I_Fair_Use** file. Delete the blank line at the end of the document. Select all of the document text. Set the **Line Spacing** to **2**, and the space **After** to **0**.

5. Select the inserted text, but not the five lines at the beginning of the document that you typed. Open the **Paragraph** dialog box, add a **0.5** inch first line indent.

6. Near the top of **Page 1**, select the four paragraphs, starting with the paragraph beginning *The purpose and character*. Create a numbered list from the selected paragraphs. Decrease the indent of the numbered list until it is aligned with the left margin of the document. Display the **Paragraph** dialog box, and set the **Special** indentation to **First line**. Set the **First line** indent to **0.5** inches.

7. Near the middle of **Page 2**, select the two paragraphs starting with the paragraph beginning *You use a very small excerpt*. Create a bulleted list from the selected paragraphs. Decrease the indent of the bulleted list until it is aligned with the left margin of the document. Modify the paragraph formatting using the procedure in Step 6.

8. Move to the end of the document. In the second-to-last paragraph, beginning with *Laws governing*, locate and select the three periods between *availability* and *many*. Display the **Symbol** dialog box, and from the **Special Characters tab**, insert an **Ellipsis** (…).

9. In the last paragraph of the document, move the first sentence—beginning with *With cases constantly*—to the end of the paragraph.

10. Display the **Find and Replace** dialog box, use it to replace **make the determinations into** with **determine** and then **Save** your document.

11. Near the top of **Page 1**, in the fourth item in the numbered list, position the insertion point to the left of the period. Insert the following **Web site** citation, using **MLA** style. Be sure to select the **Corporate Author** check box:

Corporate Author:	**United States Copyright Office**
Name of Web Page:	**Fair Use**
Year:	**2006**
Month:	**January**
Day:	**31**
Year Accessed:	**2009**
Month Accessed:	**June**
Day Accessed:	**6**
URL:	**http://www.copyright. gov/fls/fl102.html**

(Project 2I–Fair Use continues on the next page)

Content-Based Assessments

Word
chapter two   **Mastering Word**

(Project 2I–Fair Use continued)

12. Save your document. On **Page 2**, at the end of the second bullet point, use the same procedure to add the following **Web site** citation:

Corporate Author: **Stanford University**

Name of Web Page: **Copyright & Fair Use**

Year: **2004**

Year Accessed: **2009**

Month Accessed: **June**

Day Accessed: **8**

URL: **http://fairuse. stanford.edu/Copyright_ and_Fair_Use_Overview/ chapter9/9-d. html**

13. Save your document. At the end of the second-to-last paragraph of the document, locate the long quotation, which begins *"Copyright is among,"* and position the insertion point to the right of the second quotation mark. Add the following **Book** citation:

Author: **Crews, Kenneth D.**

Title: **Copyright, Fair Use, and the Challenge for Universities**

Year: **1993**

City: **Chicago, IL**

Publisher: **University of Chicago Press**

14. Add the page number **2** to the citation.

15. Save your document. Move to the end of the document and insert a manual page break. Type **Works Cited** and press Enter. **Center** the *Works Cited* title and remove the first line indent. Position the insertion point in the blank line below *Works Cited*.

16. On the **References tab**, click the **MLA** style, and then insert a **Bibliography**. Select the bibliography field, and then display the **Paragraph** dialog box. Double-space the selected text, and then add a hanging indent.

17. Save your changes. Preview the document, and then print it, or submit it electronically as directed. **Close** the file, and then **Close** Word.

 End **You have completed Project 2I**

Content-Based Assessments

 **Business Running Case**

Project 2J — Business Running Case

In this project, you will apply the skills you practiced in Projects 2A and 2B.

From My Computer, navigate to the student files that accompany this textbook. In the folder **03_business_running_case_pg37_86**, locate and open the folder for this chapter. Open and print the instructions for this project, which are provided to you in Adobe PDF format. Follow the instructions and use the skills you have gained thus far to assist Jennifer Nelson in meeting the challenges of owning and running her business.

 You have completed Project 2J ⎯⎯⎯⎯⎯⎯

Rubric

The following outcomes-based assessments are *open-ended assessments*. That is, there is no specific correct result; your result will depend on your approach to the information provided. Make *Professional Quality* your goal. Use the following scoring rubric to guide you in *how* to approach the problem and then to evaluate *how well* your approach solves the problem.

The *criteria*—Software Mastery, Content, Format and Layout, and Process—represent the knowledge and skills you have gained that you can apply to solving the problem. The *levels of performance*—Professional Quality, Approaching Professional Quality, or Needs Quality Improvements—help you and your instructor evaluate your result.

	Your completed project is of Professional Quality if you:	Your completed project is Approaching Professional Quality if you:	Your completed project Needs Quality Improvements if you:
1-Software Mastery	Choose and apply the most appropriate skills, tools, and features and identify efficient methods to solve the problem.	Choose and apply some appropriate skills, tools, and features, but not in the most efficient manner.	Choose inappropriate skills, tools, or features, or are inefficient in solving the problem.
2-Content	Construct a solution that is clear and well organized, contains content that is accurate, appropriate to the audience and purpose, and is complete. Provide a solution that contains no errors of spelling, grammar, or style.	Construct a solution in which some components are unclear, poorly organized, inconsistent, or incomplete. Misjudge the needs of the audience. Have some errors in spelling, grammar, or style, but the errors do not detract from comprehension.	Construct a solution that is unclear, incomplete, or poorly organized, containing some inaccurate or inappropriate content; and contains many errors of spelling, grammar, or style. Do not solve the problem.
3-Format and Layout	Format and arrange all elements to communicate information and ideas, clarify function, illustrate relationships, and indicate relative importance.	Apply appropriate format and layout features to some elements, but not others. Overuse features, causing minor distraction.	Apply format and layout that does not communicate information or ideas clearly. Do not use format and layout features to clarify function, illustrate relationships, or indicate relative importance. Use available features excessively, causing distraction.
4-Process	Use an organized approach that integrates planning, development, self-assessment, revision, and reflection.	Demonstrate an organized approach in some areas, but not others; or, use an insufficient process of organization throughout.	Do not use an organized approach to solve the problem.

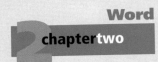

Word

chapter two

Problem Solving

Project 2K — Seminar

In this project, you will construct a solution by applying any combination of the skills you practiced from the Objectives in Projects 2A and 2B.

For Project 2K, you will need the following file:

New blank Word document

You will save your document as
2K_Seminar_Firstname_Lastname

College students are often asked to write research papers and presentations that involve information gathered from many sources. GHS Law Partners has been asked by the local college to conduct a seminar for faculty members that covers the topic of how students use the intellectual property of others. In this Problem Solving project, you will create a one-page document that outlines the topic.

Your document should consist of an introduction to the law firm and the topic, followed by a list of definitions of terms, including—but not limited to—*intellectual property, copyright, fair use,* and *plagiarism.* Add a footnote indicating your source for the definitions. Then, add a list of the topics to be covered in the order in which they will be presented. You might include topics such as quotations, downloaded pictures from the Web, and how to cite sources. Add a title to the document, and format the text appropriately. You may want to do some research on the Web or in your school library on such topics as copyrights, plagiarism, and citing sources to develop your topics.

Add the file name to the footer. Check your document for spelling and grammar errors. Save the document as **2K_Seminar_Firstname_Lastname** and submit it as directed.

 End **You have completed Project 2K** —————

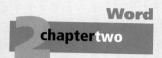

Problem Solving

Project 2L — Evaluation

In this project, you will construct a solution by applying any combination of the skills you practiced from the Objectives in Projects 2A and 2B.

For Project 2L, you will need the following file:

New blank Word document

**You will save your document as
2L_Evaluation_Firstname_Lastname**

In this project, you will write a letter that summarizes the categories and the criteria to be used in a job performance evaluation for summer interns. The letter should be addressed to Andrea Smith, 1884 Bullpen Dr., Black River, GA 30366, and should be from Michael Scott, the Office Manager of the law firm, GHS Law Partners.

Be sure to

- Use the letter style you practiced in Chapter 1.

- Research the topic in your library or on the Web. There are many sites that discuss the types of criteria used when rating employee performance. (Hint: Search for *employee evaluation* or *job evaluation*.)

- Divide the criteria into two or three categories. Introduce the categories, and then add a short list of criteria under each category.

- Use at least one special bullet symbol for a list.

Add the file name to the footer. Check the letter for spelling and grammar errors. Save the document as **2L_Evaluation_Firstname_Lastname** and submit it as directed.

End **You have completed Project 2L** ——————————

Outcomes-Based Assessments

Problem Solving

Project 2M — Trademarks

In this project, you will construct a solution by applying any combination of the skills you practiced from the Objectives in Projects 2A and 2B.

For Project 2M, you will need the following file:

New blank Word document

You will save your document as 2M_Trademarks_Firstname_Lastname

When a company has a very recognizable name that is used for a product, they often get protection for that name from the U.S. Patent and Trademark Office. Microsoft, for example, has a long list of trademarks, logos, and trade names, including Microsoft Windows® and MapVision™. To view the list, use a Web browser and go to *www.microsoft.com.* At the bottom of the Microsoft home page, click **Trademarks**. Notice that some of the items use the Registered® symbol, and some use the Trademark™ symbol.

Write a 400–600 word research paper (about two pages long) that identifies the similarities and differences between items that are identified as *registered* and those identified as *trademarked*. Your paper should follow MLA style guidelines, or other style guidelines as directed by your instructor. Use at least two references, and include a Works Cited page. Detailed information about writing in the MLA style can be found in your college library and also online. Include at least one list, two symbols, and one informational endnote or footnote. Save the research paper as **2M_Trademarks_Firstname_Lastname** and then create a footer that contains the file name. Submit the document as directed.

End You have completed Project 2M

Outcomes-Based Assessments

Problem Solving

Project 2N—Calendar

In this project, you will construct a solution by applying any combination of the skills you practiced from the Objectives in Projects 2A and 2B.

For Project 2N, you will need the following file:

New blank Word document

**You will save your document as
2N_Calendar_Firstname_Lastname**

Create a memo that contains a MEMO heading from you to the employees of GHS Law Partners listing the scheduled holidays and breaks during the upcoming calendar year. Include a date and subject header. Use the memo style you practiced in Chapter 1.

Write one or two introductory sentences indicating that this is the list of holiday and conference dates that were proposed by the GHS Personnel Committee, and agreed to by the law firm's senior partners. Consult a calendar and create a list of official holiday names and dates for next year that will be easy for the reader to scan. Add two one-week business law conferences that will be hosted by the law firm. Save the memo as **2N_Calendar_Firstname_Lastname** and then create a footer that contains the file name. Submit the document as directed.

 End **You have completed Project 2N** ⎯⎯⎯⎯⎯⎯⎯⎯⎯⎯⎯

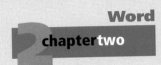

Word

chapter two | **Problem Solving**

Project 20 — APA Research Paper

In this project, you will construct a solution by applying any combination of the skills you practiced from the Objectives in Projects 2A and 2B.

For Project 20, you will need the following file:

w02O_APA_Research_Paper
2B_Law_Overview

You will save your document as
2O_APA_Research_Paper_Firstname_Lastname

In Project 2B, you edited a research paper and formatted it in the Modern Language Association (MLA) style. The other major style guide used for research papers is published by the American Psychological Association (APA). APA guidelines differ in several ways; for example, formats for margins, titles, headers, and references differ from the MLA style.

This research paper should conform to APA style. Information on the APA style is available on the Web in many places—search for *APA research paper guidelines* to find sites that provide assistance using the APA style. There are *two approaches* you can use to complete this project:

1. Open the **w02O_APA_Research_Paper** file, save the file as **2O_APA_Research_Paper_Firstname_Lastname** and follow the steps in Project 2B, formatting the text in APA format instead of MLA format.

OR

2. Open your **2B_Law_Overview** file from your Word Chapter 2 folder, save the file as **2O_APA_Research_Paper_Firstname_Lastname** and change the formatting to conform to APA guidelines.

Add the file name to the footer, and submit the document as directed.

 End You have completed Project 20 ——————————

Outcomes-Based Assessments

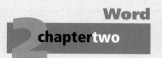
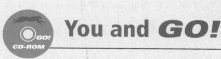
You and GO!

Project 2P — You and GO!

In this project, you will construct a solution by applying any combination of the skills you practiced from the Objectives in Projects 2A and 2B.

From My Computer, navigate to the student files that accompany this textbook. In the folder **04_you_and_go_pg87_102**, locate and open the folder for this chapter. Open and print the instructions for this project, which are provided to you in Adobe PDF format. Follow the instructions to create a flyer for a family reunion.

End **You have completed Project 2P** ————————————

GO! with Help

Project 2Q — GO! with Help

When you insert a file name in a footer, or insert the date or time in a footer or in a document, you are adding a field to that document. Fields have other uses in Microsoft Word, including calculations, indexes, and reference lists. In this project, you will explore inserting and editing fields.

1 **Start** Word. Click the **Microsoft Office Word Help** button.

2 Click the **Search arrow**, and then click **All Word**. In the **Type words to search for** box, type **field** and then click **Search**.

3 In the **Word Help** window, from the **Results** list, click **Insert and format field codes in Word**. Read the introduction, and then click the links to learn more about fields, how to insert a field, and how to edit a field.

4 If you want to print a copy of the information, click the **Print** button at the top of the **Word Help** window.

5 **Close** the Help window, and then **Close** Word.

End **You have completed Project 2Q** ————————————

Outcomes-Based Assessments

Group Business Running Case

Project 2R—Group Business Running Case

In this project, you will apply the skills you practiced from all the Objectives in Projects 2A and 2B.

Your instructor may assign this group case project to your class. If your instructor assigns this project, he or she will provide you with information and instructions to work as part of a group. The group will apply the skills gained thus far to help the Bell Orchid Hotel Group achieve its business goals.

 You have completed Project 2R ——————————

3 chapter three

Using Graphics and Tables

OBJECTIVES

At the end of this chapter you will be able to:

1. Insert and Format Graphics
2. Set Tab Stops
3. Insert and Modify Text Boxes and Shapes

OUTCOMES

Mastering these objectives will enable you to:

PROJECT 3A
Insert and Modify Graphics and Set Tab Stops

---

4. Create a Table
5. Format a Table

PROJECT 3B
Create and Format a Table

Memories Old and New

Professional and amateur artists, photographers, students, teachers, and hobbyists have made Memories Old and New one of Chicago's fastest-growing art, photography, and scrapbooking supply stores. The store carries a wide variety of premium art supplies, such as paints, pencils, cutting and framing tools, and brushes. Local photographers are featured in the small gallery, and photo restoration services and supplies are offered. For scrapbookers, the store provides the newest and highest quality books, papers, stencils, and archival supplies. Scrapbooking classes are also offered to assist customers in adding principles of art and design to their projects.

Using Graphics, Tabs, and Tables

Adding graphics enhances the effectiveness of documents. Digital images, such as those obtained from a digital camera or a scanner, can be inserted into documents. You can also create your own graphic objects by using the Drawing tools.

Tab stops are useful to horizontally align text and numbers. Use the Tab key to move text to specific tab stop locations on a line. You can set and specify the alignment of your own tab locations.

Tables present data effectively and efficiently. The row and column format of a table makes information easy to find and easy to read. A table also helps the reader organize and categorize the data. The Word table feature has tools that enable you to format text, change column width and row height, and change the background for all or part of a table. You can also modify the table's borders and lines.

Project 3A Photography Flyer

In Activities 3.1 through 3.14, you will create a flyer for an upcoming exhibition of photographs by photographer Annie DeCesare at Memories Old and New. Your completed document will look similar to Figure 3.1.

For Project 3A, you will need the following files:

New blank Word document
w03A_Photography_Flyer
w03A_Machine
w03A_Ore_Cart

You will save your document as
3A_Photography_Flyer_Firstname_Lastname

Figure 3.1
Project 3A—Photography Flyer

Objective 1
Insert and Format Graphics

Graphics include pictures, clip art, charts, and *drawing objects*—shapes, diagrams, lines, and so on. You can modify drawing objects by changing their color, pattern, border, and other characteristics.

Graphics that you insert in a document convey information in a way that plain text cannot. For additional visual interest, you can convert text to an attractive graphic format; add, resize, move and format pictures; and provide an attractive finishing touch to your document by adding a page border.

Activity 3.1 Formatting Text Using WordArt

You can insert decorative text with the *WordArt* command, and then edit and format the decorative text. WordArt is a gallery of text styles with which you can create decorative effects, such as shadowed or mirrored text.

> ## Note — Comparing Your Screen with the Figures in This Textbook
>
> Your screen will match the figures shown in this textbook if you set your screen resolution to 1024 x 768. At other resolutions, your screen will closely resemble, but not match, the figures shown. To view your screen's resolution, on the Windows desktop, right-click in a blank area, click Properties, and then click the Settings tab.

1 **Start** Word. Display formatting marks and rulers, and be sure the left and right edges of the document display. Display the **Page Setup** dialog box, and then set the **Top**, **Bottom**, **Left**, and **Right** margins to **.75"**. On the **Home tab**, in the **Styles group**, click the **No Spacing** button.

2 Type **Annie DeCesare, Photographer** and then press Enter. Notice that the last name is flagged as a spelling error. Right-click the name *DeCesare*, and then from the shortcut menu, click **Ignore All**.

3 Without selecting the paragraph mark at the end, select the first line of text. Click the **Insert tab**. In the **Text group**, click the **WordArt** button to display the WordArt gallery, as shown in Figure 3.2. In the second row, point to the second shape and notice the ScreenTip *WordArt style 8*.

Figure 3.2

WordArt button

WordArt style 8

Selected text

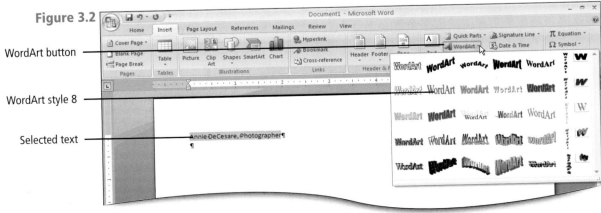

4 From the **WordArt gallery**, click **WordArt style 8**, and then compare your screen with Figure 3.3.

The Edit WordArt Text dialog box displays, and the selected text displays in the Text box. The default font size is 36 point.

Figure 3.3

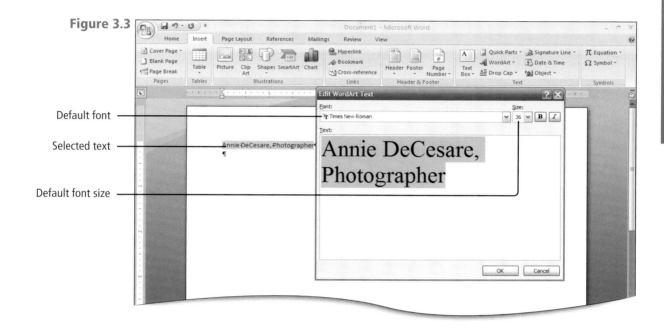

Default font

Selected text

Default font size

5 At the bottom of the **Edit WordArt Text** dialog box, click **OK**.

The WordArt contextual tools display on the Ribbon. A WordArt is a type of drawing object, and thus it displays *sizing handles*—small dark boxes with which you can manually change the size of the WordArt.

6 On the **Format tab**, in the **Size group**, click the **Shape Height button up spin arrow** as necessary to change the height of the WordArt to **0.7"**. Click the **Shape Width button up spin arrow** as necessary to change the width of the WordArt to **6.5"**.

7 In the **Arrange group**, click the **Position** button, and then under **With Text Wrapping**, in the top row of the gallery, point to the second button to display the ScreenTip *Position in Top Center with Square Text Wrapping*, and then click the button. Compare your screen with Figure 3.4.

The WordArt is centered between the left and right margins, and positioned at the top of the document. The *anchor* symbol indicates the paragraph to which the WordArt is attached and the sizing handles change to circles. Additionally, a *rotate handle* to rotate the WordArt and an *adjustment handle* to drag parts of the object into various positions display.

Figure 3.4

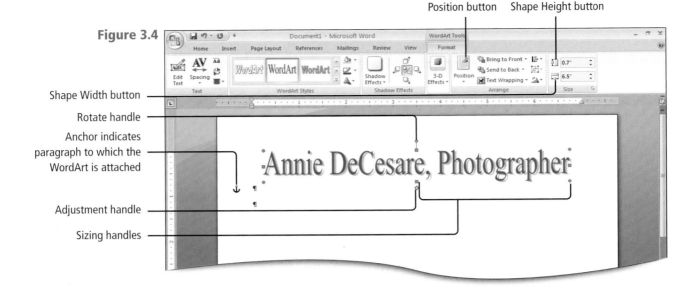

Position button   Shape Height button

Shape Width button

Rotate handle

Anchor indicates paragraph to which the WordArt is attached

Adjustment handle

Sizing handles

Annie DeCesare, Photographer

8 From the **Office** menu, display the **Save As** dialog box, click the **Save in button arrow**, and then navigate to the location where you are saving your files. In the upper right corner of the dialog box, click the **Create New Folder** button. In the **Name** box, name the new folder **Word Chapter 3** and then click **OK**.

9 In the **File name** box, delete the existing text. Using your own name, type **3A_Photography_Flyer_Firstname_Lastname** and then click **Save**.

Activity 3.2 Inserting Pictures from Files

1 Press Ctrl + End to move to the last line of the document and deselect the WordArt title. Click the **Insert tab**. In the **Text group**, click the **Object button arrow**, and then click **Text from File**. Locate and **Insert** the file **w03A_Photography_Flyer**. Delete the blank line at the end of the document.

2 If necessary, right-click any words flagged with wavy red underlines—words not recognized by the Office dictionary—and ignore all suggested corrections.

3 In the paragraph beginning *Memories Old and New*, click to position the insertion point at the beginning of the paragraph. On the **Insert tab**, in the **Illustrations group**, click the **Picture** button. Locate and **Insert** the file **w03A_Ore_Cart**. Compare your screen with Figure 3.5.

The Picture contextual tools display on the Ribbon. The Picture command places the picture in the document as an ***inline object***; that is, the picture is positioned directly in the text at the insertion point, just like a character in a sentence.

Sizing handles display around the edges of the picture; recall that sizing handles enable you to manually resize a graphic. The corner sizing handles are round and resize the graphic proportionally.

The square sizing handles in the center of each border are used to resize a graphic vertically or horizontally only, which will distort the graphic. A rotate handle, with which you can rotate the graphic to any angle, displays above the top center sizing handle.

Figure 3.5

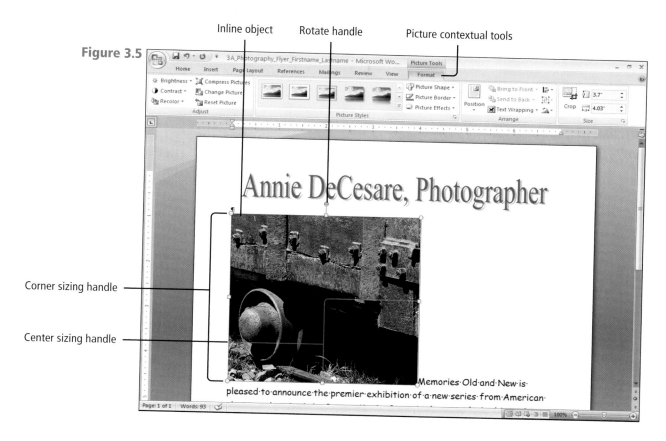

Inline object   Rotate handle   Picture contextual tools

Corner sizing handle

Center sizing handle

4 **Save** 💾 your document.

Activity 3.3 Resizing a Graphic

In this activity, you will adjust the size of the picture.

1 If necessary, click to select the ore cart picture.

2 On the lower edge of the picture, point to the center square sizing handle until the ↕ pointer displays. Drag upward until the bottom of the graphic is aligned at approximately **2 inches on the vertical ruler**. Notice that the height of the graphic has been resized, but the width remains unchanged, as shown in Figure 3.6.

Figure 3.6

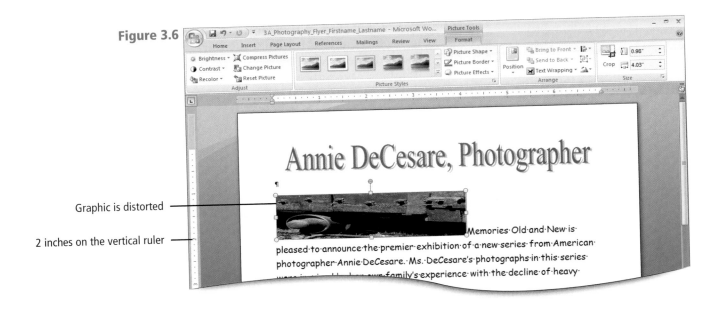

Graphic is distorted

2 inches on the vertical ruler

3 On the **Format tab**, in the **Adjust group**, click the **Reset Picture** button to return the graphic to its original size. Alternatively, on the Quick Access Toolbar, click the **Undo** button.

4 At the lower left corner of the picture, point to the round sizing handle until the pointer displays. Drag upward and to the right until the bottom of the graphic is aligned at approximately **2 inches on the vertical ruler**. Notice that the graphic is resized proportionally and not distorted.

5 In the **Adjust group**, click the **Reset Picture** button.

6 On the **Format tab**, in the **Size group**, click the **Shape Height button spin box down arrow** as necessary to change the height of the picture to **2"**. Notice that the picture resizes proportionally—the width adjusts as you change the height—as shown in Figure 3.7.

Figure 3.7

Graphic is 2 inches high and proportionally resized

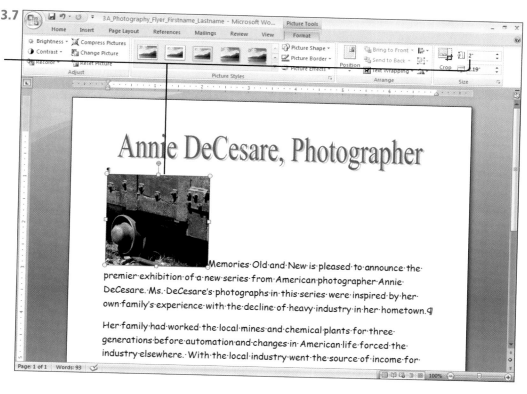

7 **Save** 💾 your document.

Activity 3.4 Wrapping Text Around a Graphic

Graphics inserted as inline objects are treated like characters in a sentence, which can result in unattractive spacing. You can change an inline object to a *floating object*—a graphic that can be moved independently of the surrounding text characters.

1 Be sure the **ore cart** picture is still selected. On the **Format tab**, in the **Arrange group**, click the **Text Wrapping** button to display the **Text Wrapping gallery**, as shown in Figure 3.8.

Text wrapping refers to the manner in which text displays around an object.

Figure 3.8

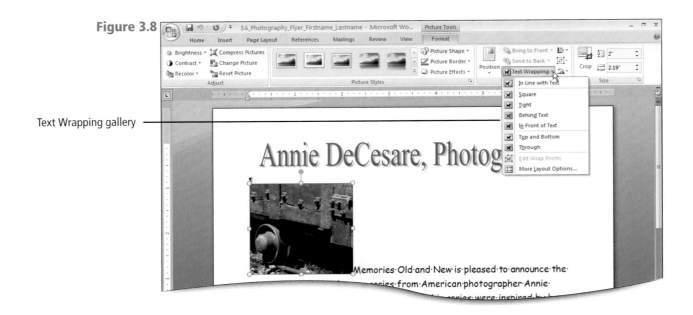

Text Wrapping gallery

2 From the **Text Wrapping gallery**, click **Square** to wrap the text around the graphic.

Square text wrapping insures that all four edges of the surrounding text will be straight. To wrap text around an irregularly shaped object use the Tight text wrap format.

3 Click to the left of *M* in the first line of the paragraph that begins *Memories Old and New* to deselect the picture. Click the **Insert tab**. In the **Illustrations group**, click the **Picture** button. Locate and **Insert** the file **w03A_Machine**.

Recall that pictures are inserted as inline objects; the inserted picture becomes the first character in the paragraph and the text is forced down in the document.

4 On the **Format tab**, in the **Arrange group**, click the **Text Wrapping** button, and then click **Square**. Compare your screen with Figure 3.9.

The text wraps around the second graphic.

Figure 3.9

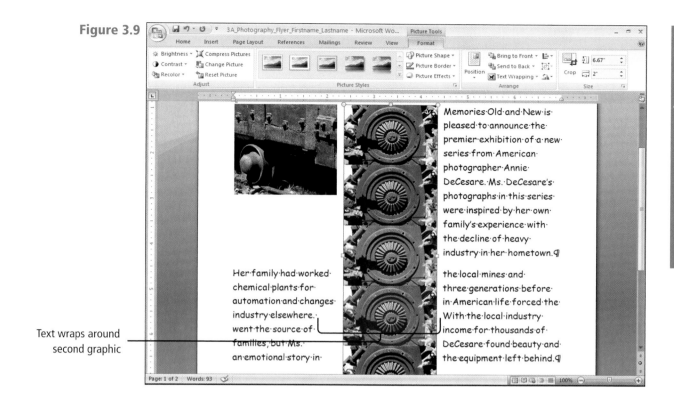

Text wraps around second graphic

5 **Save** 🖫 your document.

Activity 3.5 Moving a Graphic

1 Point anywhere in the **machine** picture to display the 🔁 pointer.

The Move pointer displays a four-way arrow, and enables you to move a floating object anywhere in the document.

2 Drag the picture to the right until the right edge of the picture is aligned at approximately **7 inches on the horizontal ruler**, and then drag downward until the top edge of the picture is aligned at approximately **2.5 inches on the vertical ruler**. Compare your screen with Figure 3.10.

Figure 3.10

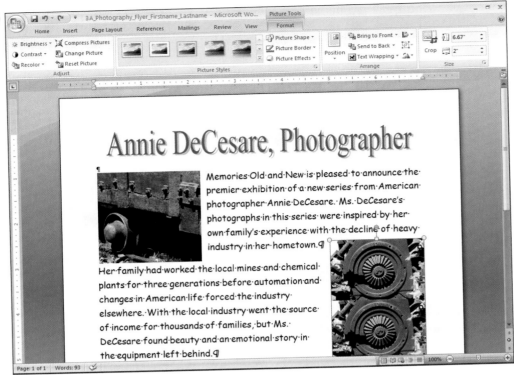

3 Move the graphics as necessary to align them in approximately the same position as those shown in Figure 3.10.

Recall that you can nudge an object in small increments—hold down Ctrl, and then press the arrow keys.

4 **Save** your document.

Activity 3.6 Applying Picture Styles

In this activity, you will use Pictures styles to add sophisticated visual features to your pictures.

1 Click to select the **ore cart** picture. Click the **Format tab**, and then in the **Picture Styles group**, point to the first picture style—**Simple Frame, White**. Notice that Live Preview displays the graphic as it would look if you clicked the *Simple Frame, White* button.

2 Point to the other picture styles to view some of the styles that are available.

3 To the right of the **Picture Styles gallery**, click the **More** button to display more available styles. Click the **Beveled Matte, White** button—the second button in the first row. Click anywhere in the document to deselect the picture, and then compare your screen with Figure 3.11.

Figure 3.11

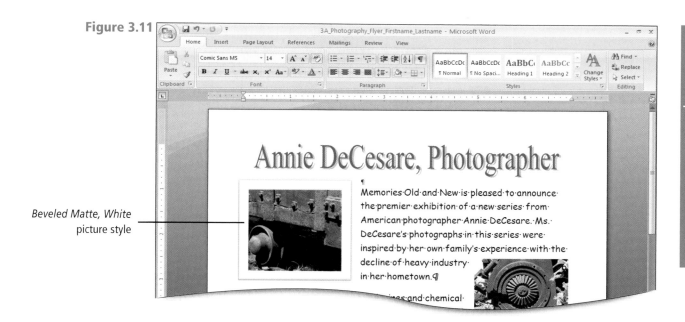

Beveled Matte, White picture style

4 Click to select the **w03A_Machine** picture. On the **Format tab**, in the **Picture Styles group**, click the **Picture Effects** button. In the **Picture Effects gallery**, point to **Soft Edges**, and then click **25 Point**. Click anywhere in the document to deselect the picture, and then compare your screen with Figure 3.12.

The Soft Edges feature fades the edges of the picture. The number of points you choose determines how far the fade goes inward from the edges of the picture. Recall that a point is 1/72 of an inch.

Figure 3.12

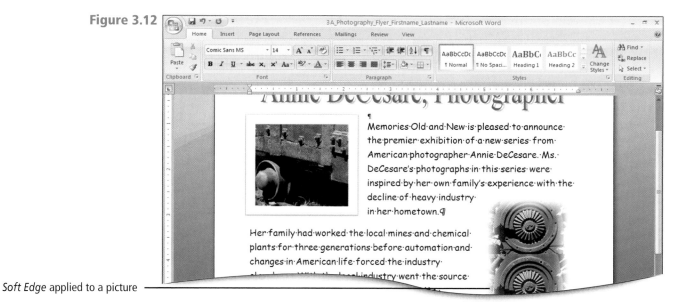

Soft Edge applied to a picture

5 From the **Office** menu, point to the **Print button arrow**, and then click **Print Preview** to see how your pictures are arranged in relation to your text.

6 On the **Print Preview tab**, in the **Preview group**, click the **Close Print Preview** button.

7 **Save** 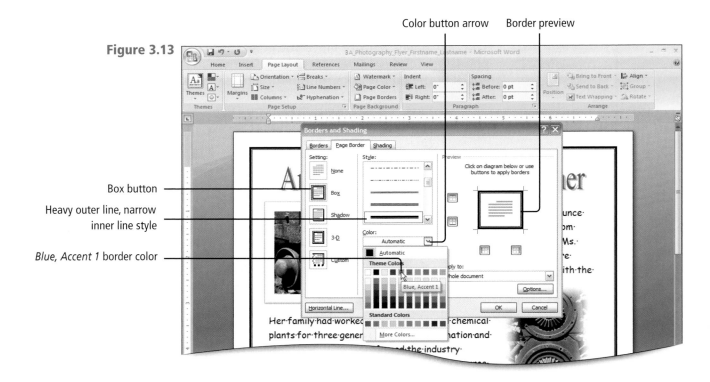 your document.

Activity 3.7 Adding a Page Border

Page borders frame a page and help to focus the information on the page.

1 Click the **Page Layout tab**, and then in the **Page Background group**, click the **Page Borders** button.

2 In the displayed **Borders and Shading** dialog box, be sure the **Page Border tab** is selected. Under **Setting**, click **Box**. Under **Style**, scroll down the list about a third of the way and click the heavy outer line with the thin inner line—check the **Preview** area to be sure the heavier line is the nearest to the edges of the page. Click the **Color arrow**, and then under **Theme Colors**, in the first row of colors, point to the fifth button—**Blue, Accent 1**. Compare your screen with Figure 3.13.

Color button arrow   Border preview

Figure 3.13

Box button

Heavy outer line, narrow inner line style

Blue, Accent 1 border color

3 Click **Blue, Accent 1**, and then at the bottom of the **Borders and Shading** dialog box, click **OK**. Notice that a border is placed around the page, about 0.5 inch in from the edge of the page, as shown in Figure 3.14.

Page border

Figure 3.14

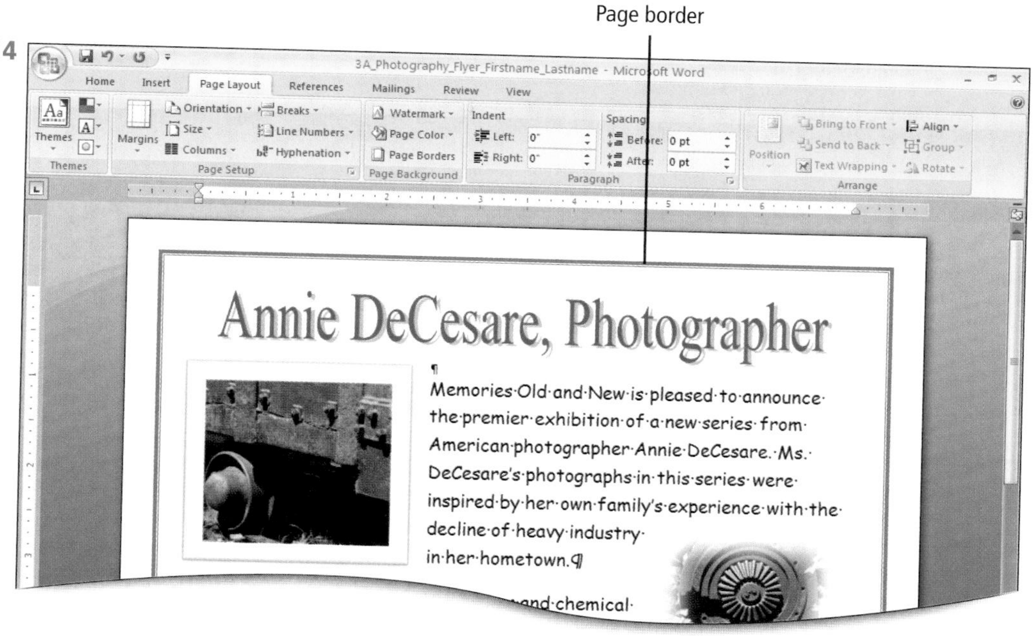

4 **Save** your document.

Objective 2
Set Tab Stops

Tab stops mark specific locations on a line of text; use tab stops to indent and align text. Press the [Tab] key to move to tab stops. In this activity, you will use tab stops to format a short table of dates and times that the photography exhibit will be open.

Activity 3.8 Setting Tab Stops and Using Click and Type

1 Take a moment to study the tab alignment options shown in Figure 3.15 and described in the table in Figure 3.16.

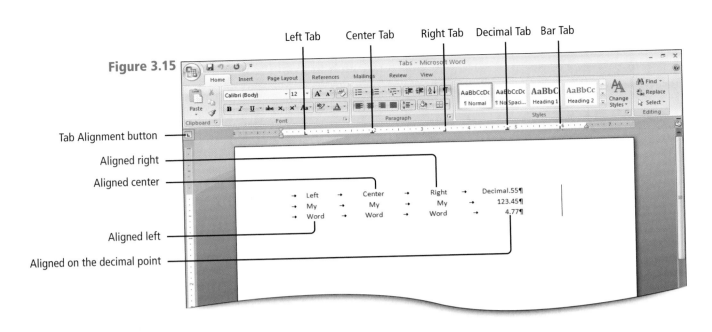

Figure 3.15

Left Tab   Center Tab   Right Tab   Decimal Tab   Bar Tab

Tab Alignment button
Aligned right
Aligned center
Aligned left
Aligned on the decimal point

Tab Alignment Options

Type	Tab Alignment Button Displays This Marker	Description
Left		Text is left aligned at the tab stop and extends to the right.
Center		Text is centered around the tab stop.
Right		Text is right aligned at the tab stop and extends to the left.
Decimal		The decimal point aligns at the tab stop.
Bar		A vertical bar is inserted in the document at the tab stop.
First Line Indent		Indents the first line of a paragraph.
Hanging Indent		Indents all lines but the first in a paragraph.

Figure 3.16

2 Scroll to the bottom of the document. Position the pointer below the text and near the left margin to display the pointer, as shown in Figure 3.17.

This is one of several **click and type pointers**; a series of pointers with lines attached in various arrangements to depict alignment. In this instance, the pointer displays left aligned horizontal lines. The shape attached to the pointer indicates what type of formatting will be applied if you double-click at the pointer location on the page.

Figure 3.17

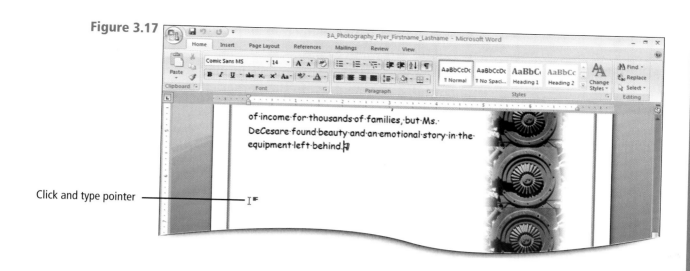

Click and type pointer

What if the click and type pointer does not display?

If you move the pointer around the blank area of the document and do not see the click and type pointer, click the Office button, and then click Word Options. Click Advanced, and then under *Editing options,* select the *Enable click and type* check box.

3 With the pointer displayed at approximately **7 inches on the vertical ruler** and at the left margin, double-click to place the insertion point.

The insertion point is positioned at the left margin. If you double-click the click and type pointer near the horizontal middle of the document, a center tab is inserted and the insertion point is positioned at the center of the line. If you double-click near the right margin, a right tab is inserted.

Because you cannot type in a blank area of a document without some type of paragraph formatting in place, click and type inserts blank lines quickly without having to press Enter numerous times—and uses the formatting of the nearest paragraph above.

4 To the left of the horizontal ruler, point to the **Tab Alignment** button and observe the *Left Tab* ScreenTip. Click the **Tab Alignment** button one time, move the mouse pointer away, and then point to the button again to display the next ScreenTip—*Center Tab.* Repeat this process to cycle through and view the ScreenTip for each of the types of tab stops, and then stop at the **Left Tab** button .

5 Move the pointer into the horizontal ruler, click at **0.5 inch on the horizontal ruler**, and then compare your screen with Figure 3.18.

A left tab stop is inserted on the ruler for the paragraph containing the insertion point. Left tab stops are used when you want the information to align on the left. By default, tab stops are set every half inch, but they do not display on the ruler. When you customize a tab as you did here, the custom tab stop overrides default tab stops that are to the left of the custom tab.

A tab stop is part of a paragraph's format and thus the information about tab stops is stored in the paragraph mark.

Left alignment tab at 0.5 inch

Figure 3.18

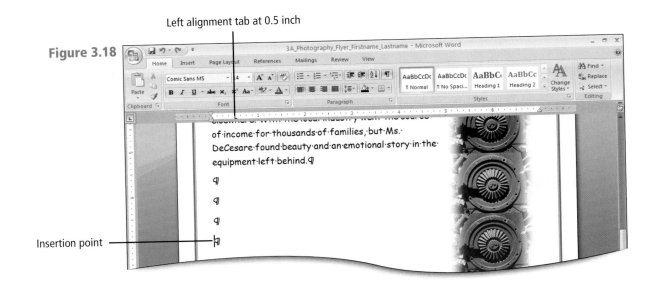

Insertion point

6 Click the **Tab Alignment** button 🔲 two times to display the **Right Tab** button ➡️. Point to **2.25 inches on the horizontal ruler**, and then click one time.

A right tab stop is inserted in the ruler. Right tab stops are used to align information on the right. As you type, the text will extend to the left of the tab stop.

7 Click the **Tab Alignment** button 🔲 six times to display the

Center Tab button 🔲. Click at **3.5 inches on the horizontal ruler**, and then click again at **4.5 inches**. Compare your screen with Figure 3.19.

Two center tab stops display on the ruler. Center tab stops are used when you want to center information over a particular point.

Figure 3.19

Center alignment tabs

Right alignment tab

Tabs set only for the line in
which the insertion point
is positioned

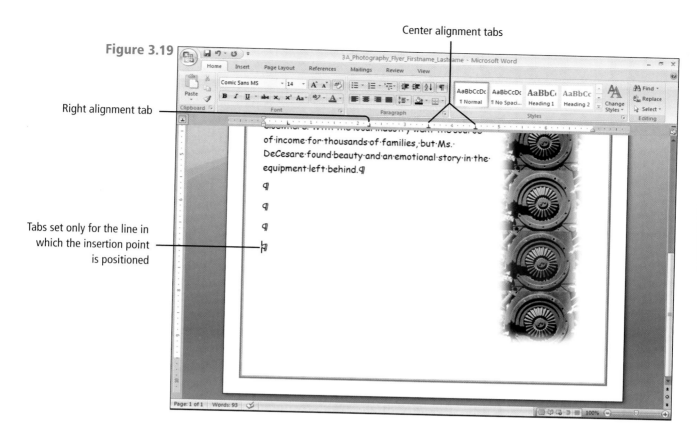

of·income·for·thousands·of·families,·but·Ms.·
DeCesare·found·beauty·and·an·emotional·story·in·the·
equipment·left·behind.¶

8 **Save** your document.

Activity 3.9 Formatting and Removing Tab Stops

Recall that tab stops are a form of paragraph formatting, and thus, the
information about them is stored in the paragraph mark to which they
were applied.

1 On the **Home tab**, in the **Paragraph group**, click the **Dialog Box
Launcher** . If necessary, change the spacing *After* to 0, and the
Line Spacing to Single, and then click **OK**. Move the pointer to any of
the tab markers on the ruler, double-click to display the **Tab** dialog
box, and then compare your screen with Figure 3.20.

The tabs you just added to the ruler display under *Tab stop position*.
In the Tabs dialog box, you have more flexibility in adding, removing,
and formatting tab stops.

Figure 3.20

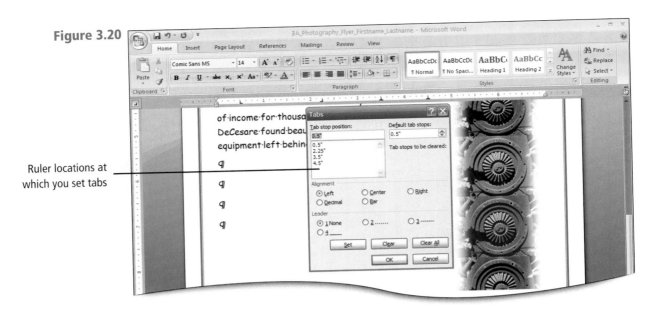

Ruler locations at which you set tabs

2 Under **Tab stop position**, click **3.5"**, and then at the bottom of the **Tabs** dialog box, click the **Clear** button.

The cleared tab stop will be removed when you click OK to close the dialog box.

3 If necessary, under **Tab stop position**, click **4.5"**. Under **Alignment**, click the **Right** option button. Under **Leader**, click the **2** option button. Near the bottom of the **Tabs** dialog box, click **Set**, and then compare your screen with Figure 3.21.

The Set button saves the change. The tab stop at 4.5 inches is changed to a right tab, and now has a *leader character*. Leader characters create a solid, dotted, or dashed line that fills the space used by a tab character. A leader character draws the reader's eyes across the page from one item to the next. Later, when you move to this location with the Tab key, a row of dots will display. When the character used for the leader is a dot, this is commonly referred to as a *dot leader*.

Figure 3.21

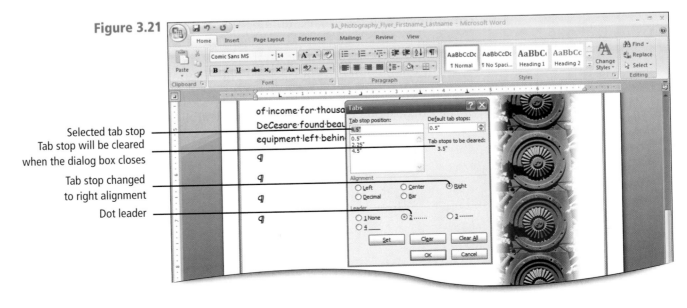

Selected tab stop
Tab stop will be cleared when the dialog box closes

Tab stop changed to right alignment

Dot leader

4 At the bottom of the **Tabs** dialog box, click **OK**, and notice that the changes are reflected in the ruler.

5 **Save** 💾 your document.

Activity 3.10 Using Tab Stops To Enter Text

1 With the insertion point positioned at the beginning of the line with the new tab stops, Press ⎆Tab, and then compare your screen with Figure 3.22.

The insertion point moves to the first tab stop, which is at 0.5 inch, and the nonprinting character for a tab—a small arrow—displays.

Figure 3.22

Tab stop

Nonprinting character indicating that the Tab key was pressed

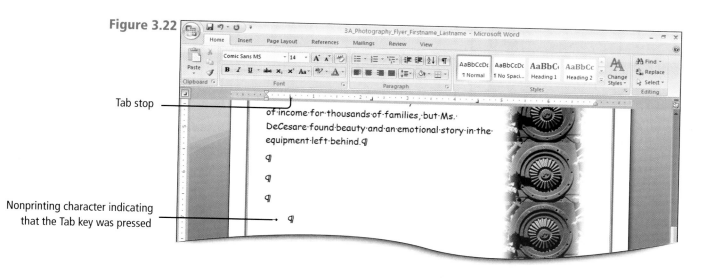

2 Type **Sunday** and notice that the left edge of the text remains aligned with the tab stop. Press ⎆Tab, and then type **July 30**

The insertion point moves to the tab stop at 2.25 inches, and the text moves to the left of the right tab mark. With a right tab, the right edge of the text remains aligned with the tab mark, and the text moves to the left.

3 Press ⎆Tab, and then type **Daytime 9 - 6** and press ⏎Enter. Compare your screen with Figure 3.23. Notice that when you press ⏎Enter, the formatting of the previous paragraph, including tab stops, is copied to the new paragraph.

A dot leader is added, helping to draw your eyes across the page to the next item.

Tab stops included in new paragraph

Figure 3.23

Dot leader

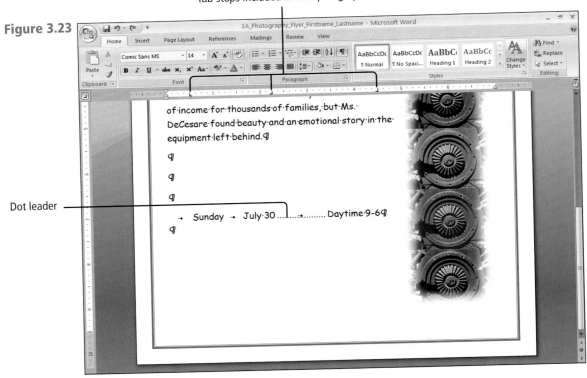

Note — Using Dot Leaders

It is sometimes tempting to hold down ⬚ on the keyboard to create a string of dots. This is not a good idea for several reasons. The periods, because of proportional spacing, may be spaced differently between rows. The periods will not line up, and, most importantly, the column on the right side of the string of periods may look lined up on the screen, but will be crooked when printed. If you need a string of dots, always insert a tab stop with a dot leader.

4 Type the following—first pressing ⎄Tab⎄ one time to indent each line— to complete the exhibition schedule, click **Save**, and then compare your screen with Figure 3.24:

| Monday | July 31 | Evening 6 - 9 |
| Tuesday | August 1 | All Day 9 - 9 |

Depending on your Word settings, when you type a hyphen surrounded by spaces, the dash may change to a longer dash.

Figure 3.24

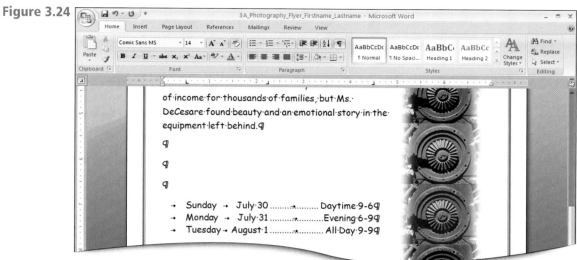

Another Way —— **To Create an Indent**

If the items in the first column of a list are indented the same amount, using a left-aligned tab, you can save keystrokes by indenting the paragraph instead. You can do this on the Home tab by clicking the Increase Indent button in the Paragraph group, or by using the Paragraph dialog box. You can also drag the Left Indent marker from the left side of the ruler and position it at the desired location. When you are finished typing the list, you can drag the marker back to the left margin position. When you use an indent at the beginning of the paragraph for a tabbed list, you do not have to press Tab before you type the first item in the list.

Activity 3.11 Moving Tab Stops

If you are not satisfied with the arrangement of your text after setting tab stops, you can reposition the text by moving tab stops.

1 Move the pointer into the left margin area, to the left of the first line of tabbed text. When the pointer displays, drag downward to select the three lines of tabbed text.

By selecting all of the paragraphs, changes you make to the tabs will be made to the tab stops in all three rows simultaneously.

2 With the three lines of tabbed text selected, point to the horizontal ruler and position the pointer so the tip of the pointer arrow is touching the **0.5-inch tab stop**. When you see the *Left Tab* ScreenTip, drag the tab stop mark to the left to **0.25 inch on the ruler**, and then release the mouse button.

3 In the horizontal ruler, point to the **4.5-inch tab stop** until you see the *Right Tab* ScreenTip. Drag the tab stop mark to the right to **4.75 inches on the horizontal ruler**. Compare your screen with Figure 3.25.

Tab stop at 0.25 inch   Tab stop at 4.75 inches

Figure 3.25

Selected text moved

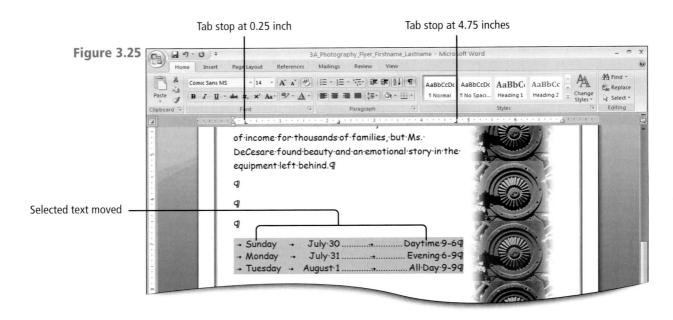

4 Click anywhere to deselect the text, and then **Save** 🖫 your document.

Objective 3
Insert and Modify Text Boxes and Shapes

In addition to graphics such as pictures and clipart, you can also add predefined shapes and text boxes to documents. A ***drawing canvas*** is provided as a work area for complex drawings; however, when inserting and formatting simple drawing objects, it is more convenient to leave the drawing canvas off.

Activity 3.12 Inserting a Text Box

A **text box** is a movable, resizable container for text or graphics. A text box is useful to give text a different orientation from other text in the document because a text box can be placed anywhere in the document in the manner of a floating object. A text box can be placed outside the document margin, resized, and moved.

1 Scroll down to display the bottom edge of the document. Click the **Insert tab**, and then from the **Text group**, click the **Text Box** button. At the bottom of the **Text Box gallery**, click **Draw Text Box**.

2 Position the ⊞ pointer at approximately **5.5 inches on the vertical ruler** and **0 inches on the horizontal ruler,** and then drag down and to the right to create a text box approximately **1.25 inches** high and **4 inches** wide. Then in the **Size group**, use the spin arrows to set the height and width precisely at **1.3** and **4** inches. Compare your screen with Figure 3.26. If you are not satisfied with your result, click the Undo button and try again.

Figure 3.26

Height of text box

Width of text box

Text box

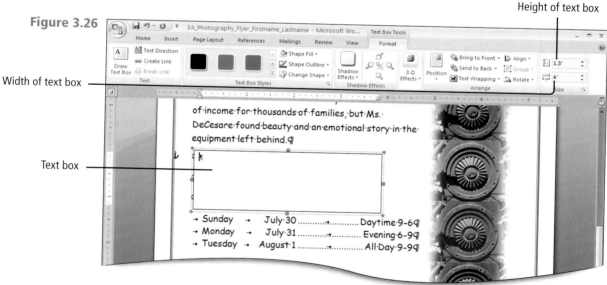

3 With the insertion point displayed in the text box, click the **Home tab**. If necessary, in the **Styles group**, click the **No Spacing** style to remove the space *After* paragraphs and change the line spacing to *Single*. Include the quotation marks as you type **"Annie DeCesare finds beauty where no one else thinks to look!"** and press Enter. Type **Chicago Arts Review**

4 In the text box, select the quote, including both quotation marks and the paragraph mark. On the Mini toolbar, click the **Font Size button arrow** 12 ▾, and then click **16**. With the text still selected, on the Mini toolbar, click the **Bold** button **B**.

5 In the text box, select **Chicago Arts Review**, and then on the Mini toolbar, click the **Italic** button I. In the **Paragraph group**, click the **Align Text Right** button. Click anywhere outside the text box, and then compare your screen with Figure 3.27.

Figure 3.27

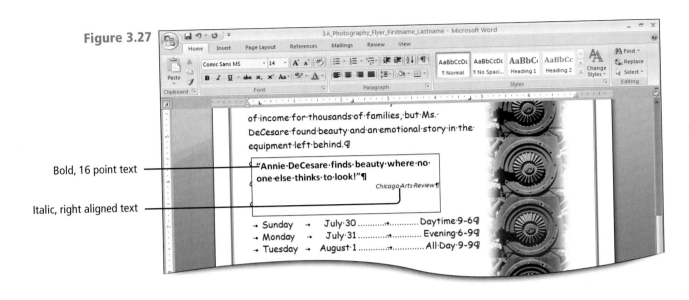

Bold, 16 point text

Italic, right aligned text

6 **Save** your document.

Activity 3.13 Moving, Resizing, and Formatting a Text Box

1 Click anywhere inside the text box so that it is selected and the text inside is deselected. Click the **Format tab**. In the **Size group**, change the **Height** of the text box to **0.9"** and the **Width** to **3.5"**.

2 Point to one of the text box borders until the pointer displays. Drag the text box down and to the right until it is centered in the same approximate location as the one shown in Figure 3.28. Position the right edge at approximately **4.5 inches on the horizontal ruler**, and the top edge at approximately **5.75 inches on the vertical ruler**.

Because the rulers show the size of the text box, but not the location of the document relative to the rest of the document, you will likely need to deselect the text box, check the position, and then move the box again.

Figure 3.28

Word | chapter 3

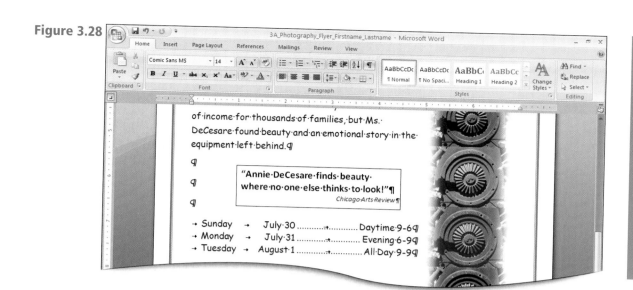

3 Click to select the text box. On the **Format tab**, in the **Shadow Effects group**, click the **Shadow Effects** button. In the **Shadow Effects gallery**, under **Drop Shadow**, in the first row, point to the fourth shadow—**Shadow Style 4**. Notice that Live Preview displays a shadow around the text box, as shown in Figure 3.29.

Because the default shadow on both the WordArt and the oval picture are down and to the right, it is good design to create a text box shadow in the same direction.

Shadow Effects gallery

Figure 3.29

Shadow Style 4

Live Preview
displays the shadow

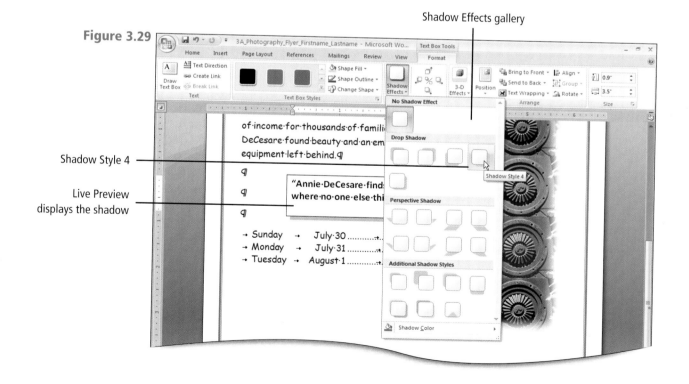

4 Click **Shadow Style 4**. In the **Shadow Effects group**, click the **Nudge Shadow Left** button 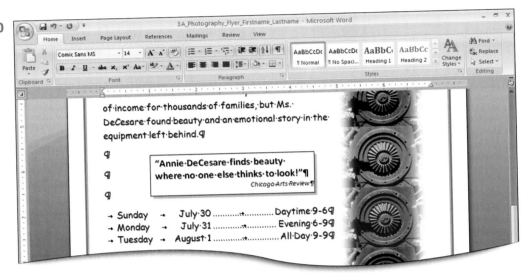 two times, and then click the **Nudge Shadow Up** button two times. Click anywhere in the document to deselect the text box, and then compare your screen with Figure 3.30.

The Nudge Shadow buttons enable you to apply precision formatting to your shadows; in this instance you made the shadow more subtle and in proportion to the shadows on the other two graphics on the page.

Figure 3.30

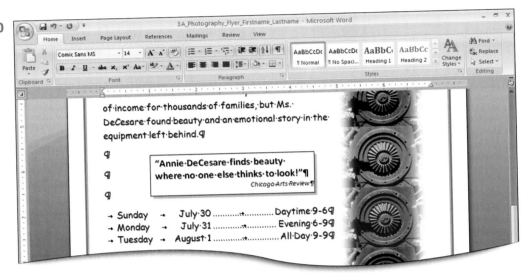

5 **Save** your document.

Activity 3.14 Inserting a Predefined Shape

Shapes are predefined drawing objects such as stars, banners, arrows, and callouts. More than 150 predefined Shapes are available with Word. In this activity, you will insert a banner shape into which you will add the address and phone number for Memories Old and New.

1 Click the **Insert tab**, and then from the **Illustrations group**, click the **Shapes** button to display the **Shapes gallery**, as shown in Figure 3.31.

Figure 3.31

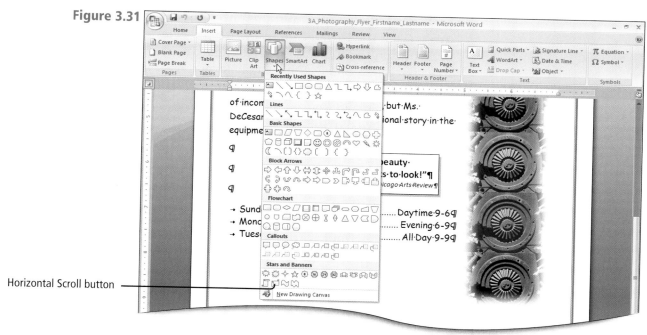

Horizontal Scroll button

2 From the displayed **Shapes gallery**, under **Stars and Banners**, in the second row, click the second shape—**Horizontal Scroll**.

3 Move the ⊞ pointer near the left margin at approximately **8 inches on the vertical ruler**. Using both the horizontal and vertical rulers as guides, drag down and to the right to create a banner approximately **1 inch** high and **3 inches** wide. Then in the **Size group**, use the **Shape Height** and **Shape Width spin box arrows** to set the **Height** precisely to **1.2"** and the **Width** to **3"**. Compare your screen with Figure 3.32. If you are not satisfied with your result, click the Undo button ↺ and begin again.

Figure 3.32

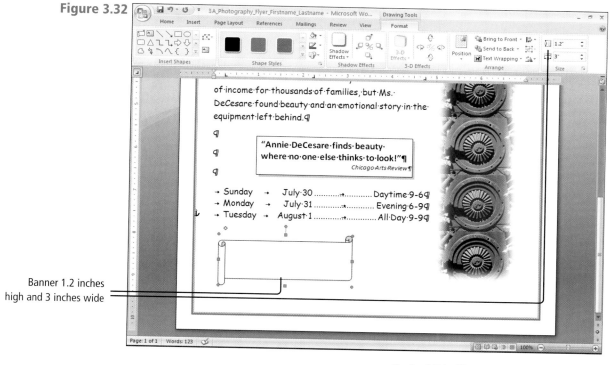

Banner 1.2 inches
high and 3 inches wide

4 Right-click the banner, and then from the shortcut menu, click **Add Text**. Click the **Home tab**. In the **Styles group**, click the **No Spacing** style button to remove the space *After* paragraphs and change the line spacing to *Single*. Type the following text, pressing Enter after each line except the last line:

Memories Old and New

220 West Randolph Street

Chicago, IL 60601

312-555-0023

5 In the banner, select the first line of text—*Memories Old and New*— and then on the Mini toolbar, click the **Bold** button. Click the **Font Size button arrow** 12, and then click **14**.

6 Select all of the text in the banner, and then on the Mini toolbar, click the **Center** button. If necessary, adjust the height of the banner to accommodate the text.

7 Click the **Format tab**, and then in the **Shadow Effects group**, click the **Shadow Effects** button. Use the technique you practiced with the text box to apply **Shadow Style 4**. Nudge the shadow **Up** two times and to the **Left** two times. Click outside of the banner to deselect it, and then compare your screen with Figure 3.33.

Figure 3.33

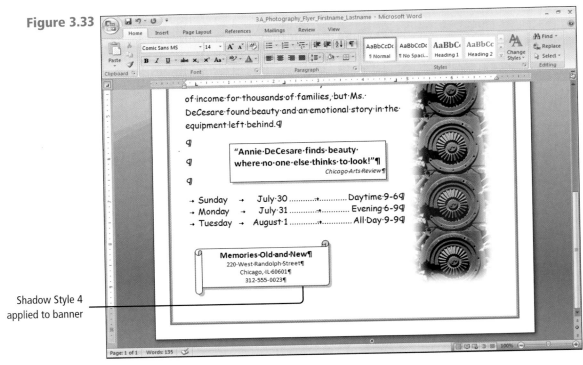

Shadow Style 4 applied to banner

8 Add the file name to the footer, and then display the **Print Preview** window to make a final check of your document. Submit the document as directed.

9 **Close** your document, and then **Exit** Word.

End You have completed Project 3A

Project 3B Price List

In Activities 3.15 through 3.24, you will create a price list for framed and unframed prints by photographer Annie DeCesare at Memories Old and New. Your completed document will look similar to Figure 3.34.

For Project 3B, you will need the following file:

w03B_Price_List

You will save your document as
3B_Price_List_Firstname_Lastname

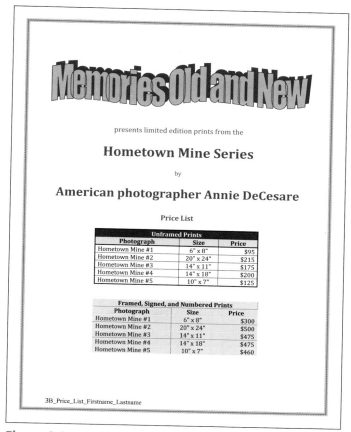

Figure 3.34
Project 3B—Price List

Objective 4
Create a Table

The table feature in Word has largely replaced the use of tabs because of its flexibility and ease of use. *Tables* consist of rows and columns and are used to organize data. You can create an empty table, and then fill in the boxes, which are called *cells*. You can also convert existing text into a table if the text is properly formatted.

To adjust a table, you can add rows or columns and change the height of rows and the width of columns. You can format the text and numbers in the cells and the backgrounds and borders of cells.

Activity 3.15 Creating and Entering Text into a Table

1 **Start** Word, and display the formatting marks and rulers. From your student files, locate and open the file **w03B_Price_List**. From the **Office** menu , click **Save As**, and then navigate to your **Word Chapter 3** folder. In the **File name** box, type **3B_Price_List_Firstname_Lastname** and press Enter.

2 In the three blank lines under *Price List*, click in the middle blank line. Click the **Insert tab**, and then in the **Tables group**, click the **Table** button. In the **Table gallery**, move the pointer to the second square in the fifth row of squares. Notice that the size of the table—2 × 5—displays at the top of the gallery, as shown in Figure 3.35.

Figure 3.35

Table size

Preview of inserted table

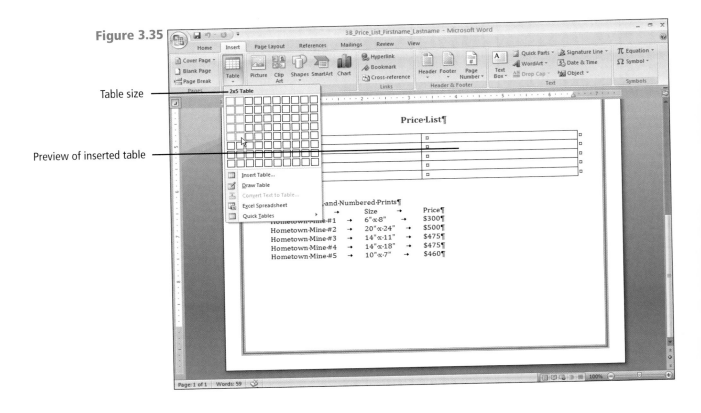

3 Click the mouse button, and then compare your screen with Figure 3.36.

A table with five rows and two columns is created at the insertion point location, and the insertion point is placed in the upper left cell. The table fills the width of the page, from the left margin to the right margin. Table Tools display on the Ribbon, and add two contextual tabs—*Design* and *Layout*.

Design tab   Layout tab

Figure 3.36

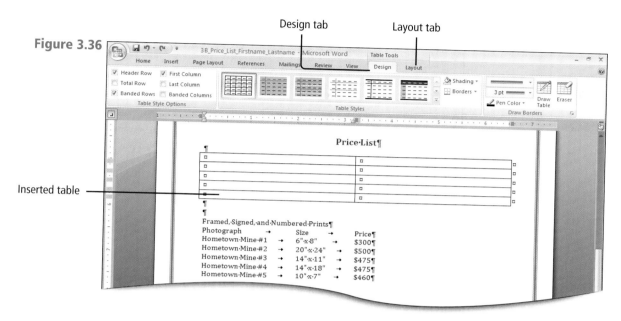

Inserted table

4 Type **Unframed Prints** and then press Tab to move to the second cell in the first row of the table.

The Tab key is used to move from cell to cell in a Word table. The natural tendency is to press Enter to move from one cell to the next. In a table, however, pressing Enter creates another line in the same cell, similar to the way you add a new line in a document. If you press Enter by mistake, you can remove the extra line by pressing ←Bksp.

5 Press Tab again to move to the first cell in the second row. Type **Hometown Mine #1** and press Tab. Type **$95** and press Tab.

6 Type the following to complete the table, but do not press Tab after the last item. Compare your screen with Figure 3.37.

Hometown Mine #2	**$215**
Hometown Mine #3	**$175**
Hometown Mine #4	**$200**

Figure 3.37

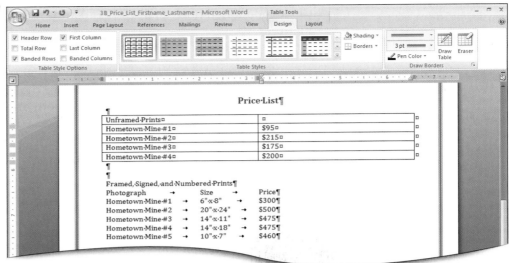

More Knowledge

Navigating in a Table

You can move to a previous cell in a table by pressing ⇧Shift + Tab. This action selects the contents of the previous cell. The selection moves back one cell at a time each time you press Tab while holding down ⇧Shift. You can also use the up or down arrow keys to move up or down a column. The left and right arrow keys, however, move the insertion point one character at a time within a cell.

Activity 3.16 Adding a Row to a Table

You can add rows to the beginning, middle, or end of a table.

1 With the insertion point in the last cell in the table, press Tab to add a new row to the bottom of the table. Type **Hometown Mine #5** and press Tab. Type **$125** and then, in the second row of the table, click anywhere to position the insertion point.

2 Click the **Layout tab**, and then in the **Rows & Columns group**, click the **Insert Above** button to insert a new row.

3 In the new row, type **Photograph** and press Tab.

When the entire row is selected, text that you type automatically begins in the cell on the left.

4 Type **Price** and then compare your table with Figure 3.38.

Figure 3.38

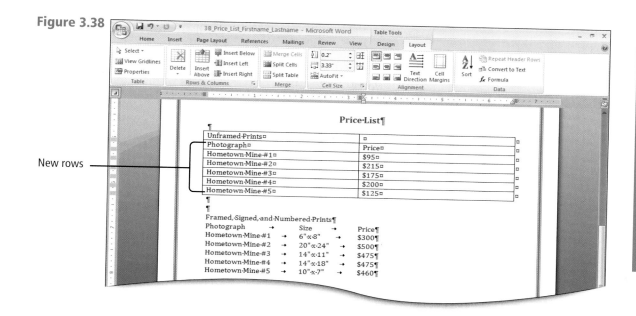

New rows

5 **Save** your document.

Activity 3.17 Changing the Width of a Table Column

1 In the first column of the table, move the pointer to the right boundary until the pointer displays, as shown in Figure 3.39.

Figure 3.39

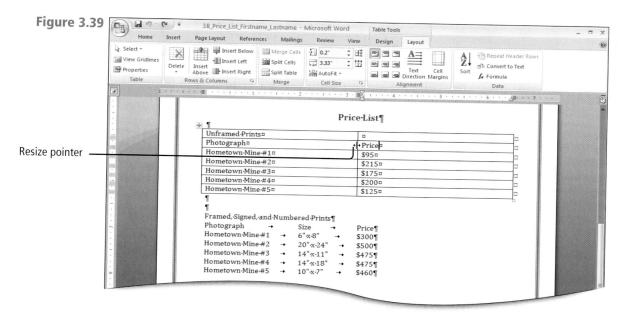

Resize pointer

2 Drag the boundary to the left until the first column's right boundary aligns at approximately **2 inches on the horizontal ruler**. Use the horizontal ruler as a guide. If only one row resizes, click the Undo button and begin again.

3 Drag the right boundary of the second column to **2.75 inches on the horizontal ruler**. Compare your table with Figure 3.40.

4 **Save** your document.

Figure 3.40

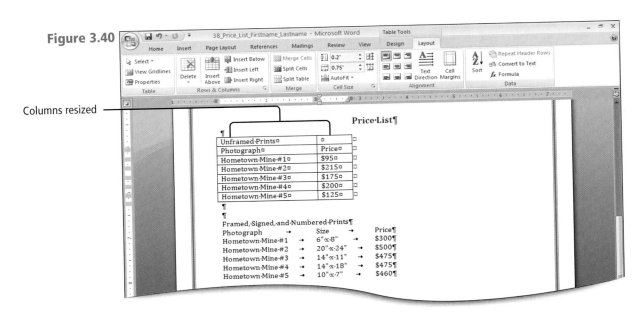

Columns resized

Activity 3.18 Adding a Column to a Table

You can add a column to a Word table in a manner similar to inserting a row.

1 In the first column of the table, click anywhere in the column to position the insertion point. On the **Layout tab**, in the **Rows & Columns group**, click the **Insert Right** button.

2 In the new column, click to place the insertion point in the second row. Type **Size** and press ↓.

3 Complete the column with the following information. The text may be too wide for the cell, and wrap to the next line in the same cell.

6" x 8"
20" x 24"
14" x 11"
14" x 18"
10" x 7"

Note — Using Straight Quotes versus Curly Quotes

When you type a quotation mark in Word, one of two characters displays—a straight quote (") or a curly quote ("). **Straight quotes** consist of two straight lines, and are used for such things as inch marks. **Curly quotes**, which have rounded sides and are more decorative, are often used for quotations. By default, when you type a quotation mark, Word's AutoCorrect feature automatically changes it to a curly quote. However, many computers will have this AutoCorrect feature turned off. The single quote mark works the same way, where a curly single quotation mark is used as an apostrophe for contractions and possessive words, while the straight single quotation mark is used for foot marks in measurements.

4 Drag the right boundary of the third column to **4 inches on the horizontal ruler**.

If you try to resize the middle column first, the right border of the table will remain fixed, thus decreasing the width of the column on the right.

5 Drag the right boundary of the second column to **3 inches on the horizontal ruler**, and then compare your screen with Figure 3.41.

Figure 3.41

New column inserted

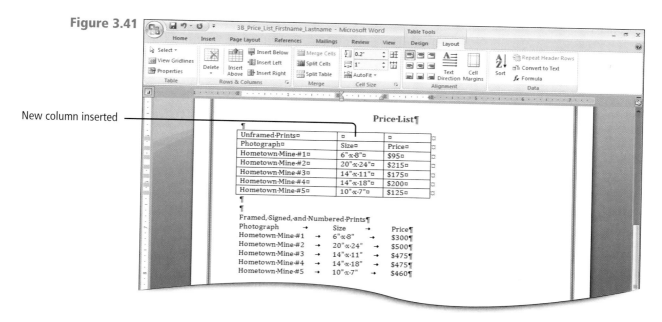

6 **Save** your document.

More Knowledge

Using Tabs in Tables

You can add tabs to a table column; doing so lets you indent items within a table cell. The easiest way to add a tab is to click on the ruler to set the location within a column. Then you can drag the tab stop indicator to change the location of the tab within the column or add the hanging indent marker so multiple lines in a list are evenly indented. To move to the tabbed location within the cell—and not to the next cell—press [Ctrl] + [Tab].

Activity 3.19 Converting Text to Tables

The Insert Table feature is useful if you are beginning a new table, but Word also provides a tool that enables you to convert existing text into a table. The text must be marked using *separator characters*—usually tabs or commas that separate the text in each line. When you convert text to a table, you can have Word optimize the column widths at the same time. You can also add blank rows or columns, if needed.

1 Scroll as necessary to view the lower portion of the document. In the block of text at the end of the document, beginning with *Framed* and continuing to the end of the document, notice the tab marks indicating where the [Tab] key was pressed, as shown in Figure 3.42.

Tab marks can act as separator characters for the purpose of converting text to a table.

Figure 3.42

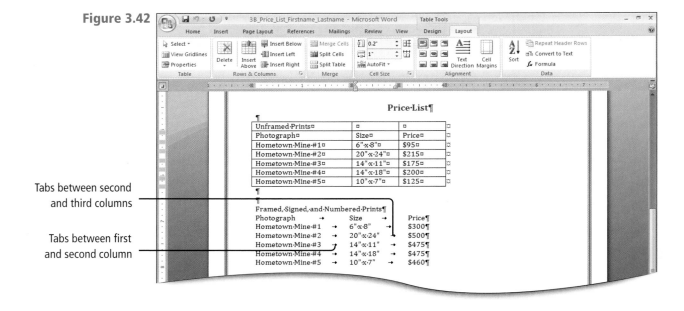

Tabs between second and third columns

Tabs between first and second column

2 Click to position the insertion point to the left of the word *Framed*, hold down ⇧Shift, and then click at the end of the last line, after *$460*. Be sure you include the paragraph mark to the right of *$460*.

3 With the text selected, click the **Insert tab**. In the **Tables group**, click the **Table** button, and then click **Convert Text to Table**. In the displayed **Convert Text to Table** dialog box, under **Table size**, click the **Number of columns up spin arrow** to change the number of columns to **3**. Then, under **AutoFit behavior**, click the **AutoFit to contents** option button.

The AutoFit to contents option instructs Word to evaluate the contents of the columns and choose appropriate column widths for each column.

4 Under **Separate text at**, click the **Tabs** option button. Compare your dialog box with Figure 3.43.

Figure 3.43

Three columns

Column width adjusts to fit contents

Separator type

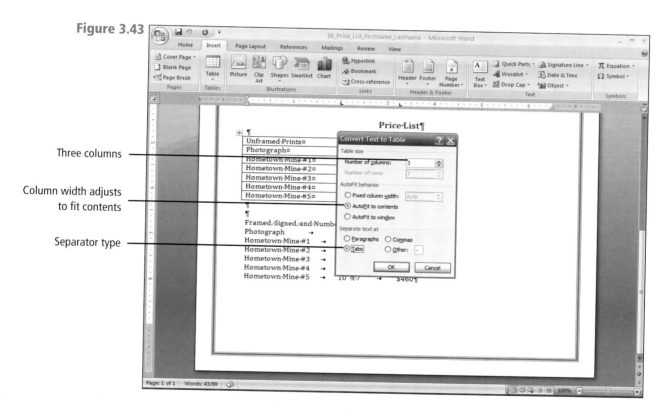

5 At the bottom of the **Convert Text to Table** dialog box, click **OK**.

Click anywhere in the document to deselect the table. **Save** 🖫 your document, and then compare your table with Figure 3.44.

The columns are set to the width of the widest item in each column.

Three columns—column widths adjust to fit contents

Figure 3.44

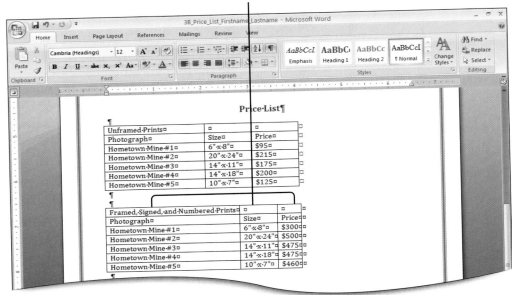

More Knowledge
Formatting Text for Easy Conversion to a Table

To format text that will eventually be converted into a table, separate the columns using a separator character. Tabs and commas are the most commonly used separators, but you can specify a number of different marks, including dashes, dollar signs, or colons. Word will not recognize a mixture of tabs and commas as separators in the same block of text. Use only one kind of separator between each column item.

Objective 5
Format a Table

You can format tables to make them more attractive and easier to read. When you type numbers, for example, they line up on the left of a column instead of on the right. With Word's formatting tools, you can shade cells, format the table borders and grid, align text, and center the table between the document margins. All of these features make a table more inviting to the reader.

Activity 3.20 Formatting Text in Cells and Shading Cells

1 In the upper table, click anywhere in the cell containing the word *Photograph*, hold down the left mouse button, and then drag to the right to select all three cells in the second row. On the Mini toolbar, click the **Bold** button **B**, and then click the **Center** button **≡**. Compare your screen with Figure 3.45.

Figure 3.45

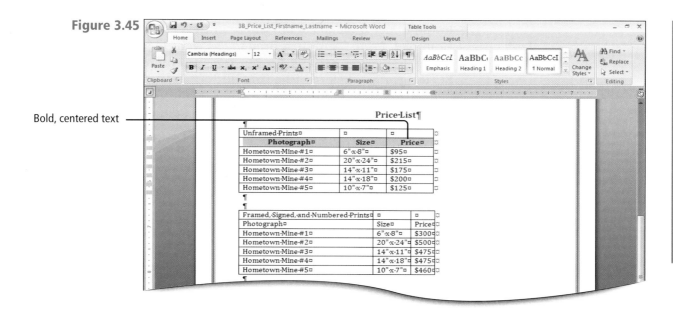

Bold, centered text

2 In the second column, click in the cell containing *6" × 8"* and then drag down to select the third cell through the seventh cell. On the Mini toolbar, click the **Center** button.

3 In the third column, click in the cell containing *$95* and then drag down to select the third cell through the seventh cell. On the **Home tab**, in the **Paragraph group**, click the **Align Text Right** button. Compare your screen with Figure 3.46.

Centered text   Right-aligned text

Figure 3.46

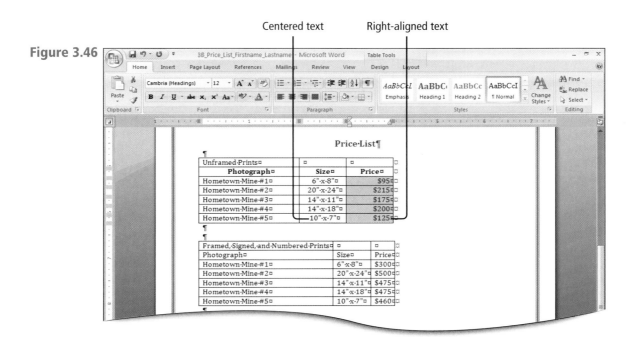

4 In the upper table, click anywhere in the cell containing the *Unframed Prints*, and then drag to the right to select all three cells in the first row. Click the **Design tab**, and then in the **Table Styles group**, click the **Shading** button. In the **Shading gallery**, near the bottom of the fourth column, point to—but do not click—**Dark Blue, Text 2, Darker 25%**. Compare your screen with Figure 3.47.

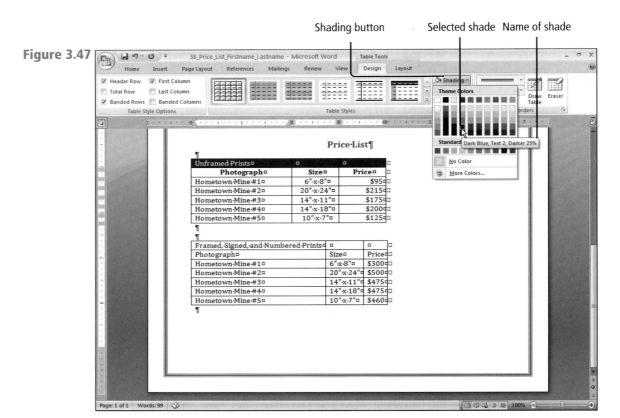

Figure 3.47

5 Click to apply **Dark Blue, Text 2, Darker 25%**.

6 In the upper table, click anywhere in the cell containing the word *Photograph*, and then drag to the right to select all three cells in the second row. On the **Design tab**, in the **Table Styles group**, click the **Shading** button. In the **Shading gallery**, click **Dark Blue, Text 2, Lighter 80%**—the second button in the fourth column. Click anywhere in the table to deselect the cells, and then compare your screen with Figure 3.48.

Figure 3.48

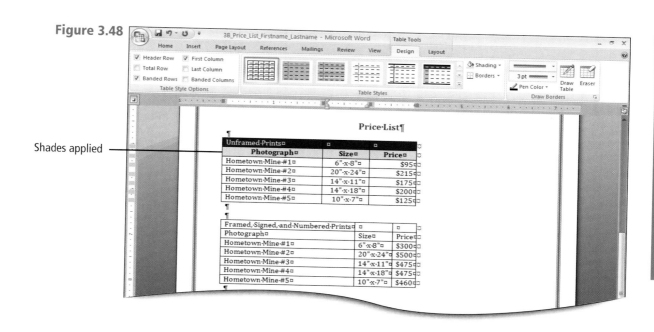

Shades applied

7 Save the document.

Activity 3.21 Changing the Table Border

You can modify or remove the border from an entire table, a selected cell, or individual boundaries of a cell.

1 In the upper table, click anywhere in the cell containing the word *Photograph*, and then drag to the right to select all three cells in the second row.

2 On the **Design tab**, in the **Table Styles group**, click the **Borders button arrow**, and then click **Borders and Shading**. Alternatively, right-click anywhere in the selected cells and click Borders and Shading.

3 In the displayed **Borders and Shading** dialog box, under **Setting**, click the **Custom** button. Click the **Width button arrow**, and then click **1 1/2 pt**. In the **Preview** area, click the bottom border of the preview diagram. Notice that the Preview area displays a bottom border that is heavier than the side or top borders, as shown in Figure 3.49.

The Custom setting enables you to change the characteristics of individual border lines, rather than change all of the borders at one time.

Figure 3.49

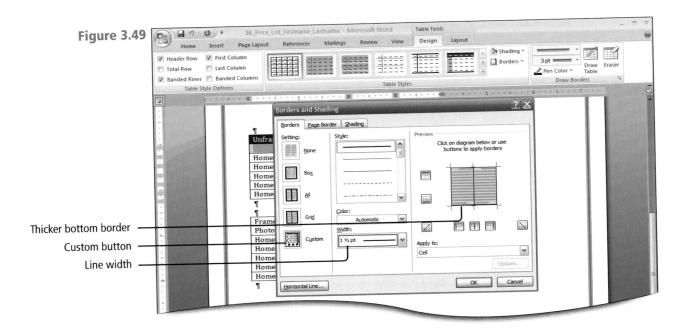

Thicker bottom border
Custom button
Line width

4 Click **OK** to change the bottom border of the selected cells. Click anywhere in the upper table, and then click the **Layout tab**. In the **Table group**, click the **Select** button, and then click **Select Table**.

5 Click the **Design tab**, and then in the **Table Styles group**, click the **Borders** button. In the displayed **Borders and Shading** dialog box, under **Setting**, click the **Custom** button, if necessary. Click the **Width button arrow**, and then click **1 1/2 pt**. In the **Preview** area, click the four outside borders, and then click **OK**.

6 Click anywhere in the document to deselect the table, and then compare your screen with Figure 3.50.

Figure 3.50

Thicker cell border

Thicker outside border

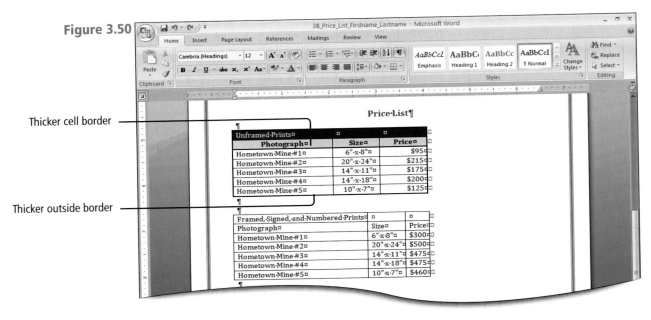

7 Save the document.

Activity 3.22 Centering a Table

1 Click anywhere in the upper table, and then click the **Layout tab**. In the **Table group**, click the **Select** button, and then click **Select Table**.

2 Click the **Home tab**, and then in the **Paragraph group**, click the **Center** button ▤.

Another Way

To Center a Table

You can center a table without selecting the table first. Right-click anywhere in the table, and then, from the shortcut menu, click Table Properties. In the Table Properties dialog box, on the Table tab, under Alignment, click Center. The Table Properties dialog box also enables you to wrap text around a table the way you wrap text around a graphic.

3 Click anywhere in the document to deselect the table, and then compare your screen with Figure 3.51.

Table centered horizontally on the page

Figure 3.51

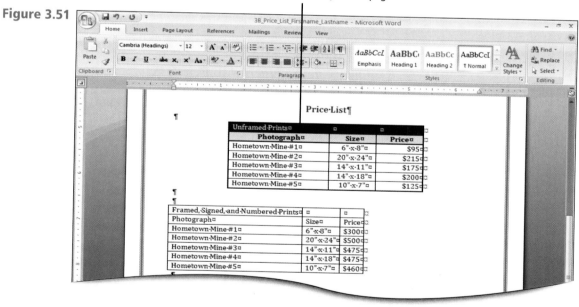

4 **Save** ▤ the document.

Activity 3.23 Merging Cells

The title of a table typically spans two or more columns. In this activity, you will merge cells so that you can position the table title across the columns.

1 In the upper table, click anywhere in the cell containing the word *Unframed Prints*, and then drag to the right to select all three cells in the first row.

2 Click the **Layout tab**, and then in the **Merge group**, click the **Merge Cells** button.

The cells are merged, and the borders between the top row of cells are removed.

3 Select the text in the top cell—**Unframed Prints**. On the Mini toolbar, click the **Bold** button **B**, and then click the **Center** button **≡**.

Another Way

To Align Text in a Table

You can use shortcut menus to align text in a table. Right-click the cell, point to Cell Alignment from the shortcut menu, and then click the alignment style you want from the Cell Alignment palette that displays. You can choose from both vertical and horizontal cell alignment options using the Cell Alignment gallery.

---

4 Click anywhere in the document to deselect the table, and then compare your screen with Figure 3.52.

Text is merged across three cells

Figure 3.52

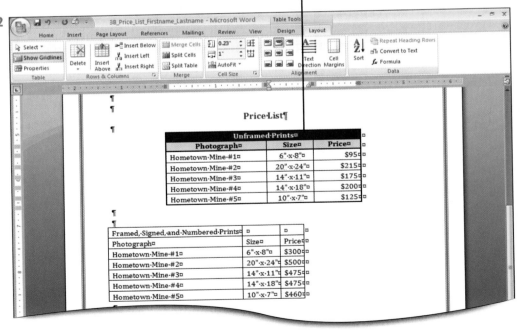

5 **Save** 🖫 the document.

Activity 3.24 Applying a Predefined Format to a Table

Word includes a number of built-in table formats with which you can quickly give your table a professional design. This is accomplished by applying a **Table Style**—a predefined set of formatting characteristics, including font, alignment, and cell shading.

1 In the lower table, click anywhere to position the insertion point within the table—you need not select the entire table to use Table Styles.

2 Click the **Design tab**. In the **Table Styles group**, point to the second Table Style—**Table 3D effects 1** and notice that Live Preview displays the table the way it would look if you clicked that style, as shown in Figure 3.53.

Live Preview displays the table style   Table 3D effects 1 style

Figure 3.53

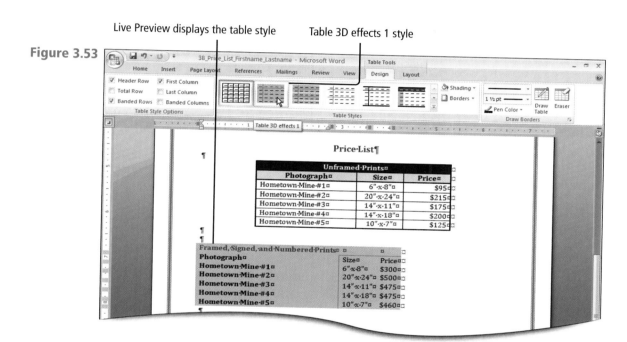

3 In the **Table Styles group**, click the **More** button ⬇. Scroll down to view the available table styles, and then point to several of the styles in the gallery. Click anywhere in the document to close the gallery.

4 In the **Table Styles group**, point to the third style—**Table 3D effects 2**—and click to apply the style. Click the **Layout tab**, and then in the **Table group**, click the **Select** button, and then click **Select Table**.

5 Click the **Design tab**. In the **Table Styles group**, click the **Shading** button, and then in the second row, click the fourth color—**Dark Blue, Text 2, Lighter 80%**.

6 Right-click the table, and then from the shortcut menu, click **Table Properties**. In the displayed **Table Properties** dialog box, on the **Table tab**, under **Alignment**, click **Center**.

7 Drag the dialog box so that you can see most of the lower table. In the **Table Properties** dialog box, click the **Column tab**. Under **Size**, click the **Next Column** button to select the first column, as shown in Figure 3.54.

First column is highlighted   Next Column button

Figure 3.54

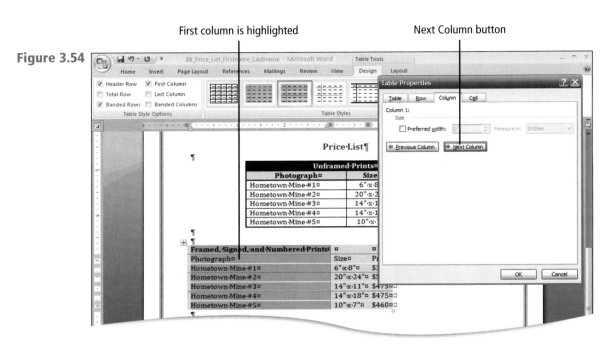

8 With the first column selected, select the **Preferred width** check box, select the text in the **Preferred width** box, type **2** and then click the **Next Column** button. Use the same procedure to make the second and third columns **1.1** inches wide, and then click **OK**.

9 Point to the first cell of the top row and drag to the right to select all three cells. Click the **Layout tab**. In the **Merge group**, click the **Merge Cells** button. In the **Alignment group**, click the **Align Center** button ▦.

10 In the second row of the table, select all three cells, and then on the Mini toolbar, click the **Bold** button **B**, and then click the **Center** button ▤.

11 In the second column, click in the cell containing *6″ × 8″*, and then drag down to select the third cell through the seventh cell. On the Mini toolbar, click the **Center** button ▤.

12 In the third column, click in the cell containing *$300*, and then drag down to select the third cell through the seventh cell. Click the **Home tab**, and then in the **Paragraph group**, click the **Align Text Right**

button 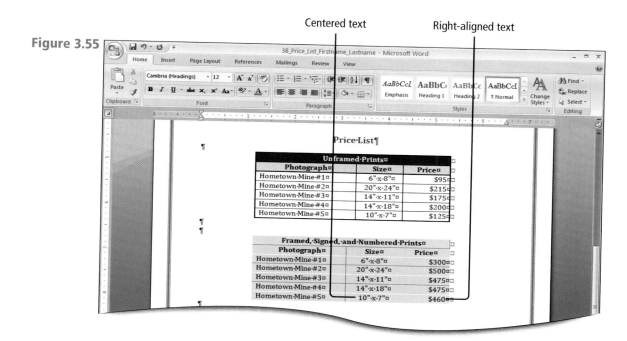. Click anywhere in the document to deselect the cells, and then compare your screen with Figure 3.55.

Centered text   Right-aligned text

Figure 3.55

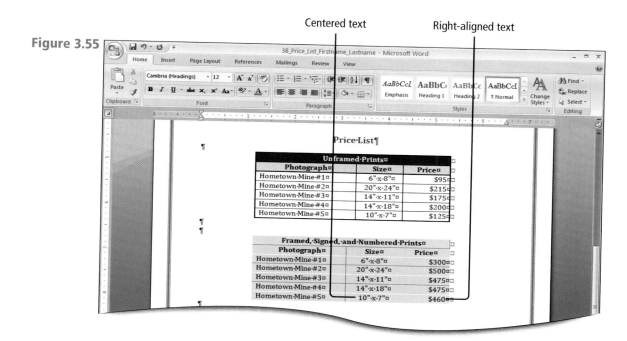

13 Add the file name to the footer, and then **Save** 🖫 your document. Submit the document as directed.

14 **Close** Your document, and then **Exit** Word.

End **You have completed Project 3B** ————————————

There's More You Can Do!

From My Computer, navigate to the student files that accompany this textbook. In the folder **02_theres_more_you_can_do_pg1_36**, locate and open the folder for this chapter. Open and print the instructions for this project, which are provided to you in Adobe PDF format.

Try IT!—Create a Chart

In this Try IT! exercise, you will insert a chart into a Word document.

Content-Based Assessments

Summary

Many graphic elements can be inserted into a Word document, including clip art, pictures, and basic shapes created with Word's drawing tools. Text can also be converted into a graphic format using WordArt.

An effective way to present information is with a tabbed list or a table. A variety of tabs can be used, such as left-aligned, decimal, centered, or right-aligned. Leader characters, such as a solid, dotted, or dashed line, can be used to fill the space created by using a tab stop.

Tables present information in a format of rows and columns. Tables can be formatted to display the information in a manner that emphasizes certain parts of the table. Text in a table can be formatted using both the Table contextual tools and Table Styles. Existing text can be converted to a table format.

Key Terms

Adjustment handle 177	**Drawing object** 176	**Sizing handle** 177
Anchor 177	**Floating object** 181	**Straight quote** 209
Cell 204	**Graphic** 176	**Tab stop** 187
Click and type pointer 188	**Inline object** 178	**Table** 204
Column chart ....⊙	**Leader character** 192	**Table Style** 219
Curly quote 209	**Pie chart** ....⊙	**Text box** 197
Dot leader 192	**Rotate handle** 177	**Text wrapping** 181
Drawing canvas 196	**Separator character** 210	**WordArt** 176
	Shapes 200	

The ⊙ symbol represents Key Terms found on the Student CD in the 02_theres_more_you_can_do folder for this chapter.

Content-Based Assessments

Matching

Match each term in the second column with its correct definition in the first column by writing the letter of the term on the blank line in front of the correct definition.

_____ **1.** A gallery of text styles with which you can create decorative effects, such as shadowed or mirrored text.

_____ **2.** An object or graphic that can be moved independently of the surrounding text.

_____ **3.** An object or graphic inserted in a document that acts like a character in a sentence.

_____ **4.** Small squares or circles in the corners of a selected graphic with which you can resize the graphic proportionally.

_____ **5.** A movable, resizable container for text or graphics.

_____ **6.** A handle on a selected graphic that can be dragged to rotate the graphic to any angle.

_____ **7.** The symbol that indicates the paragraph to which an object is attached.

_____ **8.** Predefined drawing shapes, such as stars, banners, arrows, and callouts, included with Microsoft Office, and that can be inserted into documents.

_____ **9.** Characters that form a solid, dotted, or dashed line that fills the space used by a tab character.

_____ **10.** A character used to identify column placement in text; usually a tab or a comma.

_____ **11.** A mark on the ruler that indicates the location where the insertion point will be placed when you press the Tab key.

_____ **12.** The text select (I-beam) pointer with various attached shapes that indicate which formatting will be applied when you double-click—such as a left-aligned, centered, or right-aligned tab stop.

_____ **13.** The rectangular box in a table formed by the intersection of a row and column.

_____ **14.** Rows and columns of text or numbers used to organize data and present it effectively.

_____ **15.** A command that applies one of a number of built-in table formats—resulting in a table with a professional design.

A Anchor

B Cell

C Click and type pointer

D Corner sizing handle

E Floating graphic

F Inline object

G Leader characters

H Rotate handle

I Separator character

J Shapes

K Tab stop

L Table

M Table Style

N Text box

O WordArt

Fill in the Blank

Write the correct answer in the space provided.

1. A(n) _____ symbol indicates the paragraph to which an object is attached.

2. When a graphic is selected, _____ _____ display around the edge of the graphic.

3. To align text to the contours of an irregularly shaped graphic, choose _____ Text Wrapping.

4. A banner is an example of a predefined _____ that can be inserted into a document.

5. Tab stops are a form of paragraph formatting and are stored in the _____ mark.

6. The tab alignment option that centers text around a tab stop is the _____ tab.

7. A series of dots following a tab that serve to guide the reader's eyes is known as a dot _____.

8. To move text aligned with tabs, select the text and drag the _____ _____ on the ruler.

9. To move from cell to cell across a table as you enter text, press _____.

10. To create a table in Word, click the _____ button on the Insert tab.

11. When you press Tab with the insertion point in the last cell in a table, a new _____ is added to the table.

12. On the Table Tools Design tab, click the _____ button to add gray or color to a table cell.

13. To set the alignment of a table on a page, display the Table tab of the _____ _____ dialog box.

14. A predefined set of table formatting characteristics, including font, alignment, and cell shading is called a Table _____.

15. To combine two or more cells into one cell, use the _____ _____ button on the Layout tab.

Content-Based Assessments

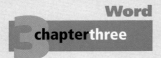
Skills Review

Project 3C—Creative Supplies

In this project, you will apply the skills you practiced from the Objectives in Project 3A.

Objectives: 1. *Insert and Format Graphics;* **2.** *Set Tab Stops;* **3.** *Insert and Modify Text Boxes and Shapes.*

In the following Skills Review, you will create a flyer for Memories Old and New that describes the range of products available at the store. Your completed flyer will look similar to the one shown in Figure 3.56.

For Project 3C, you will need the following files:

New blank Word document
w03C_Art_Supplies
w03C_Supplies

You will save your document as
3C_Creative_Supplies_Firstname_Lastname

Figure 3.56

(Project 3C–Creative Supplies continues on the next page)

Content-Based Assessments

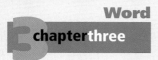

Skills Review

(Project 3C–Creative Supplies continued)

1. **Start** Word and display formatting marks and rulers. From the **Page Layout tab**, display the **Page Setup** dialog box, set the **Top** and **Bottom** margins to **1"**, the **Left** and **Right** margins to **1.25"**, and then click **OK**.

2. Type **Memories Old and New** and then press [Enter] two times. Select the text you just typed, but do not select the paragraph mark. Click the **Insert tab**. In the **Text group**, click the **WordArt** button. From the displayed **WordArt gallery**, in the second row, click the second style—**WordArt style 8**. In the **Edit WordArt Text** dialog box, click the **Font arrow**, scroll as necessary to locate, and then click **Arial**, and then click **OK**.

3. On the **Format tab**, in the **Size group**, click the **Shape Height button up spin arrow** as necessary to change the height of the WordArt to **1"**. Click the **Shape Width button up spin arrow** as necessary to change the width of the WordArt to **6"**. Display the **Save As** dialog box, navigate to your **Word Chapter 3** folder, save the document as **3C_Creative_Supplies_Firstname_Lastname** and then add the file name to the footer.

4. Close the footer area. Press [Ctrl] + [End]. Click the **Insert tab**. From the **Text group**, click the **Object button arrow**, and then click **Text from File**. Locate and insert the file **w03C_Supplies**. In the paragraph beginning *Scrapbookers*, click to position the insertion point at the beginning of the paragraph. In the **Illustrations group**, click the **Picture** button. Locate and insert **w03C_Art_Supplies**.

5. On the **Format tab**, in the **Size group**, click the **Shape Height spin box down arrow** as necessary to change the height of the picture to **1.4"**. With the graphic still

selected, on the **Format tab**, in the **Arrange group**, click the **Text Wrapping** button. From the **Text Wrapping gallery**, click **Square** to wrap the text around the graphic.

6. Point anywhere in the **w03C_Art_Supplies** graphic to display the [pointer icon] pointer, and then drag the graphic up until the top edge of the graphic is aligned with the top edge of the paragraph beginning *Memories Old and New*. Be sure the left side of the graphic is aligned with the left side of the text. With the graphic still selected, on the **Format tab**, in the **Picture Styles group**, click the third picture style—**Metal Frame**. Move the picture as necessary to match Figure 3.56.

7. Click anywhere in the document to deselect the graphic. Click the **Page Layout tab**, and then in the **Page Background group**, click the **Page Borders** button. In the displayed **Borders and Shading** dialog box, under **Setting**, click **Box**. Click the **Color arrow**, and then in the last column of colors, click the fifth button—**Orange, Accent 6, Darker 25%**. Click the **Width arrow**, click **3 pt**, and then click **OK**. **Save** your document.

8. Scroll to position the lower half of the document on your screen. Move the [pointer icon] pointer on your screen to position it at approximately **6.5 inches on the vertical ruler** and at the left margin, double-click to place the insertion point. If necessary, change the **Font** to **Cambria**, and the **Font Size** to **14**. Type **Store Hours** and press [Enter].

9. Be sure the **Tab Alignment** button displays a **Left tab**. Click on **4 inches on the horizontal ruler**. Double-click the tab stop you just added to the ruler. In the

(Project 3C–Creative Supplies continues on the next page)

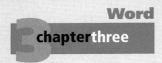

(Project 3C—Creative Supplies continued)

displayed **Tabs** dialog box, under **Tab stop position**, click to select the lower **4"**. Under **Alignment**, click the **Right** option button. Under **Leader**, click the **2** option button to add a dot leader. Click the **Set** button, and then click **OK**.

10. Display the **Paragraph** dialog box. Under **Indentation**, click the **Left spin box up arrow** to change the left margin indent to **1"**. Under **Spacing**, click the **After down spin arrow** two times to change the spacing to **0**. Click the **Line spacing arrow**, click **Single**, and then click **OK**. Type the following text, pressing Tab after the days of the week, and Enter after the time:

Monday to Friday	9 a.m. – 9 p.m.
Saturday	9 a.m. – 6 p.m.
Sunday	10 a.m. – 4 p.m.

11. Select the text *Store Hours*. On the Mini toolbar, click the **Bold** and **Center** buttons. Click the **Font Size button arrow**, and then click **16**. Select the three lines of tabbed text. Point to the horizontal ruler and position the pointer so the tip of the pointer arrow is touching the **4-inch tab stop**. When you see the *Right Tab* ScreenTip, drag the tab stop mark to the right to **5 inches on the ruler**. Click anywhere in the document to deselect the text.

12. Click the **Insert tab**, and then from the **Text group**, click the **Text Box** button. At the bottom of the **Text Box gallery**, click **Draw Text Box**. Move the ⊞ pointer to the left margin at **5 inches on the vertical ruler**. Using both the horizontal and vertical rulers as guides, drag down and to the right to create a text box approximately **1 inch** high and **3 inches** wide—then use the spin arrows in the **Size group** to size the text box precisely. With the insertion

point displayed in the text box, type **See our schedule for in-house classes. We have just added classes on scrapbooking and archival photo storage techniques.**

13. In the text box, select all of the text. On the Mini toolbar, click the **Font Size button arrow**, and then click **14**. If necessary, click the **Font button arrow**, and then click **Calibri**. Click the **Center** button. Display the **Paragraph** dialog box. Change the spacing **After** to **0** and the **Line spacing** to **Single**. With the text box still selected, on the **Format tab**, in the **Size group**, click the **Shape Width button up spin arrow** as necessary to change the width of the text box to **4"**. Click the **Shape Height button down spin arrow** as necessary to change the height of the text box to **0.8"**.

14. Point to one of the text box borders until the ⬚ pointer displays. Drag the text box down and to the right until the left edge is at approximately **1 inch on the horizontal ruler**, and the top edge is at approximately **5.5 inches on the vertical ruler**. Use Figure 3.56 as a guide. On the **Format tab**, in the **3-D Effects group**, click the **3-D Effects** button. Under **Parallel**, click the first button—**3-D Style 1**. Click anywhere in the document to deselect the text box. **Save** your document.

15. Click the **Insert tab**, and then in the **Illustrations group**, click the **Shapes** button. From the displayed **Shapes gallery**, under **Stars and Banners**, in the first row, click the twelfth button—**Curved Down Ribbon**. Move the ⊞ pointer to the left margin at **8 inches on the vertical ruler**. Using both the horizontal and vertical rulers as guides, drag down and to the

(Project 3C—Creative Supplies continues on the next page)

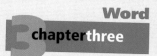
(Project 3C–Creative Supplies continued)

right to create a banner approximately **0.8 inch** high and **6 inches** wide—then use the spin box arrows in the **Size group** to size the banner precisely. Center the banner between the left and right border, and between the tabbed list and the bottom border.

16. Right-click the banner. From the shortcut menu, click **Add Text**. Type **Student and Teacher Discounts Are Available** Select the banner text, and then, on the Mini toolbar, click the **Bold** button, and then click the **Center** button. Click the **Font Color button arrow**, and then in the last column, click the last button—click **Orange, Accent 6, Darker 50%**. Click the **Font**

Size button arrow, and then click **16**. On the **Home tab**, in the **Paragraph group**, click the **Line spacing button arrow**, and then click **1.0**.

17. On the **Format tab**, in the **Text Box Styles group**, click the **Shape Fill arrow**, and then in the last column, click the third button—**Orange, Accent 6, Lighter 60%**. Click to deselect the banner, and then **Save** your document.

18. Display the **Print Preview** to make a final check of your document. Submit your document as directed.

19. **Close** your document, and then **Exit** Word.

End **You have completed Project 3C**

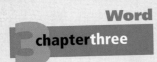

Project 3D—Sales Figures

In this project, you will apply the skills you practiced from the Objectives in Project 3B.

Objectives: 4. *Create a Table;* **5.** *Format a Table.*

In the following Skills Review, you will edit a memo about the recent photography exhibition at Memories Old and New. You will create and format a table, convert text to a table, and then AutoFormat the table. Your completed document will look similar to Figure 3.57.

For Project 3D, you will need the following file:

w03D_Sales_Figures

You will save your document as
3D_Sales_Figures_Firstname_Lastname

Figure 3.57

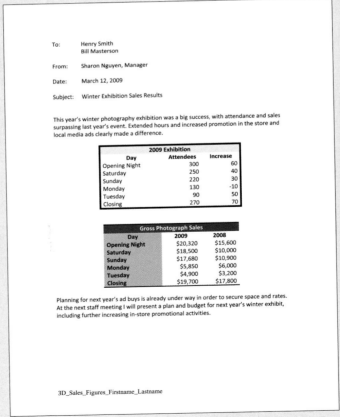

(Project 3D–Sales Figures continues on the next page)

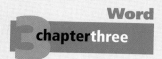

Word
chapter three   Skills Review

(Project 3D–Sales Figures continued)

1. **Start** Word. From your student files, locate and open the document **w03D_Sales_Figures**, and display formatting marks and rulers. In the three blank lines under the paragraph beginning *This year's winter*, click in the middle blank line. Click the **Insert tab**, and then in the **Tables group**, click the **Table** button. In the **Table gallery**, in the sixth row of squares, point to the second square, and then click to insert a **2-x-6** table.

2. Type **2009 Exhibition** and then press ⬇ to move to the first cell in the second row. Type **Opening Night** and press Tab. Type **300** and press Tab.

3. Type the following to complete the table, but do not press Tab after the last item.

Saturday	250
Sunday	220
Monday	130
Tuesday	90

4. From the **Office** menu, display the **Save As** dialog box, and then navigate to your **Word Chapter 3 folder**. In the **File name** box, type **3D_Sales_Figures_Firstname_Lastname** and press Enter. Add the file name to the footer area.

5. Position the insertion point in the last cell in the table, and then press Tab to add a new row to the bottom of the table. Type **Closing** and press Tab. Type **270** and then in the second row of the table, click anywhere to position the insertion point. Click the **Layout tab**, and then in the **Rows & Columns group**, click the **Insert Above** button to insert a new row. Type **Day** and press Tab. Type **Attendees**

6. In the first column of the table, move the pointer to the right boundary

until the ⬌ pointer displays. Drag the boundary to the left until the first column's right boundary aligns at approximately **1.5 inches on the horizontal ruler**. If only one row resizes, click the Undo button and begin again. In the second column, drag the right boundary to **2.5 inches on the horizontal ruler**. **Save** your document.

7. In the second column of the table, click anywhere in the column to position the insertion point. On the **Layout tab**, in the **Rows & Columns group**, click the **Insert Right** button. In the new column, click to place the insertion point in the second row. Type **Increase** and press ⬇.

8. Complete the column with the following information:

60
40
30
-10
50
70

9. In the second row, click anywhere in the first cell, and then drag to the right to select all three cells in the second row. On the Mini toolbar, click the **Bold** and **Center** buttons.

10. In the second column, click in the cell containing *300*, and then drag down and to the right to select the third cell through the eighth cell of the second and third columns, ending with *70*. Click the **Home tab**, and then in the **Paragraph group**, click the **Align Text Right** button.

11. Select all three cells in the first row. Click the **Design tab**, and then in the **Table**

(Project 3D–Sales Figures continues on the next page)

(Project 3D–Sales Figures continued)

Styles group, click the **Shading** button. Under **Theme Colors**, click the third button in the first row—**Tan Background 2**. Click the **Layout tab**, and then in the **Merge group**, click the **Merge Cells** button. Select the text in the top cell—**2009 Exhibition**. On the Mini toolbar, click the **Bold** and **Center** buttons. **Save** the document.

12. Click anywhere in the table to deselect the cells. On the **Design tab**, in the **Table Styles group**, click the **Borders button arrow**, and then click **Borders and Shading**. In the displayed **Borders and Shading** dialog box, under **Setting**, click **Box**. Click the **Width arrow**, and then click **3 pt**. In the **Apply to** box, be sure that **Table** is indicated, and then click **OK**.

13. Click the **Layout tab**. In the **Table group**, click the **Select** button, and then click **Select Table**. Click the **Home tab**, and then in the **Paragraph group**, click the **Center** button. **Save** the document.

14. In the block of text near the end of the document, beginning with *Gross Photograph Sales*, click to position the insertion point to the left of the word *Gross*, hold down ⇧Shift, and then click after the paragraph mark at the end of the line beginning *Closing*—after *$17,800*.

15. With the text selected, click the **Insert tab**. In the **Tables group**, click the **Table** button, and then click **Convert Text to Table**. In the **Convert Text to Table** dialog box, under **Table size**, click the **Number of columns up spin arrow** to change the number of columns to **3**. Under **AutoFit behavior**, click the **AutoFit to contents** option button. Then, under **Separate text at**, click the **Tabs** option button. At the bottom of the **Convert Text to Table** dialog box, click **OK**.

16. Click anywhere to position the insertion point in the lower table. On the **Design tab**, in the **Table Styles group**, click the **More** button. Under **Built-In**, in the first row, click the fifth table style—**Table Classic 2**. Right-click the table, and then from the shortcut menu, click **Table Properties**. In the **Table Properties** dialog box, on the **Table tab**, under **Alignment**, click **Center**.

17. Drag the dialog box so that you can see most of the lower table. In the **Table Properties** dialog box, click the **Column tab**. Under **Size**, click the **Next Column** button until the first column of the lower table is highlighted. Select the **Preferred width** check box, and then in the box to the right, click the spin box arrows as necessary to set the **Preferred width** to **1.5"**. Click the **Next Column** button. Use the same procedure to make the second and third columns **1"** wide, and then click **OK**.

18. In the bottom table, point to the first cell of the top row and drag to the right to select all three cells. Click the **Layout tab**, and then in the **Merge group**, click the **Merge Cells** button. In the **Alignment group**, click the **Align Center** button.

19. In the second row of the table, select the second and third cells, and then on the Mini toolbar, click the **Bold** and **Center** buttons. In the second row, in the first cell, select the text *Day*, and then on the Mini toolbar, click the **Center** button.

20. In the second column, click in the cell containing *$20,320*, and then drag down and to the right to select the third cell of the

(Project 3D–Sales Figures continues on the next page)

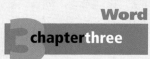

Skills Review

(Project 3D–Sales Figures continued)

second column through the eighth cell of the third column—*$17,800*. Click the **Home tab**, and then in the **Paragraph group**, click the **Align Text Right** button.

21. Display the **Print Preview** to make a final check of your document. **Save** your

changes, and then submit your document as directed.

22. **Close** your document, and then **Exit** Word.

 End **You have completed Project 3D** ⎯⎯⎯⎯⎯⎯⎯⎯⎯⎯⎯⎯⎯⎯⎯⎯⎯

Content-Based Assessments

Mastering Word

Project 3E — Modern Scrapbook

In this project, you will apply the skills you practiced from the Objectives in Project 3A.

Objectives: 1. *Insert and Format Graphics;* **2.** *Set Tab Stops;* **3.** *Insert and Modify Text Boxes and Shapes.*

In the following Mastering Word project, you will create a flyer describing a scrapbooking class to be offered at Memories Old and New. Your completed document will look similar to Figure 3.58.

For Project 3E, you will need the following files:

New blank Word document
w03E_Scrapbook

You will save your document as
3E_Modern_Scrapbook_Firstname_Lastname

Figure 3.58

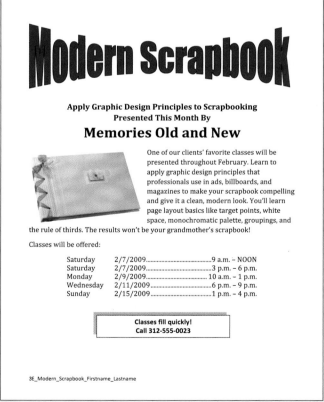

(Project 3E–Modern Scrapbook continues on the next page)

Content-Based Assessments

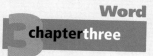
(Project 3E–Modern Scrapbook continued)

1. **Start** Word and be sure a new blank document is displayed. Display formatting marks and rulers. **Save** the document in your **Word Chapter 3** folder as **3E_Modern_Scrapbook_Firstname_Lastname** Open the document footer and add the file name to the footer. Change all four document margins to **0.75 inch**.

2. **Insert** a WordArt title using **WordArt style 4** and type **Modern Scrapbook** as the text. Change the **WordArt** size to **7 inches** wide and **2 inches** high. In the **WordArt Styles group**, click the **Shape Fill** button, and then under **Theme Colors**, click the fourth color in the first row **Dark Blue, Text 2**.

3. Click to the right of the WordArt title, and then press [Enter]. Type **Apply Graphic Design Principles to Scrapbooking** and press [Enter]. Type **Presented This Month By** and press [Enter]. Type **Memories Old and New** and press [Enter]. Select the three lines you just typed, change the **Font** to **Cambria**, **Center** the text and apply **Bold**. Change the **Font Size** of the first two lines to **16**, and change the space **After** the paragraphs to **0**. Change the **Font Size** of the third line to **28**.

4. Position the insertion point in the last blank line, change the **Font** to **Cambria**, change the **Font Size** to **14**, and then type the following text:

One of our clients' favorite classes will be presented throughout February. Learn to apply graphic design principles that professionals use in ads, billboards, and magazines to make your scrapbook compelling and give it a clean, modern look. You'll learn page layout basics like target points, white space, monochromatic palette, groupings, and the rule of thirds. The results won't be your grandmother's scrapbook!

Classes will be offered:

5. Press [Enter]. From your student files, insert the picture **w03E_Scrapbook**. Change the **Width** of the picture to **3"**, and apply **Square Text Wrapping**. Move the picture to the left margin, with the top edge even with the first paragraph you just typed—beginning with *One of our*.

6. Press [Ctrl] + [End]. Insert a **Left tab stop** at **2.25 inches on the horizontal ruler** and another **Left tab stop** at **6 inches**. In the horizontal ruler, double-click either of the new tab marks to open the **Tabs** dialog box. Select the tab stop at **6 inches on the horizontal ruler**, change the alignment to **Right**, and then add a **dot leader** to the tab stop. Display the **Paragraph** dialog box, and set the spacing **After** to **0**, and the **Line Spacing** to **Single**. Type the following text, pressing [Tab] between the weekday and the date, and between the date and the times:

Saturday	2/7/2009	9 a.m. - NOON
Saturday	2/7/2009	3 p.m. - 6 p.m.
Monday	2/9/2009	10 a.m. - 1 p.m.
Wednesday	2/11/2009	6 p.m. - 9 p.m.
Sunday	2/15/2009	1 p.m. - 4 p.m.

7. Select the tabbed text, display the **Paragraph** dialog box, and then set the **Left Indent** to **1 inch**. Click anywhere in the document to deselect the text.

8. **Draw** a **Text Box** that is aligned with the left margin, with the top edge about 0.5 inches below the tabbed text. Use the **Size** buttons to change the **Width** to **3.5"** and the **Height** to **.6"**. In the text box, type **Classes fill quickly!** and press [Enter]. Type **Call 312-555-0023 for reservations**. Select the two lines of text in the text box, and use the Mini toolbar to **Center** the text, apply **Bold**, and change the **Font Size** to **14**.

(Project 3C–Modern Scrapbook continues on the next page)

Content-Based Assessments

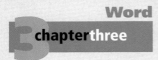
(Project 3E–Modern Scrapbook continued)

Display the **Paragraph** dialog box, and set the spacing **After** to **0**, and the **Line spacing** to **Single**. Add a **Shadow Style 1** shadow effect to the text box. On the **Format tab**, in the **Arrange group**, click the **Align** button, and then click **Align Center**.

9. Preview the document, and then print it, or submit it electronically as directed. **Save** your changes. **Close** the document, and then **Exit** Word.

 You have completed Project 3E ————————————————

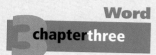

Mastering Word

Project 3F—Scrapbook Supplies

In this project, you will apply the skills you practiced from the Objectives in Project 3B.

Objectives: 4. *Create a Table;* **5.** *Format a Table.*

In the following Mastering Word project, you will edit a flyer to distribute to the scrapbooking customers of Memories Old and New. Your completed document will look similar to Figure 3.59.

For Project 3F, you will need the following file:

w03F_Scrapbook_Supplies

**You will save your document as
3F_Scrapbook_Supplies_Firstname_Lastname**

Figure 3.59

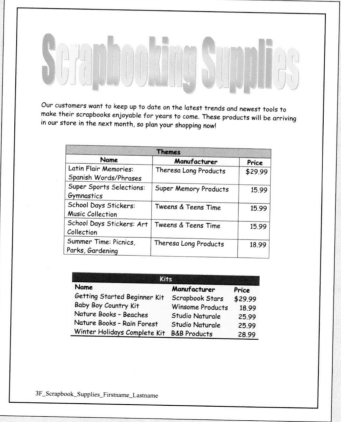

(Project 3F–Scrapbook Supplies continues on the next page)

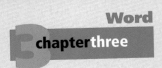

Mastering Word

(Project 3F–Scrapbook Supplies continued)

1. Locate and open the file **w03F_Scrapbook_Supplies**. Display formatting marks and rulers. **Save** the file in your **Word Chapter 3** folder as **3F_Scrapbook_Supplies_Firstname_Lastname** and add the file name to the footer. Be sure all four margins are set at **1 inch**.

2. With the insertion point at the beginning of the document, insert **WordArt** with the text **Scrapbooking Supplies** using **WordArt style 13**. Set the **Width** to **6.5 inches** and the **Height** to **1.5 inches**.

3. Move the pointer to the left of the paragraph that begins *Themes* to display the pointer, and then drag down to select all of the text through the paragraph that ends *18.99*. On the **Insert tab**, display the **Convert Text to Table** dialog box. Set the **Number of columns** to **3**, click the **AutoFit to contents** option button, and then, under **Separate text at**, choose the **Tabs** option button, and then click **OK**.

4. Display the **Table Properties** dialog box and **Center** the table. Click the **Column tab**, and then set the first two columns to **2.2 inches** wide, and set the width of the third column to **0.8 inch** wide. In the third column of the table, format all of the cells that contain numbers with the **Align Text Right** command.

5. In the first row, merge the three cells, and then apply **Center** alignment and **Bold** emphasis to the word *Themes*. **Center** and **Bold** the text in the three cells in the second row of the table. Select the first row of the table, display the **Shading gallery**, and apply **White, Background 1, Darker 25%** shading—the fourth color in the first

column. Select the second row of the table, and then from the **Shading gallery**, apply **White, Background 1, Darker 5%** shading—the second color in the first column. **Save** your document.

6. Click to place the insertion point in the blank line below the table, and then press Enter two times. **Insert** a **3-x-7** table, and then add the following text:

Kits

Name	Manufacturer	Price
Getting Started Beginner Kit	Scrapbook Stars	$29.99
Baby Boy Country Kit	Winsome Products	18.99
Nature Books - Beaches	Studio Naturale	25.99
Nature Books - Rain Forest	Studio Naturale	25.99
Winter Holidays Complete Kit	B&B Products	28.99

7. With the insertion point in the bottom table, display the **Table Styles gallery**, and then under **Built-In**, in the second row, click the second style—**Table Colorful 2**. Right-click anywhere in the lower table, point to **AutoFit**, and then click **AutoFit to Contents**.

8. Select the first column of the lower table, and then click the **Italic** button to remove the italic font style. In the second row, select the second and third cells and apply **Bold** emphasis. In the third column, apply the **Align Text Right** command to the cells that contain numbers. In the first column, remove the **Bold** font style from the last five cells.

9. Select and **Center** the lower table horizontally on the page. Select all three cells in the first row of the same table and **Merge**

(Project 3F–Scrapbook Supplies continues on the next page)

Content-Based Assessments

Mastering Word

(Project 3F–Scrapbook Supplies continued)

the cells. In the same row, select and **Center** *Kits*.

10. Add a **Box** page border, using a **1 1/2 pt** line width and the default black color.

11. Preview the document, and then print it, or submit it electronically as directed. **Save** your changes. **Close** the document, and then **Exit** Word.

 End **You have completed Project 3F** ———————————

Content-Based Assessments

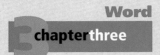
Project 3G—Photo Enhancement

In this project, you will apply the skills you practiced from the Objectives in Projects 3A and 3B.

Objectives: 1. *Insert and Format Graphics;* **3.** *Insert and Modify Text Boxes and Shapes;* **4.** *Create a Table;* **5.** *Format a Table.*

In the following Mastering Word project, you will create a handout that describes the photo enhancement services offered by Memories Old and New. Your completed document will look similar to Figure 3.60.

For Project 3G, you will need the following files:

w03G_Photo_Enhancement
w03G_Chess

You will save your document as
3G_Photo_Enhancement_Firstname_Lastname

Figure 3.60

(Project 3G–Photo Enhancement continues on the next page)

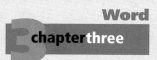

(Project 3G–Photo Enhancement continued)

1. Locate and open the file **w03G_Photo_ Enhancement**. **Save** the file in your chapter folder as **3G_Photo_Enhancement_ Firstname_Lastname** and then add the file name to the footer. Display formatting marks and rulers.

2. Position the insertion point at the beginning of the document. **Insert** a **Fun With Photos** vertical **WordArt** title using **WordArt style 12**—in the second row, the sixth style. Set the **Width** to **9 inches** and the **Height** to **.8 inch**. Note that with a vertical WordArt, the Width setting is actually the height. Add **Square** text wrapping, and then drag the WordArt title so that the upper right corner is at **0 inches on the vertical ruler** and **6.5 inches on the horizontal ruler**.

3. Position the insertion point at the beginning of the document. **Insert** the picture **w03G_Chess**, and change the **Width** to **2.5 inches**. Change the **Text Wrapping** to **Square**, and then position left edge of the picture at **3 inches on the horizontal ruler**, and the top edge of the picture level with the top edge of the text.

4. Click to place the insertion point in the blank line at the end of the document, and then press Enter. **Insert** a **2-x-6** table, and then add the following text:

Photo Service	From
Remove people from a group	$40
Add special effects	20
Change the background	40
Remove red eyes	5
Restore old photos	50

5. Display the **Table Properties** dialog box and **Center** the table horizontally on the page. Click the **Column tab**, and then set the first column to **2.5 inches** wide, and

set the width of the second column to **.6 inch** wide. In the second column of the table, format the cells that contain numbers with the **Align Text Right** command.

6. In the first row, apply **Center** and **Bold** to both cells. Select the first row of the table, display the **Shading gallery**, and add **Black, Text 1** shading—the second color in the first row. **Save** your work.

7. Click to place the insertion point anywhere in the table and display the **Borders and Shading** dialog box. Click **Box**, and then change the line width to **1 1/2 pt**.

8. Display the **Shapes gallery**. Under **Stars and Banners**, click the **Vertical Scroll** shape—the first shape in the second row. Starting at **7.25 inches on the vertical ruler**, and at **1 inch on the horizontal ruler**, draw a banner that is **3 inches** wide by **1.5 inches** high. Use the Size buttons to make the measurements exact. Right-click on the banner, click **Add Text**, and type the following:

   Memories Old and New
   220 West Randolph Street
   Chicago, IL 60601
   312-555-0023

9. **Center** the banner text, change the **Font** to **Calibri**, and increase the **Font Size** to **14**. If necessary, removing and spacing *After* the paragraphs, and set the *Line Spacing* to Single. Select the first line of text in the banner, apply **Bold**, and then change the **Font Size** to **16**. Display the **Shadow Effects gallery**, and then under **Additional Shadow Styles**, click **Shadow Style 16**. **Nudge Shadow Left** two clicks and **Nudge Shadow Up** two clicks.

(Project 3G–Photo Enhancement continues on the next page)

Content-Based Assessments

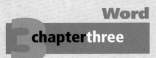
(Project 3G–Photo Enhancement continued)

10. Move the banner so that it is centered horizontally under the table, with the top edge at about **7.25 inches on the vertical ruler**. Add a **Box** page border to the document, using a **1 1/2 pt** line width and the default black color.

11. Preview the document, and then print it, or submit it electronically as directed. **Save** your changes. **Close** the file, and then **Close** Word.

 End **You have completed Project 3G** ——————————————

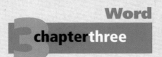

Mastering Word

Project 3H—Photo Restoration

In this project, you will apply the skills you practiced from the Objectives in Projects 3A and 3B.

Objectives: 1. *Insert and Format Graphics;* **2.** *Set Tab Stops;* **3.** *Insert and Modify Text Boxes and Shapes.*

In the following Mastering Word project, you will create a handout about photograph restoration services available at Memories Old and New. Your completed document will look similar to Figure 3.61.

For Project 3H, you will need the following files:

w03H_Photo_Restoration
w03H_Original
w03H_Quick_Restore

**You will save your document as
3H_Photo_Restoration_Firstname_Lastname**

Figure 3.61

(Project 3H–Photo Restoration continues on the next page)

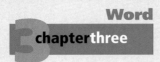

(Project 3H–Photo Restoration continued)

1. Locate and open the file **w03H_Photo_Restoration**. **Save** the file in your chapter folder as **3H_Photo_Restoration_Firstname_Lastname** and then add the file name to the footer. Display formatting marks and rulers.

2. Position the insertion point in the blank line under the title. Locate and **Insert** the picture **w03H_Original**. Reduce the **Width** of the picture to **3 inches**, and then change the **Text Wrapping** of the picture to **Square**. Click to position the insertion point in the blank line under the title, and then **Insert** the **w03H_Quick_Restore** picture. Format this second picture in the same manner you formatted the first picture. Move the second picture to the right of (and touching) the first picture—use Figure 3.61 as a guide.

3. Press `Ctrl` + `End`. Insert a **Right tab stop** at **5 inches on the horizontal ruler**. Display the **Paragraph** dialog box and set the **Left Indent** to **1 inch**. Display the **Tabs** dialog box. Add a **dot leader** to the tab stop at **5 inches on the horizontal ruler**. Type the following text, pressing `Tab` between the service and the price:

Quick Restore	$50
Major Repair	$75/hour, one hour minimum
Disaster Recovery	$75/hour + $2 per photo

4. **Save** your changes. **Draw** a **Text Box** that is aligned with the left margin, with the top edge at **8 inches on the vertical ruler**. Use the **Size** buttons to change the **Width** to **4"** and the **Height** to **.5"**. In the text box, type **Other services are available. For an estimate, contact Adrian at 312-555-0024.** Select all of the text in the text box, and use the Mini toolbar to **Center** the text and add **Bold** emphasis.

5. With the insertion point in the text box, display the **Shadow Effects gallery**. Under **Perspective Shadow**, add a **Shadow Style 8** shadow effect to the text box. Drag the text box to center it horizontally on the page, and position the top edge at about **7.75 inches on the vertical ruler**, as shown in Figure 3.61.

6. Add a **Box** page border, using a **1 1/2 pt** line width and the default black color.

7. **Save** your document. Preview the document, and then print it, or submit it electronically as directed. **Close** the file, and then **Close** Word.

End **You have completed Project 3H**

Project 3I — Student Days

In this project, you will apply the skills you practiced from all the Objectives in Projects 3A and 3B.

Objectives: 1. *Insert and Format Graphics;* **2.** *Set Tab Stops;* **3.** *Insert and Modify Text Boxes and Shapes;* **4.** *Create a Table;* **5.** *Format a Table.*

In the following Mastering Word Assessment, you will create a flyer for the Student Days celebration at Memories Old and New. Your completed document will look similar to Figure 3.62.

For Project 3I, you will need the following files:

New blank Word document
w03I_Student_Artist

You will save your document as
3I_Student_Days_Firstname_Lastname

Figure 3.62

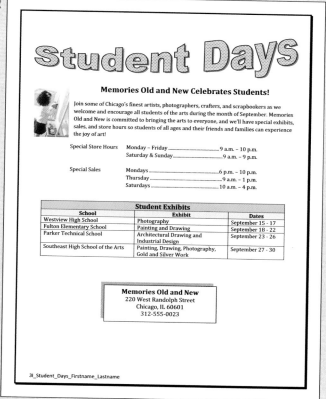

(Project 3I–Student Days continues on the next page)

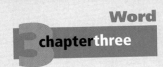

chapter three | Word

Mastering Word

(Project 3I–Student Days continued)

1. **Start** Word and be sure a new blank document is displayed. Display formatting marks and rulers. **Save** the document in your chapter folder as **7I_Student_Days_Firstname_Lastname** and add the file name to the footer. Change all four document margins to **.75 inch**. Change the **Font** to **Cambria** and be sure the **Font Size** is set to **11**.

2. **Insert** a Student Days WordArt title, using **WordArt style 23**—the fifth style in the fourth row. Change the **WordArt** size to **7 inches** wide and **1.5 inches** high.

3. Click to the right of the WordArt title, and then press ⏎. Type **Memories Old and New Celebrates Students!** and press ⏎. Select the text you just typed, **Center** the text, apply **Bold** emphasis, and then change the **Font Size** to **16**.

4. Position the insertion point in the blank line below the title you just typed, press ⏎, and then type the following text:

   Join some of Chicago's finest artists, photographers, crafters, and scrapbookers as we welcome and encourage all students of the arts during the month of September. Memories Old and New is committed to bringing the arts to everyone, and we'll have special exhibits, sales, and store hours so students of all ages and their friends and families can experience the joy of art!

5. Press ⏎. Insert a **Left tab stop** at **2.5 inches on the horizontal ruler**. Insert a **Right tab stop** at **6 inches on the horizontal ruler**. Display the **Tabs** dialog box. Add a **dot leader** to the tab stop at the **6 inches**. Type the following text, pressing ⏏ Tab between entries, and press ⏎ at the end of each line, including the last line. In the lines with no text in the first column, press ⏏ Tab. Leave the third line blank:

Special Store Hours	Monday - Friday	9 a.m. - 10 p.m.
	Saturday & Sunday	9 a.m. - 9 p.m.
Special Sales	Mondays	6 p.m. - 10 p.m.
	Thursdays	9 a.m. - 1 p.m.
	Saturdays	10 a.m. - 4 p.m.

6. Starting with the text that begins *Special Store Hours*, select the text from that point to the end of the document, but do not include the blank line at the end of the document. Display the **Paragraph** dialog box, set the **Left** indent to **1 inch**, and set the spacing **After** to **0**.

7. Press Ctrl + End, and then press ⏎. Display the **Paragraph** dialog box and set the space **After** to **0**. **Insert** a **3-x-6** table, and then add the following text:

Student Exhibits

School	Westview High School	Fulton Elementary School	Parker Technical School	Southeast High School of the Arts
Exhibit	Photography	Painting and Drawing	Architectural Drawing and Industrial Design	Painting, Drawing, Photography, Gold and Silver Work
Dates	September 15 – 17	September 18 – 22	September 23 – 26	September 27 – 30

8. Display the **Table Properties** dialog box and **Center** the table. Click the **Column tab**, and then set the first two columns to **2.5 inches** wide, and the third column to **1.5 inches** wide.

(Project 3I–Student Days continues on the next page)

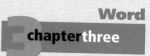

(Project 3I–Student Days continued)

9. In the first row, merge the three cells, and then **Center** and **Bold** *Student Exhibits*, and change the **Font Size** to **14**. **Center** and **Bold** the text in the three cells in the second row of the table. Select the first row of the table. On the **Design tab**, display the **Shading gallery**, and add **Orange, Accent 6, Lighter 40%** shading—the fourth color down in the last column. Select the second row of the table, display the **Shading gallery**, and add **Orange, Accent 6, Lighter 80%** shading— the second color down in the last column. **Save** your work.

10. Place the insertion point to the left of the paragraph that begins *Join some of Chicago's*, and then from your student files, insert the picture **w03I_Student_Artist**. Change the **Height** of the picture to **1.4 inches**, and then apply **Square Text Wrapping**. Move the picture to the position shown in Figure 3.62.

11. **Save** your changes. **Draw** a **Text Box** that is aligned with the left margin, with the top edge at **7.0 inches on the vertical ruler**. Use the **Size** buttons to change the **Height** to **1"** and the **Width** to **3"**. Select the paragraph mark in the text box, display the **Paragraph** dialog box, and then set the space **After** to **0** and the **Line Spacing** to **Single**. In the text box, type:

Memories Old and New
220 West Randolph Street
Chicago, IL 60601
312-555-0023

12. Select all of the text in the text box and **Center** the text. Change the **Font Size** to **12**. Select the top line of text in the text box, add **Bold** emphasis, and change the **Font Size** to **14**. Display the **Shadow Effects gallery**, and under **Drop Shadow**, click the first style—**Shadow Style 1**. Drag to center the text box under the table.

13. Add a **Shadow** page border, using a **2 1/4 pt** line width and the default black color.

14. Preview the document, and then print it, or submit it electronically as directed. **Save** your changes. **Close** the file, and then **Exit** Word.

End   You have completed Project 3I

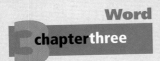

Business Running Case

Project 3J—Business Running Case

In this project, you will apply the skills you practiced from all the Objectives in Projects 3A and 3B.

From My Computer, navigate to the student files that accompany this textbook. In the folder **03_business_running_case_pg37_86**, locate and open the folder for this chapter. Open and print the instructions for this project, which are provided to you in Adobe PDF format. Follow the instructions and use the skills you have gained thus far to assist Jennifer Nelson in meeting the challenges of owning and running her business.

End **You have completed Project 3J** ———————————

Outcomes-Based Assessments

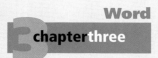

Rubric

The following outcomes-based assessments are *open-ended assessments*. That is, there is no specific correct result; your result will depend on your approach to the information provided. Make *Professional Quality* your goal. Use the following scoring rubric to guide you in *how* to approach the problem, and then to evaluate *how well* your approach solves the problem.

The *criteria*—Software Mastery, Content, Format and Layout, and Process—represent the knowledge and skills you have gained that you can apply to solving the problem. The *levels of performance*—Professional Quality, Approaching Professional Quality, or Needs Quality Improvements—help you and your instructor evaluate your result.

	Your completed project is of Professional Quality if you:	Your completed project is Approaching Professional Quality if you:	Your completed project Needs Quality Improvements if you:
1-Software Mastery	Choose and apply the most appropriate skills, tools, and features and identify efficient methods to solve the problem.	Choose and apply some appropriate skills, tools, and features, but not in the most efficient manner.	Choose inappropriate skills, tools, or features, or are inefficient in solving the problem.
2-Content	Construct a solution that is clear and well organized, contains content that is accurate, appropriate to the audience and purpose, and is complete. Provide a solution that contains no errors of spelling, grammar, or style.	Construct a solution in which some components are unclear, poorly organized, inconsistent, or incomplete. Misjudge the needs of the audience. Have some errors in spelling, grammar, or style, but the errors do not detract from comprehension.	Construct a solution that is unclear, incomplete, or poorly organized, containing some inaccurate or inappropriate content; and contains many errors of spelling, grammar, or style. Do not solve the problem.
3-Format and Layout	Format and arrange all elements to communicate information and ideas, clarify function, illustrate relationships, and indicate relative importance.	Apply appropriate format and layout features to some elements, but not others. Overuse features, causing minor distraction.	Apply format and layout that does not communicate information or ideas clearly. Do not use format and layout features to clarify function, illustrate relationships, or indicate relative importance. Use available features excessively, causing distraction.
4-Process	Use an organized approach that integrates planning, development, self-assessment, revision, and reflection.	Demonstrate an organized approach in some areas, but not others; or, use an insufficient process of organization throughout.	Do not use an organized approach to solve the problem.

Outcomes-Based Assessments

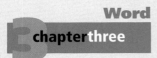
Problem Solving

Word

chapterthree

Project 3K—Books

In this project, you will apply the skills you practiced from the Objectives in Projects 3A and 3B.

For Project 3K, you will need the following file:

New blank Word document

You will save your document as
3K_Books_Firstname_Lastname

Memories Old and New carries an extensive line of books and periodicals for artists, photographers, students, teachers, and hobbyists. They have recently begun stocking a full line of scrapbooking books. In this project, you will create a flyer that includes a table of popular scrapbooking books for sale in the store.

To complete this assignment:

- Include a WordArt title, either with the name of the store, or the topic that is covered in the flyer.

- Write an opening paragraph introducing the topic.

- Create a table that consists of books on scrapbooking. The table should use at least three columns, including the author's name, the title of the book, and the book price. You should include at least six books in the table—use an online book dealer to search for appropriate titles.

- Format the table with a title that spans all of the columns and include a heading for each column. The title and column headings should be formatted distinctively.

- Include a text box with instructions for placing orders by phone.

- Include a shape with the name, address, and phone number of the store.

Add the file name to the footer. Check the flyer for spelling or grammar errors. Save the document as **3K_Books_Firstname_Lastname** and submit it as directed.

End **You have completed Project 3K** ————————————

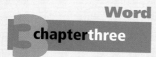

Problem Solving

Project 3L — Restoration Class

In this project, you will construct a solution by applying any combination of the skills you practiced from the Objectives in Projects 3A and 3B.

For Project 3L, you will need the following files:

New blank Word document
w03L_McArthur

You will save your document as
3L_Restoration_Class_Firstname_Lastname

Memories Old and New offers extensive photo restoration and photo recovery services. They also offer Beginner, Intermediate, and Advanced level classes on basic restoration techniques, using popular photograph manipulation software. Each level consists of two sessions that are four hours in length. Each session costs $50, and all six sessions can be taken for $250.

Create a flyer that can be handed out to customers in the store, and that contains information about the photo restoration classes. The flyer should include a decorative title, an introductory paragraph about Memories Old and New and photo restoration, and information about the classes. Format the information using a table, or using tab stops and dot leaders. You will need to include at least one text box with the name and address of the company, and one photo. If you have one or two old family photos that you would like to include, use those. Otherwise, use **w03L_McArthur**, which is included with your student files. Add a Picture Style or a Picture Effect to make the picture more visually interesting. The address information for Memories Old and New can be found in Activity 3.14.

Add the file name to the footer. Check the flyer for spelling or grammar errors. Save the document as **3L_Restoration_Class_Firstname_Lastname** and submit it as directed.

End **You have completed Project 3L** ————————

Problem Solving

Project 3M — Frames

In this project, you will construct a solution by applying any combination of the skills you practiced from the Objectives in Projects 3A and 3B.

For Project 3M, you will need the following files:

New blank Word document
w03M_Frame1
w03M_Frame2

You will save your document as
3M_Frames_Firstname_Lastname

Many people bring pictures to Memories Old and New for repair and restoration. Few people realize that the company employs experts in frame repair. In this project, you will create a flyer about picture frame repairs and refinishing offered by Memories Old and New.

Some of the frame repairs and enhancements offered, including minimum prices, are:

- Refinishing a wood frame, including stripping varnish or removing paint, which is priced by frame size and starts at $49.95.
- Adding a faux finish and distressing the wood, which is priced by project and starts at $29.95.
- Repairing plaster, which is priced by frame size and starts at $49.95.
- Repairing minor chips and scratches, which is priced by the project and starts at $29.95.
- Gilding and gold leaf, which is priced by project; prices vary.

To complete this assignment, create a flyer that includes the following:

- A WordArt title that describes the topic.
- An opening paragraph introducing the topic.
- A table using the information presented above. Format the table with a title that spans all of the columns. Each column should have a column heading. The title should be formatted distinctively.
- A text box or banner with instructions on getting an in-home estimate.
- At least one graphic with an introductory paragraph that wraps around the graphic or graphics. Two frame pictures are included with the student files.

(Project 3M–Frames continues on the next page)

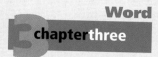

Problem Solving

(Project 3M–Frames continued)

Add the file name to the footer. Check the flyer for spelling or grammar errors. Save the document as **3M_Frames_Firstname_Lastname** and submit it as directed.

 You have completed Project 3M ⸺⸺⸺⸺⸺⸺⸺⸺⸺⸺

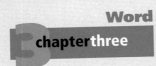

Word

chapterthree **Problem Solving**

Project 3N—Flower Show

In this project, you will construct a solution by applying any combination of the skills you practiced from the Objectives in Projects 3A and 3B.

For Project 3N, you will need the following files:

New blank Word document
w03N_Flower1
w03N_Flower2
w03N_Flower3
w03N_Flower4
w03N_Flower5
w03N_Flower6

**You will save your document as
3N_Flower_Show_Firstname_Lastname**

Memories Old and New is heavily involved in community activities. Every year, the neighborhood's small botanical garden—The Northwest Chicago Botanical Garden—sponsors a flower show, and solicits local businesses to participate and to help defray the expenses of the event. In return, participating companies receive good publicity. This year, Memories Old and New has agreed to create the event flyers.

In this project you will create a flyer advertising the event. This year's event runs from May 20 to May 25. Admission is free, and the hours are from 10 a.m. until 7 p.m. on May 20–22; 10 a.m. until 5 p.m. on May 23; and Noon to 5 p.m. on May 24–25. On the flyer, the abbreviated name of the garden—NWC Botanical Garden—should display as a decorative title. One or two paragraphs are necessary to describe the details of the event, which include a flower show and flower sale, and activities for children. A table or tabbed list is necessary to convey information about dates and times. Include at least two pictures in the flyer. You can use any flower pictures you'd like, including the six that are included with your student files. Resize the pictures as necessary, and apply special effects to the pictures that enhance the overall design of the flyer. Add a banner indicating that Memories Old and New provided the flyers and that provides information about the company. Add an appropriate page border.

Save the flyer as **3N_Flower_Show_Firstname_Lastname** and then create a footer that contains file name. Submit the document as directed.

 End **You have completed Project 3N** —————

Outcomes-Based Assessments

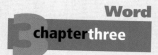

Problem Solving

Project 3O — Art Supplies

In this project, you will construct a solution by applying any combination of the skills you practiced from the Objectives in Projects 3A and 3B.

For Project 3O, you will need the following file:

New blank Word document

**You will save your document as
3O_Art_Supplies_Firstname_Lastname**

Memories Old and New started business under a different name as an artist's supply store. The business has expanded greatly, covering many more areas of the art world, but artist's supplies are still an important part of the company's business. In this project, you will create a handout of commonly used art supplies that Art Instructor Ming Han provides to her drawing students. Create a decorative title for the handout. Include an introductory paragraph that welcomes students to the drawing class and that informs them of the types of artwork that they will learn to draw, including landscapes, still lifes, animals, and cartoons. Use the Internet to research art supplies and prices, and then use your research to create a table below the introductory paragraph that lists eight to ten popular art supplies and their prices. Examples of these supplies include paint brushes, charcoal, chalk, canvas, and drawing pads. Search the Microsoft ClipArt library for one or more graphics to add to the handout. Include a text box or shape that includes the company name and address and add a page border. Save the price list as **3O_Art_Supplies_Firstname_Lastname** and then add the file name to the footer. Submit the document as directed.

End **You have completed Project 3O** ——————

Outcomes-Based Assessments

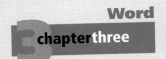
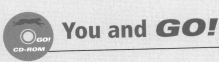 You and *GO!*

Project 3P — You and *GO!*

In this project, you will construct a solution by applying any combination of the skills you practiced from the Objectives in Projects 3A and 3B.

From My Computer, navigate to the student files that accompany this textbook. In the folder **04_you_and_go_pg87_102**, locate and open the folder for this chapter. Open and print the instructions for this project, which are provided to you in Adobe PDF format. Follow the instructions to create a resume using a table.

 End **You have completed Project 3P** ————————

GO! with Help

Project 3Q — *GO!* with Help

In this chapter, you inserted a table, and changed existing text into a table. A third way to create a table is to draw the outline and grid lines by hand. This enables you to create a table of any shape for any purpose.

1 **Start** Word. On the Ribbon, click the **Microsoft Office Word Help** button. In the **Search** box, type **draw table** and then click the **Search** button.

2 In the displayed **Search Results** task pane, click **Draw a table**. Maximize the displayed window, and at the top of the window, click the **Show All** link. Scroll through and read how to draw a table.

3 If you want, print a copy of the information by clicking the **Print** button at the top of **Word Help** window.

4 **Close** the **Help** window, and then **Exit** Word.

 End **You have completed Project 3Q** ————————

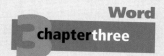

Group Business Running Case

Project 3R—Group Business Running Case

In this project, you will apply the skills you practiced from the Objectives in Projects 3A and 3B.

Your instructor may assign this group case project to your class. If your instructor assigns this project, he or she will provide you with information and instructions to work as part of a group. The group will apply the skills gained thus far to help the Bell Orchid Hotel Group achieve its business goals.

End **You have completed Project 3R** _____

chapterfour

Special Document Formats, Columns, and Mail Merge

OBJECTIVES

At the end of this chapter you will be able to:

OUTCOMES

Mastering these objectives will enable you to:

---

1. Collect and Paste Text and Graphics
2. Create and Format Columns
3. Use Special Character and Paragraph Formatting
4. Create Mailing Labels Using Mail Merge

PROJECT 4A
Create a Multicolumn Newsletter and Print Mailing Labels

---

5. Insert Hyperlinks
6. Insert a SmartArt Graphic
7. Preview and Save a Document as a Web Page

PROJECT 4B
Create and Preview a Web Page

Georgia Gardens

Gardening and lawn care in the southern United States are year-round activities. More and more people are approaching what used to be considered a chore as a rewarding and exciting hobby. Southern Home Media produces the television show *Georgia Gardens* to present information on the proven methods, newest techniques, and hottest tools for growing healthy food and creating beautiful yards and gardens. The show's hosts also travel to interesting and lovely private and public gardens throughout the United States to provide viewers a glimpse into the many possibilities that gardening provides.

Using Special Document Formats, Columns, and Mail Merge

Creating a newsletter is usually a job reserved for desktop publishing programs, such as Microsoft Publisher. Word, however, has a number of tools that enable you to create a simple and attractive newsletter that effectively communicates your message.

Newsletters consist of a number of elements, but nearly all have a title, story headlines, articles, and graphics. The text of each article is typically split into two or three columns, which is easier to read than text formatted in a single, wide column. Newsletters are often printed, but newsletters can also be designed to display as Web pages. A useful tool to couple with newsletters is mail merge, which enables you to print mailing labels.

Project 4A Garden Newsletter

In Activities 4.1 through 4.11, you will edit a newsletter for the *Georgia Gardens* subscribers. You will collect text and graphics from other documents, and then paste the collected information into a new document. You will change the text from one column to two columns, and then format the columns. You will use special text formatting features to change the font color and set off one of the paragraphs with a border and shading. Finally, you will create mailing labels for the newsletter. Your completed documents will look similar to Figure 4.1.

For Project 4A, you will need the following files:

New blank Word document
w04A_Tomatoes
w04A_Ornamental_Grasses
w04A_Pictures
w04A_Addresses

You will save your documents as
4A_Garden_Newsletter_Firstname_Lastname
4A_Mailing_Labels_Firstname_Lastname
4A_Addresses_Firstname_Lastname

Samira Ahmed
3418 Longview Drive
#320
Atlanta, GA 30309

Juanita Andersen
9000 S. Susan Creek Dr.
Chattanooga, TN 37419

Lenesha Barnett
2361 Bluebird Lane
#8
Atlanta, GA 30317

Mauro Calva
82 E. Ramona Blvd.
Woodstock, GA 30188

Taylor Dunnahoo
189 Ventura Street
Rome, GA 30161

David Feingold
1821 Alturas St.
#1442
Chattanooga, TN 37405

Duncan McArthur
3336 S. Flowers Rd.
#234
Macon, GA 31217

Jessica Pyun
1255 Miravista Street
Atlanta, GA 30309

Phillip Scroggs
1518 Orchard Place West
Hunstville, AL 35806

Cesar Vargas
1550 Glenrosa Drive
#1550
Atlanta, GA 30301

Bin Wu
676 North St. Clair St.
Hunstville, AL 35824

Georgia Gardens Newsletter

ORNAMENTAL GRASSES

As seen on *Georgia Gardens*, ornamental grasses can add new drama, texture, and color to your garden. Best of all, they tend to be very hardy and low-maintenance plants.

In the South, most ornamental grasses grow quickly in the spring and summer, bloom late in the summer and fall, and are dormant throughout the winter. They are very versatile—they can be annuals or perennials, and they can be ground covers or can reach up to 20 feet tall. Some have flowers and are brightly colored, and all have interesting textures and sway gracefully in the wind.

Ornamental grasses can be used as accent plants, but they can also be used to solve problems in your landscape. Try planting them to create a hedge, a border, or a groundcover.

Some dramatic ornamental grasses that do well in the South: Pampas Grass, which can reach up to 20 feet in height and has large silvery white flower plumes on long stems; Red Baron Japanese Blood Grass, which is about 12 to 18 inches tall and has bright red foliage in summer and fall; and Variegated Purple Moor Grass, which has purplish leaves with cream stripes.

To see more examples of how ornamental grasses can enhance your landscape, watch *Georgia Gardens*.

TOMATO TIPS

Few things taste more delicious than a freshly picked tomato from the garden in summer. With a little extra knowledge, you can help ensure a healthy tomato harvest this year.

After the last frost in your area, the soil should be warm enough to plant tomatoes. Choose a spot where the plants will receive at least six hours of sunlight each day. Due to the clay soil found in most of the South, it is recommended that you augment the soil with some peat moss or humus. You have the right mix if it crumbles when you squeeze a handful.

Be sure to dig a deep hole for the tomato plant. It should sit deeper in the ground than it does in the pot. This helps the roots grow stronger and produces a stronger plant. Add a little fertilizer to the soil before planting. Tomato plants can get very large and need extra support, so it is best to use stakes or a cage to hold them up so they won't fall over.

Water the plants well when you plant them, and then check them regularly to see if they need more water (wilted leaves are a sign that they need water). When you water, focus on the soil around the plant rather than watering the plant itself. Consider adding fertilizer after another six to eight weeks.

By following these tips, you should be able to enjoy a fruitful tomato season.

4A_Garden_Newsletter_Firstname_Lastname

Figure 4.1
Project 4A—Garden Newsletter

Objective 1
Collect and Paste Text and Graphics

You have already used the Office Clipboard, which is a temporary storage area maintained by your Windows operating system. When you perform the Copy command or the Cut command, the text that you select is moved to the Office Clipboard. From this Office Clipboard storage area, you can paste text into another location of your document, into another document, or into another Office program.

You can copy and then paste a single selection of text without displaying the Clipboard task pane. However, displaying the Clipboard task pane is essential if you want to **collect and paste** information—collect a group of graphics or selected text blocks and then paste them into a document at any time. The Office Clipboard holds up to 24 items, and the Clipboard task pane displays a preview of each item.

Activity 4.1 Using Collect and Paste To Gather Images and Text

Newsletters typically contain articles written by different people and contain graphics from various sources. Use the Office Clipboard to collect all of the components of the newsletter in one place.

> ### Note — Comparing Your Screen with the Figures in This Textbook
>
> Your screen will match the figures shown in this textbook if you set your screen resolution to 1024 x 768. At other resolutions, your screen will closely resemble, but not match, the figures shown. To view your screen's resolution, on the Windows desktop, right-click in a blank area, click Properties, and then click the Settings tab.

1 **Start** Word and display a new blank document. Display formatting marks and rulers, and be sure your screen shows both the left and right document edges. Display the **Save As** dialog box, navigate to your storage location, create a new folder named **Word Chapter 4** and then save the document as **4A_Garden_Newsletter_Firstname_ Lastname** Open the document footer and add the file name to the footer. Set the top, left, and right margins to **1 inch**, and the bottom margin to **0.5 inch**.

2 On the **Home tab**, in the **Clipboard group**, click the **Dialog Box Launcher** to display the **Clipboard** task pane. If any items display in the Clipboard, at the top of the task pane, click the **Clear All** button. At the bottom of the task pane, click the **Options** button, and then compare your screen with Figure 4.2.

The options displayed in the list enable you to display the Clipboard task pane whenever you cut or copy an object, and also enable you to collect items without displaying the Clipboard task pane.

Figure 4.2

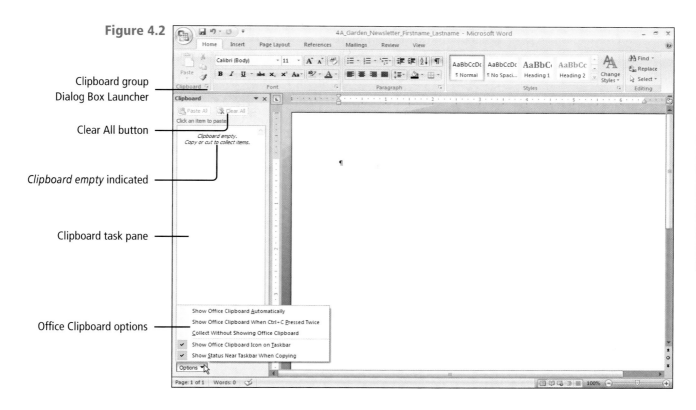

Clipboard group
Dialog Box Launcher

Clear All button

Clipboard empty indicated

Clipboard task pane

Office Clipboard options

3 Click anywhere in the document to close the **Options** list. Locate and open the file **w04A_Ornamental_Grasses**. Press Ctrl + A to select all of the text in the document, and then in the **Clipboard group**, click the **Copy** button 🖺. Press Ctrl + W to close the **w04A_Ornamental_Grasses** file. Alternatively, from the Office menu, click Close. Notice that the first few lines of text display in the Clipboard task pane, as shown in Figure 4.3.

Your saved blank document displays.

Figure 4.3

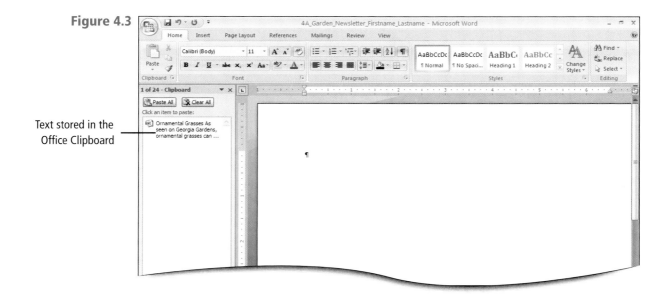

Text stored in the
Office Clipboard

4 Locate, and then open, the file **w04A_Tomatoes**. Press Ctrl + A to select all of the text in the document, and then in the **Clipboard group**, click the **Copy** button ▣. Alternatively, press Ctrl + C to copy the selected text. **Close** the **w04A_Tomatoes** file.

The copied text displays at the top of the Clipboard task pane.

5 Locate, and then open, the file **w04A_Pictures**.

This file contains no text; rather, the file contains three graphics—a WordArt title and two pictures. Recall that WordArt changes text into a decorative graphic.

6 Click to select the **Georgia Gardens Newsletter** WordArt title, and then in the **Clipboard group**, click the **Copy** button ▣ to copy it to the Office Clipboard. Use the same procedure to **Copy** ▣ the **Grass picture** on the left and the **Tomatoes picture** on the right. **Close** the **w04A_Pictures** file, and notice that the Clipboard task pane contains five items, with the most recently copied item at the top of the list as shown in Figure 4.4.

Figure 4.4

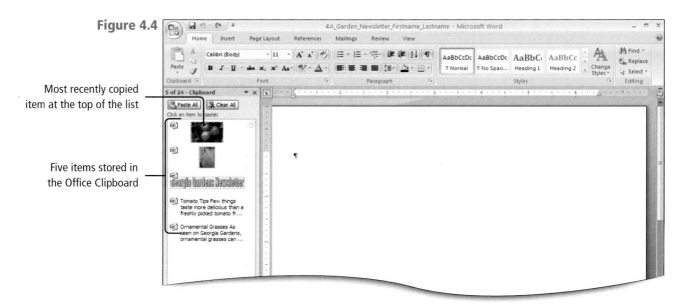

Most recently copied item at the top of the list

Five items stored in the Office Clipboard

7 **Save** 🖫 the document.

More Knowledge

Being Careful of Copyright Issues

You can collect and paste text and graphics from the Internet. However, nearly everything you find on the Internet is protected by **copyright** law, which protects authors of original works, including text, art, photographs, and music. If you want to use text or graphics that you find online, you will need to get permission. One of the exceptions to this law is the use of small amounts of information for educational purposes, which falls under Fair Use guidelines.

Copyright laws in the United States are open to different interpretations, and copyright laws can be very different in other countries. As a general rule, if you want to use someone else's material, always get permission first.

Activity 4.2 Pasting Information from the Clipboard Task Pane

After you have collected text and graphics from other documents or sources, you can paste them into your document.

1 With your **4A_Garden_Newsletter** file displayed, in the **Clipboard** task pane, locate and click the **Georgia Gardens Newsletter** WordArt title. Compare your screen with Figure 4.5.

The WordArt title is pasted into the document at the insertion point location, and also remains available in the Office Clipboard.

Figure 4.5

WordArt title is pasted at the insertion point location

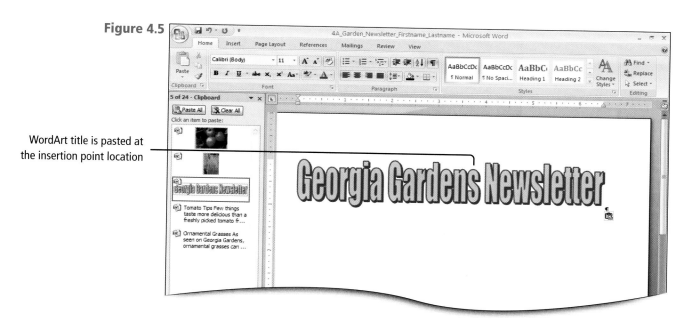

2 Press Enter. In the **Clipboard** task pane, click the text entry beginning *Ornamental Grasses* to paste the entire block of text at the insertion point.

3 In the **Clipboard** task pane, click the text entry beginning *Tomato Tips* to paste the entire block of text at the insertion point. Press ←Bksp to remove the blank line at the bottom of the inserted text.

4 Select all of the text in the document except the WordArt title. Be sure to include the paragraph mark at the end of the document.

5 Right-click the selected text, and then click **Paragraph**. In the displayed **Paragraph** dialog box, under **Spacing**, in the **After** box, click the **down spin arrow** to change the spacing to **6 pt**.

6 Under **Spacing**, click the **Line spacing arrow**, and then click **Single**. Click **OK** to close the **Paragraph** dialog box. Press Ctrl + Home to move to the top of the document, and then compare your screen with Figure 4.6.

Figure 4.6

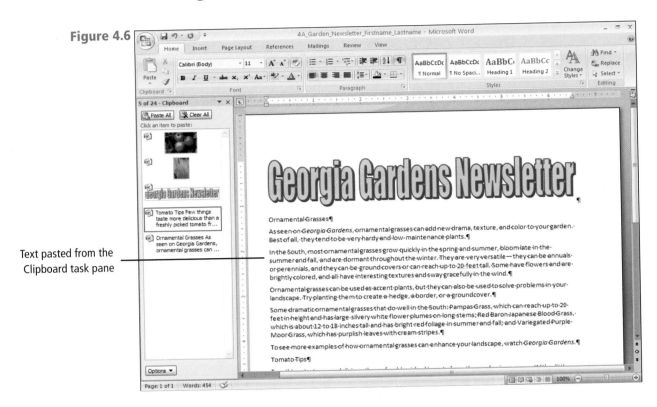

Text pasted from the Clipboard task pane

7 **Save** the document.

Objective 2
Create and Format Columns

All newspapers and most magazines and newsletters use multiple columns for articles because text in narrower columns is easier to read than text that stretches across a page. Word has a tool that enables you to change a single column of text into two or more columns, and then format the columns. If a column does not end where you want, you can end the column at a location of your choice by inserting a *manual column break*.

Activity 4.3 Changing One Column of Text to Two Columns

Newsletters are usually two or three columns wide. When using 8.5 × 11-inch paper in portrait orientation, avoid creating four or more columns because they are so narrow that word spacing looks awkward, often resulting in one long word by itself on a line.

1 Select all of the text in the document except the WordArt title. Be sure to include the paragraph mark at the end of the document.

2 Click the **Page Layout tab**, and then in the **Page Setup group**, click the **Columns** button. From the displayed **Columns gallery**, click **Two**, scroll to the top of the document, and then compare your screen with Figure 4.7.

The text is divided into two columns, and a section break is inserted below the WordArt title, dividing the one-column section of the document from the two-column section of the document. Do not be concerned if your columns do not break at the same line as shown in the figure.

Figure 4.7

Two-column format

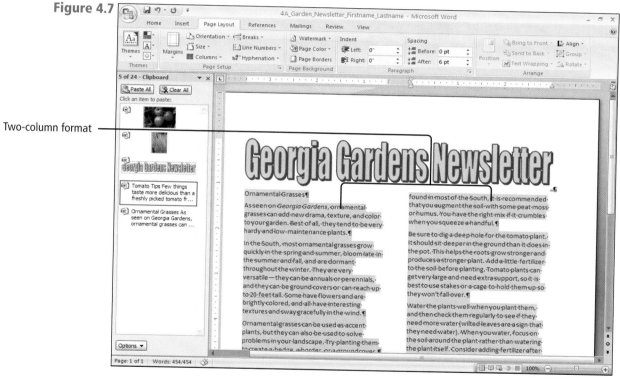

3 **Save** the document.

Activity 4.4 Formatting Multiple Columns

The uneven right edge of a single page-width column is readable. When you create narrow columns, justified text is sometimes preferable. The font you choose should also match the style of newsletter you are creating.

1 With the text still selected, click the **Home tab**. In the **Font group**, click the **Font button arrow** [Cambria ▼], scroll down the font list, and then click **Comic Sans MS**. Alternatively, you can press *c* to move to the first font beginning with that letter, and then scroll down to the desired font.

2 In the **Font group**, click the **Font Size button arrow** ~~12~~ , and then click **10**.

3 In the **Paragraph group**, click the **Justify** button ▤ . Click anywhere in the document to deselect the text, and then compare your screen with Figure 4.8.

The document displays in 10 pt. Comic Sans MS font, an informal and easy-to-read font; the text is justified.

Figure 4.8

Text justified ——

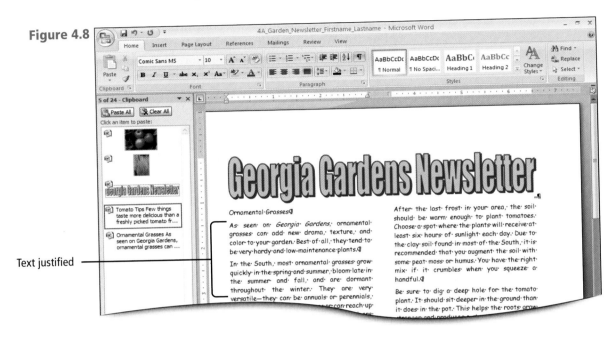

4 **Save** 🔲 the document.

More Knowledge

Justifying Column Text

Although many magazines and newspapers still justify text in columns, there is a great deal of disagreement about whether to justify the columns, or to use left alignment and leave the right edge uneven. Justified text tends to look more formal and cleaner, but it also results in uneven spacing between words, which some feel makes justified text harder to read.

Activity 4.5 Inserting a Column Break

Insert manual column breaks to adjust columns that end or begin awkwardly, or to make space for graphics or text boxes.

1 From the **Office** menu 🔲 , point to **Print**, and then click **Print Preview**. Notice that the columns end unevenly.

2 In the **Preview group**, click the **Close Print Preview** button. Scroll down, and then near the bottom of the first column, position the insertion point to the left of *Tomato Tips*.

3 Click the **Page Layout tab**, and then in the **Page Setup group**, click the **Breaks** button to display the **Page and Section Breaks gallery**, as shown in Figure 4.9.

Breaks gallery

Figure 4.9

Column break

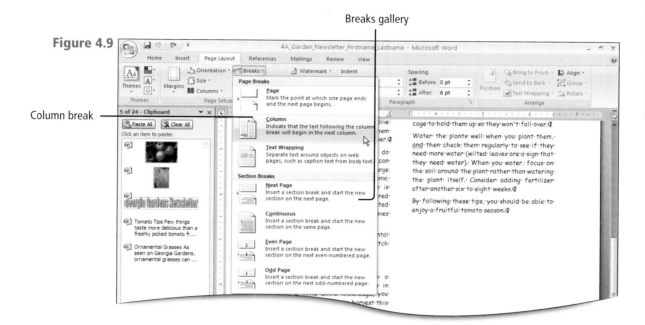

4 From the displayed **Breaks gallery**, under **Page Breaks**, click **Column**.

The column breaks at the insertion point, and the text to the right of the insertion point moves to the top of the next column.

5 From the **Office** menu, point to the **Print arrow**, and then click **Print Preview**. Compare your screen with Figure 4.10.

The columns are more even, although they still do not align at exactly the same line. The bottom alignment will be adjusted when graphics are added to the newsletter.

Figure 4.10

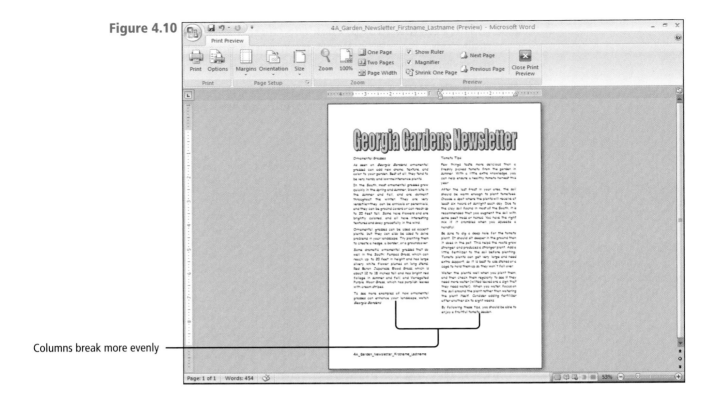

Columns break more evenly

6 In the **Preview group**, click the **Close Print Preview** button, and then **Save** 🖫 the document.

Activity 4.6 Adding Graphics to Columns

You can paste items from the Clipboard task pane at any time. Items on the clipboard remain on the clipboard throughout your Word session unless you delete them. Recall that the limit for items on the Office Clipboard is 24—if you add a 25th item, the earliest item added is removed.

1 In the first column, click anywhere to position the insertion point. In the **Clipboard** task pane, click the **grass** picture to paste it at the insertion point location.

2 Right-click the **grass** picture, point to **Text Wrapping**, and then click **Square** to wrap the text around the picture.

3 Right-click the **grass** picture, and then from the shortcut menu, click **Size**. In the displayed **Size** dialog box, under **Scale**, select the **Lock aspect ratio** check box. Under **Size and rotate** click the **Height down spin arrow** as necessary to set the picture height to **2**". Alternatively, select the value in the Height box and type *2*.

Recall that the *aspect ratio* is the ratio of the height to the width of an object. Locking the aspect ratio ensures that the proportions of the object will remain unchanged when either the height or width is changed.

4 At the bottom of the Size dialog box, click the **Close** button. Drag the picture to the left margin of the first column, with the top edge of the picture even with the top of the paragraph beginning *In the South.*

5 In the second column, click anywhere to position the insertion point. In the **Clipboard** task pane, click the **tomatoes** picture to paste it at the insertion point location.

6 Use the procedure you just practiced to set the **Text Wrapping** to **Square**. Proportionally change the **Height** to **1.2**". Drag the picture to the right margin of the second column, with the top edge at approximately **5.5 inches on the vertical ruler**, as shown in Figure 4.11. Recall that you can more precisely adjust the position of the picture by holding down Ctrl and then pressing the arrow keys.

Picture size

Figure 4.11

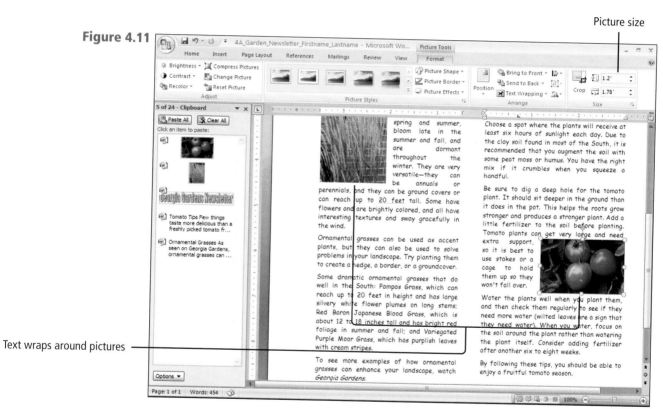

Text wraps around pictures

7 Near the top of the **Clipboard** task pane, click the **Clear All** button to remove all items from the Office Clipboard. **Close** ✕ the Clipboard task pane.

8 **Save** 🖫 the document.

Objective 3
Use Special Character and Paragraph Formatting

Special text and paragraph formatting is useful to emphasize text, and it makes your newsletter look more professional. There are various ways to call attention to specific text. One way is to place a border around a paragraph. Another is to shade a paragraph, although use caution not to make the shade too dark, because shading can make the text difficult to read.

Activity 4.7 Using Small Caps and Changing the Font Color

For headlines and titles, *small caps* is an attractive font effect. Lowercase letters are changed to uppercase letters but remain the height of lowercase letters. Titles are frequently formatted using this style.

1 Press `Ctrl` + `Home` to move to the top of the document. At the top of the first column, select the text *Ornamental Grasses*. Be sure to include the paragraph mark.

2 Right-click the selected text, and then from the shortcut menu, click **Font**. In the displayed **Font** dialog box, click the **Font color arrow**, and then under **Theme Colors**, click **Orange, Accent 6, Darker 50%**—the bottom color in the tenth column. Under **Font style**, click **Bold**. Under **Size**, click **18**. Under **Effects**, select the **Small caps** check box. Compare your screen with Figure 4.12.

The Font dialog box gives you more options than are available on the Ribbon, and enables you to make several changes at the same time.

Small caps
check box   Font size

Figure 4.12

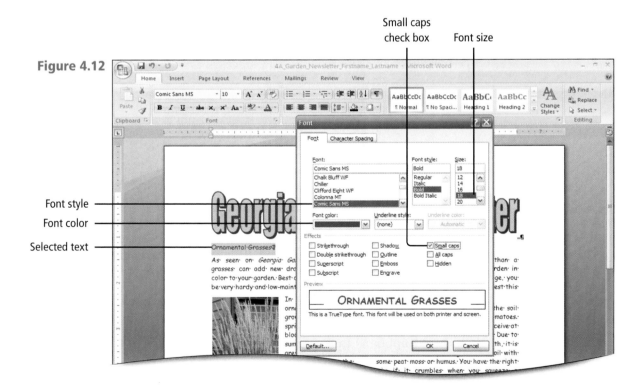

Font style

Font color

Selected text

3 At the bottom of the **Font** dialog box, click **OK**.

4 At the top of the second column, select the text *Tomato Tips*. Using the technique you just practiced, apply the same formatting that you added to the title of the first column. Alternatively, use the Format Painter. Click anywhere in the document to deselect the text, and then compare your screen with Figure 4.13.

Figure 4.13

Word | chapter 4

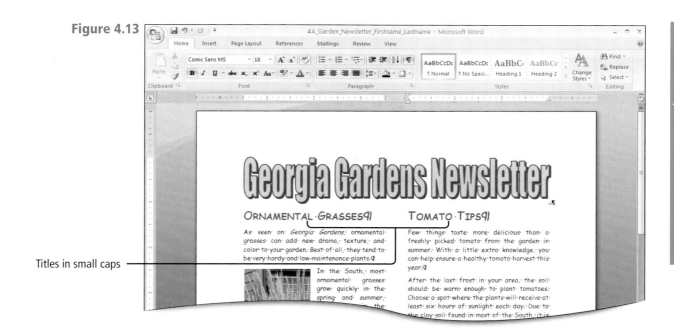

Titles in small caps

5 Save 💾 the document.

Activity 4.8 Adding a Border and Shading to a Paragraph

Paragraph borders provide strong visual cues to the reader. Shading can be used with or without borders. When used with a border, light shading can be very effective in drawing the reader's eye to the text.

1 At the bottom of the first column, in the paragraph that begins *To see more examples*, triple-click in the paragraph to select it. On the **Home tab**, in the **Paragraph group**, click the **Border button arrow**, and then click **Borders and Shading**. In the displayed **Borders and Shading** dialog box, be sure the **Borders tab** is selected. Under **Setting**, click **Box**. Click the **Width arrow**, and then click **1 1/2 pt**. Click the **Color arrow**, and then click **Orange, Accent 6, Darker 50%**—the bottom color in the tenth column. Compare your screen with Figure 4.14.

In the lower right portion of the Borders and Shading dialog box, the *Apply to* box displays *Paragraph*. The *Apply to* box directs where the border will be applied—in this instance, the border will be applied to the selected paragraph.

Figure 4.14

Border preview   *Apply to* box

Box setting

Border color

Border line width

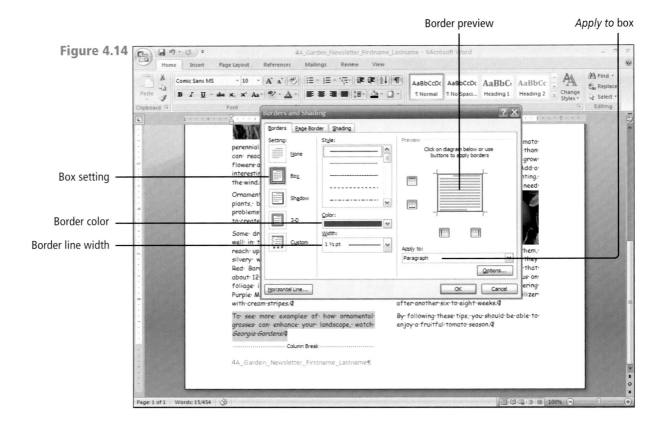

Note — Adding Simple Borders to Text

Simple borders and border edges can be added using the Border button in the Paragraph group. This button offers very little control, however, because line thickness and color depend on the previous thickness and color chosen from the Borders and Shading dialog box.

2 At the top of the **Borders and Shading** dialog box, click the **Shading tab**.

3 Click the **Fill arrow**, and then click **Orange, Accent 6, Lighter 80%**—the second color in the tenth column. At the bottom of the **Borders and Shading** dialog box, click **OK**. Click anywhere in the document to deselect the text, and then compare your screen with Figure 4.15.

Figure 4.15

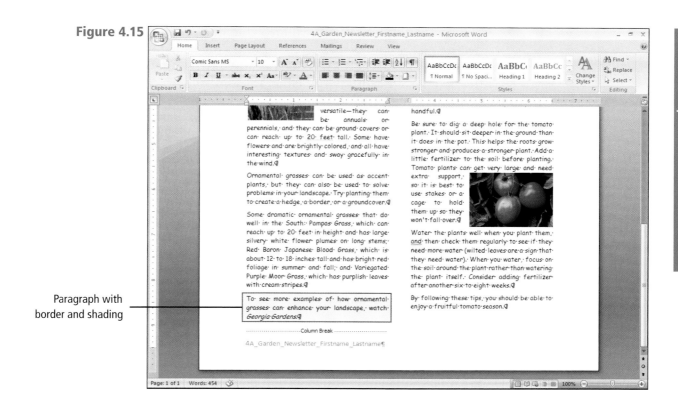

Paragraph with border and shading

4 **Save** the document, submit your file as directed, and then **Exit** Word.

Objective 4
Create Mailing Labels Using Mail Merge

Word's *mail merge* feature joins a *main document* and a *data source* to create customized letters or labels. The main document contains the text or formatting that remains constant. In the case of labels, the main document contains the formatting for a specific label size. The data source contains information including the names and addresses of the individuals for whom the labels are being created. Names and addresses in a data source might come from a Word table, an Excel spreadsheet, or an Access database.

The easiest way to perform a mail merge is to use the Mail Merge Wizard. Recall that a wizard asks you questions and, based on your answers, walks you step-by-step through a process. Labels are used to address newsletters, envelopes, postcards, disk labels, name badges, file folder labels, and so on. Sheets of precut labels can be purchased from office supply stores.

Activity 4.9 Opening the Mail Merge Wizard Template

Mail merge information can be stored in various formats and programs, including Microsoft Word tables. Such tables can be edited in the same manner as other Word tables.

The label feature in Word contains the product numbers of the standard Avery label products as well as several other label brands. Each product number is associated with a layout in Word's table format consisting of the height and width of the label. Because the product numbers predefine the label layout, the creation of labels is a simple and automated process. The first two steps in creating labels using the Mail Merge Wizard are identifying the label type and specifying the data source.

1 **Start** Word and display a new blank document. Display formatting marks, and be sure your screen shows both the left and right document edges. Display the **Save As** dialog box and in your **Word Chapter 4** folder, save the document as **4A_Mailing_Labels_ Firstname_Lastname**

2 **Open** the file **w04A_Addresses**—be sure to use w04**A** and not one of the other address files. Display the **Save As** dialog box, navigate to your **Word Chapter 4** folder, and then save the file as **4A_Addresses_ Firstname_Lastname**

A table of addresses displays. The first row contains the column names. The remaining rows contain addresses. This data file will be modified, but not submitted.

3 Click to position the insertion point in the last cell in the table, and then press Tab to create a new row. Enter the following information, and then compare your table with Figure 4.16.

First Name	Duncan
Last Name	**McArthur**
Address 1	**3336 S. Flowers Rd.**
Address 2	**#234**
City	**Macon**
State	**GA**
ZIP Code	**31217**

Figure 4.16

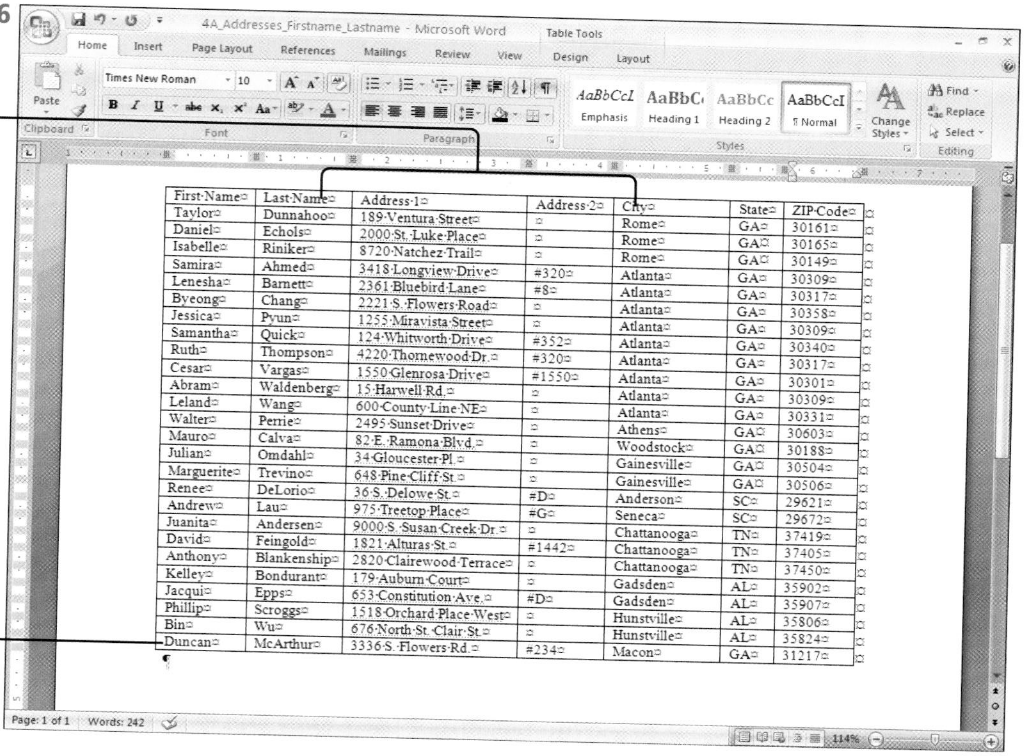

Column names ───

First Name	Last Name	Address 1	Address 2	City	State	ZIP Code
Taylor	Dunnahoo	189 Ventura Street		Rome	GA	30161
Daniel	Echols	2000 St. Luke Place		Rome	GA	30165
Isabelle	Riniker	8720 Natchez Trail		Rome	GA	30149
Samira	Ahmed	3418 Longview Drive	#320	Atlanta	GA	30309
Lenesha	Barnett	2361 Bluebird Lane	#8	Atlanta	GA	30317
Byeong	Chang	2221 S. Flowers Road		Atlanta	GA	30358
Jessica	Pyun	1255 Miravista Street		Atlanta	GA	30309
Samantha	Quick	124 Whitworth Drive	#352	Atlanta	GA	30340
Ruth	Thompson	4220 Thornewood Dr.	#320	Atlanta	GA	30317
Cesar	Vargas	1550 Glenrosa Drive	#1550	Atlanta	GA	30301
Abram	Waldenberg	15 Harwell Rd.		Atlanta	GA	30309
Leland	Wang	600 County Line NE		Atlanta	GA	30331
Walter	Perrie	2495 Sunset Drive		Athens	GA	30603
Mauro	Calva	82 E. Ramona Blvd.		Woodstock	GA	30188
Julian	Omdahl	34 Gloucester Pl.		Gainesville	GA	30504
Marguerite	Trevino	648 Pine Cliff St.		Gainesville	GA	30506
Renee	DeLorio	36 S. Delowe St.	#D	Anderson	SC	29621
Andrew	Lau	975 Treetop Place	#G	Seneca	SC	29672
Juanita	Andersen	9000 S. Susan Creek Dr.		Chattanooga	TN	37419
David	Feingold	1821 Alturas St.		Chattanooga	TN	37405
Anthony	Blankenship	2820 Clairewood Terrace	#1442	Chattanooga	TN	37450
Kelley	Bondurant	179 Auburn Court		Gadsden	AL	35902
Jacqui	Epps	653 Constitution Ave.	#D	Gadsden	AL	35907
Phillip	Scroggs	1518 Orchard Place West		Hunstville	AL	35806
Bin	Wu	676 North St. Clair St.		Hunstville	AL	35824
Duncan	McArthur	3336 S. Flowers Rd.	#234	Macon	GA	31217

New row ───

4 **Save**, and then **Close** the table of addresses; be sure your **4A_Mailing_Labels** document displays.

5 Click the **Mailings tab**. In the **Start Mail Merge group**, click the **Start Mail Merge** button, and then click **Step by Step Mail Merge Wizard** to display the **Mail Merge** task pane. Under **Select document type**, click the **Labels** option button.

6 At the bottom of the task pane, click **Next: Starting document** to display **Step 2 of 6** of the Mail Merge Wizard. Under **Select starting document**, be sure **Change document layout** is selected, and then under **Change document layout**, click **Label options**.

7 In the **Label Options** dialog box, under **Printer information**, click the **Tray arrow**, and then click **Default tray (Automatically Select)**—your wording may vary—to print the labels on regular paper, rather than feeding label pages manually. Under **Label information**, click the **Label vendors arrow**, and then click **Avery US Letter**. Under **Product number**, Scroll about halfway down the list, and then click **5160**. Compare your screen with Figure 4.17.

The Avery 5160 address label is a commonly used label. The precut sheets contain three columns of 10 labels each—for a total of 30 labels per sheet.

Project 4A: Garden Newsletter | **Word**   277

Figure 4.17

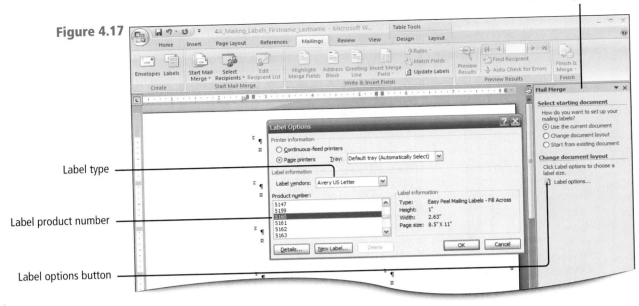

Label type

Label product number

Label options button

---

8 At the bottom of the **Label Options** dialog box, click **OK**. If a message box displays, click OK to set up the labels. At the bottom of the task pane, click **Next: Select recipients**.

The label page is set up with three columns and ten rows. The label borders may or may not display on your screen, depending on your setup. In Step 3 of the Mail Merge Wizard, you must identify the recipients—the data source. For your recipient data source, you can choose to use an existing list—for example, a list of names and addresses that you have in an Access database, an Excel spreadsheet, a Word table, or your Outlook contacts list. If you do not have an existing data source, you can type a new list at this point in the wizard.

9 Under **Select recipients**, be sure the **Use an existing list** option button is selected. Under **Use an existing list**, click **Browse**. Click the **Look in arrow**, navigate to your **Word Chapter 4** folder, select your **4A_Addresses_Firstname_Lastname** file, and then click **Open** to display the Mail Merge Recipients dialog box, as shown in Figure 4.18.

The labels in the first row of the Word table display as the column headings in the Mail Merge Recipients dialog box. In a database or Word address table, each row of information that contains data for one person is called a *record*. The column headings—for example, *Last Name* and *First Name*—are referred to as *fields*.

Figure 4.18

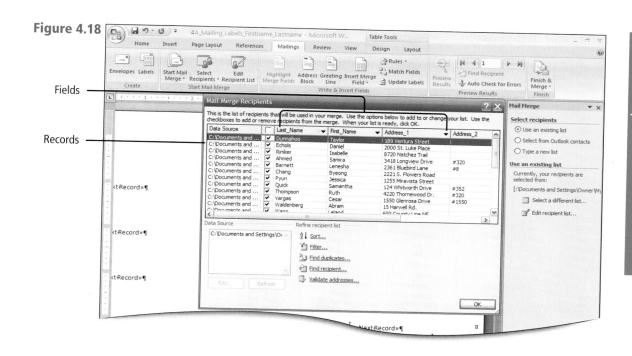

Fields

Records

10 Click the **Last_Name** field column heading to sort the records in alphabetical order by last name. In the labels document, notice that <<*Next Record*>> displays in the table cells that are visible behind the dialog box, except the first label, which is the first record.

You can sort on any of the fields by clicking the field column heading.

Activity 4.10 Completing the Mail Merge Wizard

You can add or edit names and addresses while completing the Mail Merge Wizard. You can also match your column names with preset names used in Mail Merge; for example, if the column heading for city names was *Place*, you could match that column with the *City* field to create the correct address blocks.

1 Near the bottom of the **Mail Merge Recipients** dialog box, under **Data Source**, click the file name. At the bottom of the **Mail Merge Recipients** dialog box, click **Edit**.

The Data Form dialog box displays. You can edit or delete the selected record, or use the same dialog box to add a new recipient.

2 On the right side of the displayed **Data Form** dialog box, click **Add New**. In the displayed blank record, type the following, and then compare your **Data Form** dialog box with Figure 4.19:

First Name	Harriet
Last Name	Hasty
Address 1	1875 Bullpen Dr.
Address 2	
City	Columbus
State	GA
ZIP Code	31993

Figure 4.19

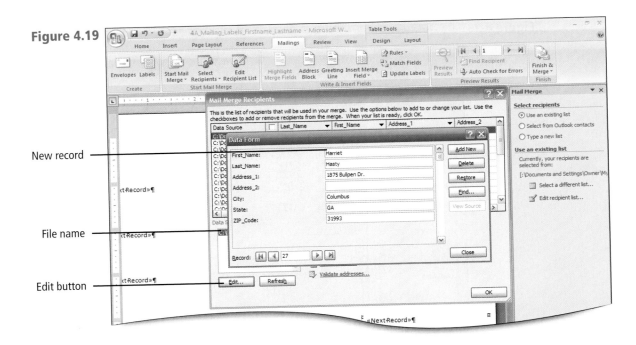

New record

File name

Edit button

> **3** At the bottom of the **Data Form** dialog box, click **Close**. Scroll through the recipient list to confirm that the record you just added is in the list. At the bottom of the **Mail Merge Recipients** dialog box, click **OK**. At the bottom of the **Mail Merge** task pane, click **Next: Arrange your labels**.

At Step 4 of the Mail Merge Wizard, Word provides various ways to arrange and add features to your labels.

> **4** Under **Arrange your labels**, click **Address block**. In the **Insert Address Block** dialog box, under **Specify address elements**, examine the various formats for names. If necessary, under **Insert recipient's name in this format**, select the **Joshua Randall Jr.** format. Compare your dialog box with Figure 4.20.

Figure 4.20

Address block preview

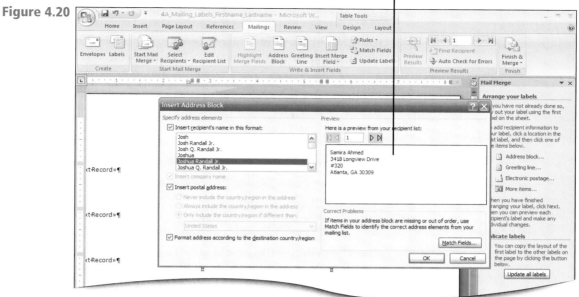

5 Near the bottom of the **Insert Address Block** dialog box, click **Match Fields**. Scroll down and examine the dialog box, and then compare your screen with Figure 4.21.

If your field names are descriptive, the Mail Merge program will identify them correctly, as is the case with the information in the *Required for Address Block* section. If you need to match a field, display the list to choose the correct field from your database or table.

Figure 4.21

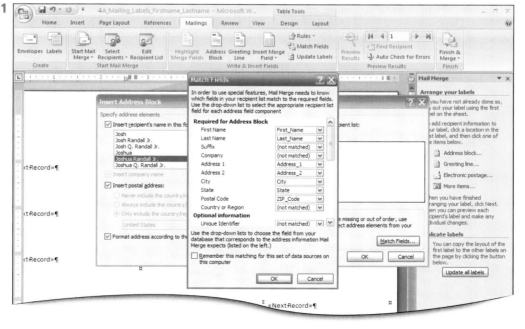

6 At the bottom of the **Match Fields** dialog box, click **OK**. At the bottom of the **Insert Address Block** dialog box, click **OK**.

The Address block is inserted in the first label space and is surrounded by double angle brackets. The *Address Block* field name displays, which represents the address block you saw in the Preview area of the Insert Address Block dialog box.

7 In the upper left corner of the document, select the <<**Address Block**>> field. Be sure to include the paragraph mark. Click the **Page Layout tab**, and in the **Paragraph group**, use the **spin box arrows** to set the **Before** and **After** boxes to **0** to ensure that the four-line addresses will fit on the labels.

8 In the task pane, under **Replicate labels**, click **Update all labels** to insert an address block in each label space for each subsequent record.

9 At the bottom of the task pane, click **Next: Preview your labels**. Notice that the labels are sorted alphabetically by the Last Name field, and that the order of the labels is from left to right and then down to the next row. If the address block lines are spaced too far apart and some of the text at the bottom of the labels is cut off, press Ctrl + A to select the entire document, and then on the Home tab, in the Styles group, click the No Spacing style. If necessary, scroll to the left to view the left edge of the page, and then compare your labels with Figure 4.22.

Some Word defaults add extra spacing after paragraphs. Changing the line spacing ensures that the address blocks will fit properly on the labels. In some cases, where there is an apartment or unit number, there are addresses on two lines. The wizard creates the lines automatically when the Address Block is inserted and centers the address block vertically on each label.

Addresses on two lines

Figure 4.22

Labels are sorted by last name

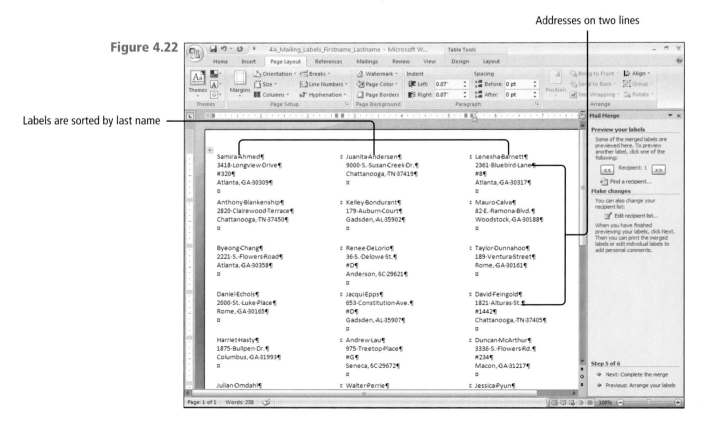

10 At the bottom of the task pane, click **Next: Complete the merge**. **Save** your labels.

Step 6 of the Mail Merge task pane displays. At this point you can print or edit your labels, although this is done more easily in the document window.

11 **Close** ☒ the Mail Merge Wizard task pane.

Activity 4.11 Previewing and Printing the Mail Merge Document

Before you print, preview your labels to be sure the information fits in the space reserved for each label.

1 Display the document footer and add the file name to the footer, and then close the footer area. From the **Office** menu 🔘 , point to the **Print arrow**, and then click **Print Preview**. Position the 🔍 pointer over the labels and click one time. Compare your screen with Figure 4.23.

Adding footer text to a label sheet replaces the last row of labels on a page with the footer text, and moves the last row of labels to the top of the next page. In this case, a blank second page is created.

Figure 4.23

Labels display at full size (100%)

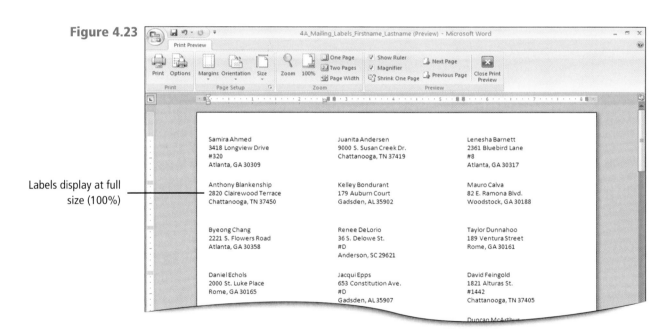

2 To submit electronically, follow your instructor's directions. Otherwise, on the **Print Preview tab**, in the **Print group**, click the **Print** button. In the **Print** dialog box, under **Page range**, click the **Current page** option button, and then click **OK**.

The labels will print on whatever paper is in the printer. In this case, unless you have preformatted labels available, you will print your labels on a sheet of paper. Printing the labels on plain paper first enables you to proofread the labels before you print them on more expensive label sheets.

3 On the **Print Preview tab**, in the **Preview group**, click the **Close Print Preview** button.

4 **Close** the document, click **Yes** to save the data source, click **Yes** to save the labels, and then **Exit** Word.

End **You have completed Project 4A** ———————————

Project 4B Television Hosts

In Activities 4.12 through 4.18 you will edit a document that introduces the hosts of the *Georgia Gardens* television show. You will add links to text and graphics, and you will add a SmartArt graphic. Finally, you will save the document as both a Word document and as a Web page. Your completed documents will look similar to Figure 4.24.

For Project 4B, you will need the following file:

w04B_Television_Hosts

You will save your documents as
4B_Television_Hosts_Firstname_Lastname
4B_Television_Hosts_Firstname_Lastname.mht

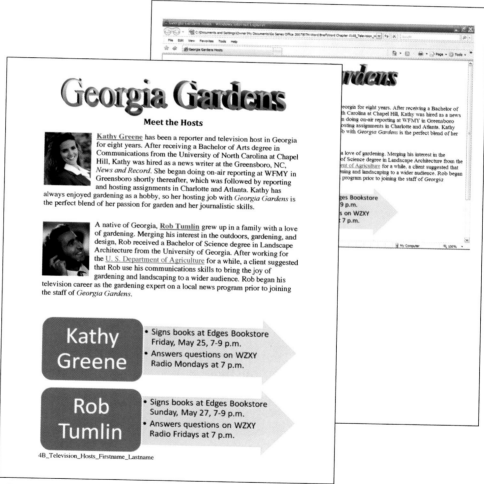

Figure 4.24
Project 4B—Television Hosts

Objective 5
Insert Hyperlinks

Organizations publish information about themselves on the Web. Microsoft Word has tools that enable the creation of Web pages directly from word processing documents. Hyperlinks can be added to move to related sites quickly. *Hyperlinks* are text or graphics that you click to move to a file, another page in a Web site, or a page in a different Web site.

Activity 4.12 Inserting Text Hyperlinks

The type of hyperlink used most frequently is one that is attached to text. Text hyperlinks usually display underlined and in blue.

1 **Start** Word. Locate and open the document **w04B_Television_ Hosts**. Display formatting marks, and be sure your screen shows both the left and right document edges. Display the **Save As** dialog box, and then save the document as **4B_Television_Hosts_Firstname_ Lastname** Open the document footer and add the file name to the footer.

2 In the paragraph to the right of the upper picture, select the text *Kathy Greene*. Click the **Insert tab**, and then in the **Links group**, click the **Hyperlink** button. Alternatively, right-click on the selected text and click Hyperlink from the shortcut menu.

3 In the displayed **Insert Hyperlink** dialog box, under **Link to**, be sure **Existing File or Web Page** is selected. In the **Address** box, type **http://www.georgiagardens.tv/hosts/greene.htm**

When you begin to type, AutoComplete may display an address in the Address box. It displays the Web address typed most recently in this dialog box. The Georgia Gardens Web addresses used in this project are not live links.

4 In the upper right corner of the **Insert Hyperlink** dialog box, click **ScreenTip**. In the **Set Hyperlink ScreenTip** dialog box, under **ScreenTip text**, type **Kathy Greene Biography** and then compare your screen with Figure 4.25.

This is the ScreenTip that will display when the pointer is moved over the hyperlink.

Figure 4.25

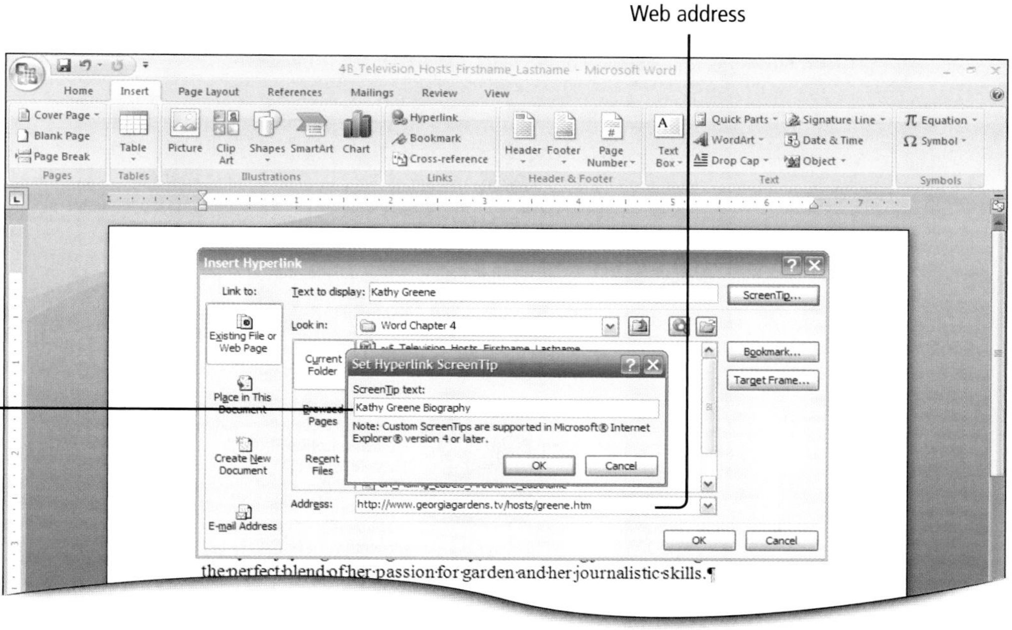

ScreenTip

5 In the **Set Hyperlink ScreenTip** dialog box, click **OK**. At the bottom of the **Insert Hyperlink** dialog box, click **OK**.

The hyperlink is recorded, and the selected text changes to blue and is underlined.

6 In the next paragraph, in the first line, select the text *Rob Tumlin*. Using the technique you just practiced, create a hyperlink to the address **http://www.georgiagardens.tv/hosts/tumlin.htm** and then as the **ScreenTip**, type **Rob Tumlin Biography**

7 In the same paragraph, select the text *U. S. Department of Agriculture.* Using the technique you just practiced, create a hyperlink to the address **http://www.usda.gov** and then as the **ScreenTip**, type **Department of Agriculture**

8 **Save** your document, and then compare your screen with Figure 4.26.

Figure 4.26

Inserted hyperlinks

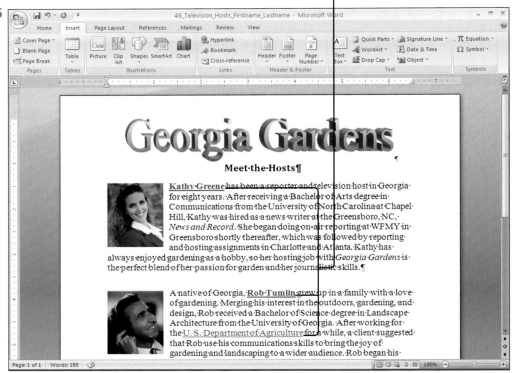

Activity 4.13 Adding a Hyperlink to a Graphic

When you point to a graphic on a Web page, if the pointer changes to the Link Select pointer ⟨⊕⟩, this indicates that a hyperlink has been added to the graphic. When you point to a hyperlink in a Word document, a ScreenTip displays with instructions for accessing the link.

1 Near the top of the document, right-click the upper picture—the picture of *Kathy Greene*—and then click **Hyperlink**.

2 In the displayed **Insert Hyperlink** dialog box, under **Link to**, be sure **Existing File or Web Page** is selected. In the **Address** box, type **http://www.georgiagardens.tv/hosts/greene.htm**

This is the same address you typed for the text in the paragraph to the right of the picture. In this document, there will be two hyperlinks to the same address for each host.

3 In the upper right corner of the **Insert Hyperlink** dialog box, click **ScreenTip**. In the **Set Hyperlink ScreenTip** dialog box, under **ScreenTip text**, type **Kathy Greene Biography** and then close both dialog boxes.

4 Click to deselect the picture. Point to the *Kathy Greene* picture and notice the ScreenTip and the Web address in the status bar, as shown in Figure 4.27. Use the same procedure to check the *Kathy Greene* text hyperlink.

Hyperlink ScreenTip

Figure 4.27

Web address in status bar

5️⃣ Right-click the lower picture—the picture of *Rob Tumlin*—and click **Hyperlink**. Using the technique you just practiced, create a hyperlink to the address **http://www.georgiagardens.tv/hosts/tumlin.htm** and then type **Rob Tumlin Biography** as the ScreenTip.

6️⃣ **Save** 💾 the document.

More Knowledge
Adding an E-Mail Hyperlink

You can also add a hyperlink to an e-mail address in a document. Select the text that you want to link to, and then display the Insert Hyperlink dialog box. Under Link to, click E-mail Address. Type the e-mail address, or select it from the Recently used e-mail addresses list. If desired, type a Subject line. You can also click the ScreenTip button to add a ScreenTip to the hyperlink.

Activity 4.14 Testing and Modifying Hyperlinks

Make changes to hyperlinks in the Edit Hyperlink dialog box, which is similar to the Insert Hyperlink dialog box.

1️⃣ Be sure you have an Internet connection. Point to the **U. S. Department of Agriculture** hyperlink and read the ScreenTip. Follow the directions to test the hyperlink.

Your computer may be configured to click to activate a hyperlink, or you may be required to hold down Ctrl, and then click the hyperlink.

2 Return to your document. Point to the **U. S. Department of Agriculture** hyperlink, and then right-click. From the shortcut menu, click **Edit Hyperlink**. At the bottom of the displayed **Edit Hyperlink** dialog box, in the **Address** box, change the address to **http://www.usna.usda.gov/Gardens/collections/friend.html** Be sure to capitalize *Gardens*.

3 In the upper right corner of the **Edit Hyperlink** dialog box, click **ScreenTip**. Change the ScreenTip to **USDA Friendship Garden** and then compare your dialog box with Figure 4.28.

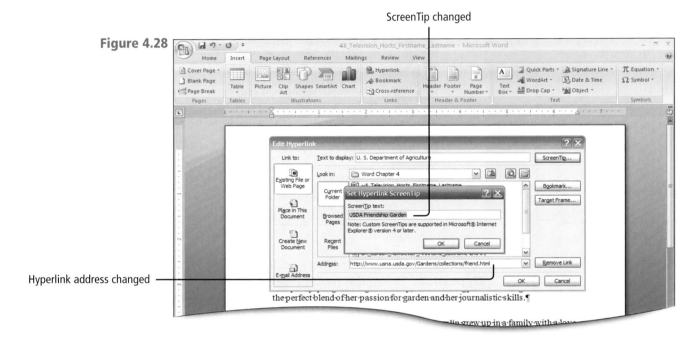

Figure 4.28

ScreenTip changed

Hyperlink address changed

Note — If the Text Displays Automatically

When you begin typing the text in the text boxes of the Edit Hyperlink dialog box, the complete text may display after typing only a few letters. This indicates that another student used the computer to complete this project and that the AutoComplete feature is turned on.

4 Click **OK** to close both dialog boxes. Point to the **U. S. Department of Agriculture** hyperlink and read the new ScreenTip. Follow the directions to test the new hyperlink address.

5 **Save** 🔲 the document.

Objective 6
Insert a SmartArt Graphic

SmartArt graphics are designer-quality visual representations of information that you can create by choosing from among many different layouts. Insert a SmartArt graphic to more effectively communicate your messages or ideas, and to add visual appeal to a document or a Web page.

Activity 4.15 Inserting a SmartArt Graphic

1 Press [Ctrl] + [End] to move to the end of the document, and then press [Enter].

2 Click the **Insert tab**, and then in the **Illustrations group**, point to the **SmartArt** button to display its ScreenTip. Read the ScreenTip, and then click the button.

3 In the displayed **Choose a SmartArt Graphic** dialog box, use the scroll bar to examine the types of SmartArt graphics available to you. When you are finished, scroll to the top of the list, and then click the first style in the fifth row—**Vertical Arrow List**. At the right of the dialog box, notice the preview and description of the graphic, as shown in Figure 4.29.

Figure 4.29

Preview and description

Vertical Arrow List SmartArt graphic

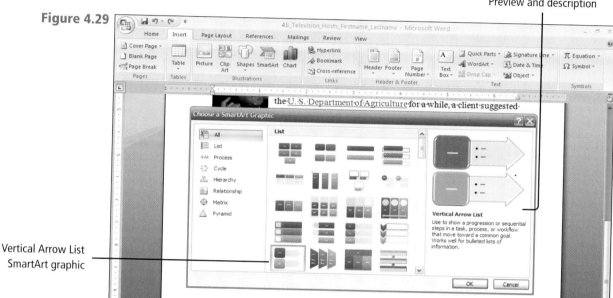

4 At the bottom of the displayed **Choose a SmartArt Graphic** dialog box, click **OK**. If the *Type your text here* box does not display, on the Design tab, in the Create Graphic group, click the Text Pane button. Compare your screen with Figure 4.30.

The SmartArt graphic is placed at the insertion point location. The graphic consists of two parts—the graphic itself, and a *Type your text here* box, into which you can type the SmartArt graphic text in outline format. On the Ribbon, two SmartArt Tools—the Design tab and the Format tab—display.

Figure 4.30

Text Pane button

Type your text here box

SmartArt Tools

Vertical Arrow List
SmartArt graphic

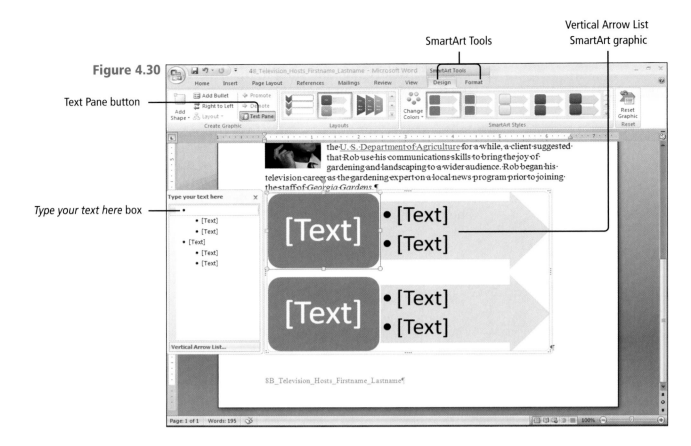

5 **Save** 🖫 your document.

Activity 4.16 Adding Text to a SmartArt Graphic

1 With the SmartArt graphic displayed on your screen, click in the first top-level bullet point. In the **Type your text here** box, type **Kathy Greene** and then press ⬇.

The ***top-level points*** are the main points in a SmartArt graphic. ***Subpoints*** are second-level bullet points. The name displays in the left SmartArt box, and the insertion point moves to the first second-level bullet. If you press the Enter key, a new bullet point will be added at the same level as the previous bullet point.

2 Type **Signs books at Edges Bookstore Friday, May 25, 7-9 p.m.** and then press ⬇. Compare your screen with Figure 4.31.

Figure 4.31

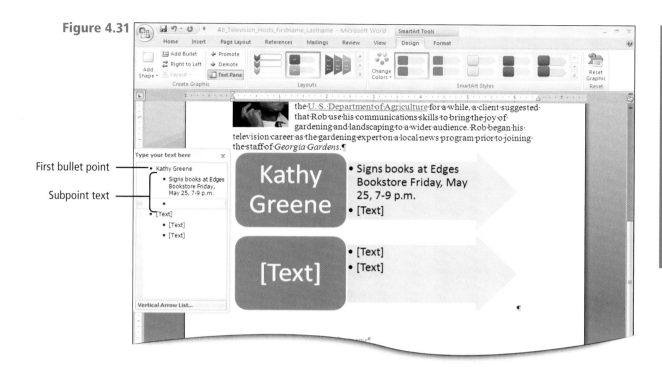

First bullet point

Subpoint text

3 Type **Answers questions on WZXY Radio Mondays at 7 p.m.** and then press Enter to add a new subpoint, and then press ↓.

4 Type **Rob Tumlin** and then press ↓. Type **Signs books at Edges Bookstore Sunday, May 27, 7-9 p.m.** and then press ↓. Type **Answers questions on WZXY Radio Fridays at 7 p.m.** and then in the **Create Graphic group**, click the **Text Pane** button to close the *Type your text here* box.

5 Move the pointer to the middle of the right border of the SmartArt graphic to display ↔ pointer, and then drag the right edge of the graphic to **6.5 inches on the horizontal ruler**. On the right side of the **Format tab**, click the **Arrange** button, click the **Position** button, and then under **With Text Wrapping**, click the **Position in Bottom Center with Square Text Wrapping** button—the middle button in the bottom row. Compare your screen with Figure 4.32.

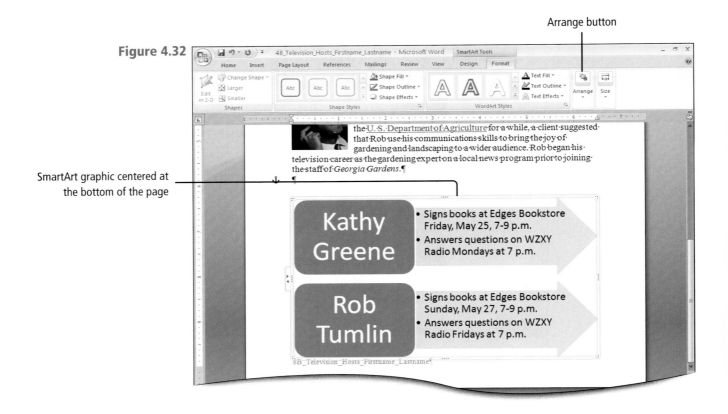

Arrange button

Figure 4.32

SmartArt graphic centered at
the bottom of the page

6 Deselect the SmartArt graphic, and then **Save** 🔲 your document.

More Knowledge
Adding More Items to a SmartArt List

After you have filled the SmartArt graphic with information, you can add
new top-level points and subpoints. In the *Type your text here* box, position
the insertion point where you want a new point. On the Design tab, in the
Create Graphic group, click Add Bullet. To move to a first-level heading
down to a subhead level, click the Demote button. To move a subpoint to a
top-level heading, click the Promote button.

Objective 7
Preview and Save a Document as a Web Page

After you have created a document to be used as a Web page, you can
see what the page will look like when displayed in a Web browser such as
Internet Explorer. A **Web browser** is software that enables you to use the
Web and navigate from page to page and site to site. You can adjust the
image and preview it until you get it exactly right. After you are satisfied
with the way your document looks when displayed in a Web browser, you
can save the document as a Web page.

Activity 4.17 Previewing a Document as a Web Page

1 Click the **View tab**, and then in the **Document Views group**, click the **Web Layout** button. **Maximize** the screen if necessary, and then scroll to the top of the page. Compare your screen with Figure 4.33.

The document displays as a Web page, although Word does not open your Web browser. Your screen may look different from the figures shown, depending on your screen size, screen resolution, and the Web browser you use.

Document previewed as Web page—
your screen may vary

Figure 4.33

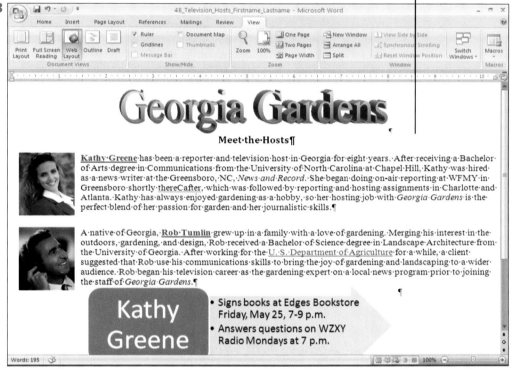

2 On the right side of the status bar, use the Zoom slider to zoom in and out to see what the Web page will look like on screens with lower or higher resolutions, or with the browser window not maximized. Notice that the font and picture sizes increase and decrease as you zoom in and out, but the word wrapping continues, and centered text remains centered. Figure 4.34 displays the look of the screen if you use a lower resolution monitor.

Figure 4.34

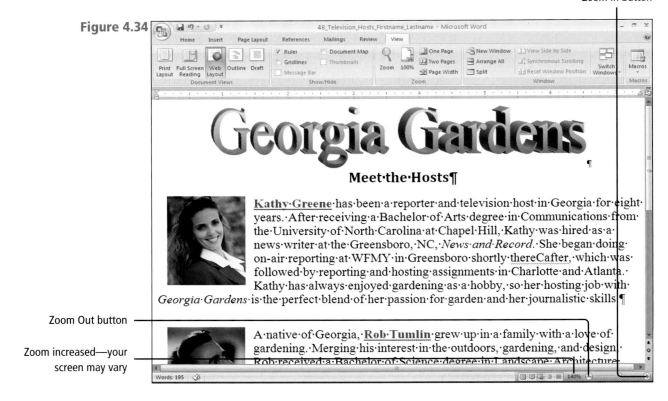

Zoom Out button

Zoom increased—your
screen may vary

3. On the **View tab**, in the **Document Views group**, click the **Print Layout** button.

4. Display **Print Preview** to check your document. Submit the Word document as directed—in the next activity, you will create a Web page using the same document.

Activity 4.18 Saving a Document as a Web Page

After you are satisfied with your document, you can save it as a Web page.

1. From the **Office** menu, click **Save As**. In the displayed **Save As** dialog box, navigate to your **Word Chapter 4** folder. Near the bottom of the **Save As** dialog box, click the **Save as type arrow**. Scroll down and click **Single File Web Page**.

The first line of the document—*Georgia Gardens*—may display as the default Page title for the Web page depending on your program settings. The default title is the first line of text in the document. If your system is set to display file extensions, *.mht* displays in place of *.docx*.

2. Near the bottom of the **Save As** dialog box, click **Change Title**. In the displayed **Set Page Title** dialog box, click to the right of Georgia Gardens, make the page title **Georgia Gardens Hosts** and then click **OK**. Compare your screen with Figure 4.35.

The text that you type in the Set Page Title dialog box will become the Web page title; that is, the title that displays in the browser title bar and displays in the Web browser's history list.

Change Title button

Figure 4.35

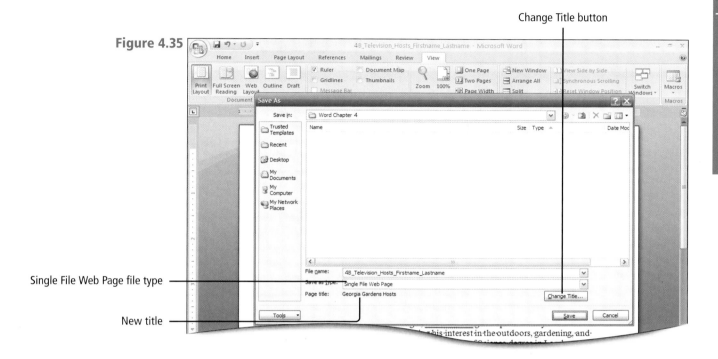

Single File Web Page file type

New title

▣ At the bottom of the **Save As** dialog box, click **Save** to save the document as a Web page.

▣ **Close** the document, and then **Exit** Word. Display the **My Computer** window, and then navigate to your **Word Chapter 4** folder. Locate and double-click the **4B_Television_Hosts_Firstname_Lastname.mht** file. If necessary, maximize the browser screen. Notice that the title you changed displays in the browser title bar, as shown in Figure 4.36.

The Web page you created will have a different file extension and file type icon to distinguish it from the Word document by the same name.

Figure 4.36

Document open in
browser window

New Web page title

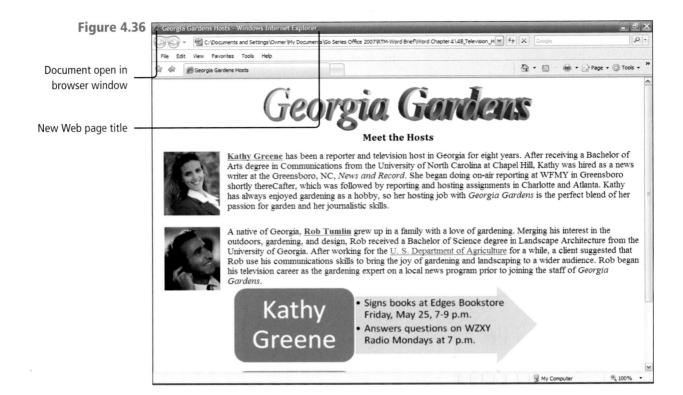

Alert! | Are you connected to the Internet?

If you are not connected to the Internet, you may see a message informing you that you are not connected, or the page cannot be displayed. Click OK or close the message box to acknowledge the message.

 Submit your Web page as directed, and then **Close** ⊠ the Web browser.

End **You have completed Project 4B** —————

There's More You Can Do!

From My Computer, navigate to the student files that accompany this textbook. In the folder **02_theres_more_you_can_do_pg1_36**, locate and open the folder for this chapter. Open and print the instructions for this project, which are provided to you in Adobe PDF format.

Try IT! 1—Adding Comments and Tracking Changes

In this Try IT! exercise, you will use Word's reviewing features to track changes made to the document and to add nonprinting comments.

Content-Based Assessments

Summary

Microsoft Word includes features you can use to create newsletters and Web pages, similar to those created by desktop publishing or Web design programs. For example, you can add borders and shading to paragraphs, and use special character formats to create distinctive headings. You can format text into multiple-column documents and add hyperlinks to a Word document and save it as a Web page. Word also assists you in creating mailing labels using the Mail Merge Wizard. Word enables you to use the collect-and-paste process to gather information from various sources and store them in the Office Clipboard. You can also create professional-looking graphics using SmartArt.

Key Terms

Collect and paste 262	**Mail merge** 275	**SmartArt** 290
Comment .... ●	**Main document** 275	**Subpoint** 292
Copyright 265	**Manual column**	**Top-level point** 292
Data source 275	**break** 266	**Track Changes** .... ●
Field 278	**Record** 278	**Web browser** 294
Hyperlink 286	**Small caps** 272	

The ● symbol represents Key Terms found on the Student CD in the 02_theres_more_you_can_do folder for this chapter.

300   Word | Chapter 4: Special Document Formats, Columns, and Mail Merge

Content-Based Assessments

Matching

Match each term in the second column with its correct definition in the first column. Write the letter of the term on the blank line in front of the correct definition.

_____ **1.** Laws that protect the rights of authors of original works, including text, art, photographs, and music.

_____ **2.** The Microsoft Office feature that enables you to place up to 24 objects on the Office Clipboard, and then paste them as needed, and in any order.

_____ **3.** A Microsoft Office program with which you can turn text into decorative graphics.

_____ **4.** An artificial end to a column to balance columns or to provide space for the insertion of other objects.

_____ **5.** A font effect, usually used in titles, that changes lowercase text into capital (uppercase) letters using a reduced font size.

_____ **6.** A category of information stored in columns in a data table.

_____ **7.** All of the fields containing information about one topic (a person or organization) and stored in a row in a data table.

_____ **8.** A Word feature that joins a main document and a data source to create customized letters or labels.

_____ **9.** The document that contains the text or formatting that remains constant in a mail merge.

_____ **10.** A list of variable information, such as names and addresses, that is merged with a main document to create customized form letters or labels.

_____ **11.** Text that you click to go to another location in a document, another document, or a Web site; the text is a different color (usually blue) than the surrounding text, and is commonly underlined.

_____ **12.** A designer-quality graphic used to create visual representations of information.

_____ **13.** The main points in a SmartArt graphic.

_____ **14.** Software that enables you to use the Web and navigate from page to page and site to site.

_____ **15.** A document that has been saved with an *.mht* extension so it can be viewed with a Web browser.

A Collect and paste

B Copyright

C Data source

D Field

E Hyperlink

F Mail merge

G Main document

H Manual column break

I Record

J Small caps

K SmartArt

L Top-level point

M Web browser

N Web page

O WordArt

Content-Based Assessments

Fill in the Blank

Write the correct word in the space provided.

1. You can store up to _____ items in the Office Clipboard.

2. To remove the items in the Clipboard task pane, click the _____ _____ button.

3. WordArt changes text into a decorative _____.

4. Microsoft Publisher is a _____ _____ program.

5. Use a(n) _____ _____ to change uneven columns into more equal lengths.

6. To change one column of text into two columns, use the _____ button on the Page Layout tab.

7. When you change from a one-column format to a two-column format, Word inserts a _____ _____.

8. Magazines and newspapers use narrower columns of text because they are easier to _____ than text that stretches across a page.

9. All of the information about a single person or business in a mail merge address file is known as a _____.

10. The column headings in a mail merge data source are known as _____.

11. In a SmartArt graphic, the main text points are the _____ points.

12. In a SmartArt graphic, the secondary points are the _____.

13. Internet Explorer is an example of _____ software.

14. To enable a user to click on text or a graphic to move to another file or a Web site, add a _____ to the text or graphic.

15. When you save a Word document as a Web page, the text that you type in the Set Page Title dialog box displays in the browser _____ bar.

Content-Based Assessments

Word

chapterfour

Skills Review

Project 4C — Trellis

In this project, you will apply the skills you practiced from the Objectives in Project 4A.

Objectives: 1. *Collect and Paste Text and Graphics;* **2.** *Create and Format Columns;* **3.** *Use Special Character and Paragraph Formatting;* **4.** *Create Mailing Labels Using Mail Merge.*

In the following Skills Review, you will use collect and paste to create a newsletter about building a trellis. You will also create mailing labels for the newsletter. Your completed documents will look similar to the ones shown in Figure 4.37.

For Project 4C, you will need the following files:

New blank Word document
w04C_Trellis_Graphics
w04C_Basic_Trellis
w04C_Rough_Trellis
w04C_Addresses

You will save your documents as
4C_Trellis_Firstname_Lastname
4C_Labels_Firstname_Lastname
4C_Addresses_Firstname_Lastname

Figure 4.37

(Project 4C–Trellis continues on the next page)

(Project 4C–Trellis continued)

1. **Start** Word and display a new blank document. Display formatting marks and rulers. Set the left and right margins to **1**", and the top and bottom margins to **0.5**". Display the **Save As** dialog box, navigate to your **Word Chapter 4** folder, and then save the document as **4C_Trellis_Firstname_Lastname** Open the document footer and add the file name to the footer.

2. On the **Home tab**, in the **Clipboard group**, click the **Dialog Box Launcher** to display the **Clipboard** task pane. If any items display in the clipboard, at the top of the task pane, click the **Clear All** button.

3. Locate, and then open the file **w04C_Basic_Trellis**. Select all of the text in the document, and then in the **Clipboard group**, click the **Copy** button. Locate, and then open the file **w04C_Rough_Trellis**. Select, and then **Copy** all of the text in the document. Locate, and then open the file **w04C_Trellis_Graphics**. **Copy** the WordArt title and the picture. Leave the **4C_Trellis** document open, but **Close** the other three files.

4. In the **Clipboard** task pane, click the **Build a Trellis** WordArt title, and then press Enter. In the **Clipboard** task pane, click the text entry beginning *Basic Trellis* to paste the entire block of text at the insertion point. In the **Clipboard** task pane, click the text entry beginning *Rough Trellis* to paste the entire block of text at the insertion point. At the bottom of the text, click the **Paste Options** button, and then click **Paste List Without Merging**—this removes the numbered list from the last three paragraphs. Press ←Bksp to remove the blank line at the bottom of the inserted text.

5. Select all of the text in the document except the WordArt title. Be sure to include the paragraph mark at the end of the document. Right-click the selected text, and then click **Paragraph**. In the displayed **Paragraph** dialog box, under **Spacing**, in the **After** box, click the **up spin arrow** to change the spacing to **6 pt**. Under **Spacing**, click the **Line spacing arrow**, and then click **Single**. Under **Spacing**, be sure the *Don't add space between paragraph of the same style* check box is cleared—you may have to click it two times to clear the check mark. Click **OK**, and then **Save** the document.

6. With the text still selected, click the **Page Layout tab**, and then in the **Page Setup group**, click the **Columns** button. From the displayed **Columns gallery**, click **Two**.

7. With the text still selected, click the **Home tab**. In the **Font group**, click the **Font button arrow**, and then click **Cambria**. In the **Font group**, click the **Font Size button arrow**, and then click **11**. In the **Paragraph group**, click the **Justify** button. Click anywhere in the document to deselect the text.

8. Click to the left of the *Rough Trellis* title, and then click the **Page Layout tab**. In the **Page Setup group**, click the **Breaks** button, and then under **Page Breaks**, click **Column**.

9. Press Ctrl + End to move to the end of the second column, and then press Enter. In the **Clipboard** task pane, click the **Trellis** picture. Click to select the **Trellis picture**, and then click the **Format tab**. In the **Size group**, click the **Shape Width up spin arrow** as necessary to set the picture width to **3**". Be sure the picture resizes proportionally. If it does not, right-click

(Project 4C–Trellis continues on the next page)

(Project 4C–Trellis continued)

the picture, and then click Size. In the displayed Size dialog box, under Scale, click the Lock aspect ratio check box. Under Original Size, click the Reset button, and then click Close.

10. Near the top of the **Clipboard** task pane, click the **Clear All** button to remove all items from the Office Clipboard. **Close** the Clipboard task pane, and then **Save** the document.

11. At the top of the first column, select the text **Basic Trellis**. Be sure to include the paragraph mark. Right-click the selected text, and then click **Font**. In the displayed **Font** dialog box, click the **Font color arrow**, and then under **Theme Colors**, click **Orange, Accent 6, Darker 50%**—the bottom color in the tenth column. Under **Font style**, click **Bold**. Under **Size**, click **20**. Under **Effects**, select the **Small caps** check box, and then click **OK**. At the top of the second column, select **Rough Trellis**. Apply the same formatting you added to the title of the first column.

12. Press Ctrl + End to move to the end of the second column, and then press Enter two times. Type **Have a gardening picture you would like to share? Send it to Rob@ georgiagardens.tv.** and then select the new paragraph. On the **Home tab**, in the **Paragraph group**, click the **Border button arrow**, and then click **Borders and Shading**. In the displayed **Borders and Shading** dialog box, be sure the **Borders tab** is selected. Under **Setting**, click **Shadow**. Click the **Width arrow** and then click **1 1/2 pt**. Click the **Color arrow**, and then click **Orange, Accent 6, Darker 50%**—the bottom color in the tenth column.

13. At the top of the **Borders and Shading** dialog box, click the **Shading tab**. Click the **Fill arrow**, and then click **Orange, Accent 6, Lighter 80%**—the second color in the tenth column. At the bottom of the **Borders and Shading** dialog box, click **OK**. **Save**, and then **Close** the document.

14. Submit your file as directed. Next, you will create mailing labels for a small group of subscribers.

15. Display a new blank document. Display the **Save As** dialog box and save the document as **4C_Labels_Firstname_Lastname** Be sure all margins are set to **1"**. Locate and **Open** the file **w04C_Addresses**. Display the **Save As** dialog box, navigate to the **Word Chapter 4** folder, and then save the file as **4C_Addresses_Firstname_Lastname**

16. Click to position the insertion point in the last cell in the table, and then press Tab to create a new row. Enter the following information:

First Name	Robert
Last Name	Hasty
Address 1	1884 Alcona Rd.
Address 2	
City	Columbus
State	GA
ZIP Code	31993

17. **Save**, and then **Close** the table of addresses; be sure your **4C_Labels** document displays. Click the **Mailings tab**. In the **Start Mail Merge group**, click the **Start Mail Merge** button, and then click **Step by Step Mail Merge Wizard** to

(Project 4C–Trellis continues on the next page)

(Project 4C–Trellis continued)

display the **Mail Merge** task pane. Under **Select document type**, click the **Labels** option button.

18. At the bottom of the task pane, click **Next: Starting document**. Under **Select starting document**, be sure **Change document layout** is selected, and then under **Change document layout**, click **Label options**. In the **Label Options** dialog box, under **Printer information**, click the **Tray arrow**, and then click **Default tray (Automatically Select)**—your text may vary. Under **Label information**, click the **Label vendors arrow**, and then click **Avery US Letter**. Under **Product number**, scroll as necessary and click **5160**.

19. At the bottom of the **Label Options** dialog box, click **OK**, and then at the bottom of the task pane, click **Next: Select recipients**.

20. Under **Select recipients**, be sure the **Use an existing list** option button is selected. Under **Use an existing list**, click **Browse**. Navigate to your **Word Chapter 4** folder, select your **4C_Addresses_Firstname_Lastname** file, and then click **Open**.

21. In the **Mail Merge Recipients** dialog box, click the **Last_Name** field column heading to sort the records in alphabetical order by last name, and then click **OK**. **Save** the document.

22. At the bottom of the **Mail Merge** task pane, click **Next: Arrange your labels**.

Under **Arrange your labels**, click **Address block**. In the **Insert Address Block** dialog box, under **Specify address elements**, examine the **Preview** area. If necessary, under **Insert recipient's name in this format**, select the **Joshua Randall Jr.** format, and then click **OK**.

23. In the upper left corner of the document, select the **<<Address Block>>** field. Be sure to include the paragraph mark. Click the **Page Layout tab**, and in the **Paragraph group**, use the **spin box arrows** to set the **Before** and **After** boxes to **0** to ensure that the four-line addresses will fit on the labels.

24. In the task pane, under **Replicate labels**, click **Update all labels**. At the bottom of the task pane, click **Next: Preview your labels**. At the bottom of the task pane, click **Next: Complete the merge**. Display the document footer, and then add the file name to the footer. **Save** your labels.

25. To submit electronically, follow your instructor's directions. Otherwise, on the **Print Preview tab**, in the **Print group**, click the **Print** button. In the **Print** dialog box, under **Page range**, click the **Current page** option button, and then click **OK**. On the **Print Preview tab**, in the **Preview group**, click the **Close Print Preview** button.

26. **Close** the document, click **Yes** to save the labels, and then **Exit** Word.

 You have completed Project 4C ——————————————

Content-Based Assessments

Skills Review

Project 4D — Lawn Care

In this project, you will apply the skills you practiced from the Objectives in Project 4B.

Objectives: 5. *Insert Hyperlinks;* **6.** *Insert a SmartArt Graphic;* **7.** *Preview and Save a Document as a Web Page.*

In the following Skills Review, you will add hyperlinks to text and a picture in a lawn care document created by the *Georgia Gardens* staff, and then add a SmartArt graphic. You will also save the document as a Web page, to be posted on the show's Web site. Your completed documents will look similar to Figure 4.38.

For Project 4D, you will need the following file:

w04D_Lawn_Care

You will save your documents as
4D_Lawn_Care_Firstname_Lastname
4D_Lawn_Care_Firstname_Lastname.mht

Figure 4.38

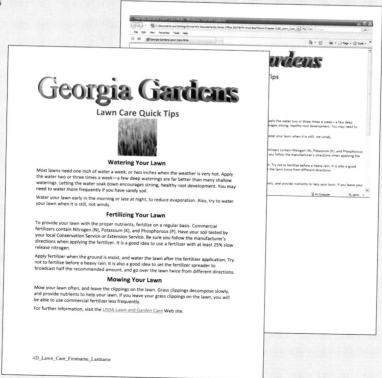

(Project 4D–Lawn Care continues on the next page)

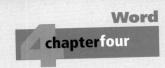
(Project 4D—Lawn Care continued)

1. **Start** Word. Locate and open the document **w04D_Lawn_Care**. Display formatting marks. **Save** the document in your **Word Chapter 4** folder as **4D_Lawn_Care_Firstname_Lastname** Open the document footer, and then add the file name to the footer.

2. In the last paragraph in the document, select the text *USDA Lawn and Garden Care*. Click the **Insert tab**, and then in the **Links group**, click the **Hyperlink** button.

3. In the displayed **Insert Hyperlink** dialog box, under **Link to**, be sure **Existing File or Web Page** is selected. In the **Address** box, type **http://www.nrcs.usda.gov/feature/highlights/homegarden/lawn.html**

4. In the upper right corner of the **Insert Hyperlink** dialog box, click **ScreenTip**. In the **Set Hyperlink ScreenTip** dialog box, under **ScreenTip text**, type **Lawn Care Tips**

5. In the **Set Hyperlink ScreenTip** dialog box, click **OK**. At the bottom of the **Insert Hyperlink** dialog box, click **OK**. **Save** your document.

6. Near the top of the document, right-click the **grass** picture, and then click **Hyperlink**. Using the procedure you just practiced, add the same address and ScreenTip, and then return to the document.

7. Be sure you have an Internet connection. Point to the *USDA Lawn and Garden Care* text hyperlink and read the ScreenTip. Follow the directions to test the hyperlink. Return to your document, and then test the hyperlink to the picture.

8. On the **View tab**, in the **Document Views group**, click the **Print Layout** button.

Display **Print Preview** to check your document.

9. Submit the Word document as directed.

10. Press [Ctrl] + [End] to move to the end of the document, and then press [Enter]. Click the **Insert tab**. In the **Illustrations group**, click the **SmartArt** button.

11. On the left side of the displayed **Choose a SmartArt Graphic** dialog box, click **Cycle**. In the middle of the dialog box, click the first SmartArt graphic—**Basic Cycle**. At the bottom of the displayed **Choose a SmartArt Graphic** dialog box, click **OK**, and then **Save** your document. The graphic will display on the second page of the document. If the *Type your text here* box does not display, on the Design tab, in the Create Graphic group, click the Text Pane button.

12. With the SmartArt graphic displayed on your screen, in the first bullet point in the **Type your text here** box, type **Water Regularly** and then press [↓].

13. Type **Fertilize As Needed** and then press [↓]. Type **Mow Often** and then press [↓]. Type **Leave Clippings** and then press [↓].

14. With the insertion point in the fifth (blank) bullet point, press [←Bksp] to remove the fifth item.

15. **Close** the *Type your text here* box. Click the **View tab**, and then in the **Document Views group**, click the **Web Layout** button. **Maximize** the screen if necessary. Scroll to the view the page.

16. From the **Office** menu, click **Save As**. In the displayed **Save As** dialog box, navigate to your **Word Chapter 4** folder. Near the

(Project 4D—Lawn Care continues on the next page)

(Project 4D–Lawn Care continued)

bottom of the **Save As** dialog box, click the **Save as type arrow**. Scroll down, and then click **Single File Web Page**.

17. Near the bottom of the **Save As** dialog box, click **Change Title**. In the displayed **Set Page Title** dialog box, type **Georgia Gardens Lawn Care Hints** and then click **OK**. At the bottom of the **Save As** dialog box, click **Save** to save the document as a Web page.

18. **Close** the document, and then **Exit** Word. Display the **My Computer** window, and then navigate to your **Word Chapter 4** folder. Locate and double-click the **4D_Lawn_Care_Firstname_Lastname.mht** file. If necessary, maximize the browser screen. Notice that the title you changed displays in the browser title bar.

19. Submit your Web page as directed, and then **Close** the Web browser.

 End **You have completed Project 4D** _____

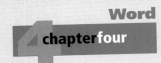

Mastering Word

Project 4E — Soil Types

In this project, you will apply the skills you practiced from the Objectives in Project 4A.

Objectives: 1. *Collect and Paste Text and Graphics;* **2.** *Create and Format Columns;* **3.** *Use Special Character and Paragraph Formatting;* **4.** *Create Mailing Labels Using Mail Merge.*

In the following Mastering Word project, you will create a newsletter for *Georgia Gardens* about dealing with different soil types. Your completed documents will look similar to Figure 4.39.

For Project 4E, you will need the following files:

New blank Word document
w04E_Soil_Types
w04E_Addresses
w04E_Soil_Graphics

You will save your documents as
4E_Soil_Types_Firstname_Lastname
4E_Mailing_Labels_Firstname_Lastname
4E_Addresses_Firstname_Lastname

Figure 4.39

Isabelle Riniker
8720 Natchez Trail
Rome, GA 30149

Taylor Dunnahoo
189 Ventura Street
Rome, GA 30161

Daniel Echols
2000 St. Luke Place
Rome, GA 30165

Cesar Vargas
1550 Glenrosa Drive
#1550
Atlanta, GA 30301

Abram Waldenberg
15 Harwell Rd.
Atlanta, GA 30309

Leland Wang
600 County Line NE
Atlanta, GA 30331

Julian Omdahl
34 Gloucester Pl.
Gainesville, GA 30504

Working with Different Soil Types

SOIL TYPES

Soil can be a gardener's best friend or worst enemy. Good quality soil is essential to the development of healthy plants. Unfortunately, few of us are lucky enough to naturally have good soil.

The three main types of soil are clay, loam, and sand. Loam is the ideal soil type. However, most Southern gardens have clay soil. To determine your soil's type, pick up a small hunk of moist soil and roll it between your fingers. If you have clay soil, you'll be able to roll the soil into a marble shape. With sandy soil, the hunk will immediately fall apart. With loam, the rolling will stick together at first but ultimately fall apart.

WHAT YOU CAN DO

If you have clay soil, you might want to rent or purchase a tiller. Clay soil

tends to be compacted, which is bad for drainage and root growth.

Organic materials, such as compost, peat moss, and manure, improve every soil type. They help bind sandy soil and break up clay soil. Add some organic material and then blend it into the existing soil.

Finally, a layer of mulch is a good idea for every soil type. It helps retain moisture and prevent weeds, and keeps the surface porous.

With a little extra attention and added materials, and a little time, you can turn your problem soil into an asset.

4E_Soil_Types_Firstname_Lastname

(Project 4E–Soil Types continues on the next page)

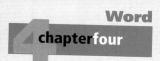

(Project 4E–Soil Types continued)

1. **Start** Word and be sure a new blank document is displayed. Display formatting marks, and be sure your screen displays both the left and right document edges. If necessary, set all document margins to **1"**. **Save** the file as **4E_Soil_Types_Firstname_Lastname** and then add the file name to the footer.

2. Display the **Clipboard** task pane, and if necessary, **Clear All** contents. Locate and open the file **w04E_Soil_Types**. Select all of the text in the document, and then **Copy** the text to the Office Clipboard. Locate and open the file **w04E_Soil_Graphics**. Select and **Copy** the **WordArt title**, the **herb garden** picture, and the **hands** picture. Leave the **4E_Soil_Types** document open, but **Close** the other files.

3. In the **Clipboard** task pane, click the **WordArt title**, and then press Enter. Use the **Office Clipboard** to insert the text beginning *Soil Types*, and then remove the blank line at the bottom of the inserted text. Select all of the text except the WordArt title. On the **Page Layout tab**, change the number of **Columns** to **Two**. On the **Home tab**, change the **Font Size** to **12**, and then **Justify** the text. Single-space the text. **Save** the document.

4. Click anywhere in the first column to deselect the text. Insert the **herb garden** picture. Display the **Format tab**, change the **Text Wrapping** to **Square**, and then change the **Height** to **2"**. Be sure the resize is proportional. Align the top edge of the picture with the left margin of the first column and the top of the paragraph beginning *The three main types*.

5. Near the end of the document, position the insertion point at the beginning of the paragraph that begins *Finally, a layer*.

Insert the **hands** picture. Display the **Format tab**, and if necessary, change the **Width** to 3". Leave the picture as an inline object, and be sure the resize is proportional. **Clear All** the items from the Office Clipboard, and then **Close** the Clipboard task pane.

6. At the top of the first column, select the title *Soil Types*, and then display the **Font** dialog box. Add **Bold** emphasis, and then change the text to **Small Caps**. Repeat this procedure with the second title—*What You Can Do*. **Save** and **Close** the document, and then submit it as directed. Next, you will create mailing labels for a group of Georgia subscribers.

7. Display a new blank document. Display the **Save As** dialog box, and then save the document as **4E_Mailing_Labels_Firstname_Lastname**. Locate and **Open** the file **w04E_Addresses**. Display the **Save As** dialog box, navigate to your **Word Chapter 4** folder, and then save the file as **4E_Addresses_Firstname_Lastname**. Add the file name to the footer.

8. Add the following row to the bottom of the table:

First Name	Henry
Last Name	Clark
Address 1	61 N. Bullpen Dr.
Address 2	
City	Woodstock
State	GA
ZIP Code	30187

9. **Save** and **Close** the table of addresses. With the **4E_Mailing_Labels** document displayed, on the **Mailings tab**, start the **Mail Merge Wizard**. Select **Labels**,

(Project 4E–Soil Types continues on the next page)

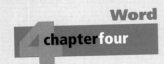

Word

chapterfour

Mastering Word

(Project 4E–Soil Types continued)

click **Next**, and then click **Label options**. Select the **Default tray (Auto Select)**—your text may vary—for the printer. Select the **Avery 5160** mailing label format.

 10. Select your **4E_Addresses_Firstname_Lastname** file as the data source, and then sort on the **ZIP_Code field**. Select the **Address Block** option, select **<<AddressBlock>>** in the upper left corner of the document, and change the

spacing **Before** and **After** to **0**, and then click to **Update all labels**. Preview your labels, adjust line spacing as necessary, and complete the merge. **Save** your labels.

11. To submit electronically, follow your instructor's directions. Otherwise, **Print** the first page of labels.

12. **Close** the document, click **Yes** to save the labels, and then **Exit** Word.

End You have completed Project 4E

Mastering Word

Project 4F—Shade Garden

In this project, you will apply the skills you practiced from the Objectives in Project 4B.

Objectives: 5. *Insert Hyperlinks;* **6.** *Insert a SmartArt Graphic;* **7.** *Preview and Save a Document as a Web Page.*

In the following Mastering Word project, you will edit a flyer about the design and use of shade gardens. Your completed documents will look similar to Figure 4.40.

For Project 4F, you will need the following file:

w04F_Shade_Garden

You will save your documents as
4F_Shade_Garden_Firstname_Lastname
4F_Shade_Garden_Firstname_Lastname.mht

Figure 4.40

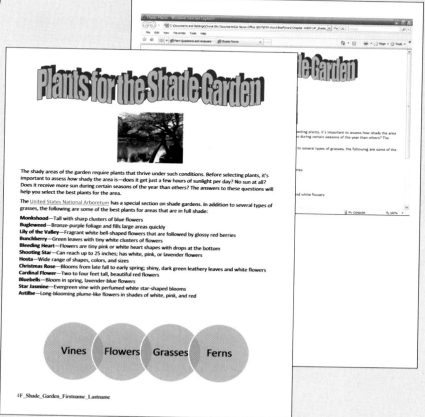

(Project 4F–Shade Garden continues on the next page)

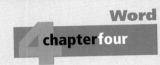

(Project 4F–Shade Garden continued)

1. Locate and open the document **w04F_Shade_Garden**. Display formatting marks, and be sure your screen displays both the left and right document edges. **Save** the file as **4F_Shade_Garden_ Firstname_Lastname** and then add the file name to the footer. Set all document margins to **0.5"**.

2. In the second paragraph in the document, select the text *United States National Arboretum*. Insert a hyperlink to the address **http://www.usna.usda.gov/ Gardens/faqs/fernsfaq2.html** Add a **Ferns in Shady Areas** ScreenTip to the hyperlink.

3. Near the top of the document, select the picture, and then insert the same hyperlink: **http://www.usna.usda.gov/ Gardens/faqs/fernsfaq2.html** Add a **Japanese Shade Garden** ScreenTip to the hyperlink. **Save** your document.

4. Be sure you have an Internet connection. Point to the *United States National Arboretum* text hyperlink and read the ScreenTip. Follow the directions to test the hyperlink. Return to your document and test the hyperlink to the picture.

5. Press Ctrl + End to move to the end of the document, and then press Enter. From the **Insert tab**, insert a **Linear Venn** SmartArt

graphic—located near the bottom of the **Relationship** graphics.

6. If necessary, open the Text pane. In the Text pane, type **Vines** and then press ⬇. Type **Flowers** and then press ⬇. Type **Grasses** and press ⬇, and then type **Ferns**

7. Move the pointer to the middle of the bottom SmartArt border to display the ⬍ pointer. Drag up until the SmartArt graphic moves to the first page of the document. On the **Format tab**, use the **Arrange** button to center the SmartArt graphic at the bottom of the page, and then click anywhere in the document to deselect it. **Close** the text pane. **Save** your document, and then submit it as directed.

8. Display the document in **Web Layout** view, and then return to **Print Layout** view. **Save** your document as a **Single File Web Page**, and then change the **Page Title** to **Shade Plants**

9. **Close** the document, and then **Exit** Word. Locate and double-click the **4F_Shade_ Garden_Firstname_Lastname.mht** file. If necessary, maximize the browser screen. Notice that the title you changed displays in the browser title bar.

10. Submit your Web page as directed, and then **Close** the Web browser.

 End **You have completed Project 4F**

Word

chapter four

Mastering Word

Project 4G — Itinerary

In this project, you will apply the skills you practiced from the Objectives in Projects 4A and 4B.

Objectives: 1. *Collect and Paste Text and Graphics;* **3.** *Use Special Character and Paragraph Formatting;* **5.** *Insert Hyperlinks;* **7.** *Preview and Save a Document as a Web Page.*

In the following Mastering Word project, you will collect information, and then create an itinerary for Rob Tumlin. You will save it as a document, and also as a Web page for the program's internal, private Web site. Your completed documents will look similar to Figure 4.41.

For Project 4G, you will need the following files:

New blank Word document
w04G_Itinerary
w04G_Itinerary_Graphics

You will save your documents as
4G_Itinerary_Firstname_Lastname
4G_Itinerary_Firstname_Lastname.mht

Figure 4.41

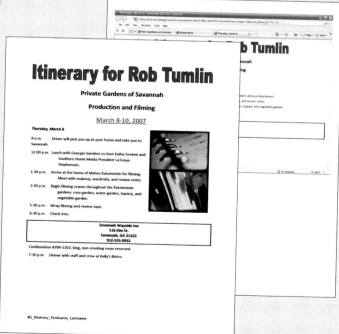

(Project 4G–Itinerary continues on the next page)

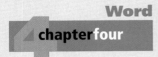
(Project 4G–Itinerary continued)

1. **Start** Word and be sure a new blank document is displayed. Display formatting marks, and be sure your screen displays both the left and right document edges. Be sure the document margins are all set to 1". **Save** the file as **4G_Itinerary_Firstname_Lastname** and then add the file name to the footer.

2. Display the **Clipboard** task pane, and if necessary, **Clear All** contents. Locate and open the file **w04G_Itinerary**. Select all of the text in the document, and then **Copy** the text to the Office Clipboard.

3. Locate, and then open the file **w04G_Itinerary_Graphics**. Select and **Copy** the **WordArt title**, and then **Copy** the **appointment book** picture. Leave the **4G_Itinerary_Firstname_Lastname** document open, but **Close** the other files.

4. In the **Clipboard** task pane, click the **WordArt title**, and then press [Enter]. Use the **Clipboard** task pane to insert the text beginning *Private Gardens*, and then remove the blank line at the bottom of the inserted text. **Center**, and then deselect the WordArt title. **Save** the document.

5. Insert the **appointment book** picture. Display the **Format tab**, change the **Height** to 3", and be sure the picture is resized proportionally. Change the **Text Wrapping** to **Square**. Align the top edge of the picture with the top edge of the paragraph *Thursday, March 8*, and align the right edge of the picture with the right document margin. **Clear All** entries in the **Clipboard** task pane, and then **Close** the task pane. Compare your screen with Figure 4.41.

6. Near the bottom of the document, select the Inn address, beginning with the line *Savannah Wayside Inn* and ending with the telephone number. On the **Home tab**, display the **Borders and Shading** dialog box. Be sure the **Borders tab** is selected. Add a **Box** border to the selected text, with a **Width** of **1 1/2 pt**. If necessary, change the box Color to Black. On the **Shading tab**, fill the box using **White, Background 1, Darker 5%**—the second color in the first column.

7. With the text still selected, **Center** the text and add **Bold** emphasis. Display the **Paragraph** dialog box, and then remove the paragraph indentation. Change the spacing **After** to **0**, and then change the **Line spacing** to **Single**.

8. Near the top of the document, select the text *March 8–10, 2007*. Insert a hyperlink to the address **http://www.georgiagardens.tv/hosts/tumlin/schedule.htm** Add a **Rob's Full Schedule** ScreenTip to the hyperlink. Move the pointer over the new hyperlink to examine the ScreenTip, but do not click the link. **Save** your document, and then submit it as directed.

9. Select, and then delete the graphic. **Save** your document as a **Single File Web Page**, and then change the page **Title** to **Thursday, March 8**

10. **Close** the document, and then **Exit** Word. Locate and double-click the **4G_Itinerary_Firstname_Lastname.mht** file. If necessary, maximize the browser screen. Notice that the shape and position of the paragraph with the box border are different—your screen may vary.

11. Submit your Web page as directed, and then **Close** the Web browser.

End **You have completed Project 4G**

Content-Based Assessments

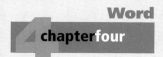

Mastering Word

Project 4H — Episode Guide

In this project, you will apply the skills you practiced from the Objectives in Projects 4A and 4B.

Objectives: 6. *Insert a SmartArt Graphic;* **7.** *Preview and Save a Document as a Web Page.*

In the following Mastering Word project, you will create a *Georgia Gardens* episode guide document that will also be used as a Web page. The focus of the document will be a SmartArt graphic. Your completed documents will look similar to Figure 4.42.

For Project 4H, you will need the following file:

New blank Word document

You will save your documents as
4H_Episode_Guide_Firstname_Lastname
4H_Episode_Guide_Firstname_Lastname.mht

Figure 4.42

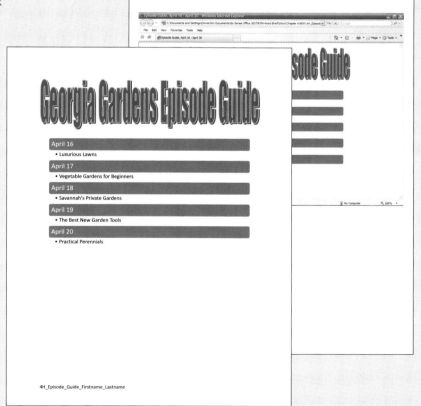

(Project 4H–Episode Guide continues on the next page)

Word

Mastering Word

(Project 4H–Episode Guide continued)

1. **Start** Word and be sure a new blank document is displayed. Display formatting marks, and be sure your screen displays both the left and right document edges. **Save** the document as **4H_Episode_Guide_Firstname_Lastname** Open the document footer, and then add the file name.

2. Add a **Georgia Gardens Episode Guide** WordArt title using **WordArt style 11**. Change the **Height** of the WordArt title to **1.5"** and the **Width** to **6.5"**. **Center** the WordArt title.

3. Create a blank line below the WordArt title, and then insert a **Vertical Bullet List** SmartArt graphic—the third style in the first row of the **List** category.

4. Use the **Type your text here** box to enter the five dates and program titles shown below. The dates should appear in the blue boxes, with the titles below the date in the white areas, as shown in Figure 4.42. After you have entered the first two dates and titles, on the **Design tab**, in the **Create Graphic group**, click the **Add Bullet**

button. Recall that you can move the bullet points up and down a level using the **Promote** and **Demote** buttons.

April 16	Luxurious Lawns
April 17	Vegetable Gardens for Beginners
April 18	Savannah's Private Gardens
April 19	The Best New Garden Tools
April 20	Practical Perennials

5. Close the **Type your text here** box. **Save** your document, and then submit it as directed.

6. **Save** your document as a **Single File Web Page**, and then change the **Page Title** to **Episode Guide, April 16 - April 20**

7. **Close** the document, and then **Exit** Word. Locate and double-click the **4H_Episode_Guide_Firstname_Lastname .mht** file. If necessary, maximize the browser screen.

8. Submit your Web page as directed, and then **Close** the Web browser.

End **You have completed Project 4H**

Project 4I — Extension Service

In this project, you will apply the skills you practiced from all of the Objectives in Projects 4A and 4B.

Objectives: 1. *Collect and Paste Text and Graphics;* **2.** *Create and Format Columns;* **3.** *Use Special Character and Paragraph Formatting;* **4.** *Create Mailing Labels Using Mail Merge;* **5.** *Insert Hyperlinks;* **6.** *Insert a SmartArt Graphic;* **7.** *Preview and Save a Document as a Web Page.*

In the following Mastering Word project, you will create a newsletter and Web page about the Georgia Gardens Extension Service. You will also complete a set of name tags for people who have confirmed that they will attend an Extension Service open house. Your completed documents will look similar to Figure 4.43.

For Project 4I, you will need the following files:

New blank Word document
w04I_Extension_Service
w04I_Extension_Service_Graphics
w04I_Addresses

You will save your documents as
4I_Extension_Service_Firstname_Lastname
4I_Extension_Service_Firstname_Lastname.mht
4I_Name_Tags_Firstname_Lastname
4I_Addresses_Firstname_Lastname

Figure 4.43

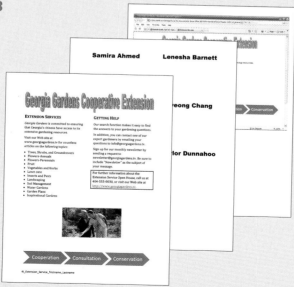

(Project 4I–Extension Service continues on the next page)

Mastering Word

(Project 4I–Extension Service continued)

1. **Start** Word and be sure a new blank document is displayed. Display formatting marks, and be sure your screen displays both the left and right document edges. **Save** the file as **4I_Extension_Service_Firstname_Lastname** and then add the file name to the footer.

2. Display the **Clipboard** task pane, and if necessary, **Clear All** contents. Locate and open the file **w04I_Extension_ Service**. Select all of the text in the document, and then **Copy** the text to the Office Clipboard. Locate and open the file **w04I_Extension_Service_Graphics**. Select and **Copy** the WordArt title, and then **Copy** the **gardening** picture. Leave the **4I_Extension_Service** document open, but **Close** the other files.

3. In the **Clipboard** task pane, click the **WordArt title**, and then press Enter. Use the **Clipboard** task pane to insert the text beginning *Extension Services*, and then remove the blank line at the bottom of the inserted text. Select all of the text except the WordArt title. On the **Page Layout tab**, change the number of **Columns** to **Two**. Change the **Font Size** to **12**, **Center** the WordArt title, and then **Save** the document.

4. Position the insertion point to the left of *Getting Help*. On the Page Layout tab, insert a column break. Press Ctrl + End to move to the end of the document. Press Enter, and then type **For further information about the Extension Service Open House, call us at 404-555-0030, or visit our Web site at www.georgiagardens.tv**. and then select the new paragraph. On the **Home tab**, display the **Borders and Shading** dialog box. Add a **Box** border to the selected text, with a **Width** of **1 1/2 pt**. On the **Shading tab**, fill the box using **White, Background 1, Darker 5%**—the second color in the first column.

5. Click anywhere in the document to deselect the text. In the paragraph with the border, select the text *www.georgiagardens.tv*. Insert a hyperlink to the address http://www.georgiagardens.tv Add a **Georgia Gardens Home Page** ScreenTip to the hyperlink.

6. Click anywhere outside the bordered text, and then from the **Clipboard** task pane, insert the **gardening** picture. Display the **Format tab**, confirm that the **Width** is **3"**, and then change the **Text Wrapping** to **Square**. Align the top edge of the picture at **6 inches on the vertical ruler**, and center it horizontally on the page, as shown in Figure 4.43. **Clear All** items from the **Office Clipboard**, and then **Close** the **Clipboard** task pane. **Save** the document.

7. At the top of the first column, select the title *Extension Services*, and then display the **Font** dialog box. Change the **Font Size** to **16**, add **Bold** emphasis, and then change the text to **Small Caps**. Repeat this procedure with the second title—*Getting Help*.

8. Position the insertion point at the bottom of the first column. From the **Insert tab**, insert a **Basic Chevron Process** SmartArt graphic—located at the beginning of the third row of the **Process** graphics.

9. In the **Text pane**, type **Cooperation** and then press ↓. Type **Consultation** and then press ↓. Type **Conservation**

10. With the SmartArt graphic still selected, display the **Format tab**. Change the

(Project 4I–Extension Service continues on the next page)

Mastering Word

(Project 4I–Extension Service continued)

Position to **Position in Bottom Center with Square Text Wrapping**—the middle button in the bottom row of the **Position gallery**. Close the **Text pane**, and then change the **Width** to **6.5**" and the **Height** to **0.7**". **Save** your document, and submit it as directed.

11. **Save** your document as a **Single File Web Page**, and then change the **Page Title** to **Extension Services** If you see a message about Small Caps changing to All Caps, click Continue.

12. **Close** the document, and then **Exit** Word. Locate and double-click the **4I_Extension_Service_Firstname_Lastname.mht** file. If necessary, maximize the browser screen. Notice that the graphics and columns are rearranged when displayed as a Web page.

13. **Close** the browser, and then submit the Web file as directed. Next, you will create name tags for the Extension Service open house.

14. **Start** Word and display a new blank document. Display the **Save As** dialog box, and then save the document as **4I_Name_Tags_Firstname_Lastname** Locate and **Open** the file **w04I_Addresses**. Display the **Save As** dialog box, navigate to your **Word**

Chapter 4 folder, and then save the file as **4I_Addresses_Firstname_Lastname** Add the file name to the footer.

15. **Close** the table of addresses. With the **4I_Name_Tags** document displayed, on the **Mailings tab**, start the **Step by Step Mail Merge Wizard**. Select the **Labels**, click **Next**, and then click **Label options**. Select the **Default tray (Automatically Select)**—your text may differ—for the printer. Select the **Avery 5095** name badge label format.

16. Select your **4I_Addresses_Firstname_Lastname** file as the data source. Select the **Address block** option. In the **Insert Address Block** dialog box, clear the **Insert postal address** check box. Then, **Update all labels**. Preview your labels, and then complete the merge. Press Ctrl + A to select all of the name tags. Change the **Font** to **Arial Black**, the **Font Size** to **22**, and then **Center** the names. Add the file name to the footer. **Save** your labels.

17. To submit electronically, follow your instructor's directions. Otherwise, **Print** the first page of name tags. **Close** the document, click **Yes** to save the labels, and then **Exit** Word.

 You have completed Project 4I

Content-Based Assessments

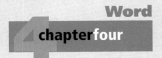

Project 4J—Business Running Case

In this project, you will apply the skills you practiced in Projects 4A and 4B.

From My Computer, navigate to the student files that accompany this textbook. In the folder **03_business_running_case_pg37_86**, locate and open the folder for this chapter. Open and print the instructions for this project, which are provided to you in Adobe PDF format. Follow the instructions and use the skills you have gained thus far to assist Jennifer Nelson in meeting the challenges of owning and running her business.

End **You have completed Project 4J** —————————

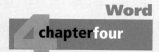

Word

Rubric

The following outcomes-based assessments are *open-ended assessments*. That is, there is no specific correct result; your result will depend on your approach to the information provided. Make *professional quality* your goal. Use the following scoring rubric to guide you in *how* to approach the problem and then to evaluate *how well* your approach solves the problem.

The *criteria*—Software Mastery, Content, Format and Layout, and Process—represent the knowledge and skills you have gained that you can apply to solving the problem. The *levels of performance*—Professional Quality, Approaching Professional Quality, or Needs Quality Improvements—help you and your instructor evaluate your result.

	Your completed project is of Professional Quality if you:	Your completed project is Approaching Professional Quality if you:	Your completed project Needs Quality Improvements if you:
1-Software Mastery	Choose and apply the most appropriate skills, tools, and features and identify efficient methods to solve the problem.	Choose and apply some appropriate skills, tools, and features, but not in the most efficient manner.	Choose inappropriate skills, tools, or features, or are inefficient in solving the problem.
2-Content	Construct a solution that is clear and well organized, contains content that is accurate, appropriate to the audience and purpose, and is complete. Provide a solution that contains no errors of spelling, grammar, or style.	Construct a solution in which some components are unclear, poorly organized, inconsistent, or incomplete. Misjudge the needs of the audience. Have some errors in spelling, grammar, or style, but the errors do not detract from comprehension.	Construct a solution that is unclear, incomplete, or poorly organized, containing some inaccurate or inappropriate content; and contains many errors of spelling, grammar, or style. Do not solve the problem.
3-Format and Layout	Format and arrange all elements to communicate information and ideas, clarify function, illustrate relationships, and indicate relative importance.	Apply appropriate format and layout features to some elements, but not others. Overuse features, causing minor distraction.	Apply format and layout that does not communicate information or ideas clearly. Do not use format and layout features to clarify function, illustrate relationships, or indicate relative importance. Use available features excessively, causing distraction.
4-Process	Use an organized approach that integrates planning, development, self-assessment, revision, and reflection.	Demonstrate an organized approach in some areas, but not others; or, use an insufficient process of organization throughout.	Do not use an organized approach to solve the problem.

Outcomes-Based Assessments

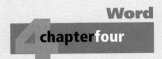

chapterfour

Problem Solving

Project 4K — Extension Classes

In this project, you will construct a solution by applying any combination of the skills you practiced from the Objectives in Projects 4A and 4B.

For Project 4K, you will need the following files:

New blank Word document
w04K_Extension_Classes

**You will save your document as
4K_Extension_Classes_Firstname_Lastname**

Georgia Gardens Extension Service offers classes on gardening and garden-related topics. The March and April schedule includes a wide variety of topics, ranging from *Pruning Basics* to *Attracting Butterflies to Your Garden*. All classes are single-day sessions, and are three hours long unless otherwise noted.

In this project, you will create a two-page newsletter announcing the upcoming classes and topics. Information about the classes can be found in a table in the file **w04K_Extension_Classes**. Open the Clipboard task pane and collect the information, or copy and paste the table information directly into your newsletter. Include a decorative title, information about where the classes are offered, and a link to the Georgia Gardens Extension Service Web site at **www.georgiagardens. tv/extension/classes.htm**. Locate a related picture or clip art image—a garden or a classroom—and add it to the newsletter. Put the class information in a two-column format. (Hint: For each class, you might want to have a title that includes the date and time, followed by the title of the class, and finally, the class description.) Format the class titles from the descriptions in a distinctive manner.

Add the file name to the footer. Check the newsletter for spelling and grammar errors. Save the newsletter as **4K_Extension_Classes_Firstname_ Lastname** and submit it as directed.

End You have completed Project 4K ————————————

Outcomes-Based Assessments

Problem Solving

Project 4L — Business Cards

In this project, you will construct a solution by applying any combination of the skills you practiced from the Objectives in Projects 4A and 4B.

For Project 4L, you will need the following files:

New blank Word document
w04L_Rob_Tumlin_Address

You will save your document as
4L_Business_Cards_Firstname_Lastname

In this project, you will create business cards for Rob Tumlin, co-host of the *Georgia Gardens* television show. Business cards are a type of label that you can create using the Mail Merge Wizard, in much the same way you created mailing labels in Project 4A. The major difference is the data source—instead of a list of different people, the data source is a Word or Access table—in this project, an Access table—that contains one name and address, repeated over and over.

Start the Step by Step Mail Merge Wizard. Using the method you practiced in Project 4A, create a set of labels that uses the default printer tray, and the 5911 Avery A4/A5 business card label type. As a data source, use the **w04L_Rob_Tumlin_Address** Access file. Use the Address Block format, and be sure to insert the company name. With the address block in place, press Enter to add a new line to the business card. In the same area where you select the Address block, select More items and add the E-mail Address field. Update all labels.

Check the business cards for spelling or grammar errors. Save the document as **4L_Business_Cards_Firstname_Lastname** and add the file name to the footer. Submit it as directed. If you are to submit a printed copy, print only records 1 through 8.

End You have completed Project 4L _____

Outcomes-Based Assessments

Word | chapter four
Problem Solving

Project 4M — Gardening Web Sites

In this project, you will construct a solution by applying any combination of the skills you practiced from the Objectives in Projects 4A and 4B.

For Project 4M, you will need the following file:

New blank Word document

You will save your documents as
4M_Gardening_Web_Sites_Firstname_Lastname
4M_Gardening_Web_Sites_Firstname_Lastname.mht

In this project, you will create a flyer and a Web page that contains a list of gardening Web sites. To complete this project:

- Add an appropriate decorative title to the document.

- Add one or more appropriate pictures or clip art graphics.

- Include lists of gardening-related Web sites, with a link to each site, and a ScreenTip with a short description of the site.

- Include at least one SmartArt graphic. The links could all be contained in the SmartArt graphic, or the graphic could relate to a particular topic contained in one of the links.

To find the gardening sources, use a Web browser and search using terms such as *flower garden*, *vegetable garden*, *shade garden*, or some other appropriate phrases. Choose several of the sites that are of interest to you.

Save the document as **4M_Gardening_Web_Sites_Firstname_Lastname** and add the file name to the footer. Submit it as directed. Then, save the document as a Single File Web Page and test your hyperlinks. Submit the Web page as directed.

End **You have completed Project 4M**

Word

chapterfour

Problem Solving

Project 4N — Junior Master Gardeners

In this project, you will construct a solution by applying any combination of the skills you practiced from the Objectives in Projects 4A and 4B.

For Project 4N, you will need the following files:

New blank Word document
w04N_Master_Gardener

You will save your document as
4N_Junior_Master_Gardeners_Firstname_Lastname

In this project, you will write a newsletter about the Junior Master Gardeners program sponsored by *Georgia Gardens*. The newsletter should contain a short article explaining what the Master Gardener program is, and then another article describing the Junior Master Gardener program. You can find information about both programs in the file w04N_Master_Gardener.

To complete this project:

- Add an appropriate decorative title to the document.

- Add one or more appropriate pictures or clip art graphics, and wrap the column text around the graphics.

- Format the articles in two-column format.

- Keep the newsletter length to one page.

- Add and format titles for both newsletter articles.

Save the document as **4N_Junior_Master_Gardeners_Firstname_Lastname** and submit it as directed. Add the file name to the footer. Check the newsletter for spelling and grammar errors, and then submit the newsletter as directed.

End **You have completed Project 4N** _____

Outcomes-Based Assessments

Problem Solving

Project 4O—Butterflies

In this project, you will construct a solution by applying any combination of the skills you practiced from the Objectives in Projects 4A and 4B.

> ### For Project 4O, you will need the following files:
>
> New blank Word document
> w04O_Butterfly1
> w04O_Butterfly2
> w04O_Butterfly3
> w04O_Butterfly4
> w04O_Butterflies

You will save your documents as
4O_Butterflies_Firstname_Lastname
4O_Butterflies_Firstname_Lastname.mht

Georgia Gardens provides classes on a variety of gardening topics. One of the classes describes how to attract and keep butterflies in your garden. In this project, you will create a one- or two-page newsletter about attracting butterflies that can be handed out at class or at the Georgia Gardens Open House. You can find information about butterflies in the file **w04O_Butterflies** and you can find more information on the Web.

To complete this project:

- Add an appropriate decorative title to the document.

- Format the articles in two-column format.

- Add several pictures to the document, and wrap the column text around the graphics. Four pictures are included with your student files—**w04O_Butterfly1** through **w04O_Butterfly4**.

- Divide the newsletter into at least two articles.

- Include a SmartArt graphic, which might include the major things you need to do to attract and keep butterflies in your garden.

- Add at least one Web link to an appropriate site.

Check for spelling and grammar errors. Save the document as **4O_Butterflies_Firstname_Lastname** and add the file name to the footer. Submit it as directed.

Save the document as a Web page. Test your Web link(s), and then submit the Web page as directed.

End You have completed Project 4O

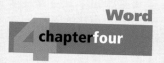

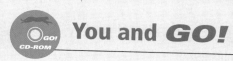

You and *GO!*

Project 4P — You and *GO!*

In this project, you will construct a solution by applying any combination of the skills you practiced from the Objectives in Projects 4A and 4B.

From My Computer, navigate to the student files that accompany this textbook. In the folder **04_you_and_go_pg87_102**, locate and open the folder for this chapter. Open and print the instructions for this project, which are provided to you in Adobe PDF format. Follow the instructions to create a family newsletter and save it as a Web page.

End You have completed Project 4P _____

GO! with Help

Project 4Q — *GO!* with Help

The Word Help system is extensive and can help you as you work. In this chapter, you created a graphic using SmartArt. There are many ways you can format a SmartArt graphics to make it better fit your needs.

1 **Start** Word. At the far right end of the Ribbon, click the **Microsoft Office Word Help** button. In the **Word Help** window, click the **Search button arrow**, and then under **Content from this computer,** click **Word Help**.

2 In the **Type words to search for** box, type **SmartArt** and then press ⏎ Enter .

3 From the list of search results, click **Change the color of a shape, shape border, or entire SmartArt graphic**. Then, scroll down and read the section on how to **Change the color of an entire SmartArt graphic**.

4 In the Tips section at the bottom of the Help window, click the link that will take you to information on how to **Apply or change a Quick Style for shapes**.

5 When you are through, **Close** the Help window, and then **Exit** Word.

End You have completed Project 4Q _____

Outcomes-Based Assessments

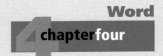

Group Business Running Case

Project 4R — Group Business Running Case

In this project, you will apply the skills you practiced from the Objectives in Projects 4A and 4B.

Your instructor may assign this group case project to your class. If your instructor assigns this project, he or she will provide you with information and instructions to work as part of a group. The group will apply the skills gained thus far to help the Bell Orchid Hotel Group achieve its business goals.

 You have completed Project 4R ——————————

Glossary

Adjustment handle A handle on a selected object that can be used to drag parts of an object into various positions.

Alignment The placement of paragraph text relative to the left and right margins.

American Psychological Association (APA) style One of two commonly used styles for formatting research papers.

Anchor A symbol that indicates to which paragraph an object is attached.

Aspect ratio The relationship of an object's height to its width. If you lock the aspect ratio, changing either the height or width will resize the object proportionally.

AutoComplete A Word feature that assists in your typing by suggesting words or phrases.

AutoCorrect A Word feature that corrects common typing and spelling errors as you type such as changing *teh* to *the.*

AutoFormat As You Type A Word feature that anticipates formatting based on what you type.

AutoText A Word feature with which you can create shortcuts to quickly insert long phrases with just a few keystrokes.

Bibliography A term used to describe a list of referenced works in a report or research paper, also referred to as Works Cited, Sources, or References, depending upon the report style.

Building block Pre-formatted content that you can add to your document, such as cover pages, pull quotes, and letterheads.

Bulleted list A list of items with each item introduced by a symbol such as a small circle or check mark—useful when the items in the list can be displayed in any order.

Bullets Text symbols such as small circles or check marks used to introduce items in a list.

Cell The rectangular box formed by the intersection of a row and column in a table.

Center alignment Text centered between the left and right margin.

Citation A list of information about a reference source, usually including the name of the author, the full title of the work, the year of publication, Web address, and other publication information.

Click and type pointer The text select (I-beam) pointer with various attached shapes that indicate which formatting will be applied when you double-click—such as a left-aligned, centered, or right-aligned tab stop.

Clip art Graphic images included with the Microsoft Office program or obtained from other sources.

Collect and paste Collect a group of graphics or selected text blocks, and then paste them into a document at any time. The Office Clipboard holds up to 24 items, and the Office Clipboard task pane displays a preview of each item.

Column chart A chart used to display changes over time, or to illustrate a comparison among items.

Comment A note that can be added to a Word document from the Review tab. Comments are not generally printed.

Complimentary closing A parting farewell in a business letter.

Contextual tab Contains related groups of commands that you will need when working with the type of object that is selected. For example, the Header and Footer Tools tab displays when you place the insertion point in a header or footer.

Contextual tool Enable you to perform specific commands related to the active area or selected object, and display one or more contextual tabs that contain related groups of commands that you will need when working with the type of area or object that is selected.

Copy Send a copy of selected text or graphics to the Office Clipboard while leaving the original intact.

Copyright Laws that protect the rights of authors of original works, including text, art, photographs, and music.

Curly quote A decorative quotation mark, with curved lines instead of the straight lines found in straight quotes.

Cut Remove selected text from a document and move it to the Office Clipboard.

Data source A list of variable information, such as names and addresses, that is merged with a main document to create customized form letters or labels.

Date line The first line in a business letter.

Document Information Panel The area of the screen just below the Ribbon that displays document properties.

Document properties The detailed information about a document that can help you identify or organize your files, including author name, title, and keywords.

Document window The Word window that displays the active document.

Dot leader A series of dots preceding a tab.

Double-click The action of clicking the left mouse button twice in rapid succession.

Draft view A simplified view of a document that does not show graphics, margins, headers, or footers.

Drag Holding down the left mouse button and moving the mouse pointer over text to select it.

Drag-and-drop A technique by which you can move selected text from location in a document to another—best used with text that will be moved a short distance, such as on the same screen.

Drawing canvas A work area for creating and editing complex figures created using the drawing tools.

Drawing object A graphic object, including shapes, diagrams, lines, and circles.

Edit Make changes to the text or format of a document.

Em dash The word processing name for a long dash in a sentence, and which marks a break in thought, similar to a comma but stronger.

Enclosure An additional document included with a letter.

Endnotes In a report or research paper, references placed at the end of the chapter containing the reference.

Enhanced ScreenTip A ScreenTip for a button that has more information than just the name, including a link to the topic in the Help system.

Field A category of information stored in columns in a data table.

Floating object An object or graphic that can be moved independently of the surrounding text.

Font A set of characters with the same design and shape.

Font styles Bold, italic, and underline used to enhance text.

Footer A reserved area for text and graphics that displays at the bottom of each page in a document or section of a document.

Footnotes In a report or research paper, references placed at the bottom of a report page containing the source of the reference.

Format Painter A Word tool with which you can copy the formatting of specific text, or of a paragraph, to text in another location in the document.

Formatting marks Characters that display on the screen, but do not print, indicating where the Enter key, the Spacebar, and the Tab key were pressed. Also called nonprinting characters.

Formatting text The process of establishing the overall appearance of text in a document.

Full Screen Reading view Displays easy-to-read pages that fit on the screen.

Gallery A visual representation of available options, activated by clicking a button on the ribbon.

Graphic A picture, clip art image, chart, or drawing object.

Group A set of command buttons related to the Ribbon tab that is currently selected.

Hanging indent An indent style in which the first line of a paragraph extends to the left of the remaining lines, an indent style that is commonly used for bibliographic entries.

Header A reserved area for text and graphics that displays at the top of each page in a document or section of a document.

Hyperlink Text that you click to go to another location in a document, another document, or a Web site; the text is a different color (usually blue) than the surrounding text, and commonly underlined.

Indenting A format for text in which lines of text are moved relative to the left and right margins, for example, moving the beginning of the first line of a paragraph to the right or left of the rest of the paragraph.

Inline object An object or graphic inserted in a document that acts like a character in a sentence.

Insert mode The mode in which text moves to the right to make space for new keystrokes.

Insertion point A blinking vertical line that indicates where text or graphics will be inserted.

Inside address The address block under the date in a business letter.

Justified alignment Text aligned on both the left and right margins.

Keyboard shortcut A combination of keys on the keyboard, usually using the [Ctrl] key or the [Alt] key, that provides a quick way to activate a command.

Leader characters Characters that form a solid, dotted, or dashed line that fills the space preceding a tab stop.

Left alignment Text aligned at the left margin, leaving the right margin uneven.

Line spacing The distance between lines of text in a paragraph.

Live Preview Changes the selected text when the pointer points to a button or list item to preview what the text will look like if the button or list item is clicked.

Mail merge A Word feature that joins a main document and a data source to create customized letters or labels.

Main document The document that contains the text or formatting that remains constant in a mail merge.

Manual column break An artificial end to a column to balance columns or to provide space for the insertion of other objects.

Manual line break The action of ending a line, before the normal end of the line, without creating a new paragraph; this is useful, for example, if your paragraph style includes space before or after paragraphs and you want to begin a new line without the space.

Margins The space between the text and the top, bottom, left, and right edges of the paper.

Mini toolbar A small box that displays above selected text or a selected object, and which contains formatting commands that can be used with the selected text or object.

Modern Language Association (MLA) style One of two commonly used styles for formatting research papers.

Navigate To move within a document.

Non-breaking hyphen A special type of hyphen that will not break at the end of a line and is useful for telephone numbers in which you normally do not want the number to be placed on two separate lines by the word wrap feature.

Non-breaking space A special type of space inserted between two words that results in treating the two words as one, and thus forcing both words to wrap even if the second word would normally wrap to the next line.

Nonprinting characters Characters that display on the screen, but do not print, indicating where the Enter key, the Spacebar, and the Tab key were pressed. Also called formatting marks.

Numbered lists A list of items with each item introduced by a consecutive number to indicate definite steps, a sequence of actions, or chronological order.

Office button Displays a list of commands related to things you can do *with* a document, such as opening, saving, printing, or sharing.

Office Clipboard A temporary storage area that holds text or graphics that has been cut or copied, and that can subsequently be placed in another location in the document or in another Office program.

Outline view A document view that shows headings and subheadings, which can be expanded or collapsed.

Parenthetical reference In the MLA report style, references placed in parenthesis within the report text that include the last name of the author or authors, and the page number in the referenced source.

Paste Move text or graphics from the Office Clipboard into a new location.

Pie chart A chart used to show items as a portion of a whole.

Point A measurement of the size of a font. There are 72 points in an inch, with 10–12 points being the most commonly used font size.

Print Layout view A view of a document that looks like a sheet of paper. It displays margins, headers, footers, and graphics.

Program tab A tab on the Ribbon that replaces the standard set of tabs when you switch to certain authoring modes or views, such as Print Preview.

Pt. Abbreviation for *point* in terms of font size.

Quick Access Toolbar (QAT) Displays buttons to perform frequently used commands with a single click. Frequently used commands in Word include Save, Undo, Redo, and Print. For commands that *you* use frequently, you can add additional buttons to the Quick Access Toolbar.

Recognizer A purple dotted underscore beneath a date or address indicating that the information could be placed into another Microsoft Office application program such as Outlook.

Record All of the fields containing information about one topic (a person or organization), and stored in a row in a data table.

References Within a report or research paper, a notation to indicate information that has been taken from another source. Also, in APA style, the title on the page that lists the sources used in the document.

Ribbon Organizes commands on tabs, and then groups the commands by topic for performing related document tasks.

Rich Text Format A universal document format that can be read by nearly all word processing programs, and retains most text and paragraph formatting. Rich Text Format documents use an *.rtf* extension.

Right alignment Text aligned on the right margin, leaving the left margin uneven.

Right-click The action of clicking the right mouse button.

Rotate handle A handle on a selected image that can be dragged to rotate the image to any angle.

Ruler Displays the location of paragraph margins, indents, and tab stops for the selected paragraph.

Salutation The greeting line of a business letter.

Sans serif font A font with no lines or extensions on the ends of characters.

ScreenTip A small box, activated by holding the pointer over a button or other screen object, which displays information about a screen element.

Scroll box Provides a visual indication of your location in a document. It can also be used with the mouse to drag a document up and down.

Selecting text Highlighting text so that it can be formatted, deleted, copied, or moved.

Separator character A character used to identify column placement in text; usually a tab or a comma.

Serif font A font that contains extensions or lines on the ends of the characters.

Shapes Predefined drawings, such as stars, banners, arrows, and callouts, included with Microsoft Office, which can be inserted into documents.

Shortcut menu A context-sensitive menu that displays commands relevant to the selected object.

Sizing handle A small square or circle in the corners and the middle of the sides of a graphic that can be used to increase or decrease the size of the graphic.

Small caps A font effect, usually used in titles, that changes lowercase text into capital (uppercase) letters using a reduced font size.

SmartArt Preformatted, designer-quality visual representations of information.

Sources A term used to describe a list of referenced works in a report or research paper, also referred to as Works Cited, Bibliography, or References, depending upon the report style.

Spin box A small box with an upward- and downward-pointing arrow that lets you move rapidly (spin) through a set of values

Spin box arrows The upward- and downward-pointing arrows in a spin box.

Split bar The gray bar that indicates the location of the border between two Word windows.

Status bar A horizontal bar at the bottom of the document window that displays, on the left side, the page and line number, word count, and the Proof button. On the right side, displays buttons to control the look of the window. The status bar can be customized to include other information.

Straight quote A quotation mark that uses straight, rather than curved, lines. Straight quotes are often used as inch marks.

Style A set of formatting characteristics—such as line spacing, space after paragraphs, font, and font style—that can be applied to text, paragraphs, tables, or lists.

Subject line The line following the subject line in a business letter that states the purpose of the letter.

Subpoint Secondary-level information in a SmartArt graphic.

Tab stop Specific locations on a line of text, marked on the Word ruler, to which you can move the insertion point by pressing the [Tab] key; used to align and indent text.

Table Rows and columns of text or numbers, used to organize data and present it effectively.

Table style A predefined set of formatting characteristics, including font, alignment, and cell shading.

Text box A movable, resizable container for text or graphics.

Text format A universal document format that retains text and paragraph marks, but does not support any text or paragraph formatting. Text format documents use a *.txt* extension.

Text wrapping The manner in which text displays around an object.

Theme A predefined set of colors, fonts, lines, and fill effects that look good together and that can be applied to your entire document or to specific items.

Title bar Displays the name of the document and the name of the program. The Minimize, Maximize/Restore Down, and Close buttons are grouped on the right side of the title bar.

Toggle button A button that can be turned on by clicking it once, and then turned off by clicking it again.

Top-level point The main text points in a SmartArt graphic.

Track Changes A Word tool that provides a visual indication of deletions, insertions, and formatting changes in a document.

Vertical scroll bar Enables you to move up and down in a document to display text that is not visible.

View options Area on the right side of the status bar that contains buttons for viewing the document in Print Layout, Full Screen Reading, Web Layout, Master Document Tools, or Draft views, and also displays controls to Zoom Out and Zoom In.

Web browser Software that enables you to use the Web and navigate from page to page and site to site.

Web Layout view A document view that shows how the document would look if viewed with a Web browser.

Word document window Displays the active document.

WordArt A gallery of text styles with which you can create decorative effects, such as shadowed or mirrored text.

Wordwrap Automatically moves text from the right edge of a paragraph to the beginning of the next line as necessary to fit within the margins.

Works Cited A term used to describe a list of referenced works placed at the end of a research paper or report when using the MLA Style.

Writer's identification The name and title of the author of a letter, placed near the bottom of the letter, under the complimentary closing.

Zoom To enlarge or decrease the viewing area of the screen.

Index

 The CD symbol represents Index entries found on the CD (See CD file name for page numbers).

Help
    Enhanced ScreenTip, 51
    searching, 52–53, 63
Home tab
    Borders and Shading, 316, 320
    Clipboard group, 96, 101, 262,
        304
    Editing group, 99, 145
    Font group, 21, 24, 60, 267–268,
        304
    No Spacing style, 65
    Paragraph group, 6, 90–92, 191,
        217, 232, 273
    Styles group, 6, 8, 59, 198
hyperlinks
    adding to graphic, 288–289
    e-mail, 289
    inserting, 286–288, 308, 314
    testing and modifying, 289–290

I

Ignore All button, 46
Ignore Once button, 46, 62
Ignore Rule button, 46
indenting
    lists, 196
    paragraphs, 124, 150
    tab lines, 188
inline object, 178
Insert group
    Date & Time button, 148
    Design tab, 32
insert mode, 17
Insert tab
    Convert Text to Table dialog box,
        238
    Header & Footer group, 60, 145,
        148
    Hyperlinks, 286
    Illustrations group, ● CD 8, 63, 178,
        182, 200–202, 228, 291
    Symbols group, 126–127, 149
    Tables group, 204–206, 211, 232
    Text group, 62, 148, 176, 178, 198,
        227
    WordArt, 241
insertion point, Word, 5
inside address, 6
Internet connection, 298
italics, 24, 65, 199

J

justify text alignment, 90, 91, 268

K

keyboard shortcut, 19
    viewing, 23

L

labels, address
    arranging, 280–281, 305–306
    formatting, 277–278, 306,
        321
    printing, 283–284, 306, 321
    updating, 282
Layout tab
    Merge group, 218, 232
    Rows & Columns group, 206–207,
        208
leader character, 192
left alignment
    tab, 188, 196, 235
    text, 90, 92
letter, parts of, 6–7
letterhead stationery, 15
line, document
    selecting, 20
    space between, 28, 131, 162,
        228
    style, creating, 131–132
list, moving quickly in, 23
lists
    bulleted, 109–110
    customizing bullets, 115–117
    ending, 113
    formatting, 113–115
    numbered, creating with
        AutoFormat, 110–113
    printing, 117
Live Preview, 21

M

Mail Merge, 260
    adding or editing names and
        addresses with wizard, 279–283,
        305–306, 321
    previewing and printing document,
        283–284
    Wizard template, opening,
        275–279
**main document, mail merge,
    275**
manual column break, 266
manual line break, 108
**Margins gallery, 13–14, 88–89,
    145**
Master Document Tools view, 36

SINGLE PC LICENSE AGREEMENT AND LIMITED WARRANTY

READ THIS LICENSE CAREFULLY BEFORE OPENING THIS PACKAGE. BY OPENING THIS PACKAGE, YOU ARE AGREEING TO THE TERMS AND CONDITIONS OF THIS LICENSE. IF YOU DO NOT AGREE, DO NOT OPEN THE PACKAGE. PROMPTLY RETURN THE UNOPENED PACKAGE AND ALL ACCOMPANYING ITEMS TO THE PLACE YOU OBTAINED THEM. *THESE TERMS APPLY TO ALL LICENSED SOFTWARE ON THE DISK EXCEPT THAT THE TERMS FOR USE OF ANY SHAREWARE OR FREEWARE ON TH E DISKETTES ARE AS SET FORTH IN THE ELECTRONIC LICENSE LOCATED ON THE DISK:*

1. GRANT OF LICENSE and OWNERSHIP: The enclosed computer programs ("Software") are licensed, not sold, to you by Prentice-Hall, Inc. ("We" or the "Company") and in consideration of your purchase or adoption of the accompanying Company textbooks and/or other materials, and your agreement to these terms. We reserve any rights not granted to you. You own only the disk(s) but we and/or our licensors own the Software itself. This license allows you to use and display your copy of the Software on a single computer (i.e., with a single CPU) at a single location for academic use only, so long as you comply with the terms of this Agreement. You may make one copy for back up, or transfer your copy to another CPU, provided that the Software is usable on only one computer.

2. RESTRICTIONS: You may not transfer or distribute the Software or documentation to anyone else. Except for backup, you may not copy the documentation or the Software. You may not network the Software or otherwise use it on more than one computer or computer terminal at the same time. You may not reverse engineer, disassemble, decompile, modify, adapt, translate, or create derivative works based on the Software or the Documentation. You may be held legally responsible for any copying or copyright infringement which is caused by your failure to abide by the terms of these restrictions.

3. TERMINATION: This license is effective until terminated. This license will terminate automatically without notice from the Company if you fail to comply with any provisions or limitations of this license. Upon termination, you shall destroy the Documentation and all copies of the Software. All provisions of this Agreement as to limitation and disclaimer of warranties, limitation of liability, remedies or damages, and our ownership rights shall survive termination.

4. DISCLAIMER OF WARRANTY: THE COMPANY AND ITS LICENSORS MAKE NO WARRANTIES ABOUT THE SOFTWARE, WHICH IS PROVIDED "AS-IS." IF THE DISK IS DEFECTIVE IN MATERIALS OR WORKMANSHIP, YOUR ONLY REMEDY IS TO RETURN IT TO THE COMPANY WITHIN 30 DAYS FOR REPLACEMENT UNLESS THE COMPANY DETERMINES IN GOOD FAITH THAT THE DISK HAS BEEN MISUSED OR IMPROPERLY INSTALLED, REPAIRED, ALTERED OR DAMAGED. THE COMPANY DISCLAIMS ALL WARRANTIES, EXPRESS OR IMPLIED, INCLUDING WITHOUT LIMITATION, THE IMPLIED WARRANTIES OF MERCHANTABILITY AND FITNESS FOR A PARTICULAR PURPOSE. THE COMPANY DOES NOT WARRANT, GUARANTEE OR MAKE ANY REPRESENTATION REGARDING THE ACCURACY, RELIABILITY, CURRENTNESS, USE, OR RESULTS OF USE, OF THE SOFTWARE.

5. LIMITATION OF REMEDIES AND DAMAGES: IN NO EVENT, SHALL THE COMPANY OR ITS EMPLOYEES, AGENTS, LICENSORS OR CONTRACTORS BE LIABLE FOR ANY INCIDENTAL, INDIRECT, SPECIAL OR CONSEQUENTIAL DAMAGES ARISING OUT OF OR IN CONNECTION WITH THIS LICENSE OR THE SOFTWARE, INCLUDING, WITHOUT LIMITATION, LOSS OF USE, LOSS OF DATA, LOSS OF INCOME OR PROFIT, OR OTHER LOSSES SUSTAINED AS A RESULT OF INJURY TO ANY PERSON, OR LOSS OF OR DAMAGE TO PROPERTY, OR CLAIMS OF THIRD PARTIES, EVEN IF THE COMPANY OR AN AUTHORIZED REPRESENTATIVE OF THE COMPANY HAS BEEN ADVISED OF THE POSSIBILITY OF SUCH DAMAGES. SOME JURISDICTIONS DO NOT ALLOW THE LIMITATION OF DAMAGES IN CERTAIN CIRCUMSTANCES, SO THE ABOVE LIMITATIONS MAY NOT ALWAYS APPLY.

6. GENERAL: THIS AGREEMENT SHALL BE CONSTRUED IN ACCORDANCE WITH THE LAWS OF THE UNITED STATES OF AMERICA AND THE STATE OF NEW YORK, APPLICABLE TO CONTRACTS MADE IN NEW YORK, AND SHALL BENEFIT THE COMPANY, ITS AFFILIATES AND ASSIGNEES. This Agreement is the complete and exclusive statement of the agreement between you and the Company and supersedes all proposals, prior agreements, oral or written, and any other communications between you and the company or any of its representatives relating to the subject matter. If you are a U.S. Government user, this Software is licensed with "restricted rights" as set forth in subparagraphs (a)-(d) of the Commercial Computer-Restricted Rights clause at FAR 52.227-19 or in subparagraphs (c)(1)(ii) of the Rights in Technical Data and Computer Software clause at DFARS 252.227-7013, and similar clauses, as applicable.

Should you have any questions concerning this agreement or if you wish to contact the Company for any reason, please contact in writing:

Multimedia Production
Higher Education Division
Prentice-Hall, Inc.
1 Lake Street
Upper Saddle River NJ 07458